INFORMATION QUALITY ASSURANCE AND INTERNAL CONTROL FOR MANAGEMENT DECISION MAKING

INFORMATION QUALITY ASSURANCE AND INTERNAL CONTROL FOR MANAGEMENT DECISION MAKING

WILLIAM R. KINNEY, JR.
University of Texas at Austin

Irwin McGraw-Hill

Boston Burr Ridge, IL Dubuque, IA Madison, WI New York San Francisco
St. Louis Brangkok Bogotá Caracas Lisbon London Madrid Mexico City
Milan New Delhi Seoul Singapore Sydney Taipei Toronto

McGraw-Hill Higher Education

*A Division of The **McGraw-Hill** Companies*

1 2 3 4 5 6 7 8 9 0 DOC/DOC 9 0 9 8 7 6 5 4 3 2 1 0 9

ISBN 0-256-22161-8

Vice president/Editor-in-chief: *Michael W. Junior*
Publisher: *Jeffrey J. Shelstad*
Developmental editor: *Kelly Lee*
Senior marketing manager: *Rhonda Seelinger*
Project manager: *Carrie Sestak*
Production supervisor: *Kari Geltemeyer*
Freelance design coordinator: *Gino Cieslik*
Supplement coordinator: *Becky Szura*
Compositor: *Carlisle Communications, Ltd.*
Typeface: *10/12 Palatino*
Printer: *R. R. Donnelly & Sons Company*

Library of Congress Cataloging-in-Publication Data

Kinney, William R.
    Information quality assurance and internal control for management
decision making / William R. Kinney, Jr.
        p.   cm.
    Supplementary materials which accompany the text: instructor's
resource manual, test bank, Web site.
    Includes index.
    ISBN 0-256-22161-8
    1. Management information systems—Auditing.   2. Decision making.
I. Title.
HD30.213.K55   2000
658.4'038—dc21   99–33629

Cover art credit:
Native Texas artist Daryl Howard (see: howard@ jump.net) uses ancient Japanese woodblock techniques and
the lens of the Musée d' Orsay's twentieth-century clockworks for "Now. . . is the Moment," a twenty-first-cen-
tury impresssion of the timeless spirit of the Louvre. The scene parallels Kinney's focus on the global and timeless demand for high-quality information and its changing expression, as information technology takes us into
the twenty-first century.

http://www.mhhe.com

Dedicated to William R. Kinney Sr. and
Linda Jo Powell

BRIEF CONTENTS

PREFACE

Information technology, globalization, and related developments have made businesses increasingly dependent on high-quality information for decision making. Business decision makers need assurance that they have relevant and reliable information available at the right time and at a reasonable cost. Assurance can be obtained from the independent assurance professionals, whose job it is to improve the quality of information for decision making, and from internal control designed to help management achieve its objectives.

A MANAGEMENT INFORMATION APPROACH

This book is about improving the quality of information for decision making as well as improving the context of the decision to be made. The book and cases focus on management's needs to reliably:

+ **inform itself** about relevant aspects of its business and protect its assets (chapters 1 through 6),
+ **inform others** about relevant aspects of its business to lower the costs of capital, production, storage, selling and distribution (chapters 7 through 10), and
+ **comply** with applicable laws and regulations (chapters 11 and 12).

We build on related topics in finance, strategy, operations management, information technology, financial statement analysis, and managerial accounting. The book is intended for:

+ Future and current **managers** who will work with information design consultants in addressing information and control problems within complex business organizations, and will deal with auditors in public reporting, securities filings, and business acquisitions
+ Future and current **bankers, investment bankers, analysts, investors, directors, and regulators** who must interpret financial statements and auditors' reports
+ Future and current **auditors, information design consultants, and other assurance professionals** who must understand business measurement, internal control, and external regulatory requirements to add value for their clients.

WHAT IS NEW HERE?

The book is unique (among auditing and assurance services books) in its orientation—that of the business decision maker. We take the perspective of top management in obtaining, evaluating, and using information, rather than the perspective of an accountant preparing information or an auditor verifying information. And although our focus is on how value is added for management (the customer), future or current auditors and accountants can benefit by understanding essential sources of value added by their services.

Enterprisewide software is the platform for analyses of an integrated financial, operating, and human resources database. This is consistent with emerging business practices that exploit information technology through new business organizations and strategies, and intregration of nonfinancial performance measures. It also allows a focus on information quality by design (error prevention), rather than by detection and correction of information errors.

Our management information approach is global and is not tied to a particular country's laws, business practices, or culture. However, principal U.S. accounting and auditing standards and business-reporting practices are illustrated as are those of selected jurisdictions is Asia and Europe. This allows appreciation of the interaction of regulatory and voluntary actions by decision makers.

The global, enterprisewide software, and information-technology-based approach is combined with initiatives of the AICPA through its Special Committee on Assurance Services and CPA Vision Project. The book is the first to fully incorporate the Vision 2000 statement through a broad range of professional services directed at information quality improvement and preservation of professional attributes. Also, the CPA's auditing activities are based on the AICPA's Engagement Risk Model, which considers the CPA firm's overall risk of association with client management. Finally, consistent with recommendations of the Accounting Education Change Commission, the book uses interactive rather than problems.

WHY INTERACTIVE CASES?

The book focuses throughout on management's use of information to improve decision making under uncertain conditions. Cases that address uncertainties and the inherent controversies and conflicts of interests underlying business transactions are central. They consider the essential roles of the independent professional assurer and verifiable objective information in reducing uncertainty and resolving the controversies. The cases emphasize the relevance, reliability, and cost of information to form mental images and make decisions.

The decisions require business information evaluation for buy/sell decisions, business valuation, performance evaluation, risk assessments (including incorrect information risk), management buyout incentives, fraud, and the hidden "codes" that auditors use to signal information quality. The cases are sometimes incomplete. Students must retrieve their own knowledge about management, business operations, contracts, and finance, and think through other individuals' self-interested behaviors in approaching the cases.

Small-group discussions and role playing are helpful in formulating approaches to the cases. Students working in small interactive groups addressing the business decisions to be made *rarely* miss the main points of the case. But students working individually and looking for a simple formula or rule to be applied often miss the main points. Thus, the interactive cases parallel real-world conditions!

WHO WILL BENEFIT FROM THIS APPROACH?

The book was written with future managers in mind; its customer orientation and broad focus on assurance services and internal control provides an excellent introduction to CPA and CA services for five-year Master of Accounting programs. Specifically, it helps financial accounting, managerial accounting, tax, and information systems students understand the roles of CPA/CAs in improving information for decision makers and the conceptual and practical problems they will face.

These same concepts that help assurance professionals understand their business are essential for MBAs who will be making business decisions under uncertainty as managers, investors, analysts, bankers, investment bankers or regulators. In addition, MBAs who want to know how to run their businesses better by informing (and protecting) themselves, informing outsiders, and complying with laws and regulations will appreciate this book's content. The book complements MBA courses such as financial statement analysis, mergers and acquisitions, managerial accounting, management information systems, and taxes for decision making.

WHAT SUPPLEMENTARY MATERIALS ACCOMPANY THE TEXT?

Instructor's Resource Manual   Authored by Bill Kinney and Linda McDaniel, University of North Carolina. Consists of solutions and recommended teaching strategies and notes for undergraduate and graduate courses.

Test bank   Authored by David Sinason at Northern Illinois University. Consists of 20 multiple choice, 10 short answer essay questions, and 2 additional cases per chapter (384 questions overall).

Web Site   A platform for communicating with your colleagues who teach this course. This web site will offer cites to current articles from the financial, professional, and scholarly press (tied to particular chapters), additional teaching strategies and resources, sample syllabi, and new content—primarily teaching cases—as users and the author share ideas.

WHO CONTRIBUTED TO THE DEVELOPMENT OF THIS TEXT?

There are many persons whose influences and efforts should be acknowledged. First, there is Bob Elliott, who has inspired my thinking about CPA services since 1972 (most recently as Chairman of the AICPA's Special Committee on Assurance Services), and Nick Dopuch from whom I learned to think about practice problems in a broad, conceptual way. Second, are the numerous students who stimulated and challenged my thinking at the University of Iowa, University of Michigan, University of Texas, and INSEAD. Third are the reviewers of this manuscript and cases including:

Urton Anderson
University of Texas at Austin

Andy Bailey
University of Illinois

Mark Beasley
North Carolina State University

Sarah E. Bonner
University of Southern California

Efrim Boritz
University of Waterloo

Joe Carcello
University of Tennessee

Charles Cullinan
Bryant College

Bill Felix
University of Arizona

Lisa Milici Gaynor
University of Texas at Austin

Charlotte Heywood
Wilfred-Laurier University

Eric Johnson
University of Texas at Arlington

Robert Kinney
Andersen Consulting

Roger Martin
Indiana University

Linda McDaniel (and her students)
University of North Carolina

Jane Mutchler
Georgia State University

Zoe-Vonna Palmrose
Southern California

Fred Phillips
University of Saskatchewan

Sally Webber
Elmhurst College

Ray Whittington
DePaul University

Especially helpful were the continuing comments of Roger Martin, Linda McDaniel, and Zoe-Vonna Palmrose—their encouraging yet stern counsel was essential in completing this project. Fourth are those at Irwin/McGraw-Hill who have been so helpful, Jeff Shelstad, Kelly Lee, and Carrie Sestak; and Linda Yancey and Dorothy Brady at the University of Texas at Austin, who provided outstanding assistance.

Fifth, I acknowledge the personal and professional roles of some of the many illustrative characters who appear in the book: Linda Jo, Tim, George, Jeff, Mamie and Willie, Nick, Phil, Kristi, Jeff, and Rob, Alex and Louis, and Elea and Olivia (the latter four being my grandchildren). Finally, Meena (Carolyn Kinney) deserves special thanks as the principal character who has shared my life for forty-plus years, and continues to provide support for and understanding of my professional endeavors.

ABOUT THE AUTHOR

William R. Kinney, Jr. is a 1963 (BS) and 1966 (MS) graduate of the accounting program at Oklahoma State University. His Ph.D. is from Michigan State University (1968). He has experience as a staff accountant with Ernst & Young in Oklahoma City and consulting experience with six national CPA firms, the Securities and Exchange Commission, and the U.S. General Accounting Office.

Since 1967, Professor Kinney has taught accounting and auditing at Oklahoma State University, the University of Iowa, the University of Michigan, INSEAD, and the University of Texas at Austin. At Iowa, Kinney was the John F. Murray Professor of Accounting and Director of the Institute of Accounting Research. In 1983 he became the Price Waterhouse Auditing Professor in the Graduate School of Business Administration at the University of Michigan where he also served as Director of the Paton Accounting Center. Since 1988, Professor Kinney has held the Charles and Elizabeth Prothro Regents Chair in Business and Price Waterhouse Auditing Fellowship at The University of Texas at Austin. In 1998, he assumed the directorship of the Texas Center for Business Measurement and Assurance Services.

Professor Kinney is author of more than 50 articles in journals such as the *Journal of Accounting Research,* the *Accounting Review,* the *Journal of Accounting and Economics,* the *Journal of Accountancy,* and the *Journal of Financial Economics.* During 1985–87 he was Director of Research for the American Accounting Association, and from 1987 to 1990 was Editor of the *Accounting Review.* He has served on the editorial boards of the *Journal of Accounting Research, Auditing: A Journal of Practice and Theory,* and *Accounting Horizons.* In 1983 and 1999 he received the Deloitte and Touche–AAA, John S. Wildman Award Medal and in 1985 he was corecipient of the AICPA–AAA Notable Contribution to the Accounting Literature award. In 1989 he received the AAA's Outstanding Accounting Educator award, and has received the Auditing Section's Distinguished Service Award (1993) and Outstanding Educator Award (1996). Professor Kinney has served on various AICPA committees including Auditing Standards Board (1981–1984) and the Special Committee on Assurance Services (1994–1996), and from 1987 to 1991 he served on the Financial Accounting Standards Advisory Council for the FASB.

TABLE OF CONTENTS

Chapter 3

Business Measurement Systems: Information Reliability and Risk Assessment   55

Chapter 4

Internal Control over Transactions   87

Chapter 5

Analytical Monitoring: Business Operations Analysis and Account Modeling Procedures   117

Chapter 6

Detailed Monitoring: Tests of Controls, Transactions, and Balances   145

SECTION II

INFORMING OTHERS

Chapter 7

Informing Outsiders: Management Assertions and Independent Certification   169

Chapter 8

Financial Statement Audits, Adjustments, and Disclosures   199

Chapter 9

Auditors' Reports and Their Interpretation   233

Chapter 10

Other Certification, Investigation, and Origination Assurance Services   259

SECTION III

PUBLIC DISCLOSURE LAWS AND REGULATIONS

Chapter 11

Regulatory Reporting and Disclosure from Management's Perspective   281

Chapter 12

Legal and Ethical Responsibilities in Public Reporting   305

1
CHAPTER

Introduction and Overview

- Do the methods used to prepare and display business information measure what I, as a business manager, need to know to run my business?
- Are the stated business measurement methods carefully applied, and the results truthfully displayed?
- Do my information and control systems produce relevant and reliable results?
- How can I reduce cost of capital, production, storage, selling, and distribution by credibly informing outsiders of my firm's condition and prospects?
- What do public disclosure and compliance regulations require of me and my firm?

These questions from top management are about the quality of information for business decision making. Most business information comes indirectly and in abstract form that must be interpreted by the decision maker. To assess the quality of information, the decision maker must understand the methods used to prepare it and have confidence about the care taken in applying the methods and displaying results.

Business managers obtain information quality assurance, in part, from information **assurance services** provided by independent professionals whose primary interest in the information is its quality—its relevance and reliability. Business managers also obtain information quality assurance and protect assets through the **internal control** process established and operated by management to help it achieve its objectives.

Assurance services can help business managers by (1) improving information relevance, (2) improving information reliability, and (3) demonstrating compliance with laws, regulations, and contracts. Assurance services can be factored into two broad types: *decision relevance analysis* (improving information relevance) and *auditing* (improving information reliability and demonstrating compliance).[1]

---

1. Independent assurance professionals can also be a direct source of relevant and reliable information for management.

1

Information for a complex business decision may encompass operating, marketing, financing, competitive, accounting, tax, regulatory, legal, behavioral, organizational, and cultural factors. Assessment of how well information displays represent real-world conditions for purposes of making a decision is the essence of **decision relevance analysis.** Included are design and evaluation of the measurement methods used to represent real-world conditions, their timeliness and completeness, and decision context.

Broadly defined, **auditing** determines whether one person's claim or assertion about a real-world condition agrees with the real-world condition (the asserted information is "reliable"). The assertion might be about the financial condition or performance of a firm, the condition of property, or the performance of a business process. Each of these assertions can be audited if measurement methods can be developed to represent real-world conditions in a reasonably consistent manner, and about which different humans will agree. For example, a description of the color of an automobile as "sea foam green" is auditable, but not the "beauty" of the color, since some observers will find "sea foam green" beautiful and others won't.

By verifying assertions, auditors facilitate activities and transactions that otherwise would not occur or would occur on less favorable terms because one party, the decision maker, doesn't fully believe the claims made by the other party, the information source. An independent auditor, whose primary interest in the claim or assertion is its quality, can increase the decision maker's perception of the reliability of the assertion.

Auditors may add value whenever two parties have a common interest in an activity or transaction, but their individual interests are in conflict and there is uncertainty about real-world conditions. Auditors can also certify compliance with regulations that are prerequisites for government-sanctioned transactions, such as security sales to the public.

Internal control over information acquisition and processing within a business can systematically provide high-quality information for routine day-to-day decision making, as well as unexpected conditions that might arise. Also, through internal control, management can prescribe checks and balances that reduce conflicts-of-interest problems within the business and protect firm assets.

About This Book

Information quality assurance and internal control for business managers are the subjects of this book. When finished, we will better understand the complexities, mysteries, and interrelation of these sometimes subtle activities and how they can add value for business managers. In particular, we can answer the five questions posed at the beginning of this chapter as well as subsidiary questions.

We will understand how business managers can use independent assurance professionals, such as certified public accountants (CPAs) and chartered accountants (CAs), to add value for themselves and their business. We will learn how decision relevance analysis can improve information relevance through better measurement methods; through customized operating, financial, tax, and regulatory information, and through advice on how systematically to acquire, verify, integrate, and summarize information.

We will learn how managers can use auditors to improve information reliability, and what another company's auditor's report means (and what it doesn't mean). And we will learn how managers can use independent auditors to convey financial, nonfinancial, and process information reliability to others to lower management's costs of capital, production, storage, selling, and distribution, as well as what auditors should be hired to do, and their obligations and limitations.

We will also understand how business managers can use internal control to assure that decisions are based on relevant and reliable information, to protect assets, and to monitor progress toward achieving objectives. Finally, we will know what laws and regulations require of managers with respect to financial reporting and internal control.

The book has two points of focus. First, the primary decision makers will be *top management*. The value of assurance services and internal control will be assessed from the perspective of management, whether management is the *user of information*; the *source of information for outside decision makers* such as investors, directors, lenders, and trading partners; or the *source of information required by law, regulations, or contract*. By understanding the value of assurance services and internal control for management, we will also better understand how managers should interpret information from others, and how information analysts, control specialists, and internal and external auditors can increase the value of their services.

Second, the *accounting system* will be the template on which analyses are built. Traditionally, the accounting record-keeping system comprises the central framework for operationalizing the internal control process, and serves as a basis for many of the information and assurance needs of management. The accounting system measures and reports to management decision-relevant financial transactions with suppliers, workers, and customers as transactions occur.

Periodic financial statements prepared using standardized accounting measurement rules and audited by an independent auditor are intended by accounting standards-setters to provide investors decision-relevant information about a business. Financial statements provide a broad basis by which management and outsiders can evaluate overall performance of a business and its management through comparison with expectations and benchmarks of comparable firms' financial statements and the same firm over time. Finally, publicly traded firms are required by law to prepare periodic financial statements using standardized accounting methods, have the statements audited by an independent auditor, and file the statements and audit report with government regulators.

Although the accounting system is the template, our assurance services approach will be broader. **Decision relevance analysis** using traditional accounting transaction measures requires that they be customized for particular decisions and integrated with nonfinancial measurements of the same underlying transactions, conditions, and events. Furthermore, external environment information that is not (yet) reflected in transactions of a business is relevant for many decisions, as is risk assessment of events that may occur in the future. Systematic collection, processing, verification, and presentation of these financial and nonfinancial business measures and risk assessments for decision making are also the subjects of **internal control** and **auditing,** and will be important to our analysis of information quality.

AN EXAMPLE: LJ APPLIANCES, INC.

Linda Jo owns and operates LJ Appliances, Inc., a chain of major appliance stores based in Iowa City, Iowa. LJ Appliances has an accounting system that is integrated with other business measurements as part of the internal control process. These systems and processes help Linda Jo increase revenues, lower costs, and protect firm assets—the example will show us how. Also, Linda Jo is considering selling her business.

Informing Management

Business Measurement Systems

When Linda Jo began her business, she purchased accounting software to help keep her books. To make the accounting information more useful for decision making, Linda Jo's outside information technology consultant (decision relevance analyst) linked information across files and departments. The decision relevance analyst wrote software that links her customer accounts receivable files (accounting system) with each customer's credit profile (credit management records), products purchased (sales analysis), and product profitability and reliability information (sales, purchasing, and service records).

Linda Jo's sales and clerical personnel rely on her integrated accounts receivables file day to day for decisions about sales authorization and collection efforts. Periodically, her credit manager analyzes the files to revise credit and collection policies. Sales management uses the sales and receivables files and external information to forecast future demand, and to design sales promotions tailored to particular classes of customers.

LJ Appliances' inventory/payables financial records are similarly integrated with supplier service and reliability information. The combined records are used day to day for pricing decisions, ordering decisions, and cash flow management. Periodically, she relates product line cost and profitability, and supplier performance evaluations to particular classes of customers to improve customer service and profitability.

The external audit (CPA) firm that audits LJ Appliances' annual financial statements worked with her information technology consultant to design a system of checks and balances to assure the reliability of her records. The design includes **internal controls** that prevent and detect accidental errors in bookkeeping and misappropriation or misuse of LJ's assets by employees.

The controls and bookkeeping establish a *recorded accountability* for receivables and inventory that helps Linda Jo determine that all cash due LJ Appliances is being collected and deposited and that inventory is not being lost or stolen. Furthermore, Linda Jo's **internal auditor** makes periodic tests of the recorded accountability by comparing recorded amounts with real-world amounts observed. The internal auditor detects and corrects errors, and since other employees know that their work will be audited, internal auditing makes them more careful and helps prevent errors. The internal auditor also monitors employees' compliance with LJ Appliances' ethical code and operating policies.

In addition to short-term operating use of the integrated accounting and operating records, Linda Jo uses quarterly and annual financial statements prepared from the accounting records for aggregate analyses of her business. She compares liquidity, profitability, and leverage ratios among her individual stores, and compares the business as a whole with financial statements of similar companies. She also relates the financial data to nonfinancial performance benchmark statistics maintained by the appliance dealers' trade association. Furthermore, in addition to using accounting data as information about her firm, Linda Jo bases store manager compensation on the accounting earnings measurements of individual stores.

Linda Jo is very pleased with her business measurement system. She believes that it is valuable in running her business, and she believes that the periodic financial statements that her internal control produces follow generally accepted accounting principles (GAAP) with essentially zero error in its application, and she knows that she hasn't intentionally misrepresented her statements.

Periodic Relevance Advice

Linda Jo meets once each quarter with her CPA to discuss the current position of the business and its possible future. They discuss the current state of the retail appliance industry, likely trends for the future, and possible risks that may threaten the business. Linda Jo benefits from her CPA firm's experience with other businesses' problems, accounting and tax regulations, information technology, and other forms of organization and cultures. The CPA offers advice on additional information that may be needed for particular decisions as well as changes in business systems.

In a recent quarterly meeting, Linda Jo and her CPA discussed how industry trends would affect the likely performance of LJ Appliances for the next quarter, and the CPA prepared forecasted financial statements under several possible scenarios. They also discussed the effect of the World Wide Web on the appliance retailing business and the possibility that a competitor company might market appliances as Amazon.com has done for books.

In reviewing LJ Appliances' systems, the CPA discussed whether it might be beneficial to formalize collection of strategic information about product demand in a data warehouse that would standardize the information collected, verify it, and make it accessible by all store managers.

The possibility of a data warehouse led to discussion of the cost and benefits of integrating LJ Appliances' business measurement system components using *enterprisewide software.* Enterprisewide software such as SAP R/3 uses a single database of company financial and nonfinancial information that can be accessed by employees in accounting, inventory control, human resources, and purchasing and by Linda Jo herself. The software offers economies of data processing as well as improved decisions since data elements from related activities can be matched to each other at low cost.

Linda Jo finds these quarterly meetings with her CPA useful in determining whether to make changes in her processes and whether to consider a change in business strategy. The conferences sometime result in additional services being acquired from the CPA firm, and other times the CPA recommends another outside consultant. Whatever the outcome, Linda Jo believes that the outside review helps improve decision context for a variety of decisions since it broadens her consideration of her business operations, opportunities for improvement, and threats to achieving her objectives.

Informing Others

Linda Jo is considering selling her business. Her initial asking price is about eight times the current year's net income based on GAAP. The prospective buyer, Tim, an external-to-the-firm decision maker, can't directly observe the value of LJ Appliances, Inc., but he can observe its information displays (such as financial and nonfinancial reports) and analyze them as if they were the real firm. Tim uses the financial statements to form a mental image or information model of the firm and its real-world conditions.

Tim believes that reliably prepared GAAP-based financial statements provide *relevant* information for making a valuation judgment, and Tim believes that internal controls over sales/receivables and cost of sales/inventory have value. In fact, Tim would be willing to pay Linda Jo's asking price if he could be reasonably confident that LJ's *financial statements* and *systems* are reliable.

But Tim doesn't fully believe Linda Jo's assertions because of her incentive to assert that her business and its systems are better than they are. Tim could gain confidence in the reliability of Linda Jo's assertions if they were audited by any of several CPAs whose reputations for *competence* and *trustworthiness* are known to him. In effect, a reputable CPA acts as an **independent assurance professional** who improves the reliability or credibility of information as perceived by Tim, the decision maker. The audit and the auditor's report raise the reliability of Linda Jo's assertions *as perceived by Tim* by making his mental image of the real-world condition of LJ Appliances, Inc., more in line with Linda Jo's beliefs.

Tim is indifferent between buying at Linda Jo's asking price if he has high confidence in Linda Jo's assertions or at a lower price if he has less confidence. Since Tim lacks confidence in the reliability of the information, he price protects himself through a lower offer (bid price) that discounts the price for what he perceives as a higher risk purchase. But Linda Jo is not indifferent. If Linda Jo can buy an independent audit for less than Tim's price discount, she will be made better off. An audit raises the quality of Linda Jo's assertions *as perceived by Tim,* and *Linda Jo benefits* through a higher bid (offer price) from Tim.

Complying with Contracts, Laws, and Regulations

Since LJ Appliances is a privately held company, it has no periodic public reporting obligations under U.S. securities acts. However, the terms of LJ Appliances' bank loan require that Linda Jo submit financial statements that comply with generally accepted accounting principles within 45 days of the end of her fiscal year. The terms also require that the statements be audited by a CPA. Audited financial statements are part of the cost of acquiring the loan.

In addition to considering whether to sell LJ Appliances, Linda Jo has also considered expanding her business through an offering of equity securities to the general public. During their quarterly meeting, Linda Jo and her CPA discussed the costs and benefits of going public and what that would imply for the way she runs her business, as well as the requirements for her accounting system to be able to support required disclosures to investors. Based on their meeting, Linda Jo decided that the costs of going public outweigh its benefits, at least for the near term.

REAL-WORLD CONDITIONS, INFORMATION, AND DECISIONS

Information obtained by means other than direct observation by the decision maker is a step away from the real-world conditions of interest and requires rules for how conditions are to be represented. All conditions can't be represented, and measurement requires specification of how the information system is to sense, measure, summarize, and display representations of the real world in abstract form such as on paper, a computer monitor display, or electronic media. In short, it requires specification of **measurement methods** for how the real world is to be represented or portrayed.

As an example, environmental sensors, processors, and cockpit instruments of a modern aircraft provide information displays that collectively allow a pilot to make essential decisions to successfully land a plane—even when flying in dense fog. The information includes measurements on the condition of the plane (engine functioning and fuel) and its external operating environment (altitude, air speed, attitude, and location coordinates). To be useful, the methods used to attach numbers to the gauges must be understood by the pilot (e.g., altitude is measured in feet versus meters) and applied with inconsequential measurement error, and the display must be free of unknown bias (e.g., a fuel gauge that, unknown to the pilot, displays five hours of fuel when the tank is empty). The pilot must also understand how various measurements are related to each other and to other conditions personally sensed by the pilot (decision context).

The usefulness of an information system and display depends on whether the mental image of real-world conditions formed in the decision maker's mind matches the real world. If the image formation is successful, the information model can be substituted for direct real-world observation by the decision maker that can greatly extend the decision maker's span of possible activities. The decision maker's mental image depends on several subtle and interrelated factors in addition to the information display itself. Specifically, it depends on the decision maker's beliefs about (a) the relevance for his or her particular decision of the methods used to prepare the display, (b) the competence and care with which the methods are applied, and (c) the trustworthiness with which the measurement results are displayed.

A business measurement system senses, processes, and prepares a display of aspects of the past, present, and possible future real-world conditions of a business according to a set of measurement methods or rules that prescribe the nature of the system. For example, an inventory accounting system senses inventory quantities on hand, looks up acquisition prices, converts quantities and prices to total cost of inventory on hand according to a cost attachment rule (such as first-in, first-out), and displays the result on a computer terminal or in an accounting report.

Figure 1–1 diagrams the essentials of a decision model based on a measurement system. The diagram is not simple, but it shows the essence of some complex and subtle relations among and between the real world, the quality of information, and how a decision maker uses both to make a decision about real-world conditions.

The first three boxes in Figure 1–1 show the basic elements of real-world conditions of interest to the decision maker (RWC), the business measurement system's quality (Q), and a displayed signal or report of the information obtained by the system (Y). Y is determined by RWC and Q (denoted Y | RWC, Q, where "|" means "given" or "based on" particular RWC and Q). Information quality, Q, depends on the decision relevance and application and display reliability of the *measurement method* used to attach numbers to RWC to form Y. Reliability of information depends on the *care* with which the methods are applied and the *trustworthiness* of the display of measurement results. In other words, information quality is a function of the measurement methods used, the care with which the methods are applied, and the trustworthiness of the display of the application results.

The decision maker observes Y and assesses what it implies about RWC. In making the assessment, the decision maker considers what he or she knows about the measurement methods and assesses the likely care in their application and the trustworthiness of the display. The decision maker may personally observe some real-world conditions and

A Decision Model: Information, Decisions, and Outcomes

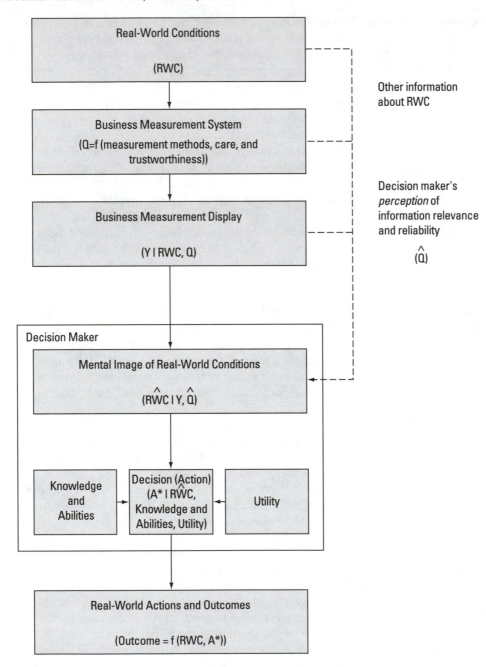

have available information from sources other than the business measurement system's display. This other information is part of the dashed line in Figure 1–1 and may confirm or deny the implications of Y. The decision maker also has perceptions about the relevance and reliability of Y that determine how much importance or value he or she will place on Y. All of these *perceptions* of information quality (denoted $\hat{Q}$) are also part of the dashed line in Figure 1–1, and perceptions of information quality vary across decision makers.

The decision maker uses the displayed information (Y) and his or her own perceptions of its quality ($\hat{Q}$) to form a "mental image" or information model of real-world conditions (R$\hat{W}$C in Figure 1–1). Then, the decision maker combines this image with his or her knowledge and decision-making abilities and his or her utility or values and preferences for future outcomes that may occur in the real world. The outcomes will be the joint result of the decision maker's action choice and the future real-world conditions that occur. Information is relevant if it helps the decision maker assess which conditions might occur and their probabilities of occurrence.

The decision maker combines all of these factors to make a decision and choose a real-world action (denoted A*). For example, the decision might be the one that maximizes the decision maker's expected satisfaction or utility based on his or her personal utility. Actions are taken to implement the decision and produce outcomes (RWC, A*)—the combination of actual real-world conditions and actions taken to implement the decision.

Different decision makers have different utilities and differ in their other knowledge and decision-making abilities. Their interpretations of information displays vary due to differences in their assessments of information quality ($\hat{Q}$)—the perceived relevance of the information displayed and its reliability. Some differences in perceived relevance are based on factors that the decision maker considers valuable (i.e., utility related), while others will be based on lack of knowledge (e.g., a decision maker who doesn't know how first-in, first-out inventory information reflects rising prices). These latter factors are part of the decision **context.**

As we shall see in the next section, assurance services and internal control can affect the mental image of real-world conditions (R$\hat{W}$C) formed by the decision maker, and thus the decisions made. This is accomplished through their impact on the information display Y and perceptions of its quality $\hat{Q}$.

ASSURANCE SERVICES AND INTERNAL CONTROL IN BUSINESS

This book explores assurance services and internal control as the means of improving the quality of information and perceptions of that quality. This section outlines concepts and uses of assurance services and internal control as they exist in current business practice. Some assurance services improve the relevance of information, and others improve reliability and perceptions of reliability. Internal control is a way for management to improve both relevance and reliability of information for internal decision making.

Assurance Services

The American Institute of Certified Public Accountants (AICPA), a trade association of independent assurance professionals in the United States, has directed attention to a broad class of information quality improvement services by defining assurance services as "independent professional services that improve the quality of information, or its context, for decision makers."[2]

The *quality of information* for decision making is improved by using *measurement methods* that better represent what the decision maker wants to know about real-world conditions (information relevance) and by raising the decision maker's confidence that the stated methods have been *carefully applied* and results *truthfully displayed* (information reliability or credibility). Information *context* quality is improved by identifying key factors, risks, and additional sources of information about real-world conditions relevant to the decision maker, by assisting with interpretation of information, and by identifying alternative actions.

Management, as *decision makers,* can benefit from purchasing assurance services that improve the quality of information for their own decisions and others within the firm. Individuals outside the firm are also decision makers. Management can benefit from purchasing assurance services that improve outside decision makers' perceptions of the reliability of information that management prepares for outsiders. *Professional services* mean that the assurance provider applies his or her expertise and judgment and that a quality of service meeting the standards of the profession can be expected by the decision maker. These characteristics affect perceived service competence, care, and trustworthiness.

Trustworthiness of information display is also related to the independence of the assurer. *Independent* means that the assurer's *only* substantive interest in the real-world conditions being measured and displayed is the *quality of information* about the real-world conditions. Assurance professionals who are hired only to improve information quality have no other substantial interest in the information. They do not cause the real-world conditions, and the real-world conditions being represented do not reflect on his or her own performance, or directly affect his or her wealth. If an assurance provider has a substantive interest in the real-world subject matter being portrayed, then the *lack* of independence would lower the decision maker's perceptions of the trustworthiness of the information display, and thus reduce its value for decision making.

Internal Control

Internal control can improve the quality of information for management, but it is not an assurance service as defined by the AICPA. Internal control has been defined as

> a process, effected by an entity's board of directors, management, and other personnel, designed to provide reasonable assurance regarding the achievement of objectives in the following categories:
>
> * effectiveness and efficiency of operations,
> * reliability of financial reporting,
> * compliance with applicable laws and regulations.[3]

Determining an organization's long-term objectives and strategies to achieve them are beyond the scope of internal control, but most other business activities are subject to in-

---

2. AICPA, "Report of the AICPA Special Committee on Assurance Services," www.aicpa.org, 1996.
3. Committee of Sponsoring Organizations of the Treadway Commission, *Internal Control—Integrated Framework* (Jersey City, NJ: COSO, 1994), p. 13.

ternal control, broadly defined. Many companies have developed business measurement systems that encompass the accounting system and related nonfinancial measures such as quantities, quality, and attitudes, and compliance systems. These measurement systems are designed to assure employee adherence to internal operating policies and ethical codes, and to external contract provisions, laws, and regulations.

In addition to providing information for decision making, internal control can help protect the assets of a business. As examples, inventory on hand at a point in time can be compared with recorded accountability for inventory in the accounting system to detect possible theft of inventory, and control procedures for payments prevent disbursement of company cash without proper authorization of the purchase and receipt of the goods.

Internal control is broader than merely measuring and monitoring day-to-day activities. Effective and efficient operations encompass internal-to-the-firm matters, as well as factors external to the firm that are not yet included in the business measurement system, or personally observed by the manager. Operating and strategic information for a business are likely to entail forecasts and risk assessments for the many possible future conditions that *might* occur rather than measurement of what *has* occurred.

Assurance Services and Information Quality

Figure 1–2 lists six broad information assurance services classified by whether the service improves information relevance, reliability, or both. Relevance-improving services are discussed below as decision relevance analysis, and reliability-improving services are discussed as auditing. Each of these services will be defined and elaborated in later chapters. All six services are encompassed in the boxes and arrows above the decision maker in Figure 1–1. Assurance services improve the decision maker's mental image of real-world conditions, but the action choice is made by the decision maker and is not an assurance service.

Decision Relevance Analysis

Decision relevance analysis improves information quality by providing measurement methods and other information that help the decision maker form a better mental image of real-world conditions about which he or she wants or needs to know. The analyst may have expertise in accounting, regulation, taxation, production, distribution, sales, finance, human resources, information technology politics, or behavioral science, or be an expert in a particular industry, culture, or region. Starting with the decision maker's objectives, the decision relevance analyst determines the information necessary for a decision and the costs and benefits of alternative information.

Some information analyses are systematic and apply to many possible decisions, such as what information to include in a customer database and the development of standards or "benchmarks" for evaluating performance. For systematic analyses, the decision relevance analyst assists with the choice of the measurement method to be applied to determine numbers to be displayed, rather than determining Y, the particular numbers themselves. The chosen methods are then systematically applied to a variety of conditions that may occur over time.

Accounting methods and accounting systems are designed systematically to sense, process, and display transactions data with customers, workers, and suppliers for internal

FIGURE 1-2

Information Quality Assurance Services

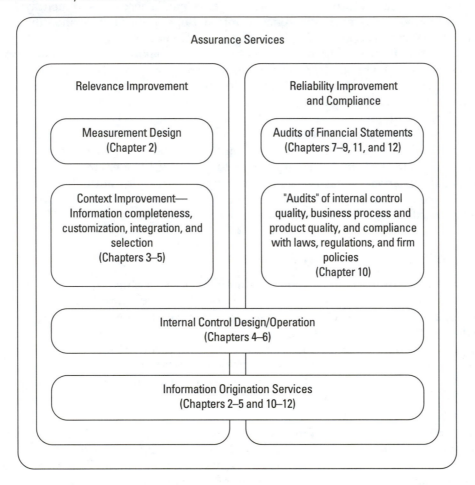

decision making on a day-to-day basis as transactions occur. In addition, periodic financial statements are prepared from systematically collected accounting transactions data and other information using GAAP-based measurement methods. GAAP-based periodic financial statements are mandated for publicly traded companies in most countries, and most countries' laws require that they be attested to (audited) by an independent auditor.

Some information analyses are one-time-only, "as needed," or ad hoc, such as information to support a specific decision about whether to sell a subsidiary or acquire a new subsidiary. Improvement in *ad hoc* information may help the decision maker use available information through better presentation, interpretation, or integration and may suggest additional information. For example, historical accounting information can be adapted, or customized, to provide predictions of future operations and performance by eliminating the effects of nonrecurring events, adding new events expected in the future, and adjusting for expected changes in events.

Auditing

Auditing, broadly defined, improves the reliability of information as perceived by the decision maker. The AICPA characterizes attestation[4] (auditing) as an expression of "a conclusion about the reliability of a written assertion that is the responsibility of another party."[5] The conclusion expressed is about the degree of correspondence between real-world conditions, as measured by stated measurement methods or measurement criteria, and the assertion by another party about real-world conditions.

Auditing by independent assurance professionals is one way to increase outsiders' confidence in the *reliability* of management's assertions about the financial and nonfinancial condition of the business and its internal control, as well as its operating effectiveness and efficiency, and its compliance with laws, regulations, and internal policies. Perceived reliability is enhanced two ways: by increasing the decision maker's confidence in the competence and care of the application of stated measurement methods and by increasing confidence in the trustworthiness of the display of measurement results.

Audits of financial statements (e.g., Y in Figure 1–1) are the most common and widely known attestation service, and GAAP comprise the measurement criteria. While GAAP are intended by accounting standards setters to provide relevant information to outside investors, GAAP-based information usually requires careful interpretation, adjustment, or customization to be made more relevant for a particular decision by a particular decision maker. More will be said in Chapter 2 about the relevance of GAAP for individual decision makers.

An auditor of financial statements obtains enough evidence to get reasonable assurance of high correspondence between the real-world condition of the firm and its financial statements as measured by GAAP. For example, reasonable assurance for quantitative aspects of financial statements of a medium-sized company may mean the auditor has about 99 percent confidence that the magnitude of misapplication of GAAP to a firm's condition is no more than about 5 to 10 percent of audited earnings using GAAP.

While GAAP are the most common measurement criteria in business, there are others. As examples, measurement criteria exist or can be specified to allow independent "assurance" to management, directors, and outsiders about the quality of internal control, the business measurement system (Q in Figure 1–1), financial forecasts, and nonfinancial events and states such as product quality and customer satisfaction.

Relevant and reliable information may be provided by an assurer acting as an information source for the decision maker. The assurer may develop and provide information to the decision maker without reference to a particular assertion of another party. Relevance is improved by applying the assurer's subject matter knowledge, and reliability or credibility is enhanced because the assurer has no substantial interest in the information except its quality (i.e., the assurer is "independent").

CPAs and CAs have been hired as information sources by decision makers to design accounting, tax, operational, or regulatory aspects of a proposed transaction; to design internal controls; to assemble or customize information for a particular decision; and to seek

---

4. The AICPA uses the term *attestation* to encompass examinations, reviews, and agreed-upon procedures applied to an assertion about any subject matter. *Auditing* as used by the AICPA refers to examination of financial statements. For simplicity, we will use auditing and attestation as equivalents without regard to the subject of the assertion.

5. AICPA, "Attestation Standards," *Statements on Standards for Attestation Engagements*, § 100.02, (1986).

information about conditions that the assurer believes might be of interest to the decision maker. They have also been hired to supervise elections, and to assemble confidential information from trade association members into aggregate performance benchmarks. Canadian CAs have been hired to independently report on the Canadian Post service performance.

Finally, assurers can improve decision context by assisting in the integration and interpretation of information from a variety of sources and the elimination of irrelevant information. For example, information from the business measurement system must be integrated with other information in making some decisions. Information integration itself sometimes leads the decision maker to reconsider his or her business strategy and important decision variables. Integration can also reveal a misunderstanding or misinterpretation of measurements and what they imply about real-world conditions. Thus, assurance services can lead to increased knowledge and information interpretation abilities by the decision maker.

TWO EXAMPLES: GEORGE'S ELECTRONIC SECURITY CORP. AND RJR NABISCO HOLDING, INC.

George's Electronic Security Corp. uses information technology to run what might be called a "virtual" company and has unusual demands for assurance services. Directors of **RJR Nabisco Holding, Inc.,** are assumed to be exploring the value of audited financial statements in a regulated reporting environment.

George's Electronic Security Corp.

Bringing high technology home security products to market at very competitive prices is central to the strategy of George's Electronic Security Corp. George's crack design staff monitors technological developments and consumer demand for home security products and then develops concepts for electronic products to meet these needs. Design engineers in Mexico create the final product design and product specifications. The products are produced to George's specifications by South Korean manufacturers under a loose operating alliance—based on only a handshake. The products are sold to Suzy's Discount Club, a major discount chain.

George's personnel have on-line electronic access to Suzy's inventory and sales records for George's products (and only George's products) at each of the chain's 150 locations across America. They use Suzy's records to prepare production schedules for the South Koreans and to coordinate just-in-time delivery of products via the United Parcel Service air freight system. George's has negotiated a special high-volume rate with UPS, which accepts shipments in South Korea and delivers directly to the freight dock at each Suzy's location. As goods are received at a Suzy's store, the chain transfers cash to George's electronically. George's then electronically transfers cash to the manufacturers.

George's uses operating agreements and information sharing with trading partners rather than relying on vertical integration of production and distribution process ownership. Information technology (IT) makes it possible to manage information instead of physical goods. IT allows George's to eliminate inventories, receivables, and cash float; outsource production capacity; and contract for human resources worldwide for optimum net value. And, although George's needs little, IT also allows new ways of acquiring capital and sharing risk through customized financing from new types of financial instruments, and from new types of investors and creditors worldwide. IT lowers the costs of production, storage, marketing, and capital by changing the organization and processes by which business is conducted. IT also changes the focus of assurance services.

Even though George's has few traditional tangible assets, the firm does have considerable market-based assets such as its relation to Suzy's as a preferred supplier, the alliance with competent South Korean manufacturers, and the human assets of the design staff. Also, George's own business measurement system and those of UPS and Suzy's have considerable value in that they make most tangible assets unnecessary. George's also generates considerable demand for assurance services.

George's *obtains assurance* about the reliability of Korean suppliers by careful consideration of each supplier's ISO 9000 certificate. ISO 9000 certificates are based on an independent auditor's evaluation of the quality control characteristics of a manufacturer and their ability to meet exacting output tolerances. George's business measurement system also monitors supplier performance on a continuing basis, tracking delivery reliability and product quality.

Reliable inventory and usage records at each Suzy's location are important to George's strategy since they allow lower costs, and Suzy's may cancel the distribution agreement if George's fails to supply their needs within a short time frame. George's monitors Suzy's information system by tracking the reliability of demand at each location as indicated by Suzy's records. George's *provides assurance* to Suzy's by agreeing to obtain an ISO 9000 report on all suppliers and a report on George's own post-sale service capabilities.

Because of its importance as a primary or core process, George's has regular reviews of its information systems. A CPA firm compares George's systems with the best practices and new technologies worldwide. Their review and recommendations give George's chief executive officer assurance that he will not lose competitive advantage and that he will be able to stay in business. Suzy's benefits by George's systems assurance because Suzy's increases its confidence that their alliance will remain viable.

RJR Nabisco Holding, Inc.

In 1997 RJR Nabisco Holding, Inc., had after-tax earnings of $381 million on revenues of $17.1 billion, using total assets of $30.7 billion and outstanding debt of $9.5 billion. As a publicly traded U.S.-based company, the U.S. securities acts require that RJR Nabisco's management make available to the Securities and Exchange Commission (SEC) and to the public U.S. GAAP-based financial statements on a quarterly and annual basis, and the latter must be audited by an independent accountant (auditor). RJR Nabisco's various debt agreements also require that audited financial statements be sent to RJR Nabisco's debt holders. To fulfill its duties, RJR Nabisco uses Deloitte and Touche, a Big Five accounting firm, as its independent auditor.

Some knowledgeable critics of auditing and the public accounting profession have made claims such as "annual audits of public companies do not add value, and they wouldn't exist if they weren't required by the securities acts." Others have said that "auditing is a commodity, so seek the lowest price when buying." Let's conduct a thought experiment and make some back-of-an-envelope calculations to test these two propositions using RJR Nabisco as an example.

Assume that the U.S. Securities Exchange Act of 1934 has just been altered to eliminate the requirement for annual independent audits of financial statements of public companies.[6] Publicly traded companies will no longer be required by law to obtain an annual audit and can issue reports for securities holders on an unaudited basis or not issue financial statements at all. In reaction to the securities law changes, RJR Nabisco's management has proposed that RJR Nabisco renegotiate its debt agreements to eliminate the annual audit provision and discontinue annual audits as a cost-cutting move. What are the possible benefits and costs of this proposal?

Consider the cost of RJR Nabisco's debt. Would current debt holders be indifferent to the annual audit requirement? Would they find valueless the Big Five auditor's assurance that the accounting principles that RJR Nabisco's uses are generally accepted and that any misstatements are likely to be less than a material amount? When MBA students and businesspersons are asked these questions, almost all say no—debt holders would demand a higher interest rate, and most say that an additional 1/4 of 1 percent interest, or 25 basis points, would be required *at a minimum*. Thus, RJR Nabisco's annual interest cost of debt would likely rise by a minimum of .0025 × $9,500,000,000, or $23,750,000.

What does an audit cost? A survey of 340 members of Manufacturers Alliance of Arlington, Virginia, revealed average 1996 audit fees of $200 per $1 million of revenues (all US$).[7] This was down from $262 per $1 million of revenues in 1993, $270 in 1989, and $330 in 1983. There were also economies of scale in auditing. For 19 survey firms with revenues of less than $100 million, audit fees averaged $1,220 per $1 million in revenues; firms with revenues from $500 million to $749 million averaged $488; and audit fees for 13 firms with revenues above $20 billion averaged $92 per $1 million in revenues. Using different methods, the most comprehensive scholarly study of audit fees found that a reasonable approximation of the typical audit fee can be calculated by multiplying by 14 the square root of a firm's total assets.[8]

Point estimates of RJR Nabisco's audit fee based on the Manufacturers Alliance study or the scholarly study's formula are under $2.5 million. Thus, even if its value were limited to interest savings alone, RJR Nabisco's annual financial statement audit is worth more than *nine times* its cost ($23.75/$2.5). Would RJR Nabisco continue to issue annually audited GAAP-based financial statements even if the securities act didn't require them? Probably so, at least if they want to maximize firm value.

Now let's consider the particular auditor chosen by RJR Nabisco, and whether auditing is a "commodity." A *commodity* is something that has common characteristics across suppliers, and any supplier is as good as any other because "all units are alike." Why do you suppose RJR Nabisco chose its particular auditor rather than "Joe's Tax, Real Estate, Insurance, and Auditing Services, Inc."? The SEC may be officially indifferent among the members of the approved class of financial statement auditors, and to satisfy its legal requirements, auditing may be a commodity. However, bondholders, analysts, directors, workers, and trading partners are unlikely to be indifferent among auditors. An auditor

---

6. This assumption may seem unrealistic, but in 1995, the U.S. House of Representatives considered a proposal that would have allowed audits on a three-year basis with major relaxations of the accounting requirements.

7. *Public Accounting Report,* November 30, 1997, p. 4.

8. D. A. Simunic, "The Pricing of Audit Services: Theory and Evidence," *Journal of Accounting Research* 18, no. 1 (1982), pp. 161–90.

with an unknown reputation (or poor reputation) for *measurement* expertise, exercise of *care*, and *trustworthiness* will add little value for management. Most believe that it is possible to differentiate between at least some audit firms by reputation.

INFORMATION ASSURANCE DEMANDS AND CONTRACTS

As we have seen, management itself is a primary beneficiary of assurance services. Management has three demands for information assurance: to inform and protect management itself, to inform outsiders, and to comply with requirements of laws, regulations, or contracts. In this section, we consider management's demands for information assurance and how *three* essentially different contract types for acquiring assurance services affect the value of assurance services.

Information Assurance Demands

To Inform and Protect Management

Management wants information assurance from or about four parties: suppliers, employees, customers, and competitors. These demands are diagrammed as inbound arrows in Figure 1–3. Management also wants assurance that management's own information, instructions, and orders are properly conveyed to the first three of these parties (outbound arrows in Figure 1–3).

FIGURE 1–3

Information Assurance Demands by Management[1]

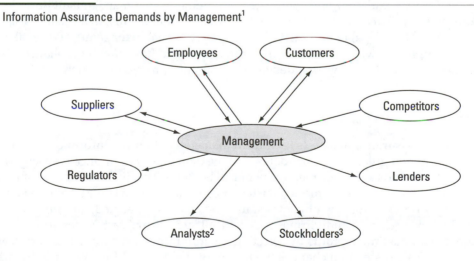

[1.] Arrowheads indicate direction of information asssurance flow.
[2.] Financial analysts and potential stockholders.
[3.] Stockholders and outside directors.

Management wants assurance that *suppliers* will be stable, high quality, and timely sources of supply. For lower costs, management wants assurance that suppliers know of management's needs for materials but that access by suppliers to other information is restricted. Management wants assurance that *employees* have followed its directives and not stolen assets. But they also want assurance that employees have been informed of management's wishes and policies.

As to *customers,* management wants assurance that they have the ability to pay for their purchases and are paying when due. But management also wants to assure customers of product quality, since customers are usually willing to pay more for a high-quality product. Finally, management wishes to have assurance that information about *competitors* is relevant and reliable, including information about technology used by competitors in manufacturing, selling, and distributing products and services.

To Inform Others

Management needs to assure *lenders* that its financial information is reliable, that it has complied with lending agreement terms, and that there are sufficient assets to cover its debts. Management can benefit if it assures *directors,* as representatives of stockholders, that managers have performed in compliance with legal requirements and with the directors' wishes, and that risks faced by the business are not excessive. *Financial analysts,* as information intermediaries for potential investors, are more likely to recommend buying a stock, other things equal, if they have confidence that management has truthfully provided information about the state of the firm, their plans, and the firm's prospects for the future—another demand for information assurance.

To Comply with Legal Requirements

There are statutory, regulatory, and contractual requirements that management provide assured information, such as audited GAAP-based financial statements, to *regulators, lenders,* and *stockholders.* These legal requirements typically specify that management is to make assertions of compliance with legal or contract provisions and have their compliance assertions attested to, or certified, by an independent assurance professional such as a CPA.

Assurance Employment Contracts

For the first two assurance demands (to inform management and to inform others), there are no government regulations or mandates, and the demand for assurance is strictly *value driven*—whatever adds value for management can be done. This includes choice of methods and choice of assurer. The same is not true for compliance with contract and legal provisions. For purposes of the law or contract, methods may be specified, and unless a particular audit firm or class of audit firm is specified, all audit firms' certificates are equal. So management can maximize profits by selecting the minimum cost supplier of certificates of compliance. This distinction changes the nature of the demand for assurance by management from (net) value maximization to cost minimization.

For the first two demands, the value of assurance services will be determined by the relevance of measurement methods, and by the reputation of the independent assurance provider for care and competence in assuring proper application and trustworthiness in display of the results—all as perceived by the decision maker. Thus, the reputation of the independent assurance provider is an important determinant of the value of assurance services. In addition, the value of assurance services depends, in part, on how the independent assurer is hired or contracted.

For analyses in this book, the assurer's job is to improve the quality of information or its context for the *benefit of management*, whether the information is for or from management. It is useful to distinguish *three* ways that they can be hired by management. The employment contract may affect outsiders' perceptions of the assurer's trustworthiness or independence, based on whether the assurer has an interest in the information other than its quality.

An information assurance provider's services can be contracted with the assurer acting as

- An information **originator** who prepares or analyzes information for management as an independent contractor (e.g., advisors who select and display information for management, design information or control systems, or determine relevant information for a particular decision).

- An information **investigator** who examines an explicit or implicit assertion about a real-world condition or process and reports findings directly to management as either an employee or an independent contractor (e.g., an internal auditor who routinely evaluates information and processes on behalf of top management, or a buy-side external auditor hired by management to evaluate another company).

- An information **certifier** who, as an independent contractor hired by management, examines management's assertions and then represents to an outside party that the assertions comply with the stated measurement criteria (e.g., a sell-side external auditor hired by management to audit financial statements prepared by management).

The three types of contracts are shown in Figure 1–4. In all three forms, there is a **source** of information (the person responsible for the real-world conditions of interest), a **decision maker,** and an **assurer.** In all cases the employment contract for the assurer is with management, even though management is sometimes the source and sometimes the decision maker (user).

The contract affects the assurer's incentives, loyalties, and legal duty to the decision maker, and leads to complications in the decision maker's evaluation of information quality. There is ambiguity or "wiggle room" in the preparation and auditing of GAAP-based financial statements. GAAP and GAAS (generally accepted auditing standards) require exercise of judgment, and judgments differ directionally across humans because of differences in the orientation or points of view of the person exercising judgment. The assurer's employment contract is one source of bias, and should be considered in interpreting the resulting information.

In an information origination contract, the subject matter of the information is the real-world condition of interest. For example, the subject matter could be the real-world condition of an asset or the performance of a person, process, or entity. The originator/assurer develops relevant information about the real-world condition. The assurer is not the source of the information because the assurer is not responsible for the real-world conditions of interest.

FIGURE 1–4

Assurance Contracts

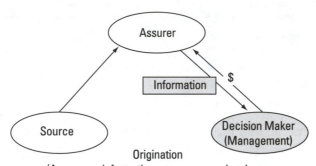

Origination
(Assurer as information source—e.g., developer
or reporter of information; or decision relevance analyst)

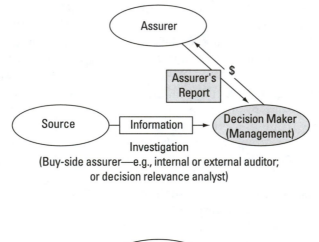

Investigation
(Buy-side assurer—e.g., internal or external auditor;
or decision relevance analyst)

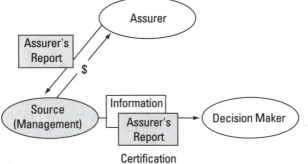

Certification
(Sell-side assurer—e.g., external auditor)

Thus, the assurer can be independent of the information because he or she has no interest in the subject matter except for the quality of information about it.[9]

The assurer as *originator* of information is a simple form of contract because the assurer's interests are clearly aligned with those of management. Since management hires the originator-assurer, management can select one with an acceptable reputation for competence and trustworthiness, and since management can instruct the assurer about its decision-making objectives, relevance of information is likely.

The assurer as *investigator* hired by management is also straightforward in that the interests of the investigator and management are aligned. Management can select an investigator-assurer with an acceptable reputation for competence and trustworthiness, and can instruct the assurer about what measurement criteria are to be applied. The buy-side investigator-assurer will report departures of the information from established criteria, as well as anything else that he or she believes would be relevant to the decision maker.

The assurer as *certifier* relationship is more subtle. In this type of contract, the information source hires the assurer to examine the source's own claims and to report findings to the user/decision maker, but the interests of the certifier-assurer and the decision maker are not necessarily aligned. Since the certificate has value to the source *only if* the user/decision maker believes that information quality is improved, management must consider the user's assessment of the decision relevance of the measurement methods and confidence in the assurer's reputation for competence and trustworthiness that affect the decision maker's assessment of information reliability.

Financial statement audits are the most common certification contract. GAAP is intended to provide decision-relevant information for investors who cannot individually dictate what information they want from management. The auditing profession and regulators such as the SEC prescribe that GAAS be followed to increase investor perceptions of auditor competence, and they prohibit certain relations between auditors and management as a means of increasing perceived independence, and thus trustworthiness.

The assurance contract form is particularly relevant when the auditor notices conditions that may be of interest to the user/decision maker, but the conditions are *not covered* by the stated measurement criteria. For example, suppose that the auditor of the financial statements of LJ Appliances notices that the company has weak controls, and by implication, LJ Appliances may face reduced future profitability. A sell-side auditor hired by Linda Jo to *certify* that her current financial statements comply with GAAP is unlikely to report the poor controls to outsiders (Linda Jo might even sue the auditor for disclosing such private information). On the other hand, a buy-side auditor hired by a potential buyer to *investigate* Linda Jo's financial statements might also be instructed to "report anything else that you think we ought to know about LJ Appliances." The buy-side auditor would likely report the poor controls to the prospective buyer that hired the auditor to investigate.

---

9. An issue that sometimes arises is whether the party that originates information can also serve as an independent assurer that takes a "second look" to investigate or certify the information. This issue will be addressed in Chapter 12.

SUMMARY

Assurance services are independent professional services that improve the quality of information, or its context, for decision makers. Independent assurance providers, who have no interest in the information except its quality, can add value for management by (a) assuring management that information for its own decision making is relevant and reliable, (b) assuring others that information provided by management is reliable, and (c) demonstrating compliance with legal requirements. Assurers can act as originators of information, as investigators on behalf of management, or as certifiers that information meets stated measurement criteria.

Information displays based on measurement methods that track essential elements of the real world and facilitate formation of useful mental images of real-world conditions can add value by providing *relevant* information for decision making. The information is *reliable* if there is negligible error in applying stated measurement rules and measurements are accurately displayed.

It is the decision maker's perception of both the *relevance* of information for the decision at hand and the *reliability* of its preparation and display that ultimately determines its value. Perceptions of relevance and reliability can be enhanced by independent assurance providers who originate, investigate, or certify elements of the information display. The decision maker's assessment of relevance and reliability will be affected by the independent assurance provider's reputation for competence and trustworthiness, as well as by the assurer's employment contract form.

Assured information displays can benefit management through (a) lower cost of capital by reducing the price-protection discount by lenders and investors and demonstrating compliance with contracts and regulations and (b) lower cost of production, selling, collection, and distribution by assuring managers and its trading partners that information can be substituted for aspects of the real-world firm.

ORGANIZATION OF THE BOOK

The remaining chapters of this book are organized along the lines of management's three demands for assurance services. **Section I (Chapters 2–6)** addresses management's needs to *inform itself* and to *protect* the firm's *assets.* In Section I there is little distinction between internal control, internal auditors, and external auditors since for internal decision-making purposes, their services are, to some extent, substitutes for each other.

Section II (Chapters 7–10) extends the concepts of Section I to include assurance services to *inform those outside the firm* such as customers, suppliers, stockholders, lenders, directors, and the board of directors. The employment contract of the assurer will be important in Section II since the user/decision maker's assessment of information relevance and reliability will be influenced by who pays the assurer.

Section III (Chapters 11 and 12) explores compliance with *laws and regulations* involving public disclosure of information and information for private contracts. Regulatory requirements and prohibitions are explored, as are alternatives for corporate governance and professional ethical codes.

CASE 1

MEENA'S PEARL DOCK

Meena assembles and sells strings of pearls at her waterfront shop on Galveston Island, Texas. One day Nick, a seafaring man unknown to Meena, appears in her shop offering to sell a bag of 1,000 pearls at a bargain price. Meena puts the contents through her "count and size" machine to confirm the number and size, but she is naturally apprehensive about the quality of the pearls. Nick claims that all 1,000 are of high quality, and he appears to be trustworthy, but he may not be around if the pearls are later discovered to be "bad."

Meena makes some mental calculations of the costs associated with buying poor-quality pearls and the benefit of the bargain price. Based on these calculations, Meena decides on a "break even" criterion for the purchase. If she can be "reasonably assured" (or believe with 95 percent confidence) that there are less than 30 bad pearls in the bag of 1,000, then she would like to make the purchase at Nick's offering price. Without such assurance, Meena is unwilling to take a chance on the transaction.

What is "relevant information" for Meena's decision?

What are three ways that Meena might become "reasonably assured" that Nick's quality claim is reliable?

Who will bear the cost of obtaining Meena's confidence?

Now suppose that the person appearing at Meena's Pearl Dock is Phil, the proprietor of an established Galveston pearl importer, Phil's Philippine Pearl Supply. Phil offers a bag of pearls equivalent to Nick's at the same price (described as a "special introductory" price) and a long-term contract guaranteeing a defect rate of less than 1 percent.

What additional assurance options or combinations are now viable?

Which seller would receive a higher (net) price for his bag of pearls, and what does this tell you about the costs and benefits of assurance?

KEY WORDS

accounting system   Personnel, procedures, and equipment that (a) measure and report the monetary value of transactions with suppliers, workers, and customers and (b) establish recorded accountability to operationalize the internal control process.

assurance services   Independent professional services that improve the quality of information, or its context, for decision makers.

attestation   An assurer's expression of a conclusion, based on application of verification procedures, about the reliability of an assertion made by another party.

auditing (broad)   Same as attestation.

auditing (narrow)   An examination of, and expression of a conclusion about, the reliability of another party's assertions that financial statements comply with GAAP.

context completeness   All relevant information about key factors, risks, alternatives, and outcomes is available to the decision maker.

decision relevance analysis   Improves information quality by providing measurements, measurement methods, and other information that help a decision maker form a better mental image of real-world conditions about which he or she wants or needs to know.

generally accepted accounting principles (GAAP)   Methods established by a standards-setting body such as the Financial Accounting Standards Board (FASB) or commonly agreed upon by professional accountants, by which to attach monetary values to economic transactions, events, and status.

independent assurer   A professional that improves the quality of information for decision making and whose *only* substantive interest in the information is its quality.

information certifier　An independent contractor hired by the information preparer to attest that the preparer's assertions comply with stated measurement criteria.

information context　All key factors, risks, and other information about real-world conditions relevant to a particular decision, including interpretation and completeness of information.

information investigator　An independent contractor or employee of a decision maker who verifies an explicit or implicit assertion made by a third party and reports a conclusion to the decision maker.

information originator　An independent contractor hired by a decision maker to provide relevant and reliable information.

internal control　A process, effected by an entity's board of directors, management, and other personnel, designed to provide reasonable assurance regarding the achievement of objectives in the following categories: effectiveness and efficiency of operations, reliability of financial reporting, and compliance with applicable laws and regulations.

quality of information　Degree to which (a) measurement methods used to prepare information can represent what a decision maker wants to know (information relevance) and (b) the stated methods have been competently applied and results truthfully displayed (information reliability or credibility).

2 CHAPTER

Business Measurement Systems: Information Relevance

- Have all key success factors been considered in my long-term strategic plan for the company?
- Do I have measures of what I need to know about all important short-term planning factors?
- Am I using the right model to predict and plan for the future?
- Are my employees being properly informed about how to carry out my plans?
- Are internal score-keeping measures adequate to evaluate performance essential to achieving my short-term and long-term objectives for the company?

All five of these questions are about content of management's information model representing the past, present, and possible future real-world condition of a business. Specifically, all five questions concern the **relevance** of information or its context for management. Decision relevance analysis by independent assurance professionals benefits management through better mental images of real-world conditions about which the manager wants to know so that he or she can make a decision. Image relevance is improved through *better measurement methods* to attach numbers to real-world conditions, or through *better understanding* of what measurements represent or mean (i.e., context).

This chapter explores answers to these and related questions about the relevance of information produced by the **business measurement system** that measures day-to-day activities of the firm. Our focus in this chapter is on how to systematically and economically obtain, customize, and interrelate information produced by the business measurement system. *External environment* information, *risk assessments,* and *reliability* of information produced by the business measurement system (e.g., possible errors in measurements) will be deferred until Chapter 3. As in Chapter 1, we will use the GAAP-based accounting system as a template for analysis.

We begin with a generic business decision model that relates accounting and other information to business planning and performance evaluation decisions. This is followed by models of the business firm and its business processes, its business measurement system, and enterprisewide software that supports all of the processes. Decision relevance assurance services, including customization and integration of accounting information for particular decisions and business measurement system design, complete the chapter.

DECISIONS USING ACCOUNTING INFORMATION

A business firm directs resources to the design, production, sale, and distribution of products and services. **Business processes** link the firm to its external **operating environment.** Specifically, business processes and internal control that support them link suppliers of the business and its workers with its customers, and are affected by competitors, regulators, capital providers, and the objectives of stockholders and others. Business processes and the operating environment are elements of the **strategic environment** of the firm.

Strategic Environment

The strategic environment of a business is comprised of longer-term external environment factors such as consumer tastes and preferences, demographics of the customer base, technological developments (substitute products and new ways of meeting old demands), and social, regulatory, and cultural factors. Long-term objectives for a corporate business entity depend on the long-term objectives of its stockholders, which typically include maximization of stock value.

Stock value depends on the ability of the business to earn more than its cost of capital, and the ability to earn more than its cost of capital depends on its available resources and long-term business strategy. In turn, business strategy defines which markets or industries the firm will enter, the scope of its activities within those markets, and how it will compete. For example, competitive strategy might focus on being the lowest cost provider of services, the largest provider, a technology leader, the highest-quality provider, or a combination of strategies. The resulting business strategy links the strategic environment and available resources to the short-term operating environment of the firm.

To succeed, the firm's strategy must exploit its sources of competitive advantage to generate results that meet the needs of stockholders through financial rewards commensurate with risks taken. It must meet the needs of trading partners: meeting the product and service needs of customers at reasonable prices, while paying competitive wages and other benefits for workers and offering financial rewards to suppliers commensurate with their investment in their products. Also, the business must comply with laws and regulations and meet threats to the continued success of the firm.

The chosen strategy will dictate the relative importance of business processes and suggest key success factors for which relevant measurements and measurement systems are needed. The business measurement system can be useful in measuring periodic progress toward successful implementation of strategies.

Operating Environment: Business Decision Model

Business strategies are implemented over multiple operating periods. Figure 2–1 shows a stylized and discrete operating decision model comprised of six steps that implement the long-term strategy each period. The first step is *obtaining information* about real-world conditions at time 0 that are relevant to conditions that may exist during period 1 and about

FIGURE 2–1

Operating Decisions, Measurement, and Evaluation

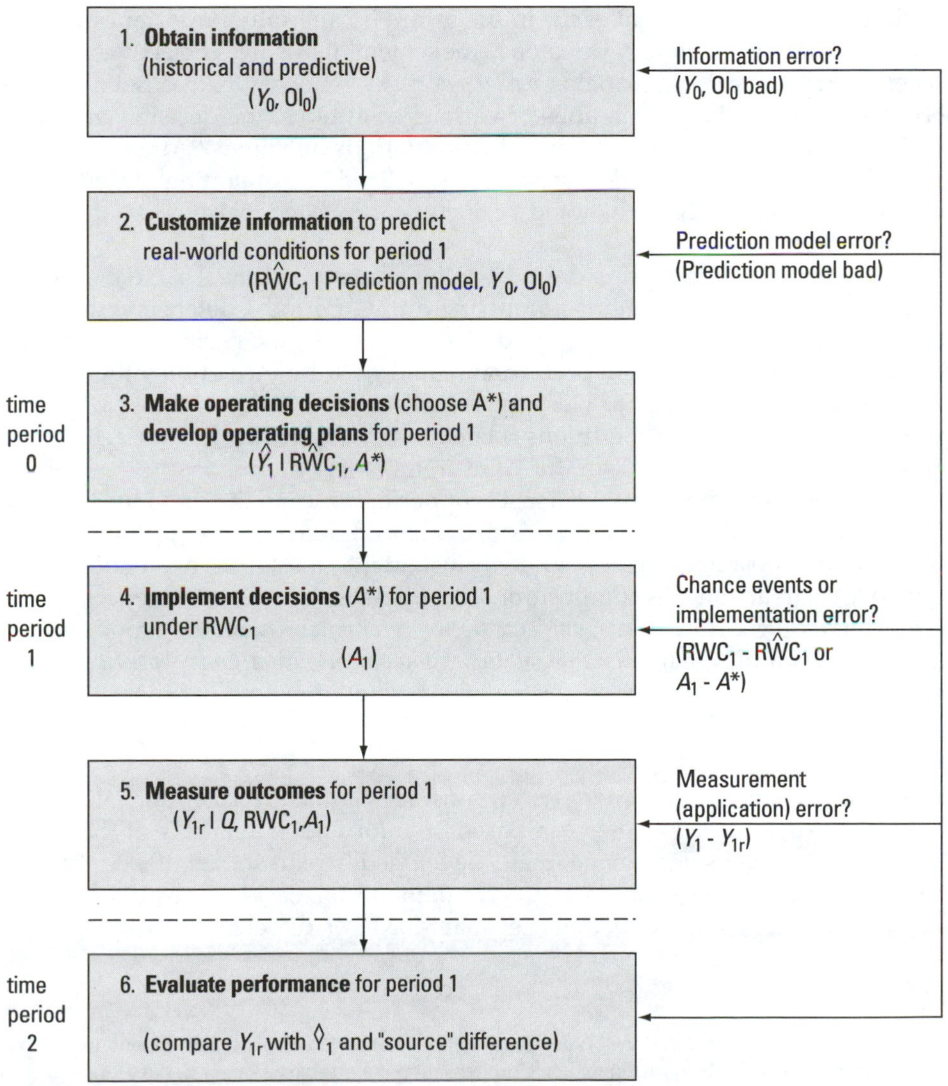

1. **Obtain information**
(historical and predictive)
(Y_0, OI_0)

Information error?
$(Y_0, OI_0$ bad$)$

2. **Customize information** to predict
real-world conditions for period 1
$(R\hat{W}C_1 \mid \text{Prediction model}, Y_0, OI_0)$

Prediction model error?
(Prediction model bad)

time period 0

3. **Make operating decisions** (choose A*) and
develop operating plans for period 1
$(\hat{Y}_1 \mid R\hat{W}C_1, A^*)$

time period 1

4. **Implement decisions** (A*) for period 1
under RWC_1
(A_1)

Chance events or
implementation error?
$(RWC_1 - R\hat{W}C_1$ or
$A_1 - A^*)$

5. **Measure outcomes** for period 1
$(Y_{1r} \mid Q, RWC_1, A_1)$

Measurement
(application) error?
$(Y_1 - Y_{1r})$

time period 2

6. **Evaluate performance** for period 1

(compare Y_{1r} with $\hat{Y}_1$ and "source" difference)

alternative courses of action that might be taken for period 1. Information obtained typically includes historical GAAP-based financial statements (Y_0, for time period 0 and prior periods), since historical accounting numbers provide some information about past actions and conditions and the relations between them. Other-than-historical-accounting information (OI_0) includes nonfinancial measures of current conditions at time 0 and internal and external forecasts of future conditions for period 1.

In step 2, Y_0 and OI_0 are customized using a prediction model to *predict* expected and other possible real-world conditions for period 1 ($R\hat{W}C$). For example, customizing Y_0 information would eliminate the effects of period 0 and prior events and conditions that are not expected to recur during period 1, and add effects of possibly unique events and conditions anticipated for period 1. Information about the probabilities of various possible real-world conditions that might occur in the future is especially important in evaluating business risks that may seriously threaten achievement of business objectives.

Then in step 3, the decision maker *makes a decision*—chooses the best set of actions (A^*) for period 1 based on the probabilities of various conditions, the decision maker's other knowledge and abilities, and his or her utility for various outcomes.[1] After making the decision, implementation *plans are developed* and formalized into operating plans for period 1. The operating plans or budgets (denoted $\hat{Y}_1$) include forecasted real-world outcomes based on the planned actions.

Step 4 is *implementing*, during period 1, A^* as planned at time 0. Actual actions taken (A_1) and actual real-world conditions occurring during period 1 determine the actual period 1 outcomes (RWC_1, A_1). During period 1, step 5 *measures* the period 1 *outcomes*, and indirectly measures implementation performance and performance of the other steps. How numbers are attached to RWC_1 to yield the recorded Y (Y_{1r}) is central to the value of the measured results. Real-world conditions related to key success factors for achieving long-run objectives are especially relevant for measurement.

Finally, step 6 is *evaluation* of all aspects of performance in the previous five steps. At step 6, the decision maker compares period 1 recorded outcomes (Y_{1r}) with planned outcomes ($\hat{Y}_1$). Decomposition of $Y_{1r} - \hat{Y}_1$ allows insight into the causes of any deviations and suggests follow-up actions. Decomposition may allow isolation of differences as *measurement error in recording, chance events, implementation error* (plans misunderstood or carelessly implemented by employees), *poor information for planning,* or a *flawed prediction model*. It may also suggest that the long-term strategy needs alteration.

LJ Appliances

To illustrate the decomposition of $Y_{1r} - \hat{Y}_1$, consider planned refrigerator sales for LJ Appliances for the first quarter of the year. Based on information available at the start of the quarter, LJ Appliances' sales management developed a plan to sell 10,000 refrigerators chainwide. The plan is based on an aggregate demand forecast (OI_0) of 100,000 refrigerators for LJ's trade area and a target market share for LJ of 10 percent (the planning model is simply aggregate demand times .1).

---

1. The decision maker's utility for various outcomes (and his or her action choices) will depend in part on the compensation plan for the decision maker. Compensation may be based on, or tied to, long-run strategy and the stockholders' objectives. As we will see, coordination of compensation and overall objectives using accounting information is one role for decision relevance analysis.

Recorded sales units for the first quarter were 9,650, so the aggregate difference between planned and recorded performance to be analyzed $(Y_{1r} - \hat{Y}_1)$ is 350. LJ's internal auditor's investigation of the difference revealed the following:

- A tornado destroyed LJ's Tulsa store, resulting in the loss of 250 planned sales.
- Aggregate demand for refrigerators in LJ's trade area was 5 percent higher than the amount predicted at the start of the first quarter.
- A new competitor takes refrigerator orders via the World Wide Web and ships from a central warehouse in Des Moines. The company was unknown prior to the start of the quarter, but is estimated to have sold 4,200 units (a 4 percent market share) in LJ's trade area during the quarter.

There are many ways to decompose these conditions. LJ's internal auditor prepared the following summary:

Planned unit sales as of start of quarter	
(100,000 × .1)	10,000
Information error	
((105,000 − 100,000) × .1)	500
Prediction model error	
(unanticipated competitor type)	−420
Chance events (unanticipated	
Tulsa tornado)	−250
Revised planned unit sales	9,830
Recorded unit sales for quarter	9,650
Unexplained difference	−180

Based on this decomposition, LJ's management can decide what it means for performance evaluation in operations, planning, and information sources. For example, management might decide that since the aggregate demand prediction was off by only 5 percent, it may not be cost-effective to try to improve the aggregate prediction process. Also, except for the new competitor and the tornado, LJ did obtain about a 10 percent market share.

The presence of a new type of competitor had a small impact the first quarter but may have a large impact in the future. Based on analysis of what the new competitor type may mean for future sales, reconsideration of LJ's operations and strategy may be appropriate. If long-term changes are deemed unnecessary, then a change should be made in the prediction model by lowering LJ's planned market share. Tornadoes and other natural disasters occur with some regularity worldwide but are not predictable as to locality or timing. The Tulsa tornado is thus unlikely to affect planning of future sales, although it may cause management to consider whether insurance is needed to mitigate risk.

Finally, the unexplained difference of 180 units could be due to error in implementing the period 1 plan, error in measuring units sold, or a large number of other causes. Given the relatively small effect of these unexplained causes in the aggregate and the cost of further investigation as to cause(s), LJ might ignore them for this period.

In this example, a nonfinancial measure was decomposed. In Chapters 3 and 5, we will consider decomposing accounting differences to evaluate performance, the risks of environmental change, and the risk of accounting errors and fraud.

A MODEL OF THE FIRM, ITS BUSINESS PROCESSES, AND THE BUSINESS MEASUREMENT SYSTEM

In order to determine what should be included in a business measurement system, the system's designer must know what factors are relevant to the decision maker or decision makers. A conceptual model of the firm can provide a basis for determining the relevant factors. This section outlines a conceptual model of a firm. The model, diagrammed in Figure 2–2, shows the external environment within which the business operates along with its **business processes** that relate the firm to its eight outside constituencies discussed in Chapter 1 (customers, suppliers, workers, competitors, lenders, directors/shareholders, analysts/potential shareholders, and regulators). Understanding the conceptual model and its elements will facilitate design of an information model of the firm through the business measurement system.

Business processes are comprised of the **core processes** of the business, **support services** that facilitate the core processes, and the **business measurement system** that provides day-to-day elements of management's information model of the firm. Business measurement systems also provide connecting links for communication and control within the organization and information required by the eight outside constituencies.

In Figure 2–2, the three business processes are surrounded by the internal control process (explored in Chapters 3 and 4) that helps people within the organization achieve their effectiveness, efficiency, and compliance objectives. The arrows show primary resource and information flows within the business and with outside constituents. For simplicity, the firm's capital assets are not shown.

Core Processes

Core processes are activities for which the firm has a competitive advantage—those activities that the firm can *do better than,* or at least as well as, any competitor. If core processes are impaired, the firm loses its competitive advantage. Core processes link workers and suppliers with customers of the firm. The core processes of most businesses are some combination of production of goods or services and the sale, distribution, and post-sale servicing of products. Because of their importance, core process performance measures are often key factors for a firm's success. Thus, they are the objects of both assurance services and internal control.

Support Services

For most businesses, support services include procurement and management of materials for production and sale of goods and services, human resources, and process technology and design services. These services facilitate the core processes but do not add unique value without the core process. For most firms, these support services are amenable to "outsourcing" (acquiring the service from outside the firm). *Core processes,* the unique process advantages of the firm, are not amenable to outsourcing. Outsourcing allows the firm to concentrate on its core processes, and may lead to demand for assurance about outsourcing quality.

FIGURE 2–2

The Firm, Its External Environment, and Its Business Processes

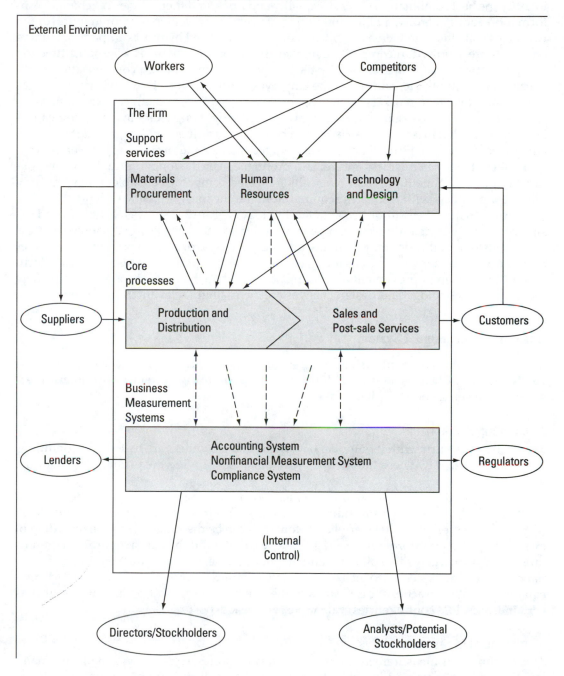

Materials procurement is often separated from production and sales management to allow specialization of effort. Efficient procurement may require worldwide searches to identify the best combination of service quality and price, and then efficient exchange of information about quantity, quality, and timing of needs to implement procurement. **Human resources** contribute an increasing portion of the value added by most companies. Human resources are acquired in competitive markets for labor and talent. This support function must find the human skills needed by the business, and then design compensation packages to attract, motivate, and retain the employees desired. Once hired, human resources must communicate to workers the plans, policies, procedures, and ethical expectations.

Technology and **organization design** are increasingly important in maintaining profitability of any business, and may even be a core process as it is for George's Electronic Security (see Chapter 1). Firms that have superior technology and design support services are more likely to stay in business and remain profitable over the longer term. In an environment of global competition, technologically informed companies are able to react quickly with new products with resources acquired from the cheapest source worldwide.

How do firms keep informed about technology? Figure 2–2 shows technology and design receiving information from competitors and customers as principal sources. For example, customer attitudes may shift toward a new product, or a new competitor may offer better service. In many businesses today, employees and suppliers are also sources of technology and design improvements as trading partners share benefits of cooperation. Timely measures of technology and design changes are increasingly relevant information.

Business Measurement System

The business measurement system routinely measures a firm's transactions, events, and conditions day to day as they occur. It includes the **accounting system, nonfinancial measurement system,** and **compliance system.**

Accounting System

Transactions of a firm with its suppliers, workers, and customers are real-world conditions occurring day to day. These transactions with outsiders provide the primary input for the accounting system.

Transactions and records of transactions also provide the basis for control of company assets through compliance procedures protecting the firm's boundaries with outsiders (e.g., authorization procedures applied before cash can be disbursed), and the recording of events provides an information model of the accountability of various parties within or outside the firm. As we'll explore in more depth in the next section, the accounting and financial reporting system also includes estimates of transactions yet to be completed, allocations of past transactions, disclosures of the effects of off-the-books conditions such as certain leases, loss contingencies, valuations, and risk exposures.

Nonfinancial Measurement System

The nonfinancial measurement system includes continuously and systematically maintained numbers measured in nonmonetary units. Some of the numbers are related to accounting system and financial statement elements (i.e., units produced and sold, hours worked, and quantities of materials used in production). Other numbers are not directly related to the accounting transactions but determine the relevance of accounting numbers. As examples, human resources has records of employee qualifications, ages, tenure with the firm, and compensation plans. Sales management has records of square footage of retail selling space, age of facilities, and trade area statistics for most outlets, while credit management has records of customer characteristics, credit qualifications, and tenure as a customer. Technology has records of when products were developed and introduced into product lines, and procurement has records of supplier delivery and quality performance, contract terms, and tenure as a supplier. Thus, the nonfinancial measurement system includes quantities of various types measured in physical units, hours, ages, and quality.

Compliance System

A firm's compliance system consists of records that meet the information demands of outside regulators including accounting requirements, tax requirements, and other compliance matters such as OSHA regulations and EPA requirements. The compliance system also incorporates mechanisms (denoted "control activities" in COSO, 1994; see Chapter 4) for assuring compliance with the firm's internal policies and procedures that protect assets, as well as ethical behavior desired. These mechanisms are applied continuously as day-to-day transactions are being processed, and are frequently required before a transaction can be completed (e.g., entry of an employee's code before release of materials).

Systems Integration: Enterprisewide Software

Accounting transactions–based records are measured or denominated in monetary units (dollars, francs, yen) and reflect a related (and varying) quantity. Payables are kept by invoice or supplier and payroll is kept by employee, while inventory is kept by product number and receivables are kept by customer.

The individual financial data elements and their aggregates are useful for controlling individual transactions and for measuring some aspects of overall performance. However, the relation of accounting numbers to nonfinancial information is often more relevant. As examples, to evaluate sales personnel efficiency, revenue per sales call is more useful than total revenue, and revenue per sales call that is less than that of competitors may signal a personnel, technology, or design problem. Decision relevance requires the capability to relate accounting system elements to various nonfinancial system elements. Also, decision relevance requires that a decision maker be able to decompose or "drill down" from an aggregate number to isolate its components that may be out of line with expectations.

Reliability of information and economic efficiency are enhanced if the compliance system is simultaneously applied as the accounting and nonfinancial systems are being applied, and the processing results are integrated across departments and across core and support processes. The 1990s have brought broad use of integrated, enterprisewide software (sometimes called enterprise resource planning (ERP) software) that can accommodate information needs of the core and support processes as well as the accounting, nonfinancial, and compliance systems.[2]

---

2. Enterprisewide software is offered by SAP AG, Oracle, PeopleSoft, Baan and Lawson, and other much smaller firms.

Fees of professional services firms to facilitate implementation of enterprisewide software including adaptation of modules for efficiency, effectiveness, and control are estimated at $5.5 billion in 1996[3] and $19 billion for 1997 and are growing at a 24 percent annual rate through 2002.[4] In contrast, aggregate revenues from accounting and auditing services of the largest 60 CPA firms in the United States have been about $7 billion per year during the 1990s. Thus, enterprise software is an increasingly important element in the overall package of information assurance and internal control for management.

To illustrate, let's consider some of the capabilities of SAP R/3, currently the largest selling enterprisewide software. SAP R/3 is based on 12 application modules that track most business processes and allow inquiries and continuous updating of a central database. To apply SAP, real-world activities of a business must be mapped to SAP's generic business process flows, which include those in Figure 2–2 but in much more detail. The generic process model allows some adaptation to unique features of a business but requires that SAP R/3's overall structure be followed. The structure matches integrated computer code that operationalizes and links each of the 12 application modules. In turn, the 12 modules access a single integrated database.

Prairie Home Corporation

Our illustration applies the Sales and Distribution (SD), Materials Management (MM), Human Resources (HR), Production Planning (PP), Controlling (CO), Treasury (TRS), and Financial Accounting (FI) modules to the sale and manufacture of a customized new home built by Prairie Home Corporation (PHC) of Anoka, Minnesota. Prairie Home offers 20 basic house plans. Customers can select a basic home plan and customize it by their choices among standardized components such as a sauna.

For sales/materials/production, the primary linking file in the central database is the Master Production Schedule that tracks home orders from their entry by sales personnel using the SD module, through delivery of title of the finished home to the sales personnel for closing. Upon entry of the customized sales order, the PP module converts the sales order into component units required for the finished product as part of Materials Requirements Planning file and schedules production. Materials management accesses the Materials Requirements Planning file to determine component and materials needs. The MM module is then used to select vendors, order materials, communicate status, and oversee delivery to production. When the goods are received, production (construction) takes place, the PP module processes completion of manufacture, and eventually the finished home order is forwarded to sales personnel for invoicing (using the SD module) and delivery to the customer.

While SD, PP, and MM are the primary modules in the illustration, others are also active. Parallel activities are in place for scheduling required labor skills using the HR and the CO modules to provide product cost and revenue analyses for the order. The SD, PP, and MM modules also generate traditional accounting entries for purchase/payment, cost of manufacture/sales, and sales/receivables used by the FI module to update financial accounting records and prepare periodic financial reports. Finally, the TR module facilitates financial and cash management including forecasting operating cash flows.

---

3. *The Wall Street Journal*, March 14, 1997.
4. Gartner Group, Stamford, CT, as reported in *Public Accounting Report*, July 31, 1998, p. 4.

Figure 2–3, part A, shows an outline of SAP R/3 as implemented by Prairie Home Corporation. It shows the client/server/database nature of the application and typical reports, or "views" of the same data for a particular order by different users. The same data elements are accessed by different users and different applications for different purposes (part B).

The essential features of enterprise software are that information and control activities for processes are integrated and use a single database, with multiple and continuous updating by employees in various departments. Also, multiple employees can access the same data, and the software has access and updating, with drill-down and reformatting capabilities. Enterprise software automates many data controls traditionally handled by different individual humans and greatly speeds processing and updating.

Figure 2–3, part B, shows aspects of PHC's home Sales Order 118 written on May 12, 1999, by sales personnel using SD. The order for a type B house with an Oley's Sauna caused PP to prepare a production order for the master production schedule. From the

FIGURE 2–3

SAP R/3 Configuration and Selected Data Views for Prairie Home Corp., as of 8/23/98

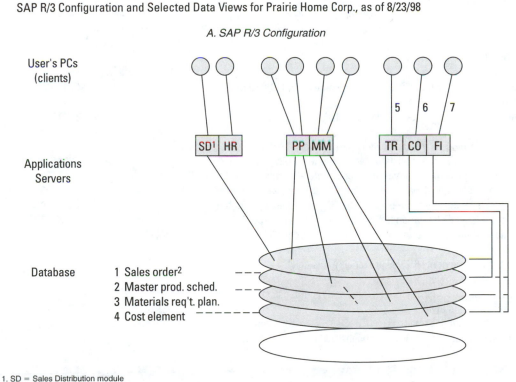

A. SAP R/3 Configuration

User's PCs (clients)

Applications Servers

SD[1] HR   PP MM   TR CO FI

5   6   7

Database
1 Sales order[2]
2 Master prod. sched.
3 Materials req't. plan.
4 Cost element

1. SD = Sales Distribution module
   HR = Human Resources module
   PP = Production Planning module
   MM = Materials Management module
   TR = Treasury module
   CO = Controlling module
   FI = Financial Accounting module
2. See Data Views in Part B.

FIGURE 2 – 3 (oont'd)

B. Selected Data Views as of August 23, 1998

1. Sales Order (S.O.):

S.O.	Order Date	House Type	Price	Custom	Delivery Date
118	5/12/99	B	$215,000	Oley's Sauna	9/15/99

2. Master Production Schedule: Production Order (P.O.) 118

Item	Quan. Std.	Quan. Act.	Act. Cost	Std. Cost	Date Issued	Date Due
Bricks	5K	5.3K	$5,300	$5,000	8/13/99	9/2/99
Oley's Sauna	1		0	0	$1,599	

3. Materials Requirements Planning (by materials item):

Item	Quan. on hand	Ave. Cost	Quan. on order 9/99	10/99	11/99
Bricks	75K	$1	220k	85K	75K	60K
Oley's Sauna	5	1,599	8	3	4	1

4. Recorded Cost Element (by order and item):

S.O.	Item	Quan.	Act. Cost	Date	Variance	Supervisor
118	Bricks	5.3K	$5,300	8/13/99	$300	G.K.

5. Cash Flow Projection for September 1999:

Sales proceeds

(sum "price" on S.O.s for 9/99 del. dates (includes P.O. 118, $215,000)) $4,831,000

Cost outlays

(sum open Prod. Orders for 9/99 dates (includes 118, $1,599))   −2,323,000

6. Variances fo 8/1/99 through 8/23/99 (various views of P.O. 118 bricks):

Sum of dollar variance for all data elements dated 8/1/99 through 8/23/99	$323,500
By house type (sum dollar variance for all data elements for house type B)*	13,800
By supervisor (sum dollar variance for all data elements supervised by G.K.)*	26,320
By item (sum dollar variance for all open P.O. data elements for bricks)*	3,230
By order (sum dollar variance for all data elements for order 118)	6,580
By data element (dollar variance for bricks for order 118)	300

7. Financial Statements 8/23/99 (materials items only):

Balance Sheet—Inventory

(sum of actual cost of inventory on hand and recorded cost elements

  for active orders at 8/23/99) $9,328,000

Income Statement—Variances

(sum dollar variance from 8/1/99 through 8/23/99)   323,500

master production schedule, MM looked up the list and timing of materials required for a B house to update the materials requirements plan, and scheduled ordering and delivery of materials. Sales, production, and materials management and procurement were all driven by the same sales order, and coordinated by the enterprisewide software.

Figure 2–3, part B, also shows the database status as of August 23, 1999, after installation of bricks on house 118. In particular, it shows the "recorded cost element," or basic data building block for cost data, which is the object of an accounting entry for the issuance of bricks from inventory and installation on house 118. The recorded cost element shows that 5,300 bricks were used, although the standard for a type B house is 5,000.

The variance of $300 is part of the recorded cost element for house 118, and records an aspect of performance by G. K., the supervisor on the house. The variance is part of other "views" of the data that can be assembled for analysis. For example, if the production manager wants to see how well PHC is performing for the month of August to-date, he or she can sum the variances across all data elements from August 1 through August 23, 1999. If the resulting total variance of $323,500 is deemed excessive relative to the manager's expectations, then he or she can "drill down" to a category of analysis to locate where costs are excessive. The subanalysis could be by house type (summing across house type to decompose the total), by supervisor, or by type of materials. Variance per house can also be calculated by relating the nonfinancial measure to the financial.

Thus, SAP R/3 helps PHC management plan, coordinate, and evaluate its activities. The enterprisewide software is a source of competitive advantage for the moment. Such software may be essential for survival in the future.

Enterprisewide software provides decision-relevant information that allows better coordination of activities, better resource utilization, better availability of information for customers, lower cost of production, and lower information processing and file maintenance cost. Even customers and suppliers may be given access to the database (recall George's access to Suzy's inventory records for George's products). Passwords and module entry codes as defined by security profiles limit who can access an application and who can update particular elements of the database.

The Accounting System as an Information Model

Because of its importance as a source of information and control for both management and external decision makers, let's consider the accounting system as an information model of a firm, its business processes, and its external environment. This analysis will allow a better understanding of the value and limitations of accounting as an information and control vehicle. It will also aid understanding of measurement method relevance.

Figure 2–4 diagrams a typical accounting system and some compliance system components comprising a major part of the measurements for the accounting information model representing the real-world core business and support processes of Figure 2–2. There are many similarities between the two figures, but also some important differences and incompleteness of representation in the accounting data. Figure 2–4 shows three boxes within the overall accounting system. The accounting and funds transfer boxes sense, measure, and process basic transactions with suppliers, workers, and customers as they occur day to day. The periodic accounting box includes allocations of other costs, point-in - time measures, and financial estimates and disclosures that are not processed day to day.

The Accounting and Compliance System and Financial Statement (Operating) Components

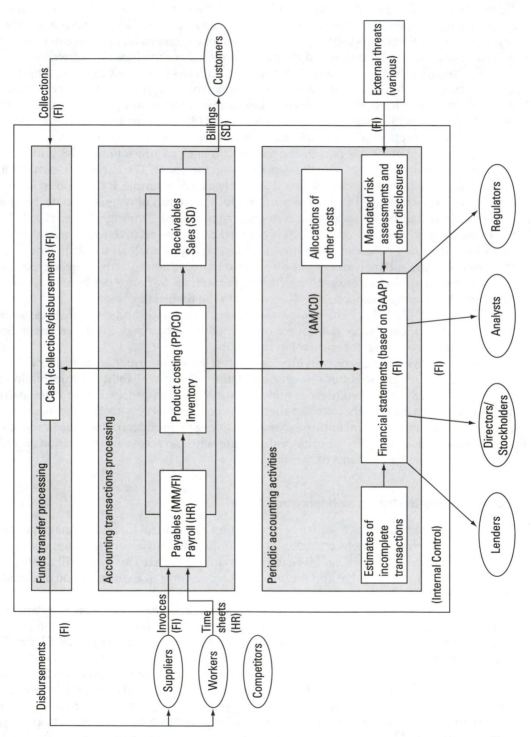

Parallel Features

Core processes and the materials procurement and human resources support processes are tracked by the accounting system. The procurement/payables processing and compliance systems (part of the MM module in SAP R/3) approve and process supplier invoices for payment and record the new asset and liability. Payroll processing and compliance (HR module) perform a similar role in approving workers' time sheets and recording the acquisition of human resources, and the receivables/sales processing and compliance systems (SD module) verify sales authorization, record the new asset, and prepare customer billings. Funds transfer processing implemented by the FI financial module in SAP R/3, receives cash from customers and, after verifying approval, disburses cash to suppliers and workers.

All of these basic accounting and compliance processes parallel a real-world transaction with persons or entities outside the firm, and all involve a natural measurement basis—cash or cash equivalents of the exchanged resources. In fact, all of these transactions are typically recorded at their cash or cash-equivalent magnitudes. The relevance for decision making of the measurements generated is obvious, and obviously useful in keeping track of payments owed and collections due the company. Less directly linked, but still parallel, is product costing that results from internal-to-the-firm transformations of materials and labor into finished product, along with the allocation of overhead costs (depreciation and allocations of corporate overhead). Product costs become costs of inventory, and inventory costs become costs of goods sold.

Differences

Some activities in Figure 2–4 have no direct counterpart in Figure 2–2. Product costing does not result from direct transactions with outsiders. Rather, the components of cost (materials, labor, and overhead) arise from internal events or transfers within the firm. In SAP R/3, product costing is initiated by the CO module based on production data via the PP module. Accounting for these internal transfers is useful in tracking responsibility (or recorded accountability) for company assets, but they do not have a natural basis for measurement. As examples, additions to the finished goods inventory could be valued using any of several historical costs to produce (following GAAP), the cost to replace component resources at the time of production, or the estimated resale value at the point of production (including estimated profit at that point and place).

There are many alternative ways to attach numbers to internally generated real-world conditions, so why is the GAAP way used? It's not because GAAP is the "theoretically correct" way to attach numbers, or that GAAP provides the most relevant measurements on average across all users of accounting numbers, and it is not necessarily the most useful for any one user. However, GAAP is the basis *mandated* by accounting authorities for attachment of numbers used in public reporting. GAAP-based measurements are required by law, regulation, and many securities exchanges and are specified in many contracts. Each of the parties specifying GAAP apparently believes that it is a useful basis, meaning that at least it meets the test of reasonable relevance for many decisions.

As elaborated later in this chapter, GAAP numbers need customization to make them *relevant* for prediction. However, customization of systematically maintained measurements such as GAAP-based accounting numbers is the cheapest way to obtain relevant information for many decisions. Enterprise software facilitates customization and makes multiple measurement methods feasible. Furthermore, some enterprise software automates foreign currency translations for easier interpretation.

Incompleteness

The most obvious omission from Figure 2–4 is the lack of accounting system provision for the technology and design functions. The primary *cost* of technology and design activities (human resources) is recorded by payroll processing, but the sources of *value* of their activities—the contact with customers and competitors—are omitted. The accounting system eventually records the success or failure of technology and design activities through revenues and expenses, but there are no natural transaction-based measures as the technology and design "condition" of the firm improves or deteriorates over time.

This diagrammatic difference points out an important limitation of traditional accounting systems: accounting omits current measures of two long-term profitability and vitality factors—technology and design. It also omits timely measurement of related market-based assets. Some companies attempt to cover these omissions through the nonfinancial measurement systems that measure customer satisfaction, and compare results with benchmarks of average performance statistics and best practices of competitors. They then try to relate exceptions to accounting system measures within the firm (e.g., class of customer and particular suppliers).

There are, of course, trade-offs in designing accounting systems. Information is more relevant for decision making if it comes earlier rather than later. However, timely measures may be expensive to obtain (such as customer satisfaction measured by interview and survey rather than by lack of sales). Also, timely measures may be less objective (less verifiable by others), less precise (as with back-of-an-envelope calculations), or more subject to measurement error (less reliable) since error detection procedures may be omitted to speed information display.

Periodic Accounting Activities

Core and support process transactions, internal transfers, and funds transfers comprise the basic books of a business and provide most of the numbers for its financial statements. The remaining numbers are **allocations** of costs, across time (depreciation—processed by the Asset Management (AM) and CO modules in SAP R/3) and across organization units; **accounting estimates** of transactions yet to be completed such as the allowance for uncollectable receivables, warranty liability, and inventory valuation reserves; and tax expense and liability calculations based on compliance requirements. These estimates and calculations are made (or updated) periodically.

In addition to numbers comprising earnings and financial condition measures, GAAP-based financial statements require **periodic disclosure** of some off–balance sheet items, such as certain types of leases, and transactions with parties related to management or the firm itself. Finally, GAAP-based financial statements require disclosure of some **risk exposures** of the firm as of the balance sheet date. Included are customer concentrations, dependence on a single supplier, loss contingencies (e.g., possible losses from a lawsuit in process), and the risk of going out of business in the near future. Thus, GAAP-based financial statements are a mixture of continuously maintained records of transactions supplemented by periodic estimates, allocations, and disclosures. Knowing how financial statements are constructed is important to users in that the statements must be deconstructed to extract their predictive and performance measurement value.

What is the cost of maintaining an accounting system, and how do costs differ across companies? A major benchmarking study conducted by the AICPA and The Hackett Group provides some answers.[5] The study collected accounting cost and activity data from more than 650 U.S. and multinational firms ranging from $50 million to $90 billion in annual revenues, including more than 40 percent of the Fortune 100.

For a firm with $1 billion annual revenues in 1996, accounting costs averaged 1.4 percent of revenues. However, for the most efficient 25 percent (the world-class firms), costs averaged only 1 percent. The typical $1 billion company processes 12,500 invoices per accounts payable employee at a cost of $3.55 per invoice processed, while the world-class companies process invoices at $.35 per invoice. For payroll, the typical payroll employee processes 23,200 payroll checks at a cost of $1.91 per check, but the world-class firm's payroll employee processes checks for an average of only $.36. Also, related to enterprise software, the world-class firm uses a single system per process while the typical firm uses between two and three. Thus, there are considerable differences in costs of accounting systems as well as potential benefits of relevance and reliability of information that they produce. Determining the optimal combination of cost and benefits from an accounting system is, of course, a potential subject of assurance services.

The accounting system, the nonfinancial measurement system, and the compliance system comprise important elements of a firm's internal control that will be the subject matter in Chapters 3 and 4.

RELEVANCE ENHANCEMENT SERVICES: DECISION RELEVANCE ANALYSIS

In the previous section, we saw the relation of business measurement systems to a conceptual model of the firm and how enterprisewide software can relate information to core and support processes. We are now ready to see how assurance services can improve the quality of information or its context using the results of the business measurement system. In particular, how can information be made more relevant for decision making? In this section, we consider aspects of three types of relevance enhancement services: (1) context improvement, (2) decision-specific information improvement, and (3) business measurement system design.

Context Improvement

A complex business decision such as a merger or whether to enter a foreign market has many dimensions—too many for one person to be informed about all of them, and may exceed the knowledge and expertise of the staffs of most companies. In these cases, information relevance is enhanced by completeness relevance services of external assurers.

As an example, consider the key factors that may affect a firm's entry into a foreign market. Some factors are business process related, and business process advantage is usually central to such an entry. Most business managers know what their core process ad-

---

5. See *Journal of Accountancy,* January 1997.

vantages are and may know how to measure and benchmark them domestically. But they do not know how their advantages will translate to success across borders. How will local customs, culture, and politics affect the firm's process advantage, and how will attitudes toward foreigners or a particular company affect it? Still other factors such as accounting, tax, and other legal and regulatory factors have important, but sometimes unique, effects in particular domiciles. Information completeness services can identity these factors. Once identified, their effects can be assessed and decisions made about whether they are controllable by management or are simply constraints.

Completeness services can also help identify alternative courses of action. Any management group is limited in its experiences. Based on their experiences with other businesses, independent experts can suggest different approaches to business organization, financing, marketing, and legal and accounting entity organization. Thus, completeness services set some boundaries on what information or action alternative may be relevant and identify the need for decision-specific information about their possible effects.

Other context improvement services include helping the decision maker make sense of available information and navigate through available information to determine its relevance. Making sense of information includes designing reports that focus the user's attention on measures of key success factors and key threats to achievement of strategic objectives. These services prevent overlooking important information or relationships in information that is available.

International CPA firms have expertise in all of these disciplines, and they have country-specific knowledge through their foreign operations. Also, because of the universality of financial statements and their experience as auditors and accounting advisors, CPAs and CAs have experience with a broad range of clients making similar decisions. They help obtain relevant measures of many of the required dimensions or design business measurement systems. When systems or measurements are not possible, they can help assess risks (see Chapter 3) and can assemble a team of advisors to ensure relevance and completeness of the dimensions of information available.

Decision-Specific Information

Some information may be sensed, measured, summarized, and displayed for only the particular decision at hand (decision-specific information). Other information for a specific decision is based on adaptation or customization of information already collected and summarized for another purpose. The most common example of customizable information is that comprising GAAP-based financial statements. In still other cases, as in a relational database maintained by enterprisewide software, decision-specific information can be developed from data sets already collected by reformatting them to be more relevant.

Information Customization

GAAP-based accounting reports are based on results of actions taken and real-world conditions for a particular time period. They do not reflect actions that might have been taken or alternative conditions that might have occurred in the past time period. Also, since accounting is historical, it cannot reflect all events, transactions, and conditions that might occur in the future. Therefore, historical accounting data must be adjusted (customized) to be useful for decision making about past performance or predicting the future. The decision relevance analyst uses his or her knowledge of how historical statements were prepared to customize accounting information for events that didn't occur in the past but may in the future, as well as for those that did but will not recur in the future.

Figure 2–5 illustrates a four-step process by which the decision relevance analyst can customize historical accounting data. The first step is decomposition of the historical accounting numbers. What transactions were executed or occurred in the past time period, and what allocations, estimates, and disclosures were made? Net income may be decomposed into cash and accrual transactions involving sales and collections of receivables, purchases and payments for materials and labor, lease payments, and allocations of overhead costs. Most accounts can be decomposed into financial and nonfinancial components. For example, revenues can be factored into prices-per-unit and units sold components.

FIGURE 2-5

Customizing Accounting Information for Prediction

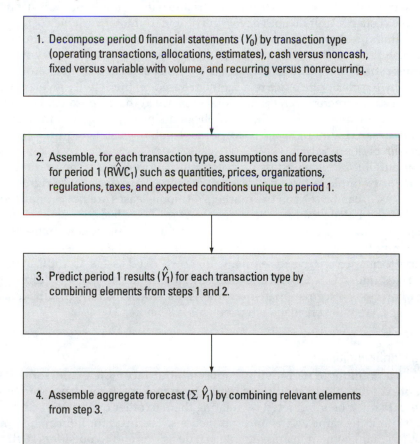

1. Decompose period 0 financial statements (Y_0) by transaction type (operating transactions, allocations, estimates), cash versus noncash, fixed versus variable with volume, and recurring versus nonrecurring.

2. Assemble, for each transaction type, assumptions and forecasts for period 1 ($R\hat{W}C_1$) such as quantities, prices, organizations, regulations, taxes, and expected conditions unique to period 1.

3. Predict period 1 results ($\hat{Y}_1$) for each transaction type by combining elements from steps 1 and 2.

4. Assemble aggregate forecast ($\Sigma\ \hat{Y}_1$) by combining relevant elements from step 3.

The second step is assembly of relevant assumptions about the future time period. What transactions are planned, at what volumes, and what are the expected environmental conditions (e.g., costs, volumes, and prices)? How will taxes be different under the planned conditions? The relevant assumptions include key factors for the coming period, and typically involve multiple alternative scenarios such as "most likely," "pessimistic," and "optimistic" conditions.

The third step is projecting each transaction type based on the planned activities and expected volumes, costs, and prices for each scenario or decision alternative. Finally, projected aggregate measures such as net cash flows, net income, or total assets are assembled by integrating the projected transaction types. To the extent that the revised numbers describe aspects of the future about which the decision maker wants to know, customized accounting information is decision relevant.

The decomposition of past transactions has several pitfalls that require consideration by decision relevance analysts. Knowledge of how the historical measurements were prepared is essential for avoiding the pitfalls. Does the transaction involve cash? Are costs fixed or variable with volume or activity? Are the amounts variable to the segment being analyzed, but fixed to the organization as a whole? In projecting transactions, many decision makers forget that fixed cost per unit is variable with volume (but is constant in total), while variable costs per unit do not vary with volume (but total variable cost changes with volume). In similar fashion, expenses that do not require outlay of cash are not relevant for predicting cash flows (with the exception of their possible effect on tax payments).

Another pitfall for assessing relevance is the level of analysis. For example, costs that are allocated by the corporate office to a segment based on the activity level of the segment are variable at the segment level, yet the total expense at the corporate level of the organization is fixed. The analysis is further complicated since the segment may transfer cash for these expenses even though, at the corporate level, no cash is required for items such as corporate-level depreciation.

A final pitfall for the analyst using accounting information is the presence of the off-book items. For example, a lease provides rights to use an asset; these rights have value and, in some cases, can be sold on the market. Yet, some leases are not capitalized as assets on a GAAP-based balance sheet. The presence of off-book leased assets requires adjustments when evaluating performance and when predicting future outcomes—segment return on (accounting) investment excludes the value of fixed assets leased and overstates measured performance relative to segments that own fixed assets. Complicated lease capitalization rules under U.S. GAAP and differences around the globe require special consideration of off-book information in interpreting statements of foreign subsidiaries or foreign companies. We will consider such problems in Chapter 11.

Integrating Nonfinancial Measures

GAAP-based accounting data provide important, but incomplete and sometimes irrelevant, measures of real-world conditions for decision making. If relevance is to be obtained, accounting data must be interpreted by relating them to other quantitative and qualitative information about the same events and transactions. The need for information integration applies both to management in making internal decisions and to outsiders such as trading partners of the firm (suppliers and customers), as well as to lenders and stockholders.

Some relevant measures can be derived from other systematically collected measures. Three examples are (a) same store sales (aggregate current period sales at stores that also operated in the prior period) as a measure of sales growth at existing locations, (b) age of product revenues (total revenues for each product divided by the number of years since its development) as a measure of product maturity, and (c) worker turnover value (average compensation of employees resigning from the firm divided by average compensation of workers remaining) as a measure of maintenance of human capital resources.

Other useful nonfinancial measures may not appear in systematically maintained records of the firm—measures such as customer attitudes toward the company, its products, and its services; worker attitudes toward the company, job satisfaction, and probability of resigning; and supplier attitudes toward the company. These nonfinancial measures tend to be related to technology and design factors. Many companies do not collect them, and those that do typically obtain them on an *ad hoc* basis since, for most companies, they are not deemed essential for day-to-day operation.

As discussed earlier, changes in technology and design factors tend not to affect current accounting transactions, but will affect them in the future. Thus, it is important to consider measuring them and to be able to relate these measures to particular types of customers, workers, and suppliers to determine their importance. For example, a decline in attitudes toward the company by a class of customers will be more important if the customer type comprises an important dollar portion of the sales and profitability of the company.

Sears, Roebuck and Company provides an example of how development of nonfinancial performance measurements of key factors can focus attention and lead to improvement in financial measures.[6] In 1992, Sears recorded a $4 billion loss in its financial statements. Part of the problem was a workforce that didn't understand the company and how their efforts determined its performance. As an example, in 1992, Sears employees typically believed that Sears' profit per revenue dollar was $.45, when the actual amount was $.02.

Over several years, Sears management conducted research on its operations and developed a model that linked financial measures of revenue and expense through a causal chain between employee attitudes, customer satisfaction, and profitability. Sears was then able to develop nontraditional, but objective, measures of these concepts and to relate them to subsequent profitability. Specifically, the model shows that a 5-unit increase in employee attitudes, as measured on the Sears measurement scale, leads to a future increase in customer satisfaction of 1.3 units, which leads to a .5 percent improvement in revenue growth in still future periods. Thus, if a particular store that has had 5 percent revenue growth shows a 5-unit increase in employee attitude as measured, then future revenue growth will be 5.5 percent for this store.

Figure 2–6 is a stylized version of the Sears model with the employee-customer-profitability links shown in bold. The nonfinancial measurements are leading indicators for future profitability at a store. Top management at Sears deems the nonfinancial measures of employee attitudes and customer satisfaction sufficiently relevant for decision making to have them audited by its external audit firm in the same manner as their financial statements. Thus, the reliability of this decision-relevant information is improved. In 1997, Sears reported a $1.5 billion profit on revenues of about $40 billion.

---

6. A. Rucci, S. Kim, and R. Quinn, "The Employee-Customer-Profit Chain at Sears," *Harvard Business Review*, January–February 1998, pp. 82–97.

FIGURE 2–6

Sears' Employee-Customer-Profit Model

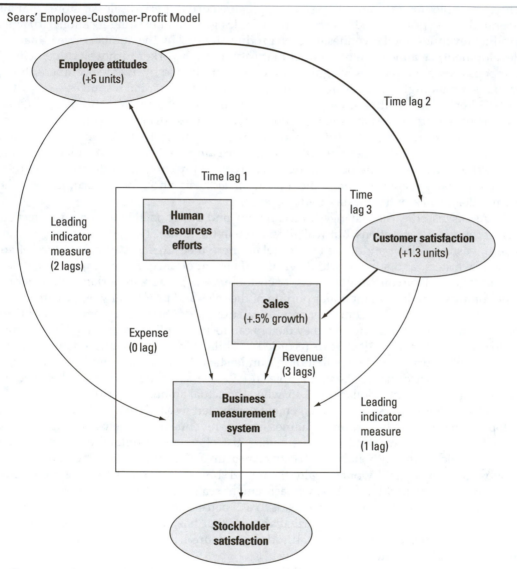

Figure 2–6 also shows that financial statements record expenditures for employee attitude improvement well before any benefit in revenue measurements, thus discouraging store managers' investment in employee attitudes. Measurement of nonfinancial variables may encourage such investment.

CPA firms have recently added measurement and analysis of a customer base as an information improvement service. For example, Arthur Andersen applies the American Customer Satisfaction Index developed by the National Quality Research Center at the University of Michigan. The index provides a uniform, cross-industry measure of consumers' perceptions of goods and services. Measurement of customer satisfaction can identify strengths and weaknesses and lead to improved profitability by building customer loyalty.[7]

Business Measurement System Design

Business measurement system design is a complex task because it requires consideration of how best to measure systematically many possible characteristics of all possible real-world conditions that might occur. Design choices encompass what to measure, how to measure it (i.e., how to attach numbers), when to measure it, and how to store and retrieve the results. Measurement system design choices that involve human behavior are particularly difficult because humans *anticipate* the measurements that result and alter their behavior to meet their own objectives.

Consider an examination score as a measure of your knowledge of business school class material. The professor wants you to maximize your knowledge about the subject matter of the course. But you know that your examination score will be used as if it were your knowledge (i.e., as a representation or model of your knowledge). So you may try to maximize your examination score rather than maximizing your subject matter knowledge—if you know that the examination will be multiple choice, then you overinvest in learning material that is amenable to testing via multiple choice questions. In choosing a testing method, a thoughtful professor considers what knowledge is measured, when it is measured, and what behavioral effects that measurement induces, along with the cost of measurement to students and professor. The choice of measurement method is a compromise of benefits and costs.

Similar dangers are present in designing business measurement systems, especially those that make multiple use of a given measurement. Top management wants lower-level managers to make decisions that help achieve the firm's long-run business objectives. But since actions that facilitate long-run performance are difficult to measure in the short run, management may use changes in periodic GAAP-based net income or return on accounting assets as if they were the long-run progress. Just like students, self-interested lower-level managers may maximize what is measured—the accounting measurement—especially if their compensation is based on accounting measures.

Costs of business measurement systems are also relevant. However, it is increasingly economical to keep measures of multiple aspects of real-world conditions and to integrate them into existing measurement systems. Information technology has lowered the cost of sensing real-world conditions, processing, summarizing, storing, and displaying the results. Multiprocess, enterprisewide software such as SAP R/3 allows integration of information from core processes and support services. But lower measurement costs may lead to overproduction of measurements. Relevance of information context can be improved by identifying elements of available information that are *not relevant* for a particular decision.

Integrating Objectives and Rewards

Consider a multiple-use measurement systems design solution for LJ Appliances that integrates measurements over time by linking forecasting, motivation, and performance evaluation. Since LJ Appliances operates a chain of retail stores in a competitive industry, its

---

7. "AA: Keep the Customer Satisfied," *Public Accounting Report,* April 15, 1998, p. 5.

profitability depends on (a) achieving high volume and (b) accurate forecasts of demand for its product so that procurement and distribution costs can be minimized. Store managers can affect sales volume achieved at their stores, and each has knowledge of future demand at his or her store (the segments) that is superior to that of top management. Top management benefits if store managers maximize store sales volume, and if they reveal to top management their true beliefs about future demand.

One way to encourage both types of behavior is to use a variable bonus plan that rewards higher segment volumes and accurate segment volume forecasts. Such a plan was originally proposed by Gonik and has been elaborated by Reichelstein.[8] The plan is based on incremental bonus rates for various forecasted volumes and a basic bonus for achieving a given level of sales.

Assume that period 1 sales demand for a particular store can be low (1,000 units), medium (1,200 units), or high (1,400 units); the price per unit is fixed at $100; and the incremental bonus rates are 5 percent, 9 percent, and 15 percent, respectively, for the three forecasted volumes. The bonus plan specifies a basic bonus to the store manager for forecasting and achieving 1,000 units is 5 percent, or $5,000. If 1,200 units are forecast and achieved, the basic bonus is $5,000 plus the equally weighted average of the low- and medium-volume incremental volume bonus rates, or 7 percent. Thus, the basic bonus for forecasting and achieving medium volume is $5,000 + (.07 × 200 × $100) = $6,400.

For each forecasted volume, the segment manager will receive an incremental bonus (penalty) of the incremental rate for the forecasted volume times actual minus forecasted volume times (fixed) selling price. For example, if 1,000 units sold are forecasted and 1,200 achieved, the bonus is $5,000 + (200 × .05 × $100) = $6,000. On the other hand, the manager's bonus is reduced if the forecast exceeds actual. To illustrate, if 1,200 units are forecasted and only 1,000 units are sold, then the bonus is $4,600. This amount is $6,400 − (.09 × 200 × $100), or the bonus for forecasting and achieving 1,200 units minus an $1,800 penalty based on the incremental bonus rate given a forecast of 1,200 units times the forecast shortfall.

Figure 2–7 diagrams the decision activities of segment and central managers and a schedule of the resulting bonus possibilities. Note that, if a store manager believes that demand will be low, medium, or high, he or she can maximize compensation by revealing that belief to central planners. Also, whatever forecast is made, if the manager can exceed the forecast, then his or her compensation will be increased—but not by as much as would have been attained if the demand had been properly forecast. For example, given a forecast of 1,000 units, the manager achieving 1,200 units sold earns $1,000 more than if 1,000 had been sold, but $400 less than if he or she had revealed 1,200 as the forecast.

Thus, we see that by joint consideration of long-term business and segment manager objectives, it is possible to design systems that achieve goal congruence between segment managers and top management. Segment managers who are motivated by compensation will maximize their pay while helping to maximize firm profits through better planning of quantities needed, closer coordination of delivery, less inventory, and faster response times for customers.

---

8. See J. Gonik, "Tie Salesmen's Bonuses to Their Forecasts," *Harvard Business Review*, May–June 1978, pp. 116–123; and S. Reichelstein, "Constructing Incentive Schemes for Government Contracts: An Application of Agency Theory," *The Accounting Review*, October 1992, pp. 712–731.

FIGURE 2-7

Information Sharing, Local Decisions, and Bonus Plan

A. Process Diagram

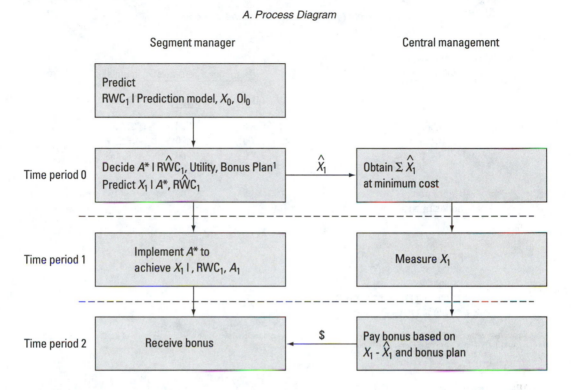

DISCLOSURE OF INFORMATION RELEVANT TO OTHERS

A final question regarding information relevance is "is it good voluntarily to disclose price and quantity information to outsiders?" Price and quantity information are useful to management in planning, implementing plans, and evaluating performance. Would the same numbers be relevant for outsiders? The answer is often yes, and management *may* benefit by providing information—information disclosure can be a source of competitive advantage.

Suppliers with knowledge of a firm's forecasted production schedule quantities can better predict their own production needs, and can produce a given level of service at lower costs and share those costs with the firm. Lenders benefit because they are better able to monitor the status of a company and the riskiness of the loan. Lenders will discount their usual interest rates to obtain such information because it lowers their costs. Likewise, the residual owners, the stockholders, can also benefit from the enriched information set—they would find it relevant for evaluating performance of a manager. They would agree to a higher bonus if the information provided better measures managerial performance.

The Jenkins Committee (1994) has recommended that companies voluntarily disclose a variety of nonfinancial measures as part of the financial reporting process.[9] Firms with

---

9. American Institute of Certified Public Accountants, *Improving Business Reporting—A Customer Focus: Meeting the Needs of Investors and Creditors* (New York, 1: AICPA), 1994.

FIGURE 2-7

(cont'd)

B. Segment Manager Compensation for Period 1

Actual Sales Achieved (X_1 in units)	Manager's Forecast ($\hat{X}_1$ in units)		
	1,000	1,200	1,400
1,000	$5,000*	$4,600	$2,800
1,200	6,000[†]	6,400[††]	5,800
1,400	7,000	8,200	8,800§
Incremental bonus rate I $\hat{X}_1$	.05	.09	.15

* $1,000 × .05 × $100
† $5,000 + (200 × .05 × $100)
†† $5,000 + (200 × .07 × $100)
§ $6,400 + (200 × .12 × $100)

1. Bonus plan (BP) rewards segment manager who chooses A* to benefit the corporation, reveals an accurate estimate of achievable demand (($\hat{X}_1$ − X_1) small), and implements actions (A_1) according to plan (A^*).

superior performance might increase firm value by providing data that reveal their performance. Yet, most companies have declined to do so, in part due to the cost of providing
the numbers, and in part because of the possible competitive disadvantage of public disclosure of information—especially information that is not disclosed by competitors. Mandated disclosure of standardized nonfinancial measures by all firms might benefit all parties, especially as costs of providing information continue to fall.

In making disclosure decisions about nonfinancial information, management must
consider the cost and benefits of the disclosure, but there may be benefits of cooperating
with competitors by sharing information. As an example, computer chip manufacturer
members of the Semiconductor Industry Association (SIA) voluntarily provide confidential order and sales data to Big Five CPA/CA firm PricewaterhouseCoopers each month.
The firm reviews each manufacturer's data and investigates questionable items. It then aggregates firm data to develop a book-to-bill ratio (value of new orders received during the
month divided by value of orders shipped) for the industry. The ratio is then transmitted
to SIA for release to the public.[10]

10. N. Fargher, "Evidence on the Information Context of the Book-to-Bill Ratio," University of Oregon, working
paper, 1997.

The book-to-bill ratio is widely used as a relevant leading indicator for the industry, both by members and outsiders. A CPA firm may have been hired for this information origination service because of its industry expertise and experience in information processing (competence) and its reputation as an auditor for maintaining confidentiality (part of trustworthiness).

An independent assurance professional may be able to add value to disclosures to others by designing relevant measures, by assembly of sensitive data as the source of information, and, as we will see in Chapters 7–10, by certifying the reliability of information prepared by management. Assurance is of consequence because with such assurance, management can lower its cost of capital, production, and distribution.

SUMMARY

Management wants to know that information about all key factors affecting the desirability of various courses of action is available when making a decision. Decision-relevant information comes from a variety of sources. Long-term business strategy, available resources, and external environmental information provide a context for operating decision making. Business measurement systems develop and systematically maintain measures of day-to-day accounting transactions, nonfinancial quantities, and compliance measures useful as an information model of the firm that can be used by management to better run the business.

Detailed transaction-based accounting information is necessary to inform management on a day-to-day basis when dealing with customers, workers, and suppliers, while periodic accounting reports can inform outsiders about aspects of the firm and GAAP-based financial statements are required to comply with contracts and legal mandates. Also, when accounting data are adapted (customized) and integrated with other information, they can facilitate planning, coordination, and implementation of plans. When integrated with nonfinancial performance measures, accounting data can assist analysis, evaluation, and motivation of performance including adequacy of plans and strategies, and even protect assets of the firm!

GAAP rules for attaching numbers to transactions are dictated by accounting standards setters whose objectives cannot encompass all decision-making needs of management. To be useful for management decision making, GAAP-based accounting numbers must be *customized* for the particular decision to be made. Relevant customization requires knowledge of how the numbers were prepared so that they can be decomposed, revised for the particular purpose, and then reassembled into relevant information for decision making.

Information is relevant to a decision maker if it conveys what he or she needs to know about real-world conditions—past, present, or future. Decision relevance analysis improves the quality of information, or its context, by improving the decision maker's mental image of real-world conditions important in making decisions. Relevance enhancement can take the form of designing systems to measure systematically what the decision maker wants to know, providing or customizing measurements prepared for another purpose, or improving context by advising on information completeness and the proper interpretation of measurements. For conditions that cannot be measured, information completeness analysis and risk assessments can also improve information context.

PRIMO CLOTHIERS, INC.

Pete Sellors is president and CEO of Primo Clothiers, Inc., a privately held corporation that owns a chain of 10 upscale men's clothing stores in state capital cities in the United States. Primo is oriented toward repeat business with ambitious legislators, bureaucrats, and lobbyists who want to make a good impression via their wardrobe. The chain has been successful in stressing service over price, and generally enjoys a very stable business after a store's clientele is established.

Primo has an unusual opportunity to invest in a joint venture in Mexico that promises a 45 percent (pre–U.S. tax) annual cash return on investment. Sellors is considering either liquidation or outright sale of the Springfield, Illinois, store to raise cash for the venture. He has come to you, a partner in Alex and Louis, CPAs, for advice. Your firm audits Primo's financial statements and has designed and installed automated accounting systems at all Primo stores.

Exhibits 1 and 2 present abbreviated historical financial statements for the Springfield store as of August 31, 1999, and a narrative providing additional information.

Required

Parts a and b are essential for your report and presentation to Sellors. Parts c and d are optional.

a. Sellors asks that you prepare calculations of the following three numbers that will be useful to him in deciding what to do.
   - Likely after-capital-gains-tax proceeds from *liquidation* of the Springfield store (i.e., assuming that the assets and liabilities will be sold or resolved item by item).
   - Likely after-capital-gains-tax proceeds if the store is sold to another party as an *operating entity*.
   - Likely *cash return lost* by Primo (i.e., the reduction in annual cash flow at the corporate level) for future years if Primo liquidates or sells the Springfield store.

b. Using your calculations in Part a and the presumed 45 percent pre–U.S. tax cash flow rate, help Sellors interpret what your calculations mean (i.e., context improvement). For example, which action looks best and what follow-up data or analyses might be useful?

c. As part of corporate-level planning, Sellors has Alex and Louis prepare forecasted financial statements for each store, based on key assumptions provided by Sellors.
   - Prepare a schedule of the forecasted financial statements for the Springfield store for the year ended August 31, 2000, assuming Primo continues to operate the store. Indicate your basis for any additional assumptions that you make.

d. Would you classify your services as a partner in Alex and Louis, CPAs, in Parts a, b, and c as attest services, assurance services, and/or consulting services? Does the classification make a difference? What knowledge and skills base is required to assist Sellors, and what comparative advantage, if any, do CPAs or CAs have as preferred providers?

KEY WORDS

accounting allocations   Systematic assignment of total cost of a transaction to particular units produced, business segment, or time period (e.g., depreciation, amortization of goodwill, assignment of overhead).

accounting estimates   Approximate measurement of transactions yet to be completed such as the allowance for uncollectable receivables, product warranty liability, inventory valuation reserves, and tax expense and liability.

EXHIBIT 1

Primo Clothiers, Inc., Condensed Financial Statements— Springfield Store (in 000s)

PRIMO CLOTHIERS, INC.
Statement of income
Year ended August 31, 1999

Retail sales (net)	$ 1527
Costs and expenses:	
Cost of sales	−1066
Operations, administration, interest	−389
Income before income taxes	$ 72
Income taxes (allocated)	−18
Net income	$ 54

Statement of Position
August 31, 1999

Assets:		Liabilities and equity:	
Cash	$ 97	Accounts payable	$ 147
Accounts receivable (net)	152	Notes payable	250
Inventory	347		
Fixtures, equipment (net)	55	Primo equity	254
	$ 651		$ 651

Statement of Cash Flows
Year ended August 31, 1999

Cash flow from operations:	
Net income	$ 54
Depreciation	5
Increase in receivables (net)	−152
Increase in inventory	−347
Increase in payables	147
Cash flow from investing:	
Purchase of equipment	−60
Cash flow from financing:	
Increase in debt	250
Increase in equity	200
Net increase in cash	$ 97

book-to-bill ratio   Monetary value for a firm or industry of new orders received for a time period divided by the value of orders shipped.

business measurement system   Personnel, procedures, and equipment that comprise an entity's accounting system, nonfinancial measurement system, and compliance system.

compliance system   Personnel, procedures, and equipment that assure compliance with laws, regulations, and internal policies.

core process   Economic activities an entity can perform better than, or at least as well as, any competitor.

enterprise resource planning software (ERP)   A set of software application modules that integrate recording and routine authorization for multiple business processes and allow continuous updating and inquiries of a central database comprising production planning, resource acquisition, personnel, sales, service, and accounting and nonfinancial records.

E X H I B I T 2

Primo Clothiers, Inc., Operations of the Springfield Store September 5, 1998, through August 31, 1999

Primo Clothiers' Springfield store was opened about a year ago in the Land o' Lincoln Shopping Mall adjacent to the state capitol and office buildings in Springfield, Illinois. The store is a division of Primo and it occupies 11,500 square feet in the 48-store indoor mall, which is the leading retail location in Springfield.

Business Operation and Prospects

In its first year of operation, the Springfield store has already developed a loyal clientele. Sales for the second half of the first year of operation were about 50 percent more than that of the first half, and Sellors believes that the sales level for the second half year can be maintained on an annual basis. Also, Sellors expects little change in costs or prices for the next several years.

The August 31, 1999, inventory is valued at cost using FIFO. Sellors believes that only about 90 percent of the August 31, 1999, stock at Springfield is needed for effective operations, but is confident that the current excess can be sold in the ordinary course of business at near-normal profit margins.

Operations, administration, and other expenses for 1999 include $35,000 for "fashion acquisition" costs. This amount is Springfield's 1 1/10 allocation of the costs of maintaining Primo's corporate-level purchasing activities in Milano and Parigi.

Retail Space

On September 1, 1998, Primo signed a 10-year noncancelable lease at $20 per square foot per year. Similar space in Springfield commands rent from $17 to $25 per square foot, and the most recent lease in Land o' Lincoln (comparable to the Primo space) was for $23 per square foot.

Recent Sales of Illinois Businesses

The current issue of *The Illinois Informer* (a Realtors' trade publication) indicates, "retail clothiers have recently sold at prices ranging from 5 to 5 1/2 times annual (pretax) operating earnings."

Financing

To help with financing and to establish a business presence in the community, Primo obtained from Illinois Central Bank a loan of $250,000. Interest at 10 percent is payable annually with the principal due at the end of five years.

enterprisewide software Same as enterprise resource planning (ERP) software.

nonfinancial measures Physical, psychological, spatial, time-based, or other nonmonetary quantitative and qualitative information about the economic states, events, and transactions that are also measured by the accounting system.

off-balance-sheet item Certain types of leases and other assets, obligations, and transactions that are not recorded in GAAP-based statements of financial position.

outsourcing Acquiring (noncore process) goods and services from a source outside the business entity.

strategic environment Longer-term factors affecting achievement of objectives external to, and relatively noncontrollable by, an entity such as consumer tastes and preferences, demographics of customer base, technological developments (substitute products and new ways of meeting old demands), and social, regulatory, and cultural factors.

support services Noncore processes that facilitate core processes, typically including procurement and management of materials for production, human resources, and technology and design services.

3
CHAPTER

Business Measurement Systems: Information Reliability and Risk Assessment

- Does my long-term strategy adequately consider possible external environment changes that would threaten achievement of business objectives?
- Are factors that might impair my business processes within reasonable limits?
- Could assets of my company be stolen?
- Do internal reports properly apply the measurement methods that I have prescribed?
- Are my assertions to outsiders in compliance with applicable standards, laws, and regulations?

All five of these questions are about possible real-world conditions that might seriously threaten a firm, including the consequences of unreliable information for decision making. This chapter explores answers to these and related questions about **risk** and the **reliability** of information produced by the *business measurement system* that measures day-to-day activities of the firm.

By its nature, risk involves more than one possible real-world condition that has occurred or might occur in the future. Thus, numbers, categories, or labels to represent risk assessments are different from business process measures of a single condition. As examples, each possible real-world condition or outcome can be represented by its probability of occurrence (a probability distribution) as low, moderate, or high, or the risk of loss of $1 million or more can be characterized as negligible or possibly serious. The latter type of risk measurement is frequently reflected by footnote disclosure in audited financial statements.

A subtle risk is the risk of being *misinformed* about real-world conditions. The risk of being misinformed (information risk) can arise from using measurement methods that are not relevant (as discussed in Chapter 2), from careless or biased application of measurement methods or their display, or from incomplete information. As used in this book, *information reliability* refers to the manner of application of stated business measurement methods and the display of the measurement results.

Reliability of numerical information has two dimensions. First, are the numbers, descriptions, or categories being attached to real-world conditions using the stated methods, and with negligible error in the measurement process? Second, does the information display correctly portray the measurements? Information reliability also applies to risk assessments, with completeness of information about risk (part of the information "context") particularly important since changed exposure to previously unimportant conditions may require rethinking options and processes strategies.

As in Chapters 1 and 2, the accounting system will be central to our consideration of risk and the business measurement system. We begin by defining business risk and relating the business decision model to various risk factors and methods of mitigating risks. Then, information reliability dimensions are explored, including accidental errors, intentional biases, misrepresentation, and fraud. Information reliability enhancement through internal control and assurance services is evaluated from management's perspective, as well as those of corporate directors, shareholders, regulators, and outside auditors.

DECISION MAKING AND RISK

Business Decision Model and Risk

The owners or managers of a business entity determine its objectives, strategies to achieve objectives, and business processes to implement strategies. Core and supporting business processes facilitate strategy implementation with the entity's suppliers, workers, capital providers, customers, and competitors. Business measurement systems are designed to measure and display key success factors for achieving objectives. The measurements facilitate planning and coordination of day-to-day activities, as well as subsequent evaluation of performance. The measurements also facilitate communication with outsiders and compliance with regulatory and ethical codes.

But measurement methods used to represent observable real-world quantities at a given point in time cannot be applied to the numerous events that *didn't* occur in the past or that *might* occur in the future. Also, an historical measurement display such as the quantity of cash on hand is subject to the risk that it is incorrectly measured or incorrectly displayed. Consideration of these possibilities and their likelihoods is necessary if business measurements are to be properly interpreted in forming images of real-world conditions for making decisions.

Uncertainty about multiple possible real-world conditions is important because it affects utility of the decision maker. Most people are not indifferent between the choice of a $500 gift and a 50/50 chance of zero or $1,000, a 10 percent chance of $5,000, or a 1 percent chance of $50,000. Each of these alternatives has an expected value of $500, yet some decision makers prefer the certain $500, while others prefer one of the gambles, and some persons prefer a .00001 chance on $5,000,000, which has an expected value of only $50! People simply differ in their preferences or utilities for the various outcomes and relative certainties of the outcomes. Most people prefer the certain $500 to any of the gambles, and most would be indifferent between a certain $500 and, say, a 50/50 chance on $2,000 or zero (the latter having an expected value of $1,000). Most people discount the value of the uncertain outcome choices, or, equivalently, they demand a premium for bearing the uncertainty of the outcome.

Uncertainty also matters in business decision making, and it also results in discounting for uncertainty. The stock of a firm with highly uncertain prospects is priced lower, other things equal, than a stock with more certain prospects. Uncertainty about a firm's prospects may be due to the markets in which the firm conducts transactions, or it may be due to uncertainty of information about the status of the firm. Real-world condition uncertainty and information uncertainty both result in discounting. More reliable information, including more reliable information about risk, can have value to the decision maker, or to those wishing to convey information to decision makers.

Business Risk

Business risk has been defined as "the threat that an event or action will adversely affect an organization's ability to achieve its business objectives and execute its strategies successfully."[1] Determination of business objectives and strategies to achieve them is beyond the scope of assurance services and internal control, and beyond the scope of this book. However, assessments of all potentially serious risks inherent in strategies and business processes are part of internal control and the subject of assurance services—both are essential for evaluating the relevance and reliability of information and its context.

A business faces many threats to achieving its objectives and to executing its strategies. In developing a comprehensive list, business risks can be classified in many ways. One useful way is

1. **External environment risks**—threats from broad factors external to the business including substitute products, catastrophic loss, changes in customers' tastes and preferences, competitors, the political environment, laws/regulations, and capital and labor availability.

2. **Business process and asset loss risks**—threats from ineffective or inefficient business processes for acquiring, financing, transforming, and marketing goods and services, and threats of loss of firm assets including its reputation.

3. **Information risks**—threats from poor-quality information for decision making within the business and erroneous information provided to outsiders.

Figure 3–1 presents more details of risks in each of the three broad categories. The external environment category includes longer-term factors external to the firm that are largely beyond management's control. Catastrophic natural events are not controllable by management, yet management can limit exposure to their effects. Similarly, management can influence environmental change to some degree through research and development of technology, advertising, and lobbying of governments. But mostly these factors are constraints to which management must react. Timely information about environmental change is important since management has more options (and probably lower cost options) if it has more time to react.

---

1. The Economist Intelligence Unit, in cooperation with Arthur Andersen, *Managing Business Risks: An Integrated Approach* (New York: EIU, 1995), p. 2.

FIGURE 3-1

Principal Business Risks by Broad Categories

External Environment	Business Processes and Asset Loss	Information
Catastrophic events (natural disasters, economic collapse, social revolution) Environmental change: Customers' tastes and preferences New (substitute) products Technology Competition Labor, materials, and capital availability and cost Political/cultural climate Laws and regulations	Inefficient or ineffective business processes Loss of assets (due to theft, fraud, erosion, accident, obsolescence): Tangible Intangible (patents, goodwill, human resources (capabilities, trust, flexibility, adaptability, morale)) Market-based (customer base, satisfaction, and loyalty; product quality, supplier quality, alliance partner reliability) Financial risk (credit, interest rate, market, currency, collateral, counterparty) Improper incentives to employees and trading partners Reputation loss (integrity risk): Unethical behavior Unacceptable practices by employees or management Illegal behaviors by management, employees, or trading partners	Operations: Unauthorized access to information Inadequate recorded accountability Internal information not relevant, reliable, complete, integrated, or accessible Financial reporting reliability: Unreliable or incomplete financial information for internal decision making or provided to outsiders Compliance: Inadequate communication of Laws and regulations for financial information, internal control, safety, human resources, and environment Internal behavior codes of expected behaviors and practices Contract requirements Inadequate *information* about failure of management, employees, or trading partners to comply with applicable laws, regulations, contracts, and expected behaviors

Assessment and control of business process risks have become increasingly important in recent years due to changes in information technology and related developments. Information technology can communicate to all parties information about changes in the environment and has reduced the time available to react to environmental change, streamlined and altered the design of business processes, and changed the optimal form of business organization. These developments have led to downsizing of businesses, with fewer employees devoted to control activities. These changes affect the nature and magnitude of risks faced. Furthermore, information technology allows operating efficiencies such as just-in-time materials arrival (eliminating materials inventory) and outsourcing of many support activities (as in George's Electronic Security in Chapter 1).

Changes in information technology have altered the underlying assets and risks of businesses. As an example of new assets and risks, consider the risk of deterioration of market-based assets such as the value of a supplier network that effectively outsources production and inventory management. Outsourcing reduces investment in equipment and labor but increases business risks when a key trading partner fails to perform. Owner/managers need to know about the risk profile of trading partners and the risks unique to their failure to perform. The changes also alter the effectiveness of traditional controls over information and safeguarding of assets.

An Example: Guiness PLC

Most of this book is about information risk, but to illustrate some of the external environment and business process risks, let's consider the case of Guiness PLC.[2] Guiness is a U.K. firm with two major business units and product lines—distilled spirits (United Distillers, Johnny Walker Black) and brewing (Guiness Brewing Worldwide, Guiness Ale)—and employs about 23,000 workers worldwide. Guiness management conducted a comprehensive risk analysis with a goal of managing "where we can, and . . . transfer risk to third parties where this is cost effective."

Business Process Risks

Guiness's business process risks are interrelated. Currency risk for Guiness is high because, for example, to be "Scotch," Scotch whiskey must be made and aged in Scotland, and the process can take up to 10 years to complete. The finished product is sold around the world in local currencies and transferred at time-of-sale currency exchanges rates. Guiness hedges its input resource commitments a year ahead and relies on brand loyalty and the related price inelasticity by raising prices to hedge final product currency fluctuations.

Brand loyalty is an important market-based asset, and risk of its loss is a very important risk. Brand loyalty is protected by effective promotion and marketing of consistently high-quality products (related to customer satisfaction risk and product quality risk). Customer satisfaction and product quality are key nonfinancial success factors that are continuously measured and closely monitored by management.

External Environment Risks

Longer-term external factors related to alcohol consumption are also important to Guiness as a maker of alcoholic beverages. Customer tastes and preferences for distilled spirits and brewed products determine aggregate demand and growth potential. Tastes and preferences vary by region, religion, and culture and over time with trends in life styles and alternative products. Guiness tries to limit the effect of changes in tastes and preferences by building its reputation for offering a premium quality product within its market.

---

2. Adapted from EIU, *Managing Business Risks*, pp. 87–91.

Cultural climate risk reflects attitudes of noncustomers as well as customers within a country, state, province, or municipality, and changes in social attitudes can also lead to increased regulation of the final product through prohibition of sale and strict liability laws (e.g., drunk driving laws). To mitigate cultural risks, Guiness has promoted responsible use of alcoholic products.

Finally, because of restrictions on Scotch whiskey production and aging, catastrophic loss risk for aging facilities is potentially important. Guiness has considered the risk of catastrophic loss of aging facilities due to, say, a plane crash. A plane crash could destroy a small aging facility and could wipe out Scotch in process for up to a 10-year period. However, Guiness management concluded that because of the large sizes of their facilities, the likelihood of catastrophic loss was virtually zero and that any reasonably possible loss magnitudes could be endured. Thus, dispersion of aging facilities to many locations is judged not worth its cost—management simply accepts the risk.

RISK IDENTIFICATION AND MITIGATION

Managing risk is essential to achieving long-term and short-term objectives of a business. One approach to risk management has been developed by Arthur Andersen and summarized in *Managing Business Risks: An Integrated Approach.* Figure 3–2 is a diagram based on its risk assessment and control steps.

Risk Identification, Sourcing, and Sizing

The first step in Figure 3–2 is identification, sourcing, and sizing of *all* potentially serious risks. To manage risk for the company as a whole, a *complete* list of risks faced by the corporation is essential. Only from a complete list can management be assured that threats to achieving its objectives are adequately assessed, reasonably contained, and economically managed.

All potentially important risks identified are then measured as to their magnitude—the monetary loss or degree of adverseness if the event occurs—and the probability that an adverse event of a given magnitude will occur. Some events are catastrophic as to potential magnitude but low in probability of occurrence, while other events have small loss magnitudes individually but have high probability of occurrence and thus may be important in the aggregate. Determining the ultimate cause(s) or source(s) of each risk is important in seeking the best solution.

Risk/Reward Trade-off and Risk Mitigation

For each potentially important risk identified, sourced, and sized, the risks versus reward trade-off is evaluated. Figure 3–2 diagrams the partitioning of risks into three risk/reward categories. Some risks are of a magnitude and probability that the risk/reward relation is acceptable at its present level. These risks are simply accepted. Other risks are of such large magnitude or probability that they are unacceptable and cannot be economically contained. These risks must be eliminated by avoiding exposure to risk through abandoning the project, or by preventing risk at the source (e.g., adopt nonpolluting technology or filter out pollutants at point of production).

F I G U R E   3 – 2

Risk Assessment and Control

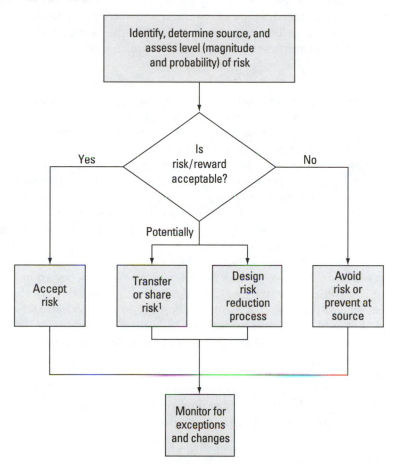

1. Hedging, derivatives, insurance, contracting, pricing, joint ventures, and alliances.

Source: Based on EIU, *Managing Business Risks: An Integrated Approach* (New York: EIU, 1995), p. 12.

Still other risks, probably most risks, may have acceptable risk return/reward trade-offs, but not without some actions by management. Some risks may be transferred to others through insurance, hedging, or derivatives or shared via joint ventures, alliances, and pricing (i.e., charging customers for the risks assumed by the firm). Risk transfer and sharing do not eliminate risk but reduce it by changing its form. For example, a variable for fixed interest rate swap based on the London Interbank Offered Rate (LIBOR) allows a firm to exchange interest payments from a variable rate loan with fixed payments of another party holding a fixed interest rate loan, thus eliminating variable interest rate risk. However, the arrangement introduces a counterparty risk that the other party will fail to fulfill its contract. Similar risks exist in varying degrees for insurance, hedging, joint ventures, and alliances. Each of these exposures creates a potential demand for assurance about the ability of the counterparty to fulfill its obligations.

Finally, many risks may be mitigated by the design of business processes that limit or otherwise reduce the risks faced. Many of the internal control procedures or control activities introduced in the next section and elaborated in Chapter 4 for control of transactions and asset protection are examples of business risk control activities.

Monitoring Risk

Whatever the route taken, the last step in risk mitigation is continued monitoring for unexpected conditions and changes in conditions. Comparison of recorded performance from the business measurement system with expected performance via plans and budgets and contemporaneous performance of competitors is a powerful way of monitoring for changes in the risk environment. Differences from expectations can be explained as to cause, or "sourced," and may point to changed environmental or business process conditions outside the limits suggested by prior risk analyses. Relevant timely measurements and decomposition as to cause allow timely reaction by management.

Figure 3–3 presents a chart showing application of the risk identification, sourcing, sizing, assessment, and response (RISSAR) approach as it might be applied by Guiness PLC. In Figure 3–3, selected potentially important risk exposures are identified and listed along with the real-world source of the risk. Each listed risk is assessed as to its possible magnitude (e.g., possible monetary loss) and the probability of a loss of that magnitude. Then, management's response to risk is entered. Some risks are avoided at the source, some are transferred or shared, and some are reduced by control procedures. All risks are monitored for changes, with some monitored on a more or less continuous basis and others only periodically.

Monitoring for changes in risks already identified can also lead to sensing new risks and changes in the risk environment. Companies that are dealing with present risks adequately may be unprepared to deal with an environmental change that presents new risks that may threaten the continued existence of the firm.[3]

INFORMATION RELIABILITY

As mentioned at the beginning of this chapter, information reliability encompasses two types of uncertainty about an information display: were the stated measurement methods carefully applied, and is the display a correct portrayal of the results? Both of these aspects (imprecision and bias) are with respect to the stated measurement methods. The choice of the stated measurement method affects the relevance of the information display, but is not part of its reliability. Irrelevant information can be reliably prepared and displayed.

Elimination of all imprecision in measurement and bias in information display would be very expensive and is not essential for a decision maker. However, a decision maker

---

3. Two subtle but pervasive risks are the risks of failure to maintain the organization's capacity to identify and exploit opportunities (Canadian Institute of Chartered Accountants, *Criteria of Control* (CoCo), CICA, 1995, para. 7), and the risk of failure to maintain the organization's resilience or capacity to respond and adapt to unexpected risks and opportunities.

Partial RISSAR [1] Chart for Guiness PLC's Business Process and External Environment Risks

Identification and Source of All Potentially Important Risks	Assess Risk		Response to Risk				
	Exposure Magnitude	Probability	Accept	Avoid	Tranfer/ Share	Reduce	Monitor
Business Process and Asset Loss							
Financial risk:							
Fluctuation in foreign currency exchange rates over next 10 years	M [2]	M			Share with customers (brand loyalty)	Hedge inputs and currency	Review quarterly
Counterparty risk for hedges	L	L	Accept				Review quarterly credit reports
Ineffective business processes:							
Product and delivery quality	M	L				Production quality controls/ delivery scheduling	Measure quality daily/weekly
Loss of assets—market-based							
Customer base	H	M				Brand image promotion	Measure customer attitudes monthly
. . .							
External Environment							
Catastrophic loss of production or storage facilities:							
Terrorists	H	L		No breweries in hostile cultures			Review political environments quarterly
Plan crash at Scotland aging facility	VH	VL	Accept				Review annually
Laws and regulations:							
Restrictive regulation adoption	M	L				"Responsible use" promotion	Review annually
. . .							

1. Risk identification, sourcing, sizing, assessment, and response.
2. VL, L, M, H, and VH denote very low, low, moderate, high, and very high magnitudes and probabilities of possible loss respectively.

would like to be reasonably confident that accidental or intentional errors and biases in the measurement and display process are immaterial to a decision, or "small enough to be ignored." One useful way to quantify reliability is an assessment of whether there is *reasonable assurance* that misstatement of displayed information is less than a *material* magnitude (or, equivalently, that there is low risk that misstatement information equals or exceeds a material magnitude).

The misstatement magnitude that is material, or "too large to be ignored," will vary across circumstances, contexts, and decision makers. One hundred dollars missing from a daily cash deposit may be too large to be ignored when controlling a particular cashier, but $10,000,000 of possible misstatement in an accounting estimate for a multinational corporation may be immaterial to an investment decision. Whatever the context, the magnitude of misinformation or misstatement that would be material to the decision maker in a particular circumstance is important because the magnitude will affect the cost of obtaining the information as well as its value.

Quantifying Information Misstatements

To define some essential concepts, let's refer to the measurement–method–application–error-free value as the true value of a datum (Y) and the value displayed as its recorded value (Y_r). For example, if first-in, first-out costing is the stated method for determining inventory cost, then the true value for the cost of inventory would be an error-free count of inventory on hand, with perfect application of purchase costs using the first-in, first-out costing assumption, and error-free multiplication and addition to yield the total cost.

The difference between recorded value and true value will be called *misstatement.* That is,

$$\text{Misstatement} = \text{Recorded value} - \text{True value}$$
$$M = Y_r - Y$$

Stated another way, recorded value is comprised of true value plus misstatement ($Y = Y_r + M$).

Misstatements in display can be due to accident in application of measurement methods or intent on the part of the preparer of the information.[4] Misstatement due to accidents in record keeping typically has an expectation of zero as overstatements and understatements are often equally likely. Information reliability for accidental misstatement involves keeping accidental measurement errors within acceptable limits (i.e., variance or spread limitation).

Intentional misstatements (fraud) by the information preparer do not have an expectation of zero, however. Intentional misstatement may be due to an attempt to hide theft of assets (misappropriation) or to create an image of better-than-actual conditions or performance (misrepresentation). For either type of intentional financial misstatement, the

---

4. Misstatement can also result from bias in applying measurement methods that require application of judgment. For example, in making accounting estimates such as the collectability of receivables, the value of inventory, or useful lives of depreciable assets, a manager may be unduly optimistic even without a conscious attempt to be misleading. Thus, even without an intent to mislead, recorded values may be biased.

recorded values for assets and income are typically greater than their true values (for example, recorded cash greater than actual cash on hand, or recorded earnings greater than true earnings as measured by GAAP). Recorded values for intentionally misstated liabilities and expenses are typically lower than their true values. Intentional misstatements, then, involve a bias of measurement or display, and control of misstatement due to intent requires bias reduction as well as variance reduction efforts.

Three Examples of Information Risk Mitigation

Let's consider three examples of *unintentional* misstatement risk, and the mitigating role of internal control and assurance services. All three examples are from LJ Appliances. The first is an example of operations inefficiency and bad information for decision-making risk, the second is an example of poor information causing loss of assets, and the third is an example of how independent information reliability assurance can add value when dealing with outside parties.

Inventory Errors

Several years ago, due to poor record keeping for individual items of inventory, LJ Appliances experienced frequent stockouts for some items, while other items had many months' supply on hand. The differences between recorded inventory amounts and the inventory on hand were both positive and negative, and they netted to approximately zero on average. However, the individual differences were important for customer satisfaction and operating efficiency. For a typical item of inventory, the probability distribution of possible errors under LJ's old system is depicted as the flatter or wider curve in Figure 3–4, part a.[5] As shown, the average error is approximately zero, but with substantial spread (variance) or high imprecision. There is a substantial risk of information error being more than a critical dollar amount k^*, where k^* is the minimum operationally important magnitude of overstatement or understatement for decision-making purposes.

Overstatements greater than k^* led to excessive unexpected inventory stockouts that disappointed customers and to rush orders at inflated costs and express delivery charges. Understatements less than $-k^*$ caused reordering of items for which there was already an adequate supply and unnecessarily raised investment in inventory.

Business and measurement process improvements included an electronic inventory recording and measurement system, and follow-up investigations to determine the cause of differences in quantities recorded and on hand. LJ Appliances was then able to reduce recorded inventory imprecision or spread to that shown in the more peaked, narrower distribution in Figure 3–4, part a. Both distributions contain the same area under the curve, but with different areas below $-k^*$ and above k^*, where area represents risk. Note that the risk of operationally important differences is much less—so much less that management deems it negligible and does not warrant the cost necessary to further reduce it. As a result of the change, LJ improved customer satisfaction, increased revenues, and lowered inventory investment.

---

5. Diagrams of probability densities in this chapter are drawn as continuous normal probability distribution for simplicity. Real-world distributions are often nonnormal, such as those skewed to the right (e.g., an L-shaped distribution). Other densities will be considered in later chapters.

FIGURE 3-4

Decision Maker's Perceived Misstatement Distribution

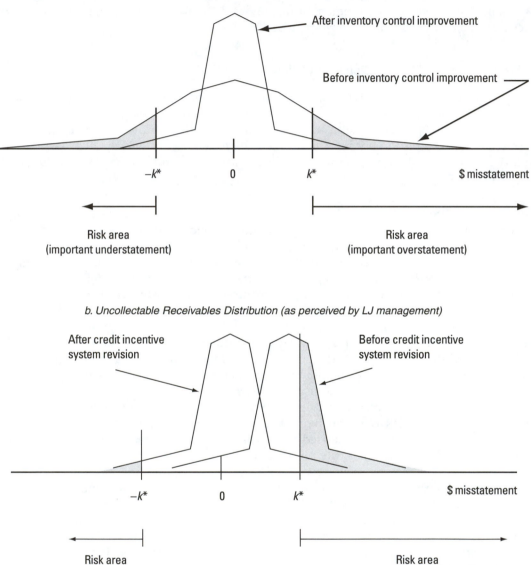

a. Inventory Misstatement Distribution (as perceived by LJ management)

After inventory control improvement

Before inventory control improvement

$-k^*$ 0 k^* $ misstatement

Risk area
(important understatement)

Risk area
(important overstatement)

b. Uncollectable Receivables Distribution (as perceived by LJ management)

After credit incentive
system revision

Before credit incentive
system revision

$-k^*$ 0 k^* $ misstatement

Risk area
(important understatement)

Risk area
(important overstatement)

FIGURE 3 – 4 (cont)

c. Aggregate Earnings Misstatement Distribution (as perceived by Tim, the prospective buyer)

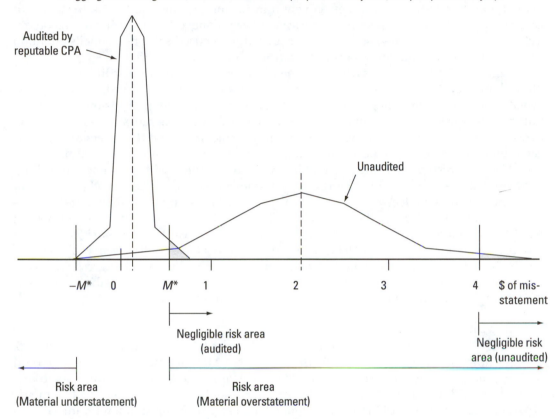

Credit Risks

Several years ago, LJ Appliances was experiencing what it considered to be excessive losses on recorded receivables due to sales to customers who did not pay their bills. An analysis of accounts written off as uncollectable showed that customers with poor prior credit histories were being accepted for credit sales by sales personnel. Discussions with sales personnel and LJ's sales manager revealed that the inability of sales personnel to obtain credit history information on potential customers at the point of sale frequently led to approval rather than risking loss of a sale. Also, sales personnel received a commission on recorded sales, not on collections from customers. Thus, the sales personnel had no disincentive to sell to weak customers.

The problem was solved by a three-pronged risk-mitigation attack. First, sales personnel were required to get approval of credit customers from the sales manager, who maintained a credit risk file based on LJ's current accounting records, on-line access to information from an independent credit service, and an efficient credit-scoring algorithm to assess credit risk. Response time on the new system was sufficient to support point-of-sale approval. Second, LJ signed agreements with Visa and MasterCard to outsource credit and collection. For customers not in LJ's file, sales personnel were allowed to accept customers using an authorized credit card, effectively transferring (selling) credit risk to the credit card company. Third, LJ's sales incentive system was changed to pay commissions on *collected* sales, not on the sale itself. The latter procedure focused sales personnel's attention on the certainty and timeliness of collection from potential customers.

Figure 3–4, part b, shows LJ management's mental image of the distribution of possible lack-of-collectability misstatements in a typical LJ customer's recorded accounts receivable before the three steps were taken. Notice that the before imprecision is not large, but there is considerable *bias* in the recorded accounts receivable measure—the errors on average are positive (overstatements), with considerable likelihood that overstatement exceeds what is considered to be an important amount (substantial area above $+k^*$).

The after results of Figure 3–4, part b, show a distribution with the same imprecision (since recorded effects of bookkeeping errors, customer disagreements, and other sources of differences were not affected), but with greatly reduced bias, and the risk of large errors is quite small. Notice also that the revised bias of recorded receivables is not zero. LJ doesn't want credit standards so restrictive as to eliminate uncollectables. If gross profit is, say, 30 percent of sales, LJ may profitably sell to customers who have at least a 70 percent probability of paying in full. Stated another way, LJ assesses the risk/reward trade-off of gross profit and bad-debt risk in choosing credit policies. The remaining bias in receivables is the basis for determining the recorded amount of bad debts allowance in LJ's financial reporting.

Bid Price Discount

In Chapter 1, Tim was considering buying LJ Appliances, Inc.; Linda Jo's ask price was $96, or eight times what she believed to be the current GAAP-based net income. What would be Tim's mental image of the distribution of possible misstatement in LJ's (unaudited) net income of $12? Tim is willing to pay eight times the "free of material overstatement" GAAP-based net income of LJ (possible understatement of earnings is not relevant to Tim's offer decision). Let's assume that he considers an earnings overstatement of less than $.50 to be immaterial and can be ignored or treated as zero. Because of Linda Jo's incentives not to be truthful in reporting LJ's net income, Tim discounts the reported amount for possible overstatement, resulting in a lower bid or offer price.

Figure 3–4, part c, shows Tim's mental image of possible earnings misstatement. Tim's point estimate (best guess) of misstatement is $2.00, with considerable variation around $2.00—in fact, dividing possible magnitudes of misstatement between those that have nonnegligible likelihood of occurring and those that have negligible likelihood shows that the negligible range starts at $4.00. To price protect himself (i.e., protect himself from offering too high a price, given his uncertainty about earnings) when figuring a bid price, Tim will treat LJ's unaudited net income of $12 as if it were a certain $8.50 (i.e., $12 − $3.50). He will offer $8 \times \$8.50 = \$68$.

Tim believes that an audit by a reputable independent CPA will lead to reasonable assurance of detection and correction of any material misstatement in LJ's reported earnings. Figure 3–4, part c, shows Tim's after-audit mental image as a tighter distribution centered on $.125, with a negligible range that starts at $.50. Thus, there is now a negligible risk that

LJ's earnings are overstated by a material amount. If audited earnings are $12, then Tim is willing to pay $8 \times \$12 = \$96$.

Thus, we see that the independent audit by a qualified CPA has two effects: reducing Tim's perceived imprecision in LJ's measurement of earnings (distribution spread or variance reduction) and reducing possible bias in its display (shifting the distribution center closer to zero). If Linda Jo's beliefs about her recorded earnings are correct (i.e., GAAP earnings are $12) and she can hire a qualified CPA to do an audit for less than $28 (i.e., $96 − $68, or $3.50 × 8), then Linda Jo will benefit from the audit.

The three cases above are only examples, but empirical studies of a large number of firms show consistent results. For example, an analysis summarizing nine studies of more than 1,500 financial statement audits over a variety of industries and a 15-year period revealed that misstatements discovered by auditors are often material by conventional measures, and average from two to eight times the minimum amount deemed to be material or "too large to be ignored."[6] Individual overstatements of earnings and assets outnumbered understatements by a ratio of at least 3 to 2. Furthermore, when analyzed by account type, recorded values for average sales and accounts receivables were overstated, inventory values were somewhat overstated on average (but with high variation across firms), and cost of sales and accounts payable were understated. All measures are consistent with overstatement of net income and assets! Thus, Tim's conclusion of increased reliability of earnings information appears justified—independent audits do, on average, reduce imprecision and bias in recorded values.

These three examples show that information reliability perceptions of a decision maker can be improved by risk assessments accompanied by process improvements, transfer of risk, and independent audits. In all three cases, imprecision and/or bias of information display of recorded values was reduced.

The risk identification, sourcing, sizing, and resolution (RISSAR) approach discussed earlier in this chapter can also be applied to information risk. In particular, the analyst lists all potentially important information risks, measures their potential magnitudes and probabilities of occurrence, and then considers means of resolving the risks. The resolution can come via acceptance, avoidance, transfer or sharing, and procedures to reduce risk. As with other risks, information is monitored for change. Figure 3–5 shows a partial RISSAR chart for LJ Appliances that illustrates how such a chart can be useful in managing information risks. As with environmental and business process risks, a complete list of possibly important exposures is essential for the approach to work.

RISK MITIGATION AND RELIABILITY ENHANCEMENT METHODS

Two principal means by which management can mitigate the consequences of risk and enhance information reliability are internal control and assurance services. In this section, we will explore the roles of internal control established by management and assurance services acquired by management from independent professionals outside the firm.

---

6. W. Kinney and R. Martin, "Does Auditing Reduce Bias in Financial Reporting," *Auditing: A Journal of Practice and Theory,* Spring 1994, pp. 149–156.

FIGURE 3-5

Partial RISSAR Chart for LJ's Appliances [1] Information Risk

Identification and Source of Potentially Important Risks	Assess Risk		Response to Risk				
	Exposure Magnitude	Probability	Accept	Avoid	Tranfer/ Share	Reduce	Monitor
Operations							
Internal information not reliable: Inventory-on-hand misstatement at item level	M	M				Item control procedures and electronic recording	Monthly review of stockout and turnover reports [1]
Poor customer credit information (accept weak credit customers and wrong employee incentives)	M	M			Accept Visa or Master Card	On-line credit reports, collection-based compensation	Monthly review of age of receivables [1]
• • •							
Financial Reporting							
Material misstatement of aggregate inventory quantities in year-end financial statements	H	L				Test-count ending inventory on hand	Examination by external auditor
• • •							

1. Internal auditors also independently monitor overall performance.

Internal Control and Risk Mitigation

In Chapter 1, **internal control** was defined as

> a process, effected by an entity's board of directors, management and other personnel designed to provide reasonable assurance regarding the achievement of objectives in the following categories
>
> ◆effectiveness and efficiency of operations,
>
> ◆reliability of financial information,
>
> ◆compliance with the applicable laws and regulations.[7]

Compared to the three broad categories of risk in Figure 3–1, the COSO definition combines the external environment and business process and asset loss risks into the effectiveness and efficiency of operations. Also included in the effectiveness and efficiency of operations is the relevance of financial information and the relevance and reliability of non-financial and compliance information. All that is left outside of the first category is the reliability of financial information and activities directed toward compliance with applicable laws and regulations. This narrow focus for the second and third categories is due to the objectives of COSO, which were to provide improved financial reporting and compliance with applicable laws and regulations by public corporations in the United States.[8]

Some auditors have characterized the three COSO categories as the three F's—the *future* of the firm, *financial* reporting, and *fraud* and illegal acts by the company. External auditors hired to audit financial statements focus on how reliably financial statement assertions comply with GAAP, and fraud is one way that assertions may be misstated. From the perspective of management, however, the future of the firm is clearly the most important category, and factoring the future into its external environment, business process and asset loss, and information components as in Figure 3–1 is important if the objectives of efficient and effective operations, broadly defined, are to be achieved.

Figure 3–6 diagrams the three COSO categories as overlapping circles with seven identifiable subcategories. Since reliability of financial reporting (category b, comprised of areas 2, 4, 6, and 7) produces GAAP-based financial statements that can be benchmarked against other firms, it is useful to analyze what is included in category b and what isn't. For example, GAAP-based historical financial statements may require footnote disclosure of the risk of possible failure of the firm in the future (area 4), but they do not include complete information about possible earnings declines in the future (represented by areas 1 and 5 that are outside category b). And GAAP measurement and disclosure criteria would cover liabilities materially understated due to failure to record possible losses from illegal acts of the firm (area 6) and the possibility of firm failure in the future due to fraud that also materially misstates fi-

---

7. COSO, 1994. Committee of Sponsoring Organizations of the Treadway Commission, *Internal Control—Integrated Framework,* Committee of Sponsoring Organizations of the Treadway Commission, (1994).

8. COSO, short for the Committee of Sponsoring Organizations of the Treadway Commission, was comprised of representatives of the AICPA, the Financial Executives Institute, the Institute of Internal Auditors, the Institute of Management Accounting, and the American Accounting Association, in response to the National Commission on Fraudulent Financial Reporting (Treadway Commission). In turn, the Treadway Commission was instituted in 1985 to identify causes of fraudulent financial reporting in an effort to reduce its incidence. Similar efforts in Canada resulted in a somewhat broader but similar Criteria of Control (CoCo), and in the U.K., the Cadbury report.

FIGURE 3-6

Internal Control Objectives Categories in COSO[1]

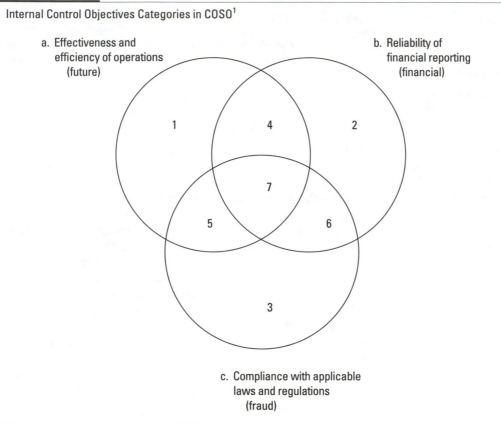

a. Effectiveness and
   efficiency of operations
   (future)

b. Reliability of
   financial reporting
   (financial)

1   4   2

7

5   6

3

c. Compliance with applicable
   laws and regulations
   (fraud)

1. GAAP criteria apply to areas 2, 4, 6, and 7, while COSO criteria apply to all seven areas.

nancial statements (area 7). But GAAP wouldn't cover fraud by employees that affects operations but is *immaterial* to financial statements (area 5) or legal compliance risks that are important for management, but are not material to financial reporting (area 3).

Internal Control Components and Limits

COSO defines five internal control components that, in combination, help achieve the three broad objectives. The five components are

> **Control environment**—the overall context within which the rest of the control process functions, including the integrity, competence, and ethical values of all people employed by the business, organization structure, and leadership.

> **Risk assessment**—the identification, sourcing, and sizing of threats to achieving the business's objectives.

> **Control activities**—policies and procedures put into place to reduce the likelihood that risk will exceed acceptable limits.

Information and communication—systematic transfer of management's operating and acceptable behaviors policies, plans, and implementation instructions, and systematic transfer of elementary data and business measurement and compliance information to those within and outside the business.

Monitoring—analysis of the functioning of other components of internal control to determine whether they provide reasonable assurance of achieving stated objectives.

Each of these components will be explored in detail in Chapter 4 in regard to day-to-day transactions of the firm. For this chapter, we will elaborate on one aspect of monitoring that relates to risk assessment.

Two things should be said about the scope of internal control. First, it does not include all aspects of management. As examples, it does not include the setting of strategic or operating objectives, long- or short-term planning, determination of how best to manage the business, or what corrective actions to take when problems are detected. These excluded management activities are simply beyond the scope of the internal control process. However, the internal control process helps achieve the objectives of these management activities by providing relevant and reliable information and protecting assets.

Second, since internal control is established and implemented primarily by management, it cannot assure those outside management that it functions effectively. While management may believe that its internal control provides reasonable assurance that stated objectives will be achieved, management may be mistaken in its beliefs about internal control quality. More important, since management is instrumental in establishing and executing internal control, it can make the process self-serving, or management may improperly "override" internal control and commit management fraud. For all of these reasons, outsiders won't fully believe management's claims about its internal control. Thus, management needs help to be able to communicate to directors, regulators, and others its beliefs that internal control is adequate and that its financial statements are reliable. Assurance services by independent professionals can facilitate this communication.

Part of the COSO effort was establishment of objective criteria for control. These criteria are analogous to GAAP as criteria for financial statement displays and allow independent assurance professionals to examine existing internal control and report whether it meets the established criteria. In this way, some of management's beliefs about the quality of internal control can be communicated to outside parties, including directors, stockholders, and regulators. Control criteria for external reporting will be elaborated in Chapter 10.

Risk and Information Reliability Assurance Services

Assurance services as defined in Chapter 1 include services directed toward improving relevance and reliability of information and its context for decision makers. Independent assurance services firms such as multinational CPA accounting firms offer three broad classes of services related to risk and information reliability enhancement: *risk-related services; design advice* for operations, financial, and compliance information systems; and *attestation services* for assertions about process or display compliance with stated criteria.

Risk-related services encompass improving information about risks faced by a business—their identification, sourcing, and sizing. Independent assurance professionals can improve the relevance, reliability, and especially the completeness of the dimensions of risk.

Management wants assurance that it is aware of all important risks and has a realistic evaluation of their possible magnitudes and impact on the business. Included are identification and evaluation of special risks (or risk levels) faced by the entity and warnings of the potential need to develop or improve formal systems for risk assessments, monitoring, and management. Corporate directors want assurance that management is informed about risks and that the directors are aware of primary risks and management's efforts to limit them. This assists directors in carrying out their oversight responsibilities on behalf of stockholders and reduces the directors' risk of being associated with the company.

Risk assessment services need not involve reporting risk assessments or attestation to outside parties, although risk assessment can be the basis for an attestation report (see Chapter 10). Outsiders, including trading partners (suppliers and customers of an entity), investors, creditors, and regulators, benefit indirectly from risk-related assurance services to management and/or directors since senior management and the directors are informed in a timely way about the risks faced by an entity. Outsiders may not need reports of risk assessment results. They may be best served by knowledge that timely risk assessments are in place and that risks are being identified, monitored, and evaluated for follow-up by senior management and oversight by directors.

The broad experiences of CPA firm specialists dealing with financial reporting for the entity as an integrated whole, and with accounting, tax, and regulatory requirements worldwide, provide a broad base of expertise. Experience with business acquisitions is also extensive as CPAs and CAs are hired to verify information, and to suggest additional information dimensions that might be relevant. Furthermore, the CPA firm's experiences with internal control and with business viability, production, financing, and markets provide additional perspectives.

Design advice related to risk has several dimensions. Because of their historical role as financial statement auditors, CPA and CA firms have experience with alternative internal control designs for financial activities as well as aspects of operations and compliance. Information technology developments have allowed automating via software many control activities that improve inherent reliability of information processing and access to assets. CPA firms have reacted by developing expertise for adapting traditional control activity designs and linking or integrating nonfinancial and compliance information. Thus, CPA/CA firms may be preferred providers of design and systems integration advice based on expertise. Furthermore, because of their reputations, adopting a CPA-suggested design may have added value to management because they can say to outsiders "we use a CPA-designed process," implying control design competence and objectivity to outside parties.

Attestation services improve reliability of information by testing it against stated criteria for measurement. Attestation (or auditing) has value if the decision maker believes that (a) the measurement criteria are relevant to the decision to be made, (b) the attestor is competent to detect material departures from the criteria in the information display (the assertion), and (c) the attestor is sufficiently trustworthy to report material departures (misstatement or omission), even if the auditor has been hired by management to certify that management has properly applied the stated measurement criteria. That is, a reputable auditor may expose misstatements made by the party that hired him or her.

The subject matter of an assertion can be particular real-world conditions (such as financial conditions—the subject matter of periodic financial statements) or a process such as internal control. For either type of assertion, criteria must be agreed upon before information can be reliably interpreted across individuals. GAAP provides widely accepted criteria for financial statements, and COSO and CoCo provide criteria for internal control. Criteria that prescribe or define measurements that are presumed relevant to the decision maker are essential for value to be added by the assertion/attestation process. Criteria for other assertions can be established for other subject matters, as we shall see in Chapters 7 and 10.

Figure 3–7 is a sketch of how an independent attestor audits a financial statement information display, with the bold boxes indicating management activities. The figure begins with the real-world condition of the firm, including its external environment as well as its business processes. Management's accounting and compliance systems then produce the recorded values and disclosures for GAAP-based financial statements.

One audit activity is the auditor's evaluation of the adequacy of the firm's internal control (elaborated in Chapter 4). Comparison of existing internal control elements with COSO or CoCo criteria helps determine whether internal control *should* produce reliable financial statements. The auditor also considers the susceptibility of an account to misstatement even if controls were not in place (denoted "inherent risk") as well as the risk of management fraud and the firm's prospects for the future. All of these activities relate to auditor assessment of the prior-to-audit risk that material financial misstatements *might occur*.

Two classes of auditing procedures attempt to detect existing misstatements. They address the risk of material misstatement in the particular recorded values this period—the risk that material misstatement *has occurred*. One class focuses on the "reasonableness" of summarized data and the other on details.

For the summary data audit activity, called analytical procedures, the auditor uses his or her expertise, overall knowledge, and knowledge of particular real-world conditions to "model the firm" in order to assess likely true financial statement values (see Chapter 5). Given the auditor's knowledge of business, and the firm, its strategy, industry, current environmental conditions, and risk profile, what would he or she expect to be the true values of the financial statement balances? Expectations can come from several sources, as we shall see in Chapter 5. If recorded values are close to the auditor's expectations of true values, then the auditor's confidence in the recorded values is increased. If the recorded values are not close to expectations, then the auditor investigates the differences to determine their cause (sourcing the difference).

A second class of auditing procedures for misstatement detection is denoted tests of details (see Chapter 6). In applying detailed detection procedures, the auditor compares individual elements of data from the recorded values (the books) with their real-world counterparts (e.g., comparing recorded values of inventory to inventory on hand to detect overstatement of recorded assets). Also, the auditor observes real-world conditions and compares them with recorded value elements (e.g., searching for unrecorded liabilities or expenses).

The combination of risk assessments, internal control failure risk assessment, and detection procedures (analytical procedures and detailed tests) gives the auditor a basis for concluding that there is a low risk of material misstatement. Thus, the auditor's perceived distribution of possible misstatement is analogous to that of Tim in the after-audit distribution in Figure 3–4, part c.

Misstatements discovered by the auditor may lead to adjustment of recorded values before the auditor concludes that there is a low risk of material misstatement in the audited

FIGURE 3-7

Assuring Information Display: Financial Statement Audits

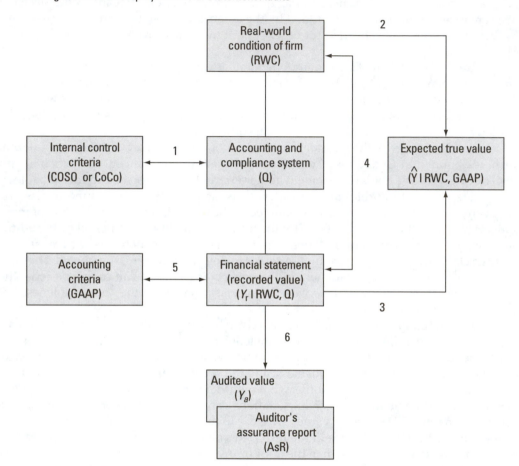

1. Comparison of internal control components with internal control criteria to assess prior-to-audit risk that financial statements (recorded value (Y_r)) might be materially misstated (internal control evaluation).

2. Auditor's expectations of true values (Y) for audit period, given RWC and measurement methods (MM) used in Q.

3. Comparison of Y_r with $\hat{Y}$ based on auditor's mental model of the firm (analytical procedures).

4. Comparison of RWC elements to Y_r elements, and Y_r elements to RWC (detailed tests).

5. Comparison of measurement methods (MM) used by Q with GAAP.

6. Conclusion about risk of materially misstated Y_a based on GAAP ($Y_a = Y_r \pm$ recorded adjustments).

display. From management's perspective, all detected misstatements are of some interest as an indication of control failure—they may be analyzed as to cause (risk sourcing and sizing) and lead to internal control process improvement. In turn, information for decision making may be improved on a continuous basis.

As internal control has improved with information technology, auditors have increased their reliance on internal control and analytical procedures. With integrated systems and enterprisewide software, internal controls can be more complete and reliable in preventing misstatements. Also, integrated databases allow more inclusive and reliable analytical procedures based on a broader information set. These developments have led to less need for extensive examination of details of business transactions by external auditors. Auditing procedures and reports will be elaborated in Chapters 5–10.

ACCOUNTING INFORMATION DECOMPOSITION AS A RISK ASSESSMENT TOOL

Financial statement components such as revenues, cost of sales, receivables, and inventory are single-number measures of real-world conditions for a period or as of a point in time. Financial statements also include footnote disclosure and audit report reference to some important risk assessments, as we shall see in Chapter 9. They do not include probability distributions of assessed uncertainty about the recorded values or probability distributions of values of possible future events. However, since the accounting system measures events and conditions that did occur, analysis of accounting information over time and across companies is useful in evaluating risk assessment performance. This is because, over time and across companies, adverse events do occur, and a decision maker can analyze records of these actual events as to cause and make process improvements.

To illustrate how accounting information can be used to evaluate risk assessment performance, let's recall the LJ Appliances example of first-quarter refrigerator sales in Chapter 2. In that example, planned (budgeted) unit sales as of the start of the first quarter were 10,000 units. To focus on quantities, let's ignore analysis of price variation by assuming that planned sales price per unit was $1,000 and actual sales prices were as predicted (true value = $1,000 per unit).

The LJ Appliances refrigerator sales planning process involved uncertainty at the planning stage about the market share the firm would achieve. LJ's management predicted a 10 percent share of the market in its trade area, but management realized that this share might vary due to many factors that are individually small and difficult to predict: chance factors such as local weather, competitors' advertising, competing events, and holidays. These factors lead to variation in realized market share in a given quarter even though nothing is wrong with LJ's performance. Random variation in market share was ignored in the planning stage but needs to be considered in the evaluation stage. This is because recorded sales for the quarter will vary somewhat from predicted, even if all key causal factors are adjusted and there is no accounting misstatement!

Assume that based on experience, management believes that the normal variation in market share due to random causes and natural period-to-period variation is approximately 2.5 percent of the predicted market share. Thus, a reasonable range, say an 80 percent confidence interval, for actual market share achieved would be .0975 to .1025 or $+/-$ 250 units, or $+/-$ $250,000.

In the example, the internal auditor analyzing planning and implementation for LJ adjusted planned sales for the effects of identifiable causes that occurred during the first quarter. In identifying causes *ex post*, the internal auditor made no distinction between those that were known to be uncertain at the beginning of the quarter (e.g., aggregate demand), those that were known to be possible, but that couldn't be predicted as to location or timing (tornadoes), and those that weren't known to be a risk (such as the new type of competitor). The revised expectation of true value for first-quarter refrigerator sales was

Original budget	$10,000,000
Adjustments for realized outcomes:	
Aggregate market information error	500,000
New competitor	−420,000
Tulsa tornado	−250,000
Revised expectation (expected true value)	$9,830,000
Reasonable range:	$9,580,000 to $10,080,000

Figure 3–8 diagrams the distribution of true value expectations.

The recorded value of $9,650,000 is $180,000 from $9,830,000, which is management's point estimate of its true value given the information that they have available at the end of the quarter. The $180,000 difference could be due to other internal or external causal factors that are valid, to accounting misstatement, or to a combination. Management would make a cost/benefit decision as to whether it is worth investigating the difference as to cause. However, management is likely to conclude that no further investigation is needed because the realized value—the recorded amount—is within a reasonable range that allows for some variation in market share even in the absence of individually important causal factors or accounting misstatement.

If LJ's recorded first-quarter sales had been $9,500,000, then investigation for other nonerror causes and possible accounting understatement would likely be undertaken by management. This is because, based on management's perceived reasonable range for true value of $9,580,000 to $10,080,000, $9,500,000 is simply too small to be easily explained by normally occurring random events. Thus, other factors (such as failure to record sales) are more likely to be the cause. Investigation would also result for recorded sales of $10,200,000, but the internal auditor would consider the risk of inflation or fictitious recorded sales.

FIGURE 3–8

LJ Management's Perceived Distribution of True Value of Refrigerator Sales for First Quarter

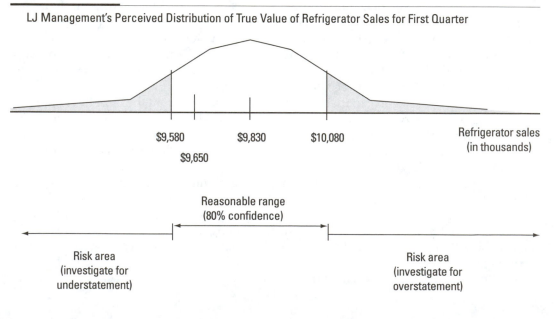

Similar analyses would also apply to planning factors such as the data inputs for planning (the forecasts of aggregate demand), the predicted market share, and the question of whether additional risk and planning factors should be incorporated into the planning process for the future. Determination of what are reasonable expectations requires judgment. Statistical tools such as confidence intervals and comparisons of realized values with confidence intervals can be used in some situations. When real-world conditions preclude formal statistical calculations, subjective estimates of reasonable ranges made by an expert business manager can be a useful input to statistical thinking about whether further investigation is economically the best action to take.

Thus, we see that historical accounting information and planned results can be analyzed for differences in planned and realized values, and for performance in assessing risk. In addition, the analysis helps management decide whether material accounting misstatement may be likely. In Chapter 5 we will see additional means of forming expectations, analyzing performance, and assessing risk.

RISK TO OUTSIDE DIRECTORS AND AUDITORS

Before summarizing this chapter, let's consider risk from the perspective of two important parties close to management: outside corporate directors and external auditors. Management has overall responsibility for effectiveness and efficiency of operation of the firm, preparation of financial statements that comply with GAAP, and compliance with applicable laws and regulations. Corporate directors are representatives of the stockholders and have oversight responsibility for corporate affairs including appointment, compensation, and retention of management. Thus, directors also have oversight responsibility for fraud or misrepresentation by management itself. Yet the board of directors does not exercise day-to-day control over management.

Outside, or independent, directors are typically prominent individuals in business, education, or government who have no management responsibilities for the corporation and no substantial financial interest in it. Because of their reputations and relative independence, outside directors typically serve on the compensation committee that approves management's compensation and the audit committee that retains and interacts with the external auditor.

Outside directors are personally concerned about their own reputations. An independent auditor with an excellent reputation for competence and trustworthiness can protect directors' reputations by reducing risk through their independent professional assurance services, and also by the auditor's association with the firm itself. In the event of materially misstated financial statements, business failure, or discovery of fraud or illegalities, the outside directors may be able to reduce perceptions of their own culpability by saying, "We hired the best consultants and auditors and they failed—what more could we have done?"

External auditors also face the risk of association with the corporation and its management. Auditors can lose reputation and be subject to legal damages by being associated with misstated financial statements, as well as fraud and business failure. Auditing procedures provide some protection against these risks, but auditors also consider the risk of management fraud and business failure before accepting clients. Increasingly, auditors are refusing to accept clients whose management appears to lack integrity and who have uncertain prospects for the future. Furthermore, as part of a financial statement audit, some auditors now analyze a client's business strategies to assess that client's ability to remain profitable. These audit-related analyses can lead to process improvements for clients as well as directing the auditor to careful consideration of risk of financial misstatement. In doing so, auditors reduce the risk of future failure and lack of compliance with applicable laws and regulations, as well as financial misstatement.

Outside directors and external auditors face an especially delicate situation when management misdeeds are discovered. As elaborated in Chapters 9 and 11, the auditor has a contractual and sometimes a statutory duty to report certain management misdeeds to the board of directors. This required communication is essential to the credibility of the financial statement certification process as a means of regulating public companies, but it is sensitive because of the often close personal relationships among and between directors, the auditor, and management. Also, the auditor has a contractual obligation to maintain confidentiality of information not required to be disclosed (see Chapter 12). Once again, the auditor with the best reputation for competence and trustworthiness is most likely to add credibility (and value) to the process.

SUMMARY

A business faces many threats to achieving its objectives. These threats, called business risks, arise from the external environment, from ineffective or inefficient business processes, from loss of assets, and from poor-quality information for decision making. External environment risks tend to be pervasive in nature. Adverse events of this type can put the company out of business or require a major change in its operation, financing, or even organization. Process level risks tend to be narrower in scope of impact than environment risks and can be dealt with on a more systematic basis because management has more ability to control them. Threats from poor-quality information for decision making include the risk of being misinformed about the external environment and process risks.

Risk assessment is primarily concerned with future possibilities or exposure to adverse outcomes. Assurance about risk assessment and mitigation can come from two principal sources: internal control established by management and assurance services acquired from independent assurance professionals. Either source can mitigate risk from the perspective of management and choice of source is a cost/benefit decision for management. However, to assure outsiders that risks are being adequately assessed and controlled, management's assertions are not fully credible because of management's interest in them. It may be economical for management to hire an independent assurance professional to certify that management has mechanisms in place to assess and mitigate risks.

Reliable information is essential for evaluating performance and identifying risks. Information reliability is improved by limiting error and bias in applying measurement rules and bias in information display. The internal control process assists management in obtaining assurance, and independent attestors can confirm the quality of internal control and help assure others about compliance of management's assertions with stated criteria. Both internal control and assurance services add value for management through risk assessment, mitigation, and communication.

The outcome of exposure to all risks is eventually reflected in an entity's historical financial statements, and some risks must be disclosed under generally accepted accounting principles and SEC rules pertaining to management discussion and analysis. Also, the accounting and compliance systems are useful in detecting loss of physical assets due to employee fraud and theft, as well as illegal and unethical acts. However, analysis and adjustment (customization) of historical measures are needed to reveal risks and risk assessment performance.

CASE 3

EXCUSEZ-MOI FLOWER EXPRESS

BACKGROUND

Excusez-Moi Flower Express (E-MFE) operates a flower delivery service through 50 outlets in metropolitan Montreal, Quebec. Each outlet operates a delivery vehicle, and all delivery expenses other than depreciation are charged to the delivery expense account. One account is maintained for each outlet.

E-MFE's internal control for delivery expenses is divided into three functional departments: Budgeting, Operations, and Internal Auditing. Exhibit 1 diagrams the functional activities and the resulting information processing risk.

Budgeting

Prior to the beginning of each quarter, the Budgeting Department meets with executives from Marketing, Operations, and Finance to assemble operating budgets for the coming quarter. They review past operations as well as plans and cost projections for the future. The operating budgets are used to plan flower purchases, promotion, and financing.

Over time, Budgeting has developed a planning model of the delivery function that predicts the average fixed delivery cost per outlet, average variable delivery costs per order, and predicted delivery volume for each outlet. One output is a quarterly total delivery cost budget for each outlet:

$$Y_p = A_p + B_p X_p \qquad (1)$$

where Y_p is predicted (budgeted) delivery cost for an outlet, X_p is the predicted volume of flower deliveries for the outlet, A_p is the pre-dicted fixed cost of delivery at each outlet, and B_p is the predicted variable cost per order delivered.

Not shown in Equation (1) is the effect of valid delivery cost factors that are neither fixed nor variable as a function of volume. Budgeting believes that the aggregate effect of these omitted factors (denoted u) is randomly distributed with a negligible effect, on the average. Since Budgeting can't predict what u will be for a particular outlet, the budgeted u (or u_p) is set at zero for each outlet. Based on experience, Budgeting can specify the likely range within which 95 percent of all u are expected to be.

Operations

The Operations Department is responsible for properly implementing all plans. For example, it is responsible for the actual delivery transactions that comprise the budget's implementation. Thus, Operations must make sure that actual transactions are authorized, properly executed in accordance with the authorization, and properly recorded, and that Excusez-Moi's assets are protected. One output of the Operations Department is the delivery expense recorded (book) values for each outlet. This book value (denoted Y_r) for an outlet can be thought of as

$$Y_r = \alpha + \beta X + u + m \qquad (2)$$

where X is the *actual* number of orders delivered by the outlet, α and β are the *actual* (but unknown) fixed and per-unit variable cost coefficients across all outlets, u is the *actual* effect of omitted variables at the outlet, and m is the *actual* accounting misstatement at the outlet.

EXHIBIT 1

Excusez-Moi Flower Express
Internal Control Overview—Delivery Expenses

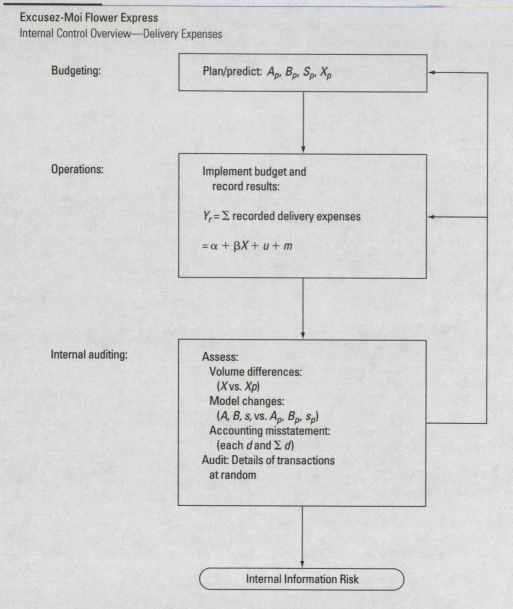

Budgeting:

> Plan/predict: A_p, B_p, S_p, X_p

Operations:

> Implement budget and
>   record results:
>
> $Y_r = \Sigma$ recorded delivery expenses
>
> $= \alpha + \beta X + u + m$

Internal auditing:

> Assess:
>   Volume differences:
>   (X vs. Xp)
>   Model changes:
>   (A, B, s, vs. A_p, B_p, s_p)
>   Accounting misstatement:
>   (each d and $\Sigma\, d$)
>   Audit: Details of transactions
>   at random

Internal Information Risk

The u term represents valid business costs, but the m term is due to accidental accounting errors, to theft, or to intent to deceive. In an accounting-misstatement-free system, m would be zero and the accounting-misstatement-free balance (Y) would be

$$Y = \alpha + \beta X + u \qquad (3)$$

Unfortunately, without investigating the details of expenses at an outlet, it is not possible to determine whether the m term is nonzero.

Internal Auditing

The Internal Auditing Department evaluates the overall performance of Budgeting and Operations by (1) comparing the recorded results of Operations with Budgeting's budgets and (2) conducting random tests of details of expense transactions.

As a quarter progresses

Internal Auditing monitors delivery reports from Operations and investigates when there are large deviations from predicted volumes at a particular outlet $(X - X_p)$. This volume analysis may result in corrective action being taken at a particular store. Internal Auditing also monitors the aggregate volume across all outlets in Montreal. The aggregate volume deviation is usually small, but if it is large, Internal Auditing may recommend actions at the corporate level such as a change in aggregate orders with the flower supplier or a change in marketing promotion for E-MFE as a whole. When corrective action doesn't appear feasible, the budgeted aggregate volume for the remainder of the quarter is revised.

At the end of the quarter

After the close of the quarter, Internal Auditing personnel review the recorded costs and volumes achieved to assess performance of Budgeting and Operations. First, they use a regression analysis of the Y_r values on X to estimate the quarter's coefficients relating volume to recorded cost (A is the estimate of α and B is the estimate of β) and the standard deviation of u (denoted s). The estimated model is of the form

$$Y_r = A + BX \qquad (4)$$

Large differences in the regression estimates (A, B, s) and A_p, B_p, and Budgeting's assessment of the variation of u lead to reconsideration of Budgeting's methods and its assumptions for the current quarter and for planning future quarters. This follow-up of the planning process allows improvement in forecasts as well as improvement in forecasting methods.

In addition to model change, volume monitoring, and implementation analyses applied to outlets in the aggregate, *for each* outlet Internal Auditing calculates

$$Y_r - (A_p + B_pX) = d \qquad (5)$$

The d for an outlet is an estimate of $u + m$, which is the sum of random but valid unexplained delivery costs and accounting misstatement. Exceptionally large positive or negative d's are investigated for possibly important accounting error or fraud (i.e., m). Specifically, the internal audit staff investigates when the calculated d is greater than $1.0 \times$ the standard error of prediction for the outlet, or less than $-1.0 \times$ the standard error of prediction.

Continuously

During the quarter, the Internal Audit staff monitors Operation's control activities, *randomly* selecting a small number of delivery expense transactions as they are being recorded and examining them for substantive validity and for evidence that the implementation controls are being applied and operating effectively.

BUDGET AND ACCOUNTING DATA

Budget and accounting data for the first quarter (Q1) of 2000 includes

a. The budget equation [Equation (1)] established before the start of Q1 of 2000 was

$$Y = \$490 + \$1.30\ X$$

and the range for 95 percent of the u's is $\pm \$115$.

b. The total budgeted volume $(\Sigma\ X_p)$ established before the start of Q1 was 89,250, or an average of 28.3 deliveries per outlet per business day (21 days per month).

c. Budgeted delivery cost and actual book values and X's for Q1 of 2000 for E-MFE and the McGill University, Old Town, and Mount Royal outlets are

		Budgeted		Actual	
		Y_p	X_p	Y_r	X
1	McGill Univ.	$ 2,830	1,800	$ 3,257	1,975
2	Old Town	3,090	2,000	3,165	1,850
	•	•	•	•	•
	•	•	•	•	•
	•	•	•	•	•
39	Mount Royal	2,709	1,707	3,169	1,697
	•	•	•	•	•
	•	•	•	•	•
	•	•	•	•	•
	Aggregate	$140,525	89,250	$160,591	94,818

d. Exhibit 2 presents data plots of volume and accounting variables along with a regression analysis using X (actual delivery volume) and Y_r (recorded delivery cost) and d for Q1 of 2000. Also, the standard deviation of X is 162.1, the correlation of X with X_p is .808, and standard errors of prediction at the McGill University, Old Town, and Mount Royal stores are $62, $61.2, and $61.8, respectively.

Required

The management of Excusez-Moi has asked you, the chief internal auditor, to analyze operation of Excusez-Moi's internal control over delivery costs for the first quarter of 2000. They want to know (a) whether there are any serious operating problems and (b) whether their planning model is adequate or needs revision.

You have available the originally predicted coefficients used by Budgeting, the book values and delivery volumes for E-MFE as a whole plus three particular outlets, and the estimated regression equation prepared by Internal Auditing at the end of the quarter using book values and actual deliveries. You also know that in reviewing entries to a few outlets selected at random, the internal audit staff noticed that each had two payments to E-MFE's collision insurance carrier. One payment was the premium for the first quar-

ter, and the other was for "additional premium based on unfavorable loss experiences" for the prior year. The latter averaged $250 per outlet and appear to be valid charges.

1. Analyze the data and cost coefficients for the firm as a whole. Does the aggregate analysis indicate any serious problems in Budgeting or Operations across all outlets?

2. Calculate likely aggregate accounting misstatement, and likely misstatement for the McGill University, Old Town, and Mount Royal outlets. Indicate which outlet(s), if any, should be investigated for possible accounting misstatement.[1]

3. Address implications of the following additional facts:

a. The internal audit staff's investigation of the recorded delivery expenses of the Mount Royal store revealed
   - Its delivery vehicle experienced a major breakdown during February causing a three-day loss of deliveries (that were diverted to other E-MFE outlets).

---

1. Hint: Suppose that the standard error of prediction for an outlet is $65. This implies that, if there is *no* accounting misstatement (i.e., m = 0), then d (d = u + 0) for about 68 percent of the outlets will be from − $65 to + $65 and for about 95 percent will be from about − $130 to +$130. Thus, an outlet with, say, d = $50 will be ignored since it is plausible that d is due to random factors (or u), and not to accounting misstatement (m.) However, if d is −$145, then either the outcome is extremely unlikely (assuming m = zero) or there is an accounting *under*statement of expenses.

EXHIBIT 2

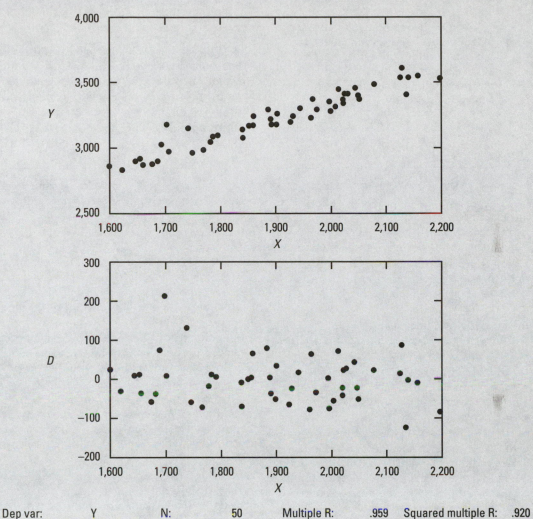

Dep var: Y   N: 50   Multiple R: .959   Squared multiple R: .920

Adjusted squared multiple R: .918   Standard error of estimate: 60.336

Variable	Coefficient	Std Error	Std Coef	Tolerance	T	P (2 Tail)
CONSTANT	848.964	101.185	0.000	.	8.390	0.000
X	1.246	0.053	0.959	.100E+01	23.431	0.000

Warning: case 39 is an outlier (studentized residual =   4.009)
Durbin-Watson D statistic   2.194
First order autocorrelation −.097

- Two payments for collision insurance as noted above (one for $225 and one for $250).
  - A repair bill for $315 dated February 10.
b. In analyzing the regression model, the Internal Auditor notices that the *d* for outlets in northern Montreal tended to be positive while those in southern Montreal tended to be negative.

c. Due to the expected arrival of warmer weather, E-MFE's Budgeting group expects higher volumes but lower operating costs for the second quarter.

4. What is your evaluation of the performance of Budgeting and Operations for the first quarter? How do you evaluate performance of the Mount Royal Store? How might the model (or modeling) be improved for the second quarter?

KEY WORDS

asset-loss risk   Threats of loss of an entity's assets including its reputation.

attestation services   Improve reliability of information by testing it against stated criteria for measurement and truthfully reporting test results.

business process risk   Threats from ineffective or inefficient business processes for acquiring, financing, transforming, and marketing goods and services.

business risk   Threat that an event or action will adversely affect a decision maker's ability to achieve his or her business objectives.

control activities   (A COSO criteria component) Policies and procedures put into place by an entity to reduce the likelihood that risks will exceed acceptable limits.

control environment   (A COSO criteria component) The overall context within which other internal control components function, including the integrity, competence, and ethical values of all people employed by the business, organization structure, and leadership.

COSO   (Short for the *C*ommittee *o*f *S*ponsoring *O*rganizations of the Treadway Commission) Criteria for evaluating quality of an entity's internal control including the components control environment, risk assessments, control activities, information and communication, and monitoring.

external environment risks   Threats from broad factors external to the business including substitute products, catastrophic loss, and changes in customers' tastes and preferences, competitors, political environment, laws/regulations, and capital and labor availability.

information and communication   (A COSO criteria component) Systematic transfer of management's policies, plans, and implementation instructions; systematic transfer of elementary data and business measurement and compliance information to those within and outside the business.

information risk   Threats from poor-quality information for decision making within an entity, and erroneous or fraudulent information provided to outsiders.

misstatement   A monetary difference due to error or fraud in the recorded value of an item and the true value of the item (value of the item if the stated measurement method were properly applied).

monitoring   (A COSO criteria component) Testing and analysis of the functioning of other components of internal control to determine whether they provide reasonable assurance of achieving stated objectives.

risk assessment   (A COSO criteria component) The identification, sourcing, and sizing of threats to achieving the business's objectives.

RISSAR   *R*isk *i*dentification, *s*ourcing, *s*izing, *a*ssessment, and *r*esponse approach to managing business risk by listing, evaluating, and responding to all potentially important risks.

4
CHAPTER

Internal Control over Transactions

- **H**ow do I know that my business measurement system gives me reliable numbers every day of the year?
- Is my company collecting all the cash that it should?
- Are my employees or others stealing from the company?
- Is the business as a whole complying with all applicable laws and regulations?
- Are employees complying with desired ethical behavior?

All of these questions about day-to-day operations can be answered through a well-designed and effectively operating internal control process for day-to-day activities in a modern business.

Chapter 4 is the first of three outlining how top management can reliably *inform itself* about business operations to obtain reasonable assurance of achieving its operating, compliance, and financial reporting objectives, and protecting the firm's assets. This chapter considers internal control over day-to-day functioning of the business through assigning responsibilities and maintaining records of accountability. Chapter 5 analyzes aggregates of recorded business operations to detect large deviations from expectations, and Chapter 6 outlines error and fraud detection procedures for individual items and transactions.

INTERNAL CONTROL CONCEPTS

As we know from Chapters 1 and 3, internal control has been defined by COSO as a process established by management and directors and other personnel of the firm to achieve the broad objectives of (a) efficient and effective operations, (b) reliable financial reporting, and (c) compliance with applicable laws and regulations. These objectives are partially overlapping, and cover a large portion of management's activities. As we will see, internal control includes day-to-day operation of business processes and business measurement processes. It does not include business decision processes.

Achievement of the three objectives of internal control is facilitated by an information model of the firm. The information model represents and displays measurements of real-world conditions that are relevant to running the business better. A relevant information model for efficient and effective operations requires that current events, conditions, and transactions of interest be sensed, measured, placed into relevant form, and then displayed for use by management and its employees. Reliable financial reporting and compliance with applicable laws and regulations are also facilitated by information displays using measurement methods specified by GAAP and by laws and regulations.

Management wants a high level of assurance that each of these information-processing steps is carefully and competently applied in unbiased fashion. Management also wants a high level of assurance that its assets are protected in order to fulfill its stewardship obligations to stockholders. Internal control over business measurements can help achieve such assurance through a reliable information model of the firm that parallels essential real-world activities for management decision making and is periodically compared with its real-world counterparts.

What's Included in Internal Control?

To illustrate what is included in internal control, Figure 4–1 shows management's activities divided into two groups: *management decision processes* and *internal control.* Management decision processes determine a multiperiod business strategy, operating plans for the current period (e.g., budgets), and resolution or follow-up actions on deviations from expected (planned) outcomes. Strategy and plans are implemented through business processes. Business processes interact with actual events, transactions, and conditions occurring during the current period to produce the actual real-world outcomes. Internal control is essential for managing much of the information to support management decision process and to protect assets.

Business transactions are a primary input for internal control, business measurement, and the accounting information model of the firm. Transactions involve exchanges between the firm and external parties. As examples, sales of products or services to a customer and purchases of products or services from suppliers are external-to-the-firm transactions involving exchanges of one asset (goods or services) for another (payment or promises to pay cash). Other inputs to the accounting system include events such as loss of assets due to natural factors and possible losses due to lawsuits, as well as conditions such as impairment of value due to changing markets.

Transactions with outside parties are ordinarily evidenced by paper or electronic business documents such as invoices, checks, receipts, and receiving reports that are signed or otherwise acknowledged by one or both parties to the exchange. Other exchanges take place within the firm. Internal exchanges include transfers of materials from a warehouse to production or from production to finished goods, and assignment of workers and overhead costs between departments. These internal transfers do not necessarily result in business documents, and thus may require special information system design provision to sense their occurrence.

F I G U R E   4 – 1

Management Decision Processes and Internal Control

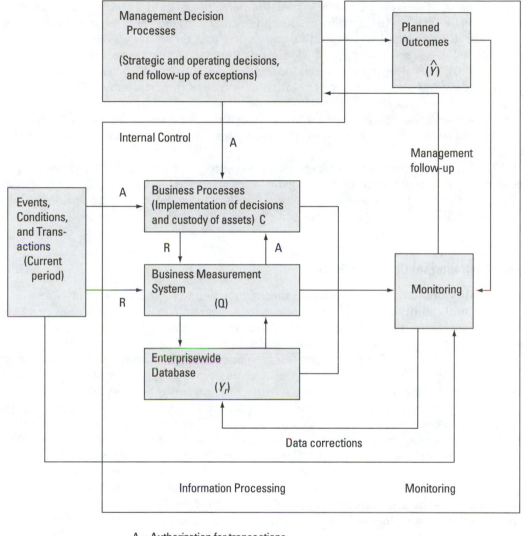

A = Authorization for transactions
B = Recording of transactions
C = Custody of assets resulting from transactions

Internal control over day-to-day transactions protects entry to business processes, including access to assets and information, as well as the accounting process that senses, measures, and records defined external transactions and internal transfers that produce the accounting record of outcomes. Documentation requirements protect access to company assets (a "boundary control") and provide a record of the activities. Entry to business processes via a sale or purchase transaction is illustrated by the "A," or authorization of transactions, arrows in Figure 4–1, while recording is labeled "R" and custody of real-world assets and obligations that are the outcomes are labeled "C."

Business processes, the business measurement system, and the enterprisewide database comprise the day-to-day information processing activities of internal control. Monitoring activities are applied after initial processing and result in corrections of data and items for follow-up by management. Monitoring involves comparisons. For example, comparison of displays of aggregated recorded accounting transactions measures with planned amounts allows analysis and decomposition of surprises in performance. Comparison of detailed recorded quantities with real-world assets as of a point in time allows determination of shortages that can be sourced as to cause, thus protecting firm assets. Monitoring can result in correction of information-processing results (database corrections) or matters for follow-up by management.

In this chapter, we will focus on internal control over day-to-day information processing of transactions, with monitoring activities addressed in Chapters 5 and 6. Specifically, Chapter 5 will explore analytical monitoring of aggregated recorded measures and Chapter 6 will consider tests of details of recorded amounts.

How Much Internal Control Is Enough?

What quality of internal control should management choose, and what level of resources should management devote to it? In concept, management considers the overall costs and expected benefits of internal control when deciding what "quality" of internal control to establish. Specifically, management considers the expected benefits of fewer and less-costly decision errors when using more reliable information and the expected reduction in possible loss of assets due to information errors. Outside parties such as capital suppliers and trading partners also have an interest in a firm's internal control quality. To the extent that management can communicate the quality of its internal controls to others, it can lower the information risk premium charged by outsiders (see Chapter 10). Also, external auditors will lower audit fees charged if they perceive internal control as reliable (see Chapter 8).

All three of these expected costs decrease as the quality of internal control increases. On the other hand, the total operating cost of internal control (outlays for personnel, equipment, and software) increases as quality increases. While internal control quality and its costs can't be precisely measured, "quality" is related to the risk of significant or "material" costs to management of decision errors due to unreliable information, asset loss, and risk premia paid to outsiders. Management faces both types of costs, and thus wishes to minimize the sum of the two.

Figure 4–2 shows a conceptual diagram of the expected decision error costs and risk premia decreasing with increasing internal control "quality." Figure 4–2 also shows internal control operating costs rising as internal control quality increases. Since management bears both types of costs, management will consider their sum in deciding what quality level of internal control is best for management. The internal control quality level chosen is the one that minimizes management's expected total cost, or ICQ* in Figure 4–2—the sum of the expected decision error costs, risk premia, and audit fees, plus the cost of internal control procedures.

FIGURE 4-2

Internal Control Quality Costs

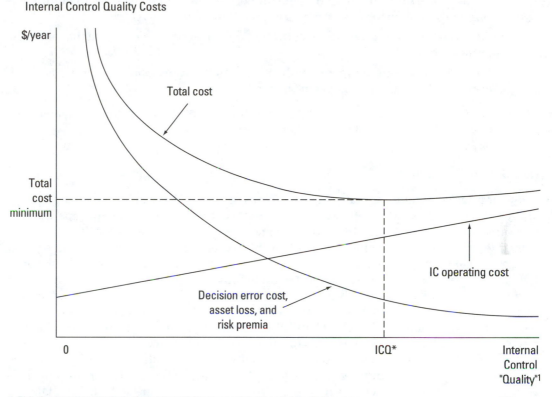

1. Risk of an important magnitude of misstatement decreases as internal control "quality" increases.

In the United States, the Foreign Corrupt Practices Act of 1977 (FCPA) requires that SEC registrants (companies registered with the SEC for the privilege of issuing securities to the general public) maintain cost-justified internal controls. Registrants must have controls whose costs are warranted by their expected benefits. One FCPA objective is improved corporate accountability, and another is improved reliability of quarterly financial information for investors (quarterly financial information is not typically audited by external auditors before its release to outsiders (see Chapter 11)).

The effect of the FCPA is uncertain because, even without the law, a profit-maximizing management would implement cost-justified controls as the economic act. However, the FCPA does focus attention on the importance of controls and the importance of justifying their cost. Some financial institutions are required to obtain an auditor's report on control compliance with specified criteria. This is an example of the regulatory/legal demand for assurance services.

The FCPA incorporates four important requirements for internal controls regarding accounting information:

- Transactions are executed in accordance with management's general or specific **authorization.**

- All transactions and other events are promptly **recorded** in the correct amount, in the appropriate accounts, and in the proper accounting period so as to permit preparation of financial statements in accordance with GAAP.

- **Access to assets and records** is permitted only in accordance with management's authorization.

- Recorded assets are **compared** with existing assets at reasonable intervals and appropriate action is taken regarding any differences.

These requirements facilitate economical preparation of GAAP-based financial statements and establish recorded accountabilities that protect firm assets.

ARC Separation Principle

The four internal accounting control requirements of the FCPA are operationalized by separating three types of duties referred to as the **ARC separation principle** (for separation of *a*uthorization and *r*ecording of transactions and *c*ustody of assets). The ARC separation principle states that an individual will not be able to perpetrate and conceal fraud or theft (and accidental errors will be reduced) if, for a particular transaction stream, he or she does not have responsibility for more than one of these activities. For example, individuals with custody of company assets such as cash can steal it, but if he or she can't reduce the recorded cash balance, then the shortage will be detected when someone else compares recorded accountability with cash on hand. Similarly, someone may authorize an improper payment, but an independently kept record may lead to discovery.[1]

Physical protective devices and computer software can facilitate separation of duties. To illustrate separation of duties and the use of physical protective devices in a simple revenue context, consider an example from the 1940s. Rudy, a five-year-old boy, is to make his first purchase by himself—a red metal toy fire engine costing 29¢. Rudy's mother cautions him to make sure he gets a cash register receipt from the sales clerk when he makes his purchase. Rudy agrees and complies with the request.

Unknown to Rudy, his insistence on a receipt allowed the store's manager to record revenue, establish accountability for cash collected by her sales clerk, and document authorization of a sale. The cash register's preparation of a printed paper receipt for Rudy also generated within the cash register a locked copy of the receipt (sales invoice), and a running subtotal of all sales for the cash register for the day. The store manager also monitored both the sales clerk and assets by looking for little boys and girls leaving the store with a fire engine, but no receipt.

At the end of the day, the sales clerk deposited total cash collected, and the bookkeeper for the store retrieved the locked copy and sales total from the cash register. The duplicate sales receipt record became the basis for recording total sales for the day, the clerk's deposit was the entry for total cash collections, and the difference was recorded as the "cashier over-and-short." If over time the (cumulative) amount of "cashier over-and-short" became large on the "short" side, the clerk would be fired. Thus, the cash register with its

---

1. A person having more than one of the ARC duties for a given transaction type is sometimes said to have "incompatible duties" (i.e., incompatible with the ARC separation principle).

locked copy of the invoice facilitated separation of authorization, recording, and custody even though a single clerk was responsible for all transactions with Rudy.

Today, conceptually similar electronic point-of-sale recording systems duplicate the cash register's functions to assist separation of duties in sales processing. For example, in fast food chain stores, the "order-taking clerk" must enter a customer's order into a point-of-sale recording device that signals the "cooks" to prepare the order. No order entry, no order. More advanced point-of-sale recording systems using bar code readers also update inventory on hand, reorder merchandise, and update product sales and customer records based on current sales recorded.

In modern enterprisewide software-based business measurement systems, separation of duties is operationalized through assignment and control of codes for accessing various computer programs and elements of the control database. For example, a salesclerk can enter a cash sale or a sale to an approved customer and can look up (read only) inventory records of available goods. However, the salesclerk cannot change a customer's receivables balance or credit limit, or alter inventory quantities except by recording a sale, because the software installer's code assignment prevents such database access by a salesclerk. The credit manager and inventory control personnel do have credit limit and inventory access code authorizations and can make changes, but they cannot initiate sales transactions.

Typical business organization also reflects these broad separation of duties following the ARC principle. Figure 4–3 shows the vice presidents for Operations, Marketing, and Human Resources having primary authorization duties, authorizing acquisition, production, and sale of goods and services comprising the core processes of the firm. The vice presidents for Finance and Information oversee the transaction recording as well as authorizing some financial functions, while the treasurer has primary responsibility for the administration and physical custody of the firm's cash. The recording function provides a record (information model) by which operations can be analyzed and compared with expectations. The recorded accountability also allows detection of shortages in cash, receivables, inventory, and fixed assets.

COSO INTERNAL CONTROL FRAMEWORK

At present, there is no single internal control document outlining standards to be applied by companies worldwide. However, the concepts in COSO have received wide acceptance. COSO describes five principal components of internal control: the **control environment, risk assessments, control activities, information and communication,** and **monitoring.** These components are important decision variables for top management in choosing the best organization design.

Control Environment

The control environment comprises the overall setting in which business is conducted within the entity. It encompasses the other four components and is pervasive in its effect. It is also the only component for which your efforts as a manager directly affect the level of control achieved.

Example Organization Chart

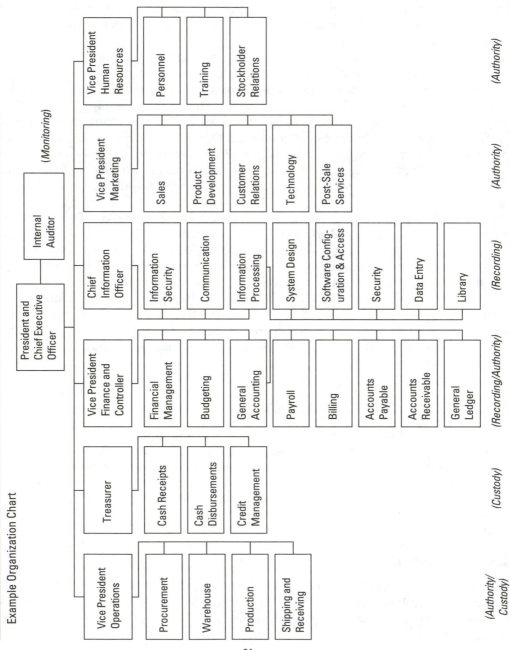

Top management is central in defining the control environment because top management's attitudes toward control are reflected in the manner in which the other four components are implemented. A weak control environment, such as one characterized by the lack of a serious attitude toward control and ethical behavior, or lack of follow-up of exceptions, can lead to ineffective results from the other components. But, even though pervasive in effect, a strong control environment does not prevent or detect errors directly— the other four components are essential.

You, as a member of top management, set the overall environment in which the other control components are applied. The attitude or seriousness of top management about internal control is especially important for the control activities and information and communication components that are carried out day-to-day as transactions are processed. Effectiveness of the control environment also depends on the people that you hire, their competence, and their integrity. Competence determines their ability to carry out responsibilities, and integrity determines how they are carried out. Employees lacking integrity are more likely to perform improperly, to steal company assets, and to misrepresent information.

Management must also decide performance monitoring practices and what follow-up action to take when exceptions are noted. Design, monitoring, and follow-up applied by management take place before or after day-to-day transactions are processed. Thus, any effect that you as management have on application of controls as transactions are being conducted is through the *perceptions of employees* applying the other four components. In a sense, the control environment is operationalized by employees' anticipation of your likely future actions, and it is the anticipation that affects day-to-day control attained. Effectiveness requires that you communicate your attitude toward control, financial reporting, and the importance of following laws and regulations as well as an established ethical code with the firm.

The control environment may also be affected by management's policies and attitudes toward performance targets, and these may have unanticipated consequences. For example, accounting information–based incentive systems such as profit sharing can encourage extra effort by employees, because extra effort is partially reflected by accounting earnings. But incentive compensation based on recorded accounting earnings also gives employees an incentive to overstate recorded earnings. During the early 1990s, top managements of at least two major U.S. firms (Woolworth Corp. and Leslie Fay Companies, Inc.) were embarrassed by lower-level employees who falsified financial records to make their firm's interim performance appear to meet top management's goals. These failures might have been prevented by better communication of ethical values versus performance measures.

Risk Assessments

Business process risk assessment concepts discussed in Chapter 3 can be applied to risk assessments for transactions processing and loss of assets of the firm. A conceptual way of considering internal control over transactions is to prepare a list of *all possible* misstatements that might arise in the conduct of a business (see Figure 3–5 in Chapter 3).

When the list of all potential risks is established, they must then be "sized" and "sourced." For those risks that are important because of size, likelihood of occurrence, or their combination, means of mitigating the risks are required. Some risks may be avoided at the source of risk by design. For example, because the risk of theft of cash due to robbery is high, a retail gasoline seller may choose to sell only by credit card, thus avoiding risk at the source.[2] For risks in the "could be" acceptable category, preventive and detective/corrective control activities applied to transactions being processed can limit risk and so can after-processing monitoring.

Control Activities

According to SAS No. 78 (a U.S. standard providing guidance for auditors on internal control reliance), control activities are "the policies and procedures that help insure that management directives are carried out." These activities can be divided into three categories applied as transactions are being processed and one applied after processing:

- *Information Processing.* Controls applied to verify accuracy, completeness, and authorization of transactions applied by financial and operating employees as transactions are being processed, and before proceeding with subsequent steps. Thus, they may prevent errors, detect and correct errors of others, and force a "precedence" order on transactions processing that protects assets (e.g., checks paying invoices for materials purchased are not prepared until notice is received that goods arrived in good condition).

- *Physical Controls.* Physical security of assets, including adequate safeguards such as secured facilities for assets and records, authorization for access to processing software and databases, and periodic counting of real-world assets and comparison with recorded amounts.

- *Separation of Duties.* Assigning different people the responsibilities of authorizing transactions, recording transactions, and maintaining custody of assets so that no person is in a position to both perpetrate and conceal errors or irregularities in the normal course of his or her duties.

- *Performance Review.* Comparison by operating employees of recorded performance with expectations based on budgets, forecasts, past performance, and nonfinancial data, and real-time investigation and corrective actions. Performance reviews are applied *after* transactions are recorded, but can detect large errors or fraud in recording as well as poor implementation of plans and environmental changes.

The two broad control activities over computers are general controls and application controls. General controls commonly cover data center operations, system and application software design and maintenance, database access, and provision for backup and restart when the system fails. Weak general controls can have a pervasive effect since they may allow strong application controls to be compromised. Strong general controls can protect the reliability of each application.

Application controls apply to the processing of individual transaction types such as sales, payroll, and materials acquisitions. These controls help assure that particular trans-

---

2. See A. Hollander, E. Denna, and O. Cherrington, *Accounting, Information Technology, and Business Solutions,* (Richard D. Irwin, 1996), p. 174, for an example of a chain of department stores operating in Russia avoiding cash theft risk by refusing to sell for cash.

actions are valid, properly authorized, and completely and accurately processed. With enterprisewide software, separation of duties is facilitated by assignment of access codes to allow particular employees access to various application program modules that access the central database. Validation of separation of duties via access codes can be accomplished by audit software that analyzes access codes for "incompatible" duties.

Information and Communication

Business measurement systems and communication are essential for all aspects of control within a business. Ethical values, plans, and expectations must be communicated to employees. Also, performance measurements and deviations from expectations must be communicated to management for evaluation and follow-up interventions leading to effective and efficient operations.

As part of the overall information system, the accounting system's methods and records are established (a) to sense, record, process, summarize, and display results of entity transactions as information about the firm for operating decisions, GAAP-based financial statements, and customized data requests; and (b) to maintain recorded accountability for related assets, liability, and equity to protect assets. As we have seen, a reliable accounting system is essential to operationalize other elements of internal control.

Monitoring

Monitoring as an internal control component is the process of assessing the quality of internal control performance over time. Performance reviews and consistency checks are made by operating personnel as transactions are processed. Reviews of recorded performance versus budgets, forecasts, prior-period performance, and operating data are made after transaction processing. Either type of review may reveal information errors, fraud, operating problems, or changed conditions. Monitoring is also facilitated by independent follow-up performance reviews by outsiders such as customer, supplier, or regulator complaints. Finally, as we'll see in Chapters 5 and 6, internal auditors monitor internal control by testing and evaluating control components, analyzing business operations, and auditing recorded results.

Inherent Limitations of Internal Control

Internal control based on the control environment, risk assessments, control activities, and information and communication processes cannot provide management with 100 percent assurance against material misstatements in accounting information and asset protection because of *inherent limitations* of these components of internal control. Six limitations are listed in International Standards on Auditing (IASC, 1995) for external auditors, and they also are relevant to top management. Three apply to all controls. Even with effective internal control, material misstatement or asset loss may arise because of

- **Human error** due to carelessness, distraction, mistakes of judgment, and the misunderstanding of management's instructions—even when employees apply prescribed procedures.
- **Collusion** of a member of lower management or an employee with parties outside or inside the entity to circumvent prescribed controls.

  • **Overriding** of an internal control by a member of lower management who has
    authority over employees applying controls.

A second group of three related limitations sometimes applies:

  ◆ Management's choice of internal control quality balances the cost of internal
    control with the expected benefits to be derived, so some misstatement will be
    optimal.

  ◆ Most internal controls tend to be directed at routine or expected transactions, so
    nonroutine or unexpected transactions may not be controlled.

  ◆ Over time, procedures may become inadequate due to changes in conditions, or
    compliance with procedures may deteriorate.

These inherent limitations have two important implications for monitoring by top management. First, there is a need for periodic and independent examination of financial
statements and operating reports produced by internal control. Second, there is a need for
continued monitoring of internal control processes.

      Top managements typically delegate some monitoring duties to an internal auditor.
The internal auditor tests control activities applied by other employees. Internal auditors
also monitor by determining the reliability of recorded financial amounts by auditing the
results of transaction processing. Specifically, they test aggregate amounts using analytical
monitoring procedures (see Chapter 5) and test details of disaggregated recorded and real-
world amounts (see Chapter 6).

TWO EXAMPLES: MATERIALS ACQUISITION AND DERIVATIVES

To illustrate the internal control components, their interrelation, and the ARC principle,
let's consider two important transaction types: the acquisition of materials for production
and derivatives.

Materials Acquisition

Traditional Processes

Figure 4–4 diagrams traditional business processes and measurement and compliance
processes for a producer (your company) and its supplier. The figure begins with a production manager who determines the materials needed for planned production (an authorization function). Materials needs are transmitted to a purchasing employee, who is responsible for finding the lowest-cost supplier of the needed materials. This activity leads
to preparation of a <u>purchase order</u>[3] that is sent to the supplier selected. The supplier then
processes the order, ships the materials, and prepares and mails an <u>invoice</u> requesting payment for the materials. The materials are received by materials department personnel, who
prepare a <u>receiving report.</u> The materials department now has custody of the materials that
eventually will be transferred to production.

---

3. Underscore indicates a business document.

Traditional Document-Based Materials Acquisition Process

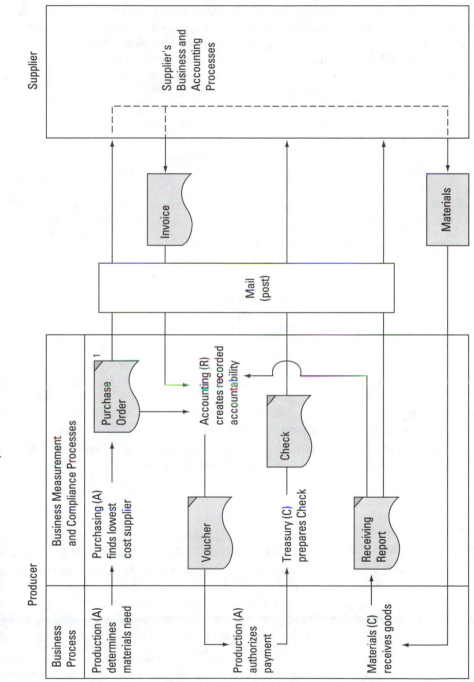

1. Indicates origination of a business document.

Cash payment processing begins when the receiving report is matched by accounting personnel with the purchase order and invoice. An accounting clerk (recording function) verifies the arithmetic accuracy of the invoice and compares price per unit with the agreed-upon price or with market prices or recent prices paid. The clerk then prepares a voucher and attaches the purchase order, receiving report, and invoice. Finally, the clerk creates a recorded accountability for the materials, records the related liability (accounts payable), and sends the voucher packet to the production manager, who reviews the documents and authorizes payment of this particular invoice by signing the voucher.

Upon receipt of a signed voucher, treasury department personnel prepare a check and mail the check to the supplier. The treasury personnel thus have custody of (access to) cash and transfer cash upon appropriate authorization by production. The recorded accountability for materials can be compared to the materials on hand in the materials department or transferred out of materials to production (as evidenced by a materials requisition signed by production personnel).

Now let's analyze the diagram for control weaknesses or incompatible duties. Can any of the personnel involved misappropriate company assets without detection?

- Materials personnel have custody of inventory, but if they steal inventory, it will be discovered when the recorded accountability from accounting (goods received less materials requisitioned by production) is compared with inventory on hand.

- Treasury personnel have custody of cash and can prepare fraudulent checks, but will be detected when other personnel compare cash on hand and in the bank with recorded cash receipts less checks supported by validly authorized vouchers.

- Accounting personnel have no access to assets, and therefore have no opportunity to steal company assets. Because of their lack of access to assets and the fact that their performance is evaluated based on the accuracy of their record keeping, accounting personnel have an incentive to keep reliable records, and the records establish accountability for assets.

- Authorizing personnel (production and purchasing personnel) can authorize transactions, but do not have direct access to firm assets.

- Production management may authorize purchase of unneeded materials, but these assets will be recorded in the asset base used to calculate the performance measure "return on investment" for production.

- The purchasing agent may choose a supplier who will overbill the company (prepare an invoice for more than the proper amount) and provide a "kickback" payment to purchasing personnel. Kickbacks require finding a supplier who will overbill and then share the overcharge with purchasing personnel. This collusion of the purchasing agent and the outside supplier may be detected by an accounting clerk reviewing prices for reasonableness before preparing a voucher, or later by an internal auditor comparing prices paid against market price quotes.

Thus we see that the separation of duties and business documents combined with the independent accounting record can protect firm assets as well as provide important information about the cost of production, assets, and liabilities. Accounting documents for transactions processing provide the basis for control of cash. Document control leads to asset control. Also, accounting documents can be related to production records to measure cost of production.

Re-engineered Processes

Enterprise software and databases integrate accounting and operating records and yield efficiencies for both accounting and operations. With enterprise software, documents are electronic and separation of duties for transactions processing is accomplished via the software.

Figure 4–5 diagrams materials acquisition for re-engineered processes based on a business contract or alliance with the supplier, electronic data interchange (EDI), and enterprise software. The contract or alliance involves sharing information between companies to lower the cost of production for the supplier with part of the savings shared with the producer.

In Figure 4–5, production management schedules production (using the production planning (PP) module in SAP). This *production schedule* is accessible by the supplier via electronic data interchange (EDI) through an independent value-added network (VAN) provider. The VAN provider is an independent firm that acts as a secure data processing agent, verifying identities of parties requesting data, transferring valid requests, and maintaining records of the transfers.

The supplier converts the planned production schedule into raw materials requirements and determines the supplier production and lead time so that the needed materials can arrive at the producer's facilities just as they are needed by the producer. The needed materials are produced by the supplier, shipped to the producer, and received by materials personnel who immediately place the materials into production.

When production personnel enter completion of production in the database, the software refers to the materials component list to determine the cash payments to be made to each supplier of materials components. Specifically, the software determines the quantity of materials that *should be* in the output and prepares an authorization for cash transfer to the supplier in the proper amount. Funds are then transferred electronically to the supplier via the VAN. The software also transmits an electronic settlement notice that details the materials for which payment is being made by the electronic funds transfer. Differences in records and goods on hand are resolved periodically (the shipment and settlement notices facilitate reconciliation of intercompany differences).

The re-engineered system differs in form from the traditional system in Figure 4–4 in that there are no paper documents accompanying the materials and there is no materials inventory. There are substantial cost savings due to better and more reliable information. The supplier saves materials production costs by knowing the timed input needs of the producer and passes part of the savings to the producer. The producer saves through lower materials acquisition costs and elimination of raw materials inventories made possible through just-in-time delivery by the supplier. Thus, the producer saves cost of production and storage as well as document processing costs. Finally, the purchasing agent is eliminated in the revised system due to the negotiation of a contract or business alliance at preset prices from a predetermined list of suppliers.

Because of closer relations between supplier and producer and the VAN that transfers data and cash and maintains records of transactions processed, the producer also has

Enterprisewide Software-Based Materials Acquisition Process Using Electronic Data Interchange

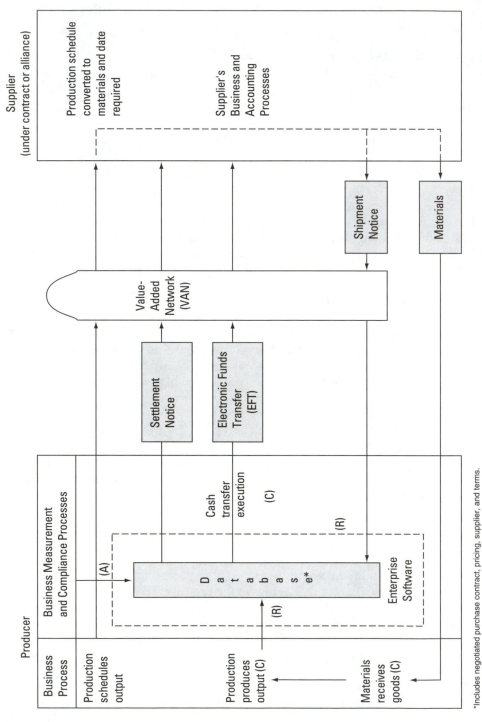

*Includes negotiated purchase contract, pricing, supplier, and terms.

additional needs for assurance services. The producer needs assurance that the supplier has access to the production schedule and conversion documents but does not have access to other producer data. The producer also needs assurance that the VAN protects access to the producer's database and transfers cash in the proper amount and only to the approved supplier. Thus, assured information systems benefit all parties involved. The need for assurance may lead to an assurer's report that the VAN has a control process that meets specified performance criteria.

In the traditional materials acquisition system of Figure 4–4, transactions control was accomplished through separation of transaction processing duties and the use of prescribed documents and control activities between persons. Transactions control procedures in the re-engineered system of Figure 4–5 are applied using computer software, and control over software requires separation of software-related duties incorporating controls within the software.

To apply the ARC principles for software-related duties, management must separate four computer processing–related activities:

- System design.
- Software component configuration and access code assignment.
- Security of access to servers, applications, and enterprise database.
- Data input.

System design and **component configuration** activities customize enterprise software for a particular company. System design determines users' needs and specifies what is to be accomplished by the enterprise software. Component configuration operationalizes the design by activating and customizing particular software components available. Component confirmation is akin to setting of channel access in home cable television networks. Since much of the operation of a computer system is not readily observable, systems design and component configuration personnel test the proposed configuration for effectiveness and agree to its validity before placing it in operation.

As an example of configuration of enterprise software for accounting, SAP R/3 can account for over 17,000 possible transaction types for various business segments and industries. This is accomplished using a menu of alternative standardized business processes and program code to operationalize these processes. The processes include production scheduling, materials management, human resources, financial accounting, and equipment maintenance, among others.

System designers choose the components applicable to their firm, and sometimes re-engineer their processes to comply with the software. Customization specifies numerical criteria for admitting transactions for processing and conditions that are to precede each of these transaction types. Customization of the software is equivalent to computer programming in a nonstandardized system. Then, personal access codes must be assigned and entered into the program to determine which person is able to initiate a particular function. Access code assignment allows implementation of ARC separation.

Security is a general control function that protects access to the software in day-to-day operation and change-management procedures to protect the software from unauthorized changes after it is placed into operation. Finally, **data input** personnel use the software daily to process transactions as authorized, but do not have access to program code or the ability to change access codes. Separation of these four duties allows separation of duties as was the case for manual systems.

Enterprisewide software allows increased data integrity since integration of data allows management or its agent (such as the internal auditor) to access transaction data at many different levels of detail to isolate the source and possible cause of unusual entries. Also, it allows detailed comparison of financial records with related nonfinancial data on the same transaction.

Furthermore, since the same basic enterprise software is used for many firms, software companies have imbedded program modules into the software itself that can evaluate control aspects of a particular application. For example, embedded routines can search the software configuration selected by a particular company for assignment of incompatible access codes, such as whether a supervisor who approves hours worked for employees also has access to human resources records. The supervisor with this access could "hire" a fictitious employee by creating an employee file and then approve hours worked on time records. Automated control evaluation helps identify the separation of duties and problems and greatly lowers the cost of testing the controls.

Derivatives

During the 1990s, derivatives became a widely used mechanism for managing some types of risk. Derivatives have also led to multimillion-dollar losses and even failure of large commercial and financial institutions. Derivatives as a means of managing risks are beyond the scope of this book. However, internal control over derivatives is relevant, since control is essential to achieving management's objectives, and control involves the ARC principle. In fact, major losses due to derivatives in the 1990s were, to a large extent, due to inadequate internal control.

Derivatives include financial instruments whose value is derived from the value of an underlying asset, liability, reference rate, or index. For example, a company borrowing $10 million with a variable interest rate may convert to a fixed interest rate by engaging in a variable-for-fixed interest rate swap. The swap might involve exchange of interest payments on a "notional" amount, such as $10 million, and the value of the London Interbank Offered Rate of interest (LIBOR). Thus, the value of the swap can be derived from LIBOR, and as LIBOR fluctuates, the value of the swap and the amount by which the value might change over a period of time (sometimes called the "value at risk") will also fluctuate.[4]

To see how the ARC principle can facilitate control over derivatives such as an interest rate swap, Figure 4–6 shows five parties within the firm, the outside (counter) party with whom interest payments are exchanged, and the underlying basis information (LIBOR) that fluctuates over time. Top management sets objectives for derivatives using the swap and sets limits on risk exposure. These objectives and limits are communicated to the trader (in the finance department) authorized to negotiate derivatives and to the internal auditor who monitors performance of the process (see arrows labeled 1 in Figure 4–6).

---

4. See T. Linsmeier and N. Pearson, "Quantitative Disclosures of Market Risk in the SEC Release," *Accounting Horizons,* March 1997, pp. 107–35.

ARC Principle for Derivatives

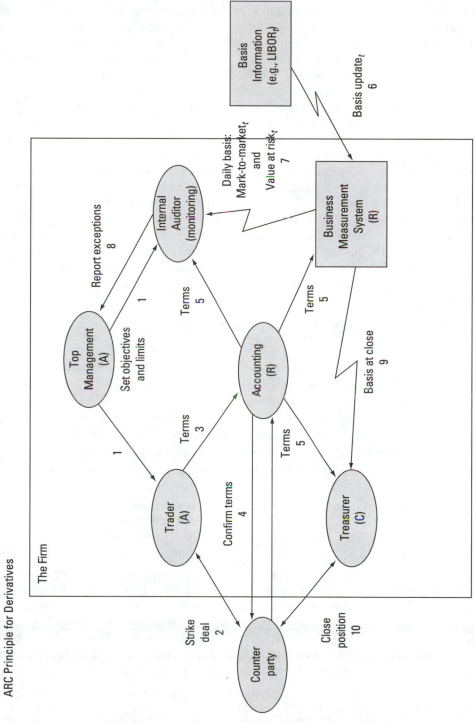

The trader negotiates terms of the swap with an outside counter party (arrow 2), and communicates terms of the transaction to accounting personnel (arrow 3), who independently confirm terms with the counter party (arrow 4). Accounting then records the terms and thus informs the treasury department, the internal auditor, and the business measurement system of the terms of the transaction (arrows labeled 5). The business measurement system will then obtain access to LIBOR and calculate the value of the derivative position and the value at risk on a daily basis (arrow 6).[5]

The internal auditor monitors the derivative portfolio position by comparing its measured value against the objectives and limits set by top management (arrow 7). If the limits are exceeded, then the internal auditor reports the breach to top management for a decision about follow-up actions (arrow 8). When the position comes due or is to be closed, treasury department personnel (cash custody) calculate the settlement amount and transfer or receive cash to settle the position (arrows 9 and 10).

Information technology and complex calculations are used to measure the value and value at risk of derivative financial instruments. However, the ARC principle still applies and allows control. Specifically, separation of authorization for objectives and limits from authorization for day-to-day trades, and independent confirmation and recording of transaction terms, independent measurement for monitoring, and settlement allow management of risk and protection of company assets.

FINANCIAL MISSTATEMENTS: ERRORS AND FRAUD

As discussed in Chapter 3, financial misstatements are differences between the true (measurement-method-application-error–free) value for a transaction or balance and its recorded value (misstatement = recorded value − true value). Misstatements have many possible causes, but they can be divided into three broad categories:

1. Errors by employees or management—accidental misstatement in sensing, measurement, classification, or calculation, or omission from display.

2. Misappropriation fraud—intentional misstatement of recorded amounts by employees, ordinarily accompanied by theft of company assets such as cash, inventory, or fixed assets.

3. Misrepresentation fraud—intentional overstatement of recorded assets, understatement of recorded liabilities, or use of improper accounting methods or biased accounting estimates with the intent of overstating a performance measure such as net income or an activity base such as total assets or equity.

Figure 4–7 classifies each as to intent, person(s) responsible, whether assets are missing, and expected effect on net assets and net income. The classifications are useful because they have different implications for how best to control the misstatement. For example, errors may or may not involve loss of firm assets—accidental failure to record and bill a customer for services rendered may lead to failure to collect cash due the company, but the accidental recording of 100 units of inventory as 10 units does not by itself mean that 90 units are lost. Also, all parties involved (operating personnel, accounting clerks, all levels of man-

---

5. Daily calculation of value of position and value at risk may not be needed for a simple swap, but the valuation of a portfolio of derivatives, hedges, and positions taken can be complex and warrant daily measurement and monitoring.

FIGURE 4-7

Errors and Fraud by Employees and Lower Management

		Fraud	
	Errors	Misappropriation	Misrepresentation
Intentional misstatement?	No	Yes	Yes
Expected effect on recorded earnings and net assets (over/understated)	Either	Overstated	Overstated[1]
Assets lost?	Maybe	Yes	No[2]
Management initiated?	No	Rarely	Frequently
Effectiveness of risk assessment, control activities, and performance review	High	Mixed[3]	Low
Effectiveness of monitoring by internal auditor	High	High	Moderate[4]

1. Expected misrepresentation could be understatement in situations such as a management buyout.

2. Assets may be lost indirectly if bonuses are paid on the basis of overstated recorded performance.

3. Lower-level managers may override control activities implemented by their subordinates and may falsify performance reviews.

4. Even an "independent" internal auditor who reports to the CEO may be ineffective in detecting biases in lower management's judgments about accounting estimates (see Chapter 6).

agement, and even the internal and outside auditors) have an interest in limiting accidental misstatements.

On the other hand, fraud may involve loss of assets, and the perpetrator of fraud can be expected to attempt to hide the fraud by misinformation and deceit. For employee fraud, both higher management and the auditors have the same interests in detection. However, if top management commits fraud, it will often be very difficult for the internal or the outside auditor to detect the fraud because top management has much discretion to mislead the auditor, override controls, and even intimidate its employees.

Misappropriation fraud is typically perpetrated by employees and lower levels of management. On the other hand, financial misrepresentation fraud is typically perpetrated by higher-level managers, and even by top management. Since this book takes the perspective of top management, we will not consider the risk that you as a member of top management will either misappropriate assets or misrepresent financial measures. We will consider the risk that lower-level managers who have responsibility for overseeing some prescribed control activities might commit fraud, and we will consider the risk that top management in a subsidiary or another company may commit fraud. Finally, in later chapters we will address the external auditor's consideration of the risk of fraud by top management.

Internal Control Design

In concept, the most important single control against error and both types of fraud is the initial recording of assets as they are acquired by the firm, such as revenues due the firm for a sale on account. A complete record of sales amounts establishes the amount due the company that can be accounted for as being in one of three categories at any point in time: cash collected and on hand or deposited in the bank, accounts receivable awaiting collection, and accounts receivable written off as uncollectable. The balances in each of these can be independently validated by management by comparing them to the cash account, verifying ending receivables, and reviewing the basis for customer accounts written down to zero. Then, total cash collected can be accounted for at any time as cash currently on hand, plus the sum of properly authorized cash disbursements for materials and payroll.

Because of their importance, revenue controls are designed to ensure complete recording of revenues. In part, this is because detection of omitted revenues is difficult since management may have little reason to expect collections and, therefore, will be unlikely to discover the failure to collect cash. Also, subsequent detection and correction procedures are likely to fail if revenue recording is incomplete, because others don't know of the existence of the sale. Similar completeness problems exist for purchases of inventory—a manager may omit a purchase and the related payable to raise recorded net income and net assets.

Historically, the economics of misstatement prevention versus detection and correction tended to favor the latter. However, development of low-cost electronic sensors has lowered the cost of automated measurements, and the lowered costs of transmitting and storing electronic images and documents, along with lower-cost computing power, have led to a cost advantage for error prevention. These developments make it possible to imbed more controls in software applied at the point of data entry and to record and evaluate more aspects of transactions and balances. Also, accidental processing mistakes are not likely to be repeated in the related processes such as nonfinancial measurements, and concealment of intentional misstatements requires the ability of the perpetrator to violate controls on all related measurements and processes.

Empirical Data on Fraud

Aggregate data to evaluate the seriousness of accidental data processing mistakes are difficult to obtain. Business firms do not publicly disclose mistakes made in routine data processing day to day, and auditors do not publicly report what they note in conducting audits after the fact. Thus, it is difficult to evaluate the "inherent risk" of accidental mistakes arising in the accounting process, or the effectiveness of controls in preventing and detecting such mistakes.

Empirical data on the relative incidence and magnitude of employee fraud are also limited. However, KPMG Peat Marwick, a Big Five CPA firm, recently surveyed the largest 2,000 (by revenues) public companies in the United States, asking them to report their experiences with employee fraud. They also asked 2,250 smaller companies with revenues of $50 million or more as well as 750 not-for-profit organizations for the same information. The data were voluntarily reported and probably understate the rates of fraud even for these companies. Also, of course, the most clever frauds remain undiscovered. But, despite these limitations, the data give some indication of how well controls over employee fraud are working.

Of the firms and organizations responding to the 1998 KPMG survey, 62 percent reported at least one type of fraud, and the median fraud loss per incident was $116,000. The survey did not report the number of respondents, so the portion of firms experiencing a particular fraud type can't be determined. However, it did report the number of frauds and average losses by fraud type. The largest average losses ($3,177,000 per fraud) were attributed to medical/insurance claims, with 29 respondents reporting such frauds. The second highest average losses ($1,239,000 per fraud) were financial statement–related, but with only 12 firms reporting. These frauds probably involved managers at a fairly high level. Credit card fraud was the third highest, with 48 organizations averaging $1,126,000 per incident. On the other hand, losses due to forged or altered checks, inventory theft, and false invoices averaged $624,000, $346,000, and $250,000 each, while diversion of sales kickbacks and expense account fraud and payable fraud losses ranged from $180,000 to $26,000.

What detected the frauds? Fifty-one percent of respondents said that it was their internal controls, and 43 percent said that internal auditors detected it (explanations totaled more than 100 percent because many firms reported more than one fraud). Thus, normally operating control procedures were often effective. However, nonroutine notification of the frauds by another employee or customers, as well as special investigations, were mentioned by 35 to 58 percent of the firms, while accidental discoveries or receipt of an anonymous letter were each mentioned by about 35 percent of the firms. Only 4 percent of the firms indicated that their external auditors discovered a fraud while conducting a year-end financial statement audit. This is not surprising since external auditors would not be expected to find immaterial misstatements.[6]

The KPMG survey also shows that poor internal controls were the most frequently mentioned factor allowing frauds to occur (about 60 percent), while factors affecting inherent limitations of internal control reliance by management were also important. More than one-third said that frauds arose when managers overrode prescribed controls, 3 in 10 said there was collusion between employees, and 2 in 10 said there was collusion between employees and outside parties. These latter results show the need for management to monitor results, since, by definition, internal controls are not effective against collusion and management override of controls.

INFORMING YOURSELF ABOUT INTERNAL CONTROL

Top management itself has limited skills in evaluating internal control and very limited time available to conduct evaluations. They must depend on others to make the evaluations. Others include internal auditors and external auditors, but how can a member of top management know if he or she should believe the evaluations of auditors? The answer depends on whether the entity is under your direct control.

Internal Auditors

For your own company, you can hire an internal auditor to act as your monitoring agent. Chapter 5 explores analytical monitoring of transaction summaries by internal auditors to identify deviations from management's expectations (possibly indicating internal control failure), and Chapter 6 presents monitoring of details comprising the summaries to identify misstatements in particular items and possible need to correct internal control processes.

---

6. External auditors are more likely to detect frauds that are material to interpreting the financial statements, which, for most firms in the survey, would be several million dollars or more (see Chapters 7–9).

Monitoring activities by internal auditors are an especially important part of internal control because of the investigative competence and independent point of view that internal auditors can bring to the evaluation of business processes. Internal auditors are trained in investigation procedures and business processes. Thus, they are competent to investigate. Also, typically they have no interest in the business processes or information displays being investigated—their only interest is the reliability of information. Thus, their findings are more likely to be objective and trustworthy than would be a report from someone who is reporting on his or her own activities, or whose compensation or performance evaluations depend on the information display.

Figure 4–3 showed the internal auditor reporting to the president and chief executive officer. Some internal auditors do report to the CEO, but others report to the chief financial officer, and still others to operating division officers. The level of reporting may affect the nature and timeliness of information that you as a member of top management receive. This is because an internal auditor reporting to a lower level of management may have an interest in the division information other than its quality.

To illustrate, an internal auditor working for the head of an operating division may readily report the division's operating or internal control problems to the division head. But the same auditor will find it difficult to report those findings to central management because they might reflect poorly on the internal auditor's boss. Any such reports are likely to be diluted and delayed in transmission. Divisional internal auditor reporting of fraud or misfeasance by the division's management is even more problematic.

The expected reliability of internal auditors as a source of information about internal control and lower-level management's performance depends in part on their lack of a substantial interest in the information other than its quality. Internal auditors of a division can be a reliable source of information about the division, but care must be taken to assure their independence (see Chapters 11 and 12 for elaboration).

External Auditors

You can also obtain information about the effectiveness of internal control in your own firm from your external auditor hired to audit your financial statements. While external auditors don't conduct a complete evaluation of internal controls when conducting a financial statement audit, they do issue letters to management indicating any important control process weaknesses that are noted in the financial statement audit. Also, at the completion of the audit, they meet with top financial management (and often the chief executive officer and other operating officers) to discuss any important differences noted during the audit between true values and recorded values (called "audit differences"). Large audit differences may be the result of inadequate internal controls.

External auditors do not ordinarily communicate with persons or groups that are not associated with the firm being audited except through the auditor's report. As we will see in Chapters 7–9, audited financial statements do not necessarily mean that internal controls are adequate for day-to-day business operations since the external auditor may be able to complete an audit even when controls are poor. However, external auditors can also be hired to audit and report specifically on internal controls (see Chapter 10).

In an engagement to express an opinion on internal control, the auditor will examine the internal controls in relation to COSO criteria, and report any material weaknesses found as well as describe other "reportable" conditions that may be less important, but still of interest. These reports are especially important for corporate directors who have oversight responsibilities (see Chapter 11). As a member of top management, you may want to hire an external auditor to conduct such an examination and report results to both you and your audit committee. The first assures you, and the second shows your stewardship over corporate affairs. Also, when evaluating potential investments in other companies, you may want to know whether their audit committees receive such assurance.

AN INTERNAL INFORMATION RISK MODEL

Let's summarize the components of internal control by developing a conceptual model of the overall risk faced by top management that it will have materially misstated financial information for internal decision making. The model is conceptual because there are too many interrelated elements to be fully operational, but the relation among components will be useful in understanding the process.

The risk of material misstatement of a particular element of internal information used by top management will be called *internal information risk.* For internal information to be materially misstated, three things must happen in the internal control process: first, material misstatement must arise in the sensing/measuring recording process; second, internal control procedures applied day to day must fail to prevent or detect and correct the misstatement; and third, any after-transactions-processing error detection (monitoring) procedures must fail to detect and correct the misstatement.

Risk assessments are directed toward assessing the risk of material misstatements arising in the accounting process; control activities plus information and communication procedures are directed toward prevention, and detection and correction of misstatements that do occur. The risk of failure of these day-to-day information processing activities must be augmented by an allowance for inherent limitations of internal control. This is because, by definition, internal control activities applied day to day cannot be effective against collusion, human failures, and management override of controls. The combination of these risks will be called *information processing risk.*

The risk of material internal information misstatement (denoted IIR) can then be approximated as information processing risk (IPR) multiplied by the *monitoring failure risk (MFR)* that management's and the internal auditor's monitoring procedures independently applied *after transactions processing* will fail to detect the misstatement. This simple characterization of comprehensive control risk as IPR $\times$ MFR = IIR is instructive since it shows the conceptual relations of internal information risk components.

In practice, the IIR model is difficult to apply because the individual component risks (IPR and MFR) are each conditional on the *expected* level of the other and are difficult to assess. For example, risk assessments must be considered in light of any related control activities that are expected to be applied. The risk of theft of an uncontrolled cash inventory of $100,000 is high, but because of this high risk assessment, management designs effective internal controls over cash so that control risk is low, and the product of the two risks is also low.

On the other hand, the risk of theft of a $100,000 inventory of steel I-beams for building construction is relatively low, and therefore internal controls over I-beams are less stringent than controls over cash. Similarly, employees applying transaction processing controls will be more careful day to day if they believe that post-processing analytical monitoring and auditing procedures will detect (and possibly punish) any misstatements. So low MFR leads to low IPR. Stated another way, employees anticipate the control procedures that are expected to follow their own activities. In an environment in which effective follow-up procedures are expected, employees are more likely to be careful (and truthful) in their work.

Stringency

Management's objectives regarding internal control are likely to be more stringent than those of outsiders. As an example, external auditors are responsible for detecting and correcting material misstatements where "material" might be 5 to 10 percent of the firm's earnings. From management's perspective, an error of 1 percent or even .5 percent of earnings might be important enough to initiate follow-up actions. Also, an acceptable risk of misstatement of a given magnitude is likely to be lower for management than for outsiders. Thus, as a practical matter, an internal control system sufficiently reliable for management's decision processes and asset protection needs will be more than adequate for outside parties.

SUMMARY

Internal control is the process that assists management in achieving its operating, financial reporting, and compliance objectives. Accounting control–related activities improve the quality of information for decision making by assuring the reliable application of specified measurement methods to attach numbers to business processes. Accounting control–related activities also provide a recorded accountability through which company assets can be protected.

Internal control has five interrelated components that collectively provide assurance that risk of adverse events is assessed and economically mitigated. Mitigation activities include risk assessments and control activities applied as transactions are being processed, communication of measurements and evaluations by operating personnel, and after-processing monitoring by internal auditors. Top management oversees design of controls, sets the environment in which other controls are applied, and is the ultimate follow-up vehicle when problems arise. Control design is based on the separation of functions: authorization of action, maintenance of recorded accountability of assets and other results of actions, and custody of assets.

Inherent limitations on control reliance by top management arise because of accidental human failure to properly perform prescribed control duties, collusion among different parties, and override of controls by one with managerial discretion in applying controls. These inherent limitations necessitate monitoring of controls and results of control application by top management or its agent, such as an internal auditor. When internal auditors are used to monitor, freedom from interests other than the reliability of internal controls is essential. Independence of internal auditors is facilitated by reporting to a high level such as the CEO and audit committee of the board of directors.

CASE 4

MAMIE'S PIE FRONTIER

Mamie makes specialty fruit pies and sells them to retail customers and gourmet restaurants in Austin, Texas. Her store is staffed by five commission salesclerks and a sales manager. Retail customers make cash purchases and restaurants buy on credit. All sales are entered by salesclerks into a computer work station/cash drawer in the sales room. The work station is tied to a small computer system in Mamie's office. Exhibit 1 shows the credit sales and credit limit computer operations.

When making a sale to a retail customer, the salesclerk enters, at the work station, his or her employee code along with the type of pie and dollar amount. Cash is collected by the clerk; the computer prints a receipt for the customer and enters the amount in the computer's daily sales file. At the end of the sales day, a designated clerk counts the cash in the cash drawer, subtracts the $300 needed for the working change fund, and takes the remainder to Mamie's cashier, who signs for it in the salesclerk's receipt book.

Restaurant sales require workstation entry of the customer's account number. The computer looks up the account number to determine that it is valid and that the amount owed to date plus the intended purchase is less than the customer's credit limit. If above the limit, then the clerk is instructed to have the customer discuss the matter with the sales manager or Mamie herself. Raising the credit limit file entry for a customer requires knowledge of the employee code and password of either the sales manager or Mamie.

The sales manager has responsibilities for hiring, training, and supervising salesclerks and for sales promotions and customer complaints. At the end of each day, the sales manager meets with the principal baker to review sales stockouts and overages for the day and to plan pie production for the next day. Both the baker and sales manager are eligible for a year-end profit-sharing bonus.

Restaurant sales are paid by mail or electronic cash transfer. For mail receipts, Mamie's secretary opens all mail and enters the customer number and check amount into her work station. The entry credits the customer's account and updates the Cash on Hand and Accounts Receivable totals. Checks are then forwarded to Mamie's cashier.

As the last act of the day, the cashier deposits all cash received for the day and makes a computer work station entry for the total deposited. The computer then makes entries to Cash in Bank for the total entered by the cashier, to Sales for the sales file total (and sales subtotals by type of pie and employee number), to Receivables for the amount entered by Mamie's secretary, and to Cash Over/Short for any difference. At the end of the month, Mamie reconciles the bank account balance as well as the total deposits and disbursements per bank.

Required*

Mamie wants to know whether she has any serious weaknesses in her internal control over cash receipts and whether they appear to be cost effective. She has asked you to prepare a report and presentation for her. In preparing your report, you might consider the following questions.

a. Does Mamie appear to have adequate control over revenue recording and cash collection? How does she achieve separation of authorization, recordkeeping, and custody?

b. How can Mamie tell if the salesclerks are pocketing cash collected from customers? How does Mamie know that her secretary or the cashier is not stealing cash? How can Mamie tell if sales employees are failing to record substantial cash sales?

c. Does the sales manager have incompatible duties? Can Mamie tell if commission amounts paid salesclerks are too high?

---

*Preparation of a RISSAR (Risk Identification, Sourcing, Sizing, and Resolution) table may help analyze the case. That is, identify all risks of cash receipts and commissions misstatements and indicate how Mamie's avoids, shares/transfers, or reduces and monitors each of them.

EXHIBIT 1

Mamie's Pie Frontier Credit Sales

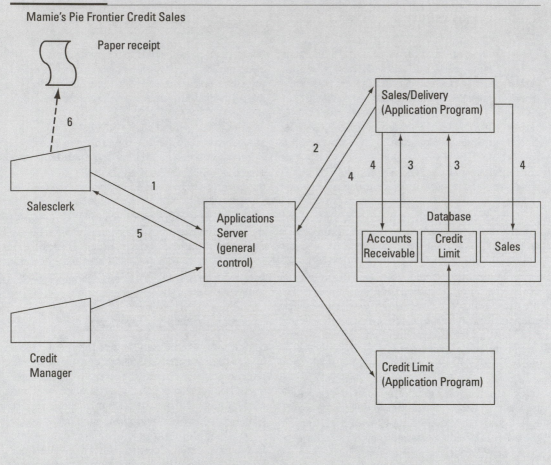

KEY WORDS

ARC principle for software-related duties Requires separation of (a) system design; (b) software component customization and access code assignment; (c) access to servers, applications, and enterprise database; and (d) data input.

ARC separation principle (For separation of *a*uthorization and *r*ecording of transactions, and *c*ustody of assets) States that an individual can't perpetrate and conceal fraud or theft (and accidental errors will be reduced) if he or she does not have responsibility for more than one of these activities for a particular transaction stream.

collusion Cooperation among or between members of lower management, an employee, or outside party to circumvent prescribed internal controls.

control override Circumvention of an internal control by a member of management who has authority over employees applying internal controls.

derivative A financial instrument whose value depends upon (is derived from) the value of an underlying asset, liability, reference rate, or index.

errors Accidental misstatements due to mistakes of sensing, measurement, classification, calculation, or omission from display.

Foreign Corrupt Practices Act of 1977 (FCPA) Among other features, requires that SEC registrants maintain cost-justified internal controls.

information processing risk (IPR) Threat that risk assessments, control activities, and information and communication controls applied to verify accuracy, completeness, and authorization of transactions as they are being processed will fail to prevent or detect material misstatement.

internal information risk (IIR) Threat of "material" misstatement of internal information used by decision makers within a business.

misappropriation fraud Intentional misstatement of recorded amounts by management or employees accompanied by theft of company assets such as cash, inventory, or fixed assets.

misrepresentation fraud Intentional misstatement by management or employees (typically overstatement of recorded assets, understatement of recorded liabilities, use of improper accounting methods, or biased accounting estimates) with the intent of misstating a performance measure such as net income or an activity base such as total assets or equity.

monitoring failure risk (MFR) Threat that analytical and detailed monitoring procedures independently applied after transactions processing will fail to detect any material misstatement.

performance review Comparison by operating employees of recorded performance with expectations based on budgets, forecasts, past performance, and nonfinancial data, and real-time investigation and corrective action.

physical controls Physical security over tangible assets, processing software, and databases, and periodic comparison of real-world assets with recorded amounts.

separation of duties Assigning different persons the responsibilities of authorizing transactions, recording transactions, and maintaining custody of assets to operationalize the ARC principle.

CHAPTER

Analytical Monitoring: Business Operations Analysis and Account Modeling Procedures

- **H**ow is my business doing relative to the competition?
- Are we experiencing unforeseen problems or good fortune?
- How can operations be improved in the future?
- Might my accounting records be materially in error?
- Is asset theft possibly a big problem?

All five questions are answerable by analytical monitoring of recorded performance. Business operations analysis of financial statement elements as an attention-directing tool (focusing on areas of higher-than-average risk of poor operations) addresses the first three questions, and what auditors call analytical procedures address the latter two. Both types of analytical monitoring involve forming expectations about what should be the aggregated recorded values for a period of time or at a particular date, and investigating deviations from expectations as to likely cause.

Analytical monitoring has become increasingly important in recent years due to the effects of information technology (IT). IT has increased the inherent reliability of routine accounting transaction processing to the extent that large-scale, detailed testing of final balances is not essential. Also, IT has lowered the cost of recording and integrating nonfinancial measures of performance that can be used in more powerful analytical procedures on which to base conclusions about financial measures. Finally, with IT, more sophisticated mathematical models can be operationalized. Many of these models have been automated for financial and nonfinancial records as well as internal control operating statistics.

We begin with a discussion of analytical monitoring concepts that underlie expectations formation. This is followed by an example of business operations analysis to understand activities for a period and to identify areas of special operating and misstatement risks. We conclude with consideration of account modeling procedures for a single account using expert judgments and regression analysis to help isolate any possible misstatements that might be material.

ANALYTICAL MONITORING CONCEPTS

In healthy living organisms, certain relationships among and between organism characteristics are expected. In a healthy human, there are norms and an expected relation between height and weight for a person of a given age and sex. Also, there are expected relations for blood pressure, temperature, resting heart rate, and metabolism. These measurements and relations can be analyzed by a physician to diagnose departures from a healthy organism.

Measurements and relations between and among them can be compared to (a) benchmark data from a population of healthy individuals of the same age and sex, (b) the same individual at prior points in time, and (c) expectations based upon any interventions since the last measurement for the particular patient (such as medication regimen). Also, measures can be compared for consistency across measures.

In a healthy business, certain relations among data are also expected. For example, gross profit should bear a close relation to pricing policies, revenues and receivables should reflect a reasonable collection period, and payables should reflect both resource acquisition and cash management objectives. Presence of these expected relations in recorded values and relations to physical measures can be evidence of both the health of the company and a lack of need to take corrective action. Also, recorded values close to expected values are consistent with there being no material accounting misstatement in the recorded values.

To assess relative health, the need to take corrective action, or the likelihood of possible misstatement, the internal auditor or analyst applying analytical monitoring uses his or her knowledge of the business and expected relations to form an expectation of the true (accounting error–free) value of the account balance. The expectation ($\hat{Y}$) is conditional on the *information available* to the analyst and the *model used* to form the expectation. Then, the expectation is compared to the current year's recorded value (Y_r).

For a "small" difference between recorded value and excepted true value ($Y_r - \hat{Y}$ negligible), the recorded value may be accepted as needing no intervention or not materially misstated. Large differences warrant investigation for possible causes such as unexpected events, changes in expected relationships, and financial misstatement due to fraud or accounting error. The investigation stage proceeds in sufficient detail for the analyst to be satisfied that the difference is adequately understood and that no further follow-up action is necessary.

Analytical monitoring focuses on summaries of transactions or summaries of subsidiary balances. In this chapter, we will consider two broad approaches to analytical monitoring: business operations analysis (BOA) and account modeling procedures (AMP). Business operations analysis might be applied to quarterly balances by comparing the ratio of total recorded accounts receivable at quarter end to total recorded sales for the quarter with various expectations of what the ratio should be. This analysis might identify unexpected events or heightened risk of misstatement in either accounts receivable or sales. An analyst or auditor applying account modeling procedures might estimate a statistical regression model that relates a single account such as sales to factors that are causally or logically related to it such as cost of sales, units shipped, and customer orders filled.

In contrast, to test details of individual recorded items comprising receivables and sales, the auditor might verify individual balances with customers, or examine particular sales documents or cash collections (see Chapter 6). Thus, while analytical monitoring may provide evidence about the likelihood of monetary error in an *aggregated* account or group of accounts, tests of details are usually needed to determine whether *particular items* are in error. Analytical monitoring provides less direct and less conclusive evidence about individual account component validity.

Figure 5–1 diagrams analytical monitoring procedures and shows the relation of each of the expectations and consistency bases to the account balance being considered. It continues the diagram in Figure 4–1 to show the application of analytical monitoring procedures. Note that analytical monitoring procedures are applied only to information in the information model—without direct reference to real-world assets, liabilities, or income or expense transactions of the firm. Analytical monitoring involves comparisons among and between different aggregates of information. Comparison of recorded values with real-world amounts is the domain of tests of details (both details of recorded values and details of transactions processing).

Figure 5–1 shows comparisons of recorded values (Y_r) with expectations of what the true (recording error–free) balance should be ($\hat{Y}$). Expectations are based on information from one or more of several sources. For example, expectations can be based on planned values of Y determined at the start of the period (denoted X_1 in Figure 5–1), other financial values recorded during the time period (X_2), nonfinancial information such as physical and time quantities recorded during the period (X_3), and information from outside the firm such as information about competitors' current activities (X_4).

Business operations analysis and account modeling procedures differ on the information used to form expectations and the model that is used to transform information into expectations. BOA tends to use a broad range of information that is more aggregated and may analyze several accounts in combination. AMP uses a narrower range of more detailed information to form expectations about a single account, but it is more precise about expectations for that particular account.

The auditor/analyst applying analytical monitoring faces four possible outcomes depending on whether he or she decides to investigate and the true state of an account balance or business process. The auditor who decides not to investigate an account may have (1) **correctly decided not to investigate** an account that is within acceptable limits or (2) made an **incorrect acceptance** error (by not investigating an account that is materially misstated or an out-of-control process). The auditor who decides to investigate may have (1) **correctly decided to investigate** an account that is materially misstated or out of control or (2) made an **incorrect investigation** (by investigating an account that is within acceptable limits). Figure 5–2 shows the cross-classification of outcomes and shows the auditor subject to only one error type for each possible decision.

The cost of an incorrect investigation error is the cost of a fruitless search for a misstatement or process defect that does not exist. The cost of an incorrect acceptance error is future loss due to incorrectly relying on financial information that is materially in error or continuation of a process that is out of control. The cost per incorrect investigation is a lot less than the cost of an incorrect acceptance of an out-of-control process or balance. However, numerous incorrect investigations are also costly. Thus, balancing the expected costs and benefits of investigation is an important consideration in designing analytical monitoring systems.

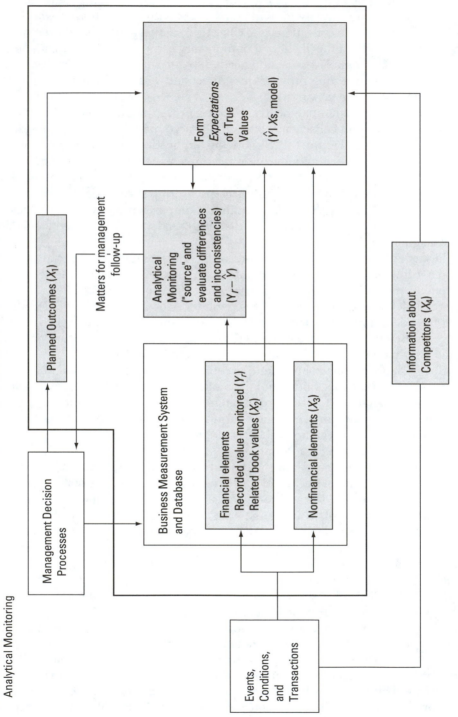

FIGURE 5–2

Possible Investigation Decision and Error Condition Outcomes

	Error Condition	
	Account (Process) Is within Acceptable Limits	**Account (Process) Is Materially Misstated (Out of Control)**
Investigation Decision		
Do not investigate	Correct decision	Incorrect acceptance
Investigate	Incorrect investigation	Correct decision

The expected value of a monitoring system depends on the true state of the account balance or process, the costs of investigating (not investigating), and conditional probabilities of investigating. The monitoring approach affects the probabilities or risks of investigating or not investigating. One characteristic of good analytical monitoring is low risk of (incorrectly) investigating when the account or process is within acceptable limits and low risk of (incorrectly) accepting when the account or process is out of control. Unfortunately, monitoring approaches that lead to low risks of both types often involve costly data to form expectations and costly models to transform data into expectations. Most companies use a combination of analytical monitoring approaches. They use BOA across several accounts to evaluate how implementation of plans is progressing and to identify operating problems or very large accounting misstatements. AMP is also used but only on particularly important accounts to isolate areas for follow-up with detailed tests.

Relation of Analytical Monitoring to Internal Information Risk

Chapter 4 discussed management's risk of materially misstated internal information (IIR) as the product of information processing risk (IPR) and monitoring failure risk (MFR). IPR results from the control environment, risk assessments, control activities, and information and communication procedures applied in the internal control process. IPR arises because, even though internal controls applied day to day are working as designed, they may fail in preventing, detecting, and correcting accounting misstatements and theft of assets. For example, day-to-day controls may fail by accident, through collusion, or through override of controls by management. IPR is an assessment of the risk that material information misstatement *might* exist prior to the application of monitoring procedures by top management or its agent, the internal auditor.

Analytical monitoring helps the internal auditor assess the risk that material misstatement of recorded values *has* occurred. Activities and accounts that have high risk of material misstatement are then investigated as to source or cause. The investigation may identify an operating problem or changes in the environment leading to a business process revision or revision of operating plans. The investigation may also lead to testing the details of accounting records and possible correction of the database.

Monitoring failure risk (MFR) is the risk that *all* monitoring activities will fail to detect existing material misstatement(s) or out-of-control process(es). The risk of incorrect acceptance of a materially misstated account when analytically monitoring adds to MFR because the account is not investigated or subjected to extended tests of details. Thus, the combination of analytical monitoring and tests of details *reduces* the risk of material misstatement in recorded amounts and thus *reduces* the risk that erroneous data will affect decisions.

BUSINESS OPERATIONS ANALYSIS

As the title suggests, business operations analysis, or BOA, involves forming broad expectations about what *should be* the true values of a set of related operating account balances, given the plans of management and the auditor/analyst's knowledge of unplanned events that arose during the period. Business operations analysis is conducted assuming that the book values are free of material misstatement (consideration of misstatement will follow). The analyst is trying to understand whether, how, and why the business's recorded values might differ from expectations due to operating causes.

Expectations Formation

To apply business operations analysis, the analyst forms expectations of the true value of each of the accounts being monitored. These expectations are typically based on budgeted revenues for the period that consider planned or projected business activities including external events adjusted for unexpected events that occurred during the period.

Analysis of deviations of recorded values from expectations based on planned results is the most commonly applied analytical tool within a business. These techniques were used by LJ Appliances' management in analyzing refrigerator units sold in Chapter 3. The analyst begins by adjusting the current period's planned amounts for changes known to have arisen since the current period plans were developed (e.g., adjusting for unexpected volume differences or the entry of new competitors or explained changes in costs).

When plans are not available, business operations analysis sometimes uses projections of historical data on the same account or set of accounts as the basis for expectation formation. In its simplest form, the expectation is simply the audited value of the account for the previous period. More sophisticated techniques include adjustment of last year's value for known differences this period, and inclusion of several years' values is often useful to estimate a trend over time. Trend estimation averages out year-to-year random fluctuations.

Historical comparisons suffer from an important limitation: the analyst may fail to consider factors that *should* differ from period to period and lead to changes in recorded values. This risk is especially high when the recorded versus expected comparison is a simple change analysis, or a comparison of this year's recorded value with last year's audited value. If the amounts are numerically close, then the analyst may incorrectly conclude that there is no difference from expectation although last year's value should have been adjusted for a significant change that occurred during the year.

A third source of information for expectation formation (or adjustment of planned results) is comparative statistics from competitors for the current time period. This expectation basis includes the effect of industrywide factors occurring during the current period, but fails to adjust for unique factors for the company itself. Thus, it will adjust for increased aggregate demand for the industry, but will fail to incorporate estimates of the effect of unique actions the company may have taken to increase its market share or to reduce costs. Competitor comparisons are difficult to apply in practice because of the lack of comparable and sufficiently disaggregated competitor data on a timely basis.

Data Consistency Analysis

In addition to comparing current period recorded values with expectations for the period, the internal auditor also makes data comparisons that are analogous to consistency checks of various health characteristics of an individual human. Rather than predicting a particular variable, they examine consistency of values across a set of variables all measured at the same point in time. Thus, they are implicitly multivariate in nature. The comparisons are across related account balances, and may compare dollar figures with related nonfinancial measures of stocks on hand or flows of transactions, goods, or hours. If the values are inconsistent with each other, then there is increased risk that at least one of them is misstated.

Related Account Comparisons

In the absence of accounting misstatement, there are certain relations expected between the recorded values of related accounts of a healthy business. For example, many companies follow a pricing policy that marks up cost of inventory to determine a selling price, implying a relation between sales and cost of sales. Similarly, firms have a target rate of inventory turnover implicit in their policies of meeting customer demands at a reasonable investment in inventory. These policies imply a target level of inventory turnover (cost of sales divided by ending inventory).

A useful analytical monitoring procedure is a consistency comparison of each account under examination with related accounts on the same financial statement (i.e., within the income statement or within the balance sheet) and between statements (an income statement account relative to its related balance sheet accounts). Consistency comparisons are especially useful in explaining changes in accounts that are due to simple scale-of-operations differences since the related accounts and amounts will be self-scaling to some degree.

A useful technique for internal auditors, external auditors, and other analysts incorporates business operation and accounting relationships into a structured analysis of related account balances. In particular, the analyst calculates ratios of account balances that are related to each other either by a business process or as part of an accounting entry. Figure 5–3 shows the approach by diagramming the primary operating accounts for a typical commercial firm or operating segment.

In Figure 5–3, the bold arrows indicate accounting entries that become account balances. By calculating ratios reflecting each arrow, the analyst may discover inconsistencies or departures from expectations. For example, material omitted purchases of inventory on account would be reflected in the end-of-period accounts as the understatement of both accounts payable and cost of sales. An analyst who calculates cost of sales/sales, inventory turnover(cost of sales/ending inventory), and inventory financed(ending inventory/ending accounts payable) is likely to see a pattern of deviations from expectations. Similarly,

FIGURE 5–3

Primary Ratios for Analytical Monitoring of Operations

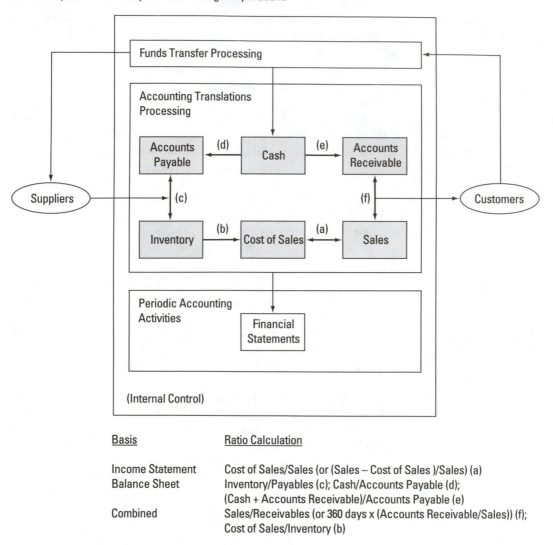

Basis	Ratio Calculation
Income Statement	Cost of Sales/Sales (or (Sales – Cost of Sales)/Sales) (a)
Balance Sheet	Inventory/Payables (c); Cash/Accounts Payable (d); (Cash + Accounts Receivable)/Accounts Payable (e)
Combined	Sales/Receivables (or 360 days x (Accounts Receivable/Sales)) (f); Cost of Sales/Inventory (b)

entry of fictitious credit sales or overpricing of the ending inventory will be reflected in other patterns of deviations from expectations.

Consideration of departures from expectations and inconsistencies can lead to "analytical investigation" to explain the differences. Explanations may lead to correction of the accounts, changes in the business measurement system (or its personnel), or perhaps improvements in operations.

The structured ratio analysis exploits the fact that *all* misstatements must be reflected in the accounts as overstatements or understatements—and each misstatement affects two accounts (with multiple chances for discovery). Furthermore, the technique works better the larger and more important the misstatement magnitude because the deviations and patterns will be more apparent in the pattern analysis.

Nonfinancial Comparisons

Enterprisewide software and integrated databases have made operational sophisticated consistency analyses and other analytical monitoring procedures based on the relation of dollar-based accounts with related physical quantities. Examples are unit costs of production, quantity of input to units of output, and measures of physical capacity utilization compared with dollar-based measures of capacity utilization in the accounting system.

With reasonably good controls over dollar values and physical quantities, the capability to understand business operations via an information model is greatly enhanced. By refining original expectations based on strategy and planning assumptions, an analyst can isolate sources of difference in expectation to improve expectation amounts for the current period, and possibly identify the need to change planning or strategic assumptions.

To the extent that recorded balances remain far from expectations even after investigation for operating explanations, the analyst must consider the possibility of accounting error or fraud. For these accounts, the analyst reconsiders the effectiveness of control activities and the need for analytical procedures and testing of details to determine whether material misstatement exists. Thus, we see that business operations analysis focuses on understanding what has happened to the business this period, while data consistency analysis and analytical procedures focus on the possibility of accounting misstatement.

A BUSINESS OPERATIONS ANALYSIS EXAMPLE: LJ APPLIANCES

To illustrate the use of business operations analysis and data consistency analysis, let's continue the example of Chapter 3 that analyzed LJ Appliances' first quarter operations. LJ's internal auditor used an information model of the firm as the basis for analysis.

In Chapter 3, the internal auditor determined that a reasonable expectation for total first quarter refrigerator revenues for LJ Appliances was $9,850,000. This number was based on sales as originally planned before the start of the quarter and was adjusted for unanticipated events that took place during the quarter. Thus, the adjusted amount is the analyst's first pass at a best estimate of the true value of revenues for LJ Appliances for the first quarter based on information at the end of the quarter. Also, recall that in Chapter 3 the analyst concluded that recorded revenues of $9,650,000 were "close enough" to rule out the need for further analytical investigation.

Figure 5–4 shows excerpts of income statement and balance sheet recorded values for LJ Appliances for the first quarter. Specifically, the figure shows recorded revenues, cost of sales, and gross profit, plus the ending inventory and accounts payable balances. Figure 5–4 also shows comparable dollar values from the first quarter of the prior year and the adjusted expectations for the quarter based on the adjusted sales expectation, planned cost of sales for the revised output level, and expected ending balances for accounts payable and total inventory amounts based on LJ's operating policies and experience. Finally, it presents recorded quantity data for refrigerators as well as for recorded sales and costs of goods sold.

FIGURE 5-4

Business Operations and Data Consistency Analysis

LJ APPLIANCES, INC.
First Quarter Results (as recorded)
(dollars and units in 000s)

a. Business Operations Analysis: Recorded versus Expectations

	Recorded	Planned (as revised)	Last Year Actual	Recorded/ Planned (revised)	Recorded/ Last Year
Revenue	$9,650	$9,850	$7,750	0.98	1.25
Cost of sales	7,660	7,880	6,225	0.97	1.23
Gross profit	1,990	1,970	1,525	1.01	1.30
Inventory (end)	810	712	650	1.19	1.31
Accounts payable (end)	840	890	790	0.94	1.06

b. Business Operations Analysis: Financial Ratios

	Recorded	Planned (revised)	Last Year
Revenue/Revenue	1.00	1.00	1.00
Cost of sales/Revenue	0.79	0.80	0.80
Gross profit/Revenue	0.21	0.20	0.20
Cost of sales/Inventory	9.01	11.07	9.58
Accounts payable/Inventory	0.99	1.25	1.22

c. Data Consistency Analysis: Financial versus Nonfinancial Results
   Production Records (units):

	Units	Dollars per Unit	
Inventory (beginning)	0.80	$ 812.50	
Purchased	9.70	810.31	
Total available	10.50	810.48	
Inventory (ending)	1.05	809.52	
Sold	9.45	810.58	(unit cost using Production Records)
	9.45	$1,021.10	(unit revenue using Production Records)
Sales Records (units):			
Sold	9.65	$ 793.78	(unit cost using Sales Records)
	9.65	1,000.00	(unit revenue using Sales Records)

Business Operations Analysis

LJ Appliances projected adjusted revenues of $9,850,000 and projected cost of sales of $800 per unit sold. Projected ending inventory ($712) is based on average acquisition prices for the quarter and LJ Appliances' economic order quantity model for inventory. The inventory model suggests that a 25 percent increase in revenues ought to be accompanied by an increase in inventory of about 10 percent. Ending payables are based on the expectation that the inventory financed ratio (accounts payable/inventory) will remain constant at the level that existed in the past.

Aggregated recorded financial amounts in panel *a* show revenues and cost of sales less than planned, but the resulting gross profit is above planned, with ending inventory much greater than planned and payables less than planned. The ratios of panel *b* tell much the same story: gross profit rate better than planned due to lower-than-expected cost of sales, but inventory turnover (cost of sales/ending inventory—a measure of efficiency) is lower than expected. The turnover result is due to inventory greater than LJ's inventory model predicted based on efficient inventory management. Thus, a tentative BOA conclusion is that inventory procurement performance may be better than expected (resulting in a lower cost per unit than planned), but inventory management needs improvement (resulting in higher levels of inventory on-hand than planned).

The only other unexpected, or inconsistent, relation in dollars is the lower-than-expected inventory financed ratio (ending payables/ending inventory). These BOA conclusions are tentative because the risk of materially misstated recorded values hasn't yet been assessed.

Data Consistency Analysis

In comparing ratios of aggregate accounting numbers for LJ Appliances, differences appear to be small. Sales are less than the budgeted sales but are within a reasonable range, given that the expectations were not precise. Revenue expectations were necessarily imprecise because very little information was used in making the projections. Also, sales are inherently difficult to predict since they depend on planned activities for the business as well as activities of competitors, customers, and other environmental factors.

Given the difference in budgeted revenues, however, recorded cost of sales was at 79 percent of recorded revenues, which is favorable and reasonably close to the planned cost-of-sales rate. The related balance sheet accounts are at least close to the level planned at the start of the period. Therefore, the business operations analyst might conclude that there are no significant adjustments needed to operations, nor changes in the planning process for the future. The difference in turnover is seemingly large, but may be within a reasonable range for turnover, since, historically, balance sheet–based ratios tend to fluctuate much more than do income statement–based ratios.

Panel *c* of Figure 5–4 relates nonfinancial data, physical units, to dollars. Specifically, panel *c* takes quantity data from purchasing, inventory, and sales records to calculate unit cost of purchases, inventory, and cost of sales. Inventory records show a beginning inventory of 800 refrigerator units at a unit cost of $812.50 and purchases of 9,700 at an average cost of $810.31. Ending inventory of 1,050 units was (FIFO) priced at the most recent purchase prices of $809.52 (the declining prices may reflect volume discounts on the increased volume).

Using production records for quantities, cost of sales per unit is $810.58 ($7,660,000/9,450) and implied revenue per unit is $1,021.16 ($9,650,000/9,450). But sales records show a volume of 9,650 refrigerators sold, which implies cost of sales per unit of $793.78 ($7,660,000/9,650), and revenue per unit of $1,000 ($9,650,000/9,650). The nonfinancial records of quantity sold are *inconsistent* with each other, leading to inconsistent costs and revenue per unit.

Based on this preliminary analysis, the analyst should reconsider why recorded cost of sales and payables might be low. There are several possible causes, but one has been relatively frequent for many companies. The combination of lower-than-expected cost of sales, inventory turnover, and inventory financed is consistent with an omitted purchase of merchandise for resale. In fact, the results are consistent with an incoming shipment of 200 refrigerators (at quarter-end prices of $809.52) *not* being recorded as a credit purchase. This would result in understatement of both recorded cost of sales and ending payables by about $162,000.

If accounts were adjusted for the omitted credit purchase by adding $162,000 to accounts payable and cost of sales, then the ratios would be similar to expectations and internally consistent, as shown in Figure 5–5. Misstatements must be incorrectly recorded (or

FIGURE 5–5

Business Operations and Internal Consistency Analysis (corrected)

LJ APPLIANCES, INC.
First Quarter Results (corrected)
(dollars and units in 000s)

a. *Business Operations Analysis: Corrected versus Expectations*

	Corrected	Planned (as revised)	Last Year Actual	Recorded/ Planned (revised)	Recorded/ Last Year
Revenue	$9,650	$9,850	$7,750	0.99	1.25
Cost of sales	7,822	7,880	6,225	0.99	1.26
Gross profit	1,828	1,970	1,525	0.93	1.20
Inventory (end)	810	712	650	1.14	1.25
Accounts payable (end)	1,002	890	790	1.13	1.27

b. *Business Operations Analysis: Financial Ratios*

	Corrected	Planned (revised)	Last Year
Revenue/Revenue	1.00	1.00	1.00
Cost of sales/Revenue	0.81	0.80	0.80
Gross profit/Revenue	0.19	0.20	0.20
Cost of sales/Inventory	9.66	11.07	9.58
Accounts payable/Inventory	1.24	1.25	1.22

c. *Internal Consistency Analysis: Financial versus Nonfinancial Results*

Production Records as corrected (units):

	Units	Dollars per Unit	
Inventory (beginning)	0.80	$ 812.50	
Purchased	9.90	810.29	
Total available	10.70	810.46	
Inventory (ending)	1.05	809.52	
Sold	9.65	810.56	
	9.65	$1,000.00	(unit revenue using Production Records)
Sales Records (units):			
Sold	9.65	$ 810.56	(unit cost using Sales Records)
	9.65	1,000.00	(unit revenue using Production Records)

be omitted) somewhere, and for accounting data they must appear (or be omitted) in two places because of the self-balancing, double-entry feature of accounting.

The overall conclusion of the business operations analysis and data consistency analysis for LJ Appliances for first-quarter financial results indicates that results are about as expected with two exceptions. First, ending inventory appears higher than would be expected given an effectively operating inventory control model. This warrants investigation of operations to determine if there are continuing problems with inventory management.

Second, comparisons of recorded values with expectations as well as data consistency analyses of financial ratios and financial with nonfinancial data suggest a material omission of credit purchases. Thus, the internal auditor should assess a higher-than-normal risk of the possibility of this type of error and consider the adequacy of controls over recording of refrigerator purchases. In planning detailed tests, the auditor would extend the search for unrecorded purchases and unrecorded liabilities (these techniques are discussed in Chapter 6). In less clear-cut cases (where the evidence may suggest omitted credit purchases, but not as conclusively), the auditor might consider the controls over omitted purchases as well as more detailed testing.

Risk Assessment by Account

The results of business operations analysis and data consistency analysis must be integrated into an assessment of risk of accounting misstatement for each account. Two outcomes are possible from the internal auditor's analyses. The auditor may decide that the combination of information processing risk plus business operations analysis and data consistency analysis suggests normal-for-the-account risk of misstatement, or it may suggest above normal (heightened) risk of misstatement. For normal risk accounts, the auditor continues monitoring with planned account modeling or detailed test procedures. For heightened risk, however, the auditor extends planned account modeling or detailed tests of particular recorded items to address the possible misstatement indicated. Thus, the auditor's risk-reduction procedures are concentrated in areas of above-normal risk. The next section considers account modeling procedures as evidence, and Chapter 6 addresses the use of tests of details for monitoring.

ACCOUNT MODELING PROCEDURES

As discussed in Chapter 4, there are several inherent limitations of internal control over day-to-day operations that affect top management's reliance on internal controls to prevent, detect, and correct accounting errors and fraud. These limitations imply that a minimum level of analytical or detailed evidence be obtained for all areas. And for areas of heightened risk, the auditor would extend tests beyond the minimum.

There are two broad ways to obtain evidence about the substantive correctness of recorded values. One is to test details of recorded amounts comprising account balances. This method is explored in depth in Chapter 6. An alternative way, called "account modeling procedures," is to model individual accounts by considering causal relations that should be reflected in the true value of the account. The base data for account modeling procedures is usually more disaggregated than it is for business operations analysis because more precise data allow more precise expectations to be formed, thus allowing better identification of any misstatements.

Causal modeling of account balances is a difficult task. Modeling is difficult because economic activity itself is complex, comprised of many controllable and uncontrollable events. Accounting data are further complicated because some parties involved may have intent to mislead or defraud.

On the other hand, analytical models can provide convincing evidence that recorded values are not likely to be misstated by an important amount, leading to a substantial cost savings over tests of details. Furthermore, the process of developing the model itself can lead to insights about the business processes resulting in the account balance. Finally, analytical models are *better* at indicating some types of errors than are tests of details. For example, an account model may suggest omission of transactions recording (understatements of recorded values) or duplicate recording of valid amounts (overstatements). Neither of these errors is likely to be detected by auditing the recorded details of the account.

Account modeling procedures tend to work well in situations for which controls are good and operations are "reasonably predictable." Reasonably predictable means that reliable data are available that are causally related to the account balance under audit, and, therefore, the expected relation between data elements can be modeled and used in forming expectations.

The expectations modeling problem has two dimensions—formation of the expectation itself and the closeness or imprecision of the expectation. Imprecision can be thought of as a reasonable range of values within which the recorded value might fall due to normal chance variation and still be correctly stated. Within the range, the auditor is willing to conclude that the difference is due to random or nonsystematic (and nonmisstatement) factors. The variation might be explainable in particular circumstances, but the auditor believes that the value of further explanation is not worth the likely cost of investigation.

Recorded values beyond this range would be unreasonable and therefore subject to investigation. An important question for analytical procedures as evidence, then, is how to determine expectations, and especially how to quantify the imprecision of expectations. The latter problem is often the more difficult problem because precise expectations require reliable and reasonably detailed data to operationalize the expectations. Also, it is difficult for the available data to yield a range of imprecision that is small enough to indicate the presence of material misstatement when the account is materially misstated.

To illustrate approaches to account modeling procedures for monitoring, let's consider two examples. The first is a bank's internal auditor trying to decide whether recorded interest income needs further auditing, and the second is a multinational corporation wishing to decide whether the total recorded sales of a subsidiary need further auditing or can be accepted without further auditing. The first example uses objective methods to quantify the expectation but judgmental methods to determine expectation imprecision. The second uses statistical analysis to estimate both the expectation and the related imprecision.

Judgmental Methods: Fifth Carolina Bancshares, Inc.

Fifth Carolina Bancshares, Inc. (FCB), is a publicly traded bank holding company whose principal subsidiary operates about 50 banks in North Carolina and South Carolina. The accounting processes for FCB are centralized in Raleigh, as are credit administration and credit quality assessment. As of the end of the current year, loans secured by real estate comprised 59 percent of FCB's loan portfolio, with commercial, financial, and agricultural loans comprising 15 percent, loans to individuals comprising 23 percent, and other loans and lease receivables comprising 3 percent. The average interest rates were relatively constant and credit quality remained stable throughout the year. Furthermore, the internal auditor of FCB believes that controls over interest income are good.

Interest income recorded on loans for the current year is $191,047 (in thousands throughout), and net income is $48,400. The auditor believes that a misstatement of interest income of $4,500 would be large enough to require adjustment (i.e., material). Therefore, the auditor plans to conduct detailed tests if estimated misstatement might reasonably equal or exceed $4,500. In applying analytical procedures, the auditor calculates estimated misstatement by subtracting his or her expectation of interest income (described below) and adds a "reasonable amount" to allow for imprecision of the method.

To address the existence, completeness, and accuracy (valuation) of loan interest income, the following account modeling procedure was applied by the FCB internal auditor. The expectation for interest income was calculated based on an analysis of the weighted average interest rate for the year applied to the average daily performing loan volume for FCB. The auditor validated the daily performing loan volume and average interest rate figures by comparing the numbers to other records in FCB and to average interest rate statistics for the region prepared by a banking authority.

Now let's consider two levels of aggregation for expectations formation. The first level considers the weighted average and the average daily performing loan volume on an *annual* basis across *all types* of loans. The results of this analysis are presented in Figure 5–6 and show expected interest income of $189,762 and the difference between recorded and expected of $1,285. Compare this analysis with Figure 5–7, which uses the same method but calculates expected interest income *each quarter* for *each type* of loan and sums the individual estimates to get an aggregated expectation. Thus, both methods use the same calculation formula and the same underlying data. They differ only on the level of aggregation used in forming the expectations.

"How close is close enough" depends on precision of expectation, which depends, in part, on the level of data aggregation. Which level of aggregation do you think leads to a more precise or narrower range of reasonable values? This question was posed to expert

FIGURE 5–6

Fifth Carolina Bancshares, Inc., Loan Interest Expectations
Annual Estimate Aggregated over All Loans ($ in 000s)

Average daily performing loan volume	$1,606,838
× Weighted average interest rate for the year	11.8097%
Expected interest income	$ 189,762
Recorded interest income	191,047
Difference	$ (1,285)

Source: McDaniel, L. and W. Kinney, "Incorporating Imprecision Judgments in Analytical Auditing," Working paper, 1999.

FIGURE 5-7

Fifth Carolina Bancshares, Inc., Loan Interest Expectations
Quarterly Estimates by Loan Type ($ in 000s)

	Loans Secured by Real Estate	Commercial, Financial, and Agricultural Loans	Loans to Individuals	All Other Loans and Lease Receivables	
First Quarter					
Average daily performing loan volume	$916,278	$263,782	$374,213	$50,507	
× Weighted average interest rate (quarterly basis)	2.97%	2.72%	3.14%	2.56%	**First Quarter**
Expected interest income	$ 27,212	$ 7,175	$ 11,750	$ 1,293	$47,431
Recorded interest income	27,303	7,228	12,656	1,332	48,520
Difference	$ (91)	$ (53)	$ (906)	$ (39)	$ (1,089)
Second Quarter					
Average daily performing loan volume	$918,113	$269,859	$374,225	$48,596	
× Weighted average interest rate (quarterly basis)	2.95%	2.71%	3.15%	2.58%	**Second Quarter**
Expected interest income	$ 27,083	$ 7.313	$ 11,788	$ 1,254	$47,438
Recorded interest income	27,131	7,409	11,772	1,226	47,538
Difference	$ (48)	$ (96)	$ 16	$ 28	$ (100)
Third Quarter					
Average daily performing loan volume	$908,024	$263,791	$373,115	$51,935	
× Weighted average interest rate (quarterly basis)	2.97%	2.70%	3.15%	2.55%	**Third Quarter**
Expected interest income	$ 26,967	$ 7,122	$ 11,753	$ 1,324	$47,167
Recorded interest income	27,030	7,143	11,701	1,349	47,224
Difference	$ (63)	$ (21)	$ 52	$ (25)	$ (57)
Fourth Quarter					
Average daily performing loan volume	$926,368	$261,437	$374,245	$52,864	
× Weighted average interest rate (quarterly basis)	2.96%	2.72%	3.16%	2.59%	**Fourth Quarter**
Expected interest income	$ 27,419	$ 7,111	$ 11,826	$ 1,369	$47,726
Recorded interest income	27,435	7,098	11,840	1,391	47,765
Difference	$ (16)	$ 13	$ (14)	$ (22)	$ (39)
Total Difference for the Year	$ (218)	$ (157)	$ (852)	$ (58)	$(1,285)

bank auditors, with each auditor given either the annual balance analysis or the quarterly and loan type analysis. Auditors receiving the imprecise data believed that a reasonable range for how far the true value might vary from the expectation was ± 2.2 percent of the expectation of $189,762 (or about $4,200), while the expert bank auditors seeing the precise data believed that a reasonable range was about ± 1.4 percent (or $2,680).

Taking the point estimate of misstatement ($1,285), plus the reasonable range, gives an upper limit for a reasonable recorded value of $5,485 for the annual data (imprecise) group and an upper limit of $3,965 for the quarterly data (precise) group. Since materiality, or the allowable misstatement for recorded interest income, is $4,500, the auditor using quarterly data would conclude that the recorded interest income is sufficiently valid to accept without further auditing. However, an auditor using annual data who believes that the reasonable range might be as high as $5,485 could not accept the recorded amount as materially error-free. This auditor would want to investigate further to determine the correctness of the recorded amount. Thus, we see that even with subjective or judgmental methods, the imprecision inherent in an estimation method can be incorporated into a decision model for monitoring.

Experience often allows experts to develop sound judgments about the width of a reasonable range of variation based on the method and data available. A relevant question is, "Can mathematics help experts do a better job, or can they help less-experienced personnel emulate experts?" The following example says yes.

Regression Analysis: Chickasaw Sales Corp.

Amy is the internal auditor for Chickasaw Sales Corp. Four years ago, Chickasaw installed an improved accounting system but has continued to use an old audit monitoring process based on rather extensive tests of details.

Amy wishes to evaluate whether regression analysis could be used to estimate a causal model of the sales account and use the modeling to assess the correctness of recorded revenues. If the model is considered viable, then Amy would substitute the statistical model results for detailed evidence collected by auditors in the field. Amy believes a revenue misstatement of $8 would be material to Chickasaw. Therefore, she will accept analytical procedure evidence as sufficient if estimated misstatement plus a "reasonable range" estimate is less than $8.

As a basis for forming expectations of true values for monthly sales for the current year, Amy has available three years of prior audited data on sales and units sold by month. As a first pass estimate, Amy regresses recorded monthly sales for the three audited years (36 months) against recorded quantities sold. The model is simple, but the result seems good: the R^2 for the model was .79, indicating that 79 percent of the variation in sales could be "explained by" or "related to" variation in units sold. Also, the standard error of the estimate (which is the standard deviation of the unexplained part of the model) was $1.56.

Figure 5–8 plots the regression's estimated residuals (recorded values minus predicted values from the model, the d's) for Chickasaw for all 48 months: months 1–36, the base on which the model is estimated, plus the 12 months (unaudited) to which the model's intercept and slope estimates were applied.

In examining the unexplained residuals, Amy noticed that the residuals for the second quarter of each year (months 4, 5, 6, months 16, 17, 18, and months 28, 29, 30) tended to be larger than those for the other three quarters. On investigation, she found that the second quarter tends to be a high demand or "peak season" during which higher prices are charged. Therefore, Amy revised the model to include an indicator variable set to 0 for quarters 1, 3, and 4 and to 1 for quarter 2. With this revised model, Chickasaw sales were described as

$$Y = A + B_1X_1 + B_2X_2 + d$$

┌IGU∩E 5-8

Chickasaw Sales Corp. Plot of Estimated d's $(d = Y_r - (A + BX))$

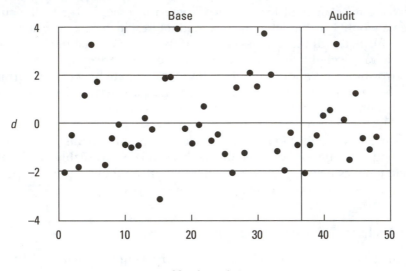

Month number

where Y is audited revenue for the month (months 1 through 36), X_1 is units sold for the month, X_2 is the quarter indicator variable, and d is the "unexplained" or "random" part of monthly sales, plus any uncorrected accounting misstatement for the month (i.e., a random portion (u) and an accounting error portion (m)).

The R^2 for this model was .85, with a standard error of $1.06. Thus, the revised model explained a larger portion of the total variation in revenues and had a much smaller standard deviation of the unexplained portion. The standard deviation of the unexplained portion is comparable to the "reasonable range" in a subjective estimate and can serve as a measure of the imprecision in the estimate. Figure 5–9 shows the residuals (estimated d's) of the revised model. Note that the spread is less for the revised model.

To complete her work, Amy calculated the sum of the unexplained amounts for months 37 through 48. That is, she summed the individual estimates of d by month to get a point estimate of aggregate misstatement for the year. Amy's logic is as follows: $d = u + m$, where u is the true value of sales not explained by volume and quarter, and m is accounting misstatement for the month. The u portion fluctuates randomly month to month, and sums to zero over time. The standard error of the regression for the base period (months 1–36), measures the usual (non error) random variation since these months have been "audited," and any important m's were corrected. Misstatement in the audit period, on the other hand, is not as likely to be random, and could sum to an unacceptable amount.

The estimated d's summed to −$2.05 for the prediction period (the audit period months 37 through 48).[1] The prediction period sum uses the coefficients from the audited base pe-

---

1. For the base period (months 1–36), the d's sum to zero by construction, since regression estimation forces the sum of the residuals for the base period model to 0 (i.e., it minimizes the sum of square deviation which, in turn, constrains the sum of the deviations to 0).

FIGURE 5-9

Chickasaw Sales Corp. Plot of Estimated d's $(d = Y_r - (A + B_1X_1 + B_2X_2))$
No Misstatement

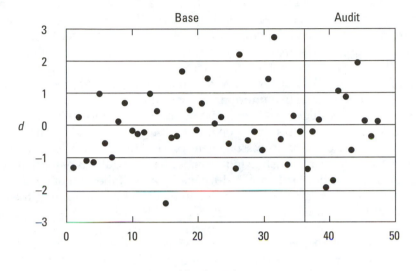

Month number

riod, and applies them to the new data. The results for the audit (prediction) period, are based on the expectation using the prior period average relation between volume and revenues (A and the Bs) applied to the current period volumes which have been independently determined. The model shows that the estimated aggregate misstatement (for the year) is −$2.05.

The point estimate of misstatement (−$2.05) is clearly immaterial when compared to materiality of $8.00, but Amy wanted to allow for "reasonable" imprecision in her estimates. So Amy calculated an upper confidence limit on possible misstatement.[2] This estimate is comprised of the point estimate plus a reasonable range based on the standard error of regression calculation for the total for the year. Amy decided that "reasonable" means 16 percent risk of an incorrect accept decision so the approximate Z factor applied to the standard error is 1.0. The estimated standard error for the total is about $4.3.[3] Thus, the upper limit on misstatement is: −$2.05 + $4.3 = $2.25. Since $2.25 is clearly less than $8, Amy would be justified in accepting the recorded values.

Now let's consider cases where there *is* material misstatement in the monitoring (audit) period. Specifically, let's assume that one or more months in the audit period contain misstatement totaling $8.00. That is, the recorded values Y_r are greater than the true values of Y by a total of $8. How would the materially overstated recorded data look in plots, and how would Amy's calculations behave?

---

2. In concept, analytical procedures can be applied simultaneously to identify exceptions in either an upward or downward direction. In practice, however, they are usually applied to one direction at a time because the analyst is usually more concerned with misstatements in one direction than the other. Also, most follow-up procedures depend on the direction of an identified difference.

3. The standard error for the year is about four times the monthly standard error for monthly data using a 36-month base period.

Figure 5–10 presents plots of the estimated d values for three separate situations assuming that $8.00 has been added to one of the months (panel a), that $2.00 has been added to each of four months (panel b), and that $.67 has been added to all 12 months (panel c). For all three cases, the estimated d's sum to $5.95 (i.e., $-2.05 + $8.00) as the point estimate of misstatement for the year. Examination of the plots clearly shows the misstatement for the concentrated error case, but for the latter two, the error is harder to see by mere inspection. However, in all cases, Amy's upper confidence limit calculation for possible misstatement is the *same*—it is $5.95 + $4.3 = $10.25, which is clearly above $8, implying that there is greater than 16 percent risk of material overstatement of recorded revenue for the year.

The results above tell us two important things about statistical analysis. First, the human eye is not always sufficiently discriminating to locate material misstatement. Second, Amy's statistical calculation depends not on the distribution of misstatements across months but solely on the total amount of misstatement present in the recorded values. Finally, it should be noted that Amy may wish to follow up with investigations of particular months in some cases (such as month 38 in Figure 5–10, panel a), even if the sum of the d's is small.

Overall, we see that regression analysis can be useful in quantifying the expectation of an account and the imprecision in expectations. With good controls, reliable data series for the base period, and reasonably stable operations, causal regression models of account activity can serve as an effective tool for monitoring for possible misstatement of interim and segment account balances. Furthermore, the methods can be automated by software and can be used by less expert auditors than can judgmental methods.

FIGURE 5–10

Chickasaw Sales Corp. Plot of Estimated d's $(d = Y_r - (A + B_1X_1 + B_2X_2))$
Aggregate Misstatement of $8 in Months 37–48

a. Month 38 overstated by $8.

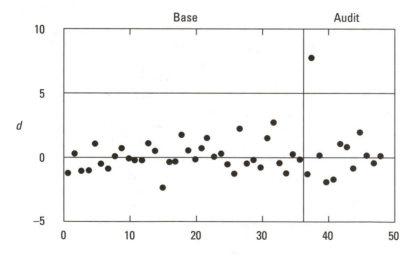

FIGURE 5 – 1 0 (continued)

b. Months 37–40 overstated by $2.

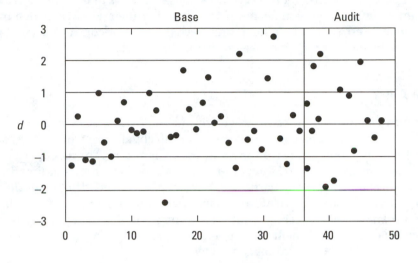

Month number

c. Months 37–48 overstated by $.67

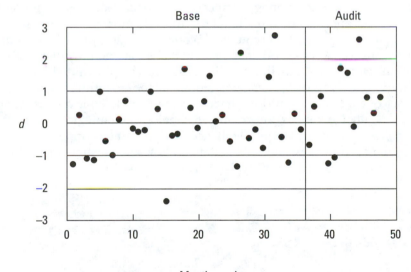

Month number

FINAL REVIEW MONITORING

There is one more use of analytical monitoring that prudent managers and internal auditors apply. It is a final critical analysis, or analytical review of the final balances resulting
after business operations analysis, data consistency analysis, analytical procedures as evidence, and tests of details have been applied.

After all of these monitoring procedures have been applied, the analyst reconsiders the final recorded values while considering all the other facts he or she has learned in the monitoring process and asks the question, "Do these numbers make sense?" If a number or relationship is unusual, are you (as top management or their agent) satisfied that it is not due to accidental error, fraud, or some unexpected or out-of-control business process? If you are, then the monitoring process is complete.

SUMMARY

Internal control comprised of the control environment, risk assessments, control activities, information, and communication processes can effectively prevent, detect, and correct many kinds of misstatements as well as fraud and theft of company assets that arise in day-to-day transactions processing. However, these methods have inherent limitations due to human failure, collusion among parties, and management override of control, among others. These inherent limitations create a demand for monitoring of recorded results by management or management's agent, the internal auditor. Monitoring by internal auditors includes the use of analytical methods applied to aggregates of recorded values, as well as tests of details of individual account components.

Analytical monitoring consists of three types of activities: business operations analysis to isolate operating problems and other unexpected events for the company and period as a whole, data consistency analysis to isolate inconsistent or illogical relations among recorded data through which management can assess heightened risk of misstatement for particular accounts, and account modeling procedures to more precisely assess risk of material misstatement in particular accounts. Account modeling procedures require use of more detailed and precise data and analytical methods than do the other analytical monitoring methods. However, it can, in some circumstances, be substituted for detailed examination of individual items comprising an account balance to reduce audit cost.

All types of analytical monitoring have become more reliable and economical to apply with the advent of lower-cost information technology and integrated systems. The economical combination of internal control reliance, analytical monitoring for risk assessment, account modeling procedures, and tests of details allows management to limit internal information risk to an acceptably low level at reasonable cost.

CASE 5

COUNT D' VALEUR CHEMISTS SHOPS

Count d' Valeur Chemists Shops (CdV) is a chain of science-based toy and novelty stores owned and operated by two brothers from a family of native Iowans with a flamboyant lifestyle. Their business has grown from one store in 1996 to 10 stores by the end of 1999. Their business strategy is to offer the very latest in science (and science-fiction) toys and novelties at low prices with aggressive sales tactics in their well-placed stores (all are in trendy shopping malls).

After a period of substantial growth, competition stiffened during 2000 and the brothers tabled their active expansion to tighten controls over operations. They focused on inventory management and sought assistance from Alex and Louis, CPAs (their independent auditor), to redesign their system. Management feels that it was successful during fiscal year 2000 because inventory was lower at year end, resulting in substantially increased inventory turnover (based on ending inventories). Furthermore, management is proud that it has continued to realize its target 100 percent markup on cost of their merchandise.

The 1999 and 2000 audited consolidated income statements for Count d' Valeur are shown in Exhibit 1, and a statement of store contributions to consolidated earnings is in Exhibit 2 along with components of each store's receivables and payables. The financials have been audited by Alex and Louis, CPAs, who gave them a favorable audit report for both 1999 and 2000.

Your Assignment

Your employer, We're Easy Money, Inc., is considering acquiring Count d' Valeur Chemists Shops as of June 30, 2000. WEMI management wants you to conduct a preacquisition review of CdV's financial statements and audit results and inform them of any accounting or auditing problems. Due to the nature of toy and novelty retailing, WEMI is especially concerned about the CdV inventory.

To facilitate negotiation of the sale, the brothers have given Alex and Louis permission to waive audit confidentiality and to fully cooperate with you in answering questions about the company and their audit. Your assistant met with the Alex and Louis partner in charge of the CdV audit. Her notes are attached as Exhibit 3, along with her calculation of selected ratios and Z-values calculated using your firm's generalized audit software and your assistant's expectations (attached as Exhibits 4 and 5).

Due to time constraints, your work will be limited to analyses of data, rather than detailed tests. In formulating your report for WEMI, you should

- Evaluate whether inventory appears to be "materially" overstated at any stores or in the aggregate. (Explain your reasoning.)

EXHIBIT 1

Audited Consolidated Earnings

COUNT D' VALEUR CHEMISTS SHOPS[1]
Summary of Consolidated Earnings
(Years Ended April 30, 1999 and 2000)
(dollars in 100s)

	1999		2000	
Sales[2]		$106,893		$108,299
Cost of sales:				
Beginning inventory	$ 8,972		$ 9,953	
Purchases	54,727		52,986	
	$63,699		$62,939	
Ending inventory[3]	9,953		8,445	
Cost of sales		53,746		54,494
Gross profit		$ 53,147		$ 53,805
Operating expenses (direct)		31,962		29,976
Net contribution of stores		$ 21,185		$ 23,829
Corporate expenses (total)		9,455		9,123
Net income		$ 11,730		$ 14,702

1. Count d' Valeur Chemists Shops is a Subchapter S corporation and is taxed as such under the Internal Revenue Code of 1954.

2. The attached statement of contribution and working capital components by store is unaudited.

3. All inventories are valued at the lower of cost or market. Cost is calculated using the first-in, first-out method.

EXHIBIT 2

Unaudited Contribution to Earnings and Working Capital Components by Store

COUNT D'VALEUR CHEMISTS SHOPS
Net Contribution by Store
(Year Ended April 30, 2000)

	Sales	Beginning Inventory	Purchases	Ending Inventory	Cost of Sales	Gross Profit	Operating Expenses	Net Contri- bution
Store 1	$ 11,372	$1,009	$ 5,456	$ 894	$ 5,571	$ 5,801	$ 3,056	$ 2,745
Store 2	10,990	982	5,370	688	5,664	5,326	2,996	2,330
Store 3	10,615	968	5,133	816	5,285	5,330	2,973	2,357
Store 4	12,052	979	5,938	966	5,951	6,101	3,126	2,975
Store 5	10,488	1,005	5,066	822	5,249	5,239	2,947	2,292
Store 6	11,653	980	5,806	918	5,868	5,785	3,092	2,693
Store 7	11,800	1,035	5,804	838	6,001	5,799	3,111	2,688
Store 8	10,995	1,016	5,468	901	5,583	5,412	3,007	2,405
Store 9	9,509	1,022	4,667	915	4,774	4,735	2,864	1,871
Store 10	8,825	957	4,278	687	4,548	4,277	2,804	1,473
Consolidated	$108,299	$9,953	$52,986	$8,445	$54,494	$53,805	$29,976	$23,829

WORKING CAPITAL COMPONENTS
(Year Ended April 30, 2000)

	Beginning Cash	Ending Cash	Beginning Receivables	Collections	Ending Receivables	Beginning Payables	Disburse- ments	Ending Payables
Store 1	$ 3	$ 3	$ 42	$ 11,366	$ 48	$ 883	$ 5,459	$ 880
Store 2	3	3	42	10,993	39	889	5,388	871
Store 3	3	3	40	10,609	46	880	5,175	838
Store 4	3	3	46	12,050	48	979	5,950	967
Store 5	3	3	38	10,478	48	835	5,077	824
Store 6	3	3	44	11,643	54	956	5,797	965
Store 7	3	3	45	11,803	42	944	5,807	941
Store 8	3	3	41	10,977	59	890	5,481	877
Store 9	3	3	39	9,506	42	823	4,656	834
Store 10	3	3	33	8,828	30	739	4,266	751
Consolidated*	$3,225	$3,436	$410	$108,253	$456	$8,818	$53,056	$8,748

*Includes corporate cash balances.

♦ Determine what additional investigation, if any, you would recommend to WEMI before they agree to buy CdV.

To assist your analysis, you should consider what overstatements might occur in ending in- ventory and, if they have occurred, how they would affect the account values and ratios of ac- count values. Also, while you may use the ratios calculated by your assistant, you should recom- pute, analyze, and include in your solution *at least one* set of Z-values using an expectation based on your own knowledge and reasoning.

EXHIBIT 3

Your Partner's Notes of Her Meeting with Alex and Louis and Her Review of Their Work Papers

Count d'Valeur's Inventory Procedures

Purchasing—Accounting for purchasing is conducted at the firm's home office in Sioux City, Iowa, but store managers are allowed great discretion in ordering unique items that they believe will sell in their own stores. Thus, there is no common chainwide product list, and inventory on hand is established on a physical or periodic basis.

Inventory Quantities—To strengthen control and to allow its store personnel to concentrate on operations, Count d'Valeur relies on an independent inventory counting firm to determine inventory quantities at each store. At fiscal year end, the outside firm sends two count specialists to each store. Each specialist has a hand-held computer designed for efficient recording of product codes, retail prices, and counts. Each specialist walks the aisles counting every product code item encountered. The count, price, and item code are then entered into the hand-held inventory computer.

At the end of the counting process, the memory contents of each hand-held computer are read into a PC program that matches the two sets of counts and identifies exceptions. The two specialists then physically locate the exception items, recount the stock, and enter a corrected amount. The PC then prepares a written inventory quantity and retail price summary for the store manager and also prepares a diskette with the same information. The diskette is forwarded by overnight express to the home office in Sioux City, Iowa.

Pricing and Obsolescence—In Sioux City, the inventory quantities on the diskettes are matched by computer against purchase records to price the inventory at first-in, first-out cost. Items without purchase records are noted for follow-up to complete the purchase/accounts payable records. The extended amounts are then summarized and entered as the general ledger inventory amounts. A lower-of-cost-or-market assessment is made by calculating inventory turnover by product groupings summarized across stores. All items with more than four months' supply are then reviewed by one of the brothers to assess whether an accounting adjustment is needed, and whether the store manager should be contacted to discuss the overstock problem.

Alex and Louis's Auditing Procedures

Alex and Louis's auditors reviewed Count d'Valeur's internal controls over inventory and were satisfied that they were well designed.

The auditors arranged with CdV management to observe the outside count team's procedures at stores 2 and 7. Also at both locations, A&L auditors randomly selected a substantial number of items, independently counted them, and noted the counts in their work papers. They observed no exceptions in procedure by the outside count personnel and observed only inconsequential quantity differences when their own counts were traced and compared with those in the final inventory summary that supported the CdV financial statements. During their store visits, A&L auditors obtained a copy of the count/price diskette and also looked for out-of-the-way, musty, or dusty inventory and found none.

The store visits were followed by testing of the pricing, summarization, and "months supply on hand" calculations that CdV personnel made at the home office. They were satisfied that the calculated totals and LoCoM adjustment were adequate for the two stores observed, and for the other eight as well. Alex and Louis conducted overall analytical procedures by comparing the CdV balances and ratios with those for toy and novelty stores nationwide. Their comparison revealed that CdV has lower merchandise markup percentages than 80 percent of the industry, but has been able to maintain their gross profit rate during 2000 while the industry average has fallen by about 1.5 percent. Also, median inventory turnover for the industry has risen from 4.5 to 4.8 over the same period. The auditors concluded that management's explanations for the differences from the industry were reasonable.

EXHIBIT 4

Your Assistant's Analytical Procedures Comparing CdV's Ratios with Various Expectations

Your assistant used a generalized audit software package (GAS) called AuditMagic. The APRat (for Analytical Procedures-Ratio) feature of AuditMagic allows the analyst to enter expectations for a ratio of a multi-outlet organization. The software then calculates the ratio by location, compares it with the expected ratio (that the software user supplied), and calculates a Z-score. The Z-score is calculated by subtracting the expectation from the recorded value of the ratio at each location and dividing by the standard deviation calculated across all the outlets. That is:

Z = (Recorded value of ratio − Expectation of ratio)/Standard deviation of ratio across locations

APRat also allows the auditor to specify critical values for the ratio and "flags" ratios beyond these cutoff values for a given probability or risk level. For example, a cutoff value of .84 (i.e., .84 standard deviation) would flag Z-values in the 20 percent upper tail, and a cutoff of 1.64 would leave 5 percent in the upper tail, as shown below.

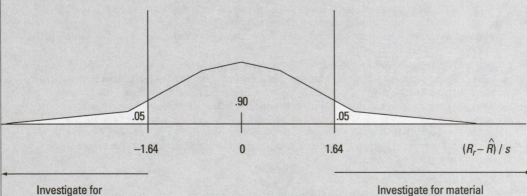

Your assistant has used various bases for her expectations. In some cases, she has used the target for Count d'Valeur, and in other cases, she has used the audited value of the ratio for the prior period. In still other cases, she adjusted the value for last year for known changes in the industry for the current audit year.

Exhibit 5 presents your assistant's output from APRat. The ratios selected involve inventory since the primary concern of your client is that inventory is overstated, and it involves accounts that are related to inventory such as cost of goods sold, purchases, and accounts payable. Your assistant has set the software to flag transactions in the 5 percent upper tail or the 5 percent lower tail, either of which may be consistent with inventory overstatement.

EXHIBIT 5

Audit Software Output Ratio

APRat (copyright AuditMagic)
Client: CdV
Expectation = **Client target**
Date: 4/30/00

Ratio 1

Segment	Cost of Sales % (CS/S)		
	Book Value		Z
1	0.489		−1.19
2	0.515	*	1.81
3	0.497		−0.25
4	0.493		−0.73
5	0.500		0.05
6	0.503		0.42
7	0.508		1.01
8	0.507		0.92
9	0.502		0.24
10	0.515	*	1.81
Company	0.503		
Std. Dev.	0.0085		
Expectation	.5000		

APRat (copyright AuditMagic)
Client: CdV
Expectation = **Last year company audited**
Date: 4/30/00

Ratio 2

Segment	Asset Mix (AR/INV)		
	Book Value		Z
1	0.053		−0.05
2	0.056		0.41
3	0.056		0.36
4	0.049		−0.65
5	0.058		0.66
6	0.058		0.73
7	0.050		−0.59
8	0.065	*	1.74
9	0.045		−1.22
10	0.043		−1.56
Company	0.054		
Std. Dev.	.0066		
Expectation	0.054		

APRat (copyright AuditMagic)
Client: CdV
Expectation = **No change**
Date: 4/30/00

Ratio 3

Segment	INV Growth (INV/INVbeg)		
	Book Value		Z
1	0.886		−1.26
2	0.700	*	−3.31
3	0.842	*	−1.73
4	0.986		−0.14
5	0.817	*	−2.01
6	0.936		−0.70
7	0.809	*	−2.10
8	0.886		−1.25
9	0.895		−1.15
10	0.717	*	−3.12
Company	0.848		
Std. Dev.	0.0903		
Expectation	1.0000		

APRat (copyright AuditMagic)
Client: CdV
Expectation = **Last year company audited**
Date: 4/30/00

Ratio 4

Segment	INV Turnover (CS/INV)		
	Book Value		Z
1	6.231		1.07
2	8.232	*	3.65
3	6.476		1.38
4	6.160		0.98
5	6.385		1.27
6	6.392		1.28
7	7.161	*	2.27
8	6.196		1.02
9	5.217		−0.24
10	6.620		1.57
Company	6.452		
Std. Dev.	0.7748		
Expectation	5.4000		

EXHIBIT 5   Continued

Audit Software Output Ratio

APRat (copyright AuditMagic)			APRat (copyright AuditMagic)		
Client: CdV			Client: CdV		
Expectation = **Last year company audited**			Expectation = **INV Growth Rate**		
Date: 4/30/00			Date: 4/30/00		
Ratio 5			**Ratio 6**		
INV Financed (INV/AP)			**AP Growth (AP/APbeg)**		
Segment	Book Value	Z	Segment	Book Value	Z
1	1.015	−1.32	1	0.996	* 7.84
2	0.789	* −3.98	2	0.979	* 6.95
3	0.973	* −1.82	3	0.952	* 5.49
4	0.998	−1.52	4	0.987	* 7.37
5	0.997	−1.54	5	0.986	* 7.32
6	0.951	−2.08	6	1.009	* 8.52
7	0.890	* −2.79	7	0.996	* 7.85
8	1.027	−1.19	8	0.985	* 7.25
9	1.097	−0.37	9	1.013	* 8.73
10	0.914	* −2.51	10	1.016	* 8.88
Company	0.9653		Company	0.9920	
Std. Dev.	0.0851		Std. Dev.	0.0189	
Expectation	1.1287		Expectation	0.8485	

KEY WORDS

account modeling procedures Analytical monitoring with expectations formed by representing individual accounts using data that is causally or logically linked to the true value of the account.

analytical monitoring Forming expectations about what should be the aggregate recorded values for a period of time or at a particular date, and investigating deviations from expectations as to likely cause.

business operations analysis Analytical monitoring using expected business operation and accounting relationships such as ratios of account balances that are related to each other either by a business process or an accounting entry.

data consistency analysis Analytical monitoring by examining data relationship consistency across a set of financial and nonfinancial variables all measured at the same point in time.

final review monitoring End-of-period analysis of balances resulting after business operations analysis, data consistency analysis, account modeling procedures, and tests of details have been applied.

incorrect acceptance Not investigating an account that is materially misstated or an out-of-control process.

incorrect investigation Investigating an account or process that is within acceptable limits.

6 CHAPTER

Detailed Monitoring: Tests of Controls, Transactions, and Balances

- ◆ **H**ow do my internal auditors know that assets aren't missing and that controls really work?
- ◆ Why can't I just wait for the external auditor to audit details?
- ◆ What will happen if I don't have adequate monitoring of details?
- ◆ How much detailed monitoring is enough?
- ◆ What instructions should I give my internal auditor?

In contrast to analytical monitoring that is sometimes applied by top management itself, top management has little direct involvement in detailed monitoring. Yet it is detailed control procedures that prevent errors and fraud in individual items as they are being processed, and other detailed controls and tests of selected transactions and balances that detect and correct on a timely basis many errors and frauds that do occur. Thus, details and monitoring of details are important to management.

In this chapter, we explore detailed monitoring concepts applied by internal auditors. We consider tests of computer-based controls that process transactions and detailed auditing of the resulting transactions and balances. Finally, we consider how judgments and test results are combined into an overall conclusion, or confidence about the resulting balances and financial displays.

DETAILED MONITORING CONCEPTS

In Chapter 4, we saw how top management can assure itself that it is obtaining reliable financial and other information day to day through the use of well-designed and effectively operating internal controls over transactions as they are being processed. In Chapter 5, we saw how management can use analytical monitoring procedures to identify significant unexpected changes in business operations as well as likely misstatement in accounting records. However, internal control over transactions processing can't prevent or detect and correct all misstatements. And analytical monitoring procedures by themselves typically can't find misstatements in individual recorded items, although they can suggest heightened risk that such errors might occur or that they have occurred. So more monitoring is needed, and detailed monitoring of controls, transactions, and balances fills the need.

A short answer to the question "How does the internal auditor know that recorded inventory is really there and that controls really work?" is that the internal auditor conducts tests of details of the application of prescribed controls and recorded results and compares recorded results with real-world quantities on hand. Overall, the internal auditor relies on a combination of internal control testing and evaluation, analytical monitoring, and tests of details to provide assurance that prescribed controls are being applied to individual transactions and that the results of data processing are reliable.

Some tests of details are applied routinely to confirm that day-to-day processing controls are being properly applied, and some determine that the recorded results are correct. Tests of details are also used for follow-up investigations when analytical monitoring indicates high risk of material misstatement but can't locate particular items in error. Thus, tests of details are the ultimate fallback procedure that provides the evidence that misstatement is or is not present in particular recorded amounts.

Before computers were used to process transactions, internal auditors' testing of details focused on an item-by-item examination of business documents and comparison of recorded amounts with underlying real-world evidence. Extensive testing of details of individual items was necessary because each item was processed manually, and humans might make mistakes on any item. For example, auditors examined purchase records to see that a paid invoice was accompanied by a purchase order and a receiving report as prescribed by the system's designer. They also periodically compared recorded inventory quantities with real-world quantities on hand and vice versa.

Most data processing control activities are now embedded in computer software, and the same processing and controls are applied to huge classes of transactions. Also, electronic sensors may continuously monitor inventory quantities on hand. Therefore, testing of controls has shifted from item-by-item examination to testing computer programs that process classes of data. Testing typically includes verifying the controls over computer processing duties (such as separating system design from system configuration and access code assignment), determining that unauthorized software changes have not been made, and testing the resulting software and their application.

Computer processing controls, integrated databases produced by enterprisewide software, and improved analytical monitoring reduce the need for extensive detailed tests of results. However, the results of computer processing are still spot-checked on a very limited basis to verify that processing is proper and to determine the substantive correctness of balances that result. For example, the auditor might confirm a recorded receivables balance directly with the customer or observe quantities of a particular type of inventory on hand as of a given date.

Accounting Considerations

Before considering detailed auditing procedures, it is useful to review the types of numbers that comprise financial statements and the misstatements that might be present in them. In Chapter 2, we considered four types of numbers appearing on public financial statements:

- **Hard numbers**—numbers attached to physical and fiscal quantities of items that result from primary transactions such as cash, receivables, inventory, fixed asset additions, accounts payable, and the related revenues and cost of sales.

- **Allocations**—numbers that spread primary transaction amounts over time, segments, or units produced such as depreciation expense, accumulated depreciation amounts, and amortization of goodwill, and assignment of overhead.

- **Accounting estimates**—quantification of transactions or losses that may occur in the future or may have occurred already such as allowance for doubtful accounts, warranty expense, reserves for inventory losses, and other contingent losses.

- **Uncertainties**—disclosure of possible losses that cannot be quantified as a point estimate but have an effect on interpretation of financial statements because of the explicit variance of outcomes that may arise in the future.[1]

These four types of numbers are different in their nature, origin, and quantifiability. They also differ in the manner in which the auditor can verify their substantive correctness. These differences imply applicable control activities and auditing procedures will differ.

In addition to the four types of numbers on financial statements, there are five possible aspects of these numbers that might be in error. U.S. auditing standards list five assertions implicitly being made by management when they purport that their financial statements comply with GAAP. While internal reports for management do not necessarily purport to follow GAAP, the same concepts apply. The five assertions are

- **Existence** (or occurrence)—the transactions, events, conditions, or assets exist or occurred as purported in the accounting records.

- **Ownership** (or obligations)—the firm owns the asset claimed (or has the right to use it) or has an obligation to pay or render service.

- **Valuation**—all items are valued using GAAP as to both method of measurement and precision of application (i.e., no material misstatement).

- **Completeness**—all items that should be recorded have been recorded (e.g., all liabilities and all expenses are recorded).

- **Disclosure and presentation**—the numbers and disclosures are presented in a form that complies with GAAP, including related informative disclosures such as risks and uncertainties.

These five assertions are potentially applicable to all assets, liabilities, revenues, and expenses. However, they typically apply differentially to particular items. For example, existence, ownership, and valuation are primary concerns for assets such as accounts receivable and inventory, while completeness will be more important for liabilities such as accounts payable and for recorded expenses. Detailed auditing procedures reflect these differences.

Auditing Procedures

Figure 6–1 diagrams the essential subject matter for detailed tests. It shows real-world conditions comprised of real-world assets, liabilities, and revenues and expenses as the starting

---

1. The measurement of uncertainty disclosure can be thought of as 0 or 1, or no material uncertainty present versus material or greater uncertainty present.

FIGURE 6-1

Computer Processing of Accounting Data

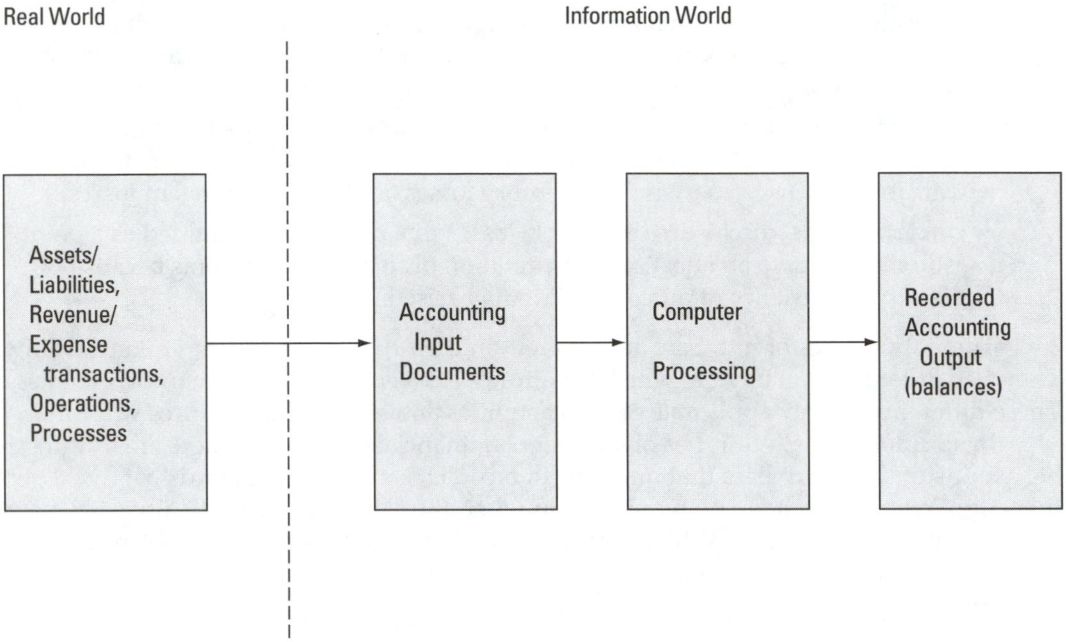

Real World   Information World

point, followed by source document inputs to the accounting process and processing of information (by computer). Finally, the resulting account balance outputs in the database (including financial statement balances, supporting detailed accounts such as customer accounts, inventory quantities on hand, and amounts owed to particular suppliers) complete the diagram. Auditor testing of details can involve comparisons within, between, and among these four components.

Figure 6–1 shows that there are four elements in the process of developing accounting data and divides them between the real world and a parallel information world. If the auditor wants to verify that the recorded accounting output in the information world is correct, he or she can look toward the real-world conditions that support the output, or to the steps in between (the input documents and computer processing of data). Auditing procedures for details follow this same logic. Some audit procedures compare recorded output with real-world conditions, others compare the output with documentary inputs, and still others verify that processing is correct.

There are five broad types of auditing procedures or "building blocks" through which the internal auditor validates output of an accounting process. These building blocks can provide the auditor with a basis for a judgment that the accounts do not contain material misstatement.

- **Observation**—visual examination or "eyeballing" of physical assets and visual examination of business processes or accounting processes as they are taking place.

- ♦ **Inquiry**—asking questions of company personnel (managers as well as employees) about what they do or have done and how they do it, and asking outsiders such as customers, suppliers, bankers, warehouse operators, and attorneys to confirm aspects of a recorded transaction or that a recorded asset is being held by the outsider.

- ♦ **Examination**—visual or electronic inspection or reading of documents such as invoices, vouchers, and contracts and tracing and comparing amounts within the accounting system.

- ♦ **Reprocessing**—reperforming the processing of input data, recalculation of allocations, or reperformance of internal control procedures (such as price verification, addition and multiplication, and reconciliation of parallel records such as bank statements and cash records).

- ♦ **Analysis**—analytical monitoring of accounting output, computer operating statistics, and input relations and reconciliation of related records (such as sales versus cost of sales and units produced versus units sold).

The first four procedures verify details and the fifth addresses aggregates of details.

AN EXAMPLE: LJ APPLIANCES' INVENTORY AND COST OF SALES

To illustrate the application of detailed auditing procedures and how they can produce evidence that accounting output is valid, let's again consider LJ Appliances. In particular, let's consider the verification of a "hard number"—LJ Appliances' ending inventory balance. The number will be verified directly by tests of details of the recorded balance and indirectly by detailed tests of the controls that produced the balance.

Detailed Tests of Transactions and Balances

Figure 6–2 extends Figure 6–1 to include arrows that illustrate auditing procedures and the evidence they produce. While the example in Figure 6–2 is limited to inventory, it shows the four detailed auditing procedures as they might be applied to all five assertions about inventory, as well as some evidence about the related cost of sales and accounts payable.

Figure 6–2 shows an arrow from the accounting output records to the real world operationalized by selecting product types from the database and then *observing* the quantities of inventory on hand for the selected types. The auditor can also *inquire* about (confirm) inventory quantities held by others such as inventory on consignment or inventory held by an outside warehouser. Observation of inventory on hand or confirmed by direct auditor contact with outsiders gives assurance that the recorded inventory exists. Periodic counting of all inventory is a common procedure that verifies inventory processing and is required by most tax authorities. An auditor's selective observation of inventory quantity details also facilitates reliable counting by warehouse workers, just as pop quizzes encourage careful preparation by students.

Another observation arrow connects the real world to the accounting output record. This arrow represents the auditor's observation of particular elements of real-world inventory on hand and tracing of it forward to the recorded output. This tests for completeness of

FIGURE 6-2

Detailed Auditing Procedures
LJ Appliances—Inventory

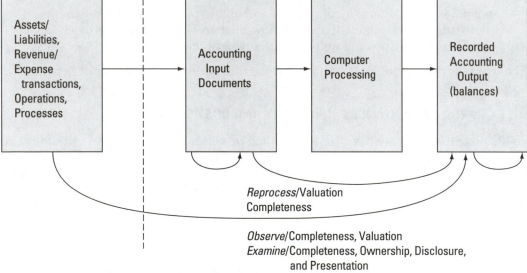
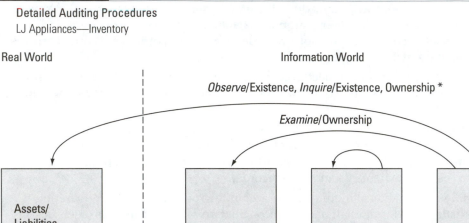

Real World   Information World

Observe/Existence, *Inquire*/Existence, Ownership *

Examine/Ownership

Assets/
Liabilities,
Revenue/
Expense
   transactions,
Operations,
Processes

Accounting
Input
Documents

Computer
Processing

Recorded
Accounting
Output
(balances)

Reprocess/Valuation
Completeness

Observe/Completeness, Valuation
Examine/Completeness, Ownership, Disclosure,
            and Presentation

*Coded as: *audit procedure* / assertion tested

recorded inventory and, perhaps, completeness of recorded accounts payable. For example, if the inventory item observed is not recorded as inventory, then recorded inventory is incomplete. If purchase of the omitted item was not recorded, then recorded accounts payable may be incomplete.

Observation of items selected from inventory on hand can also provide assurance that recorded inventory is valued according to GAAP. For example, the auditor will assess whether inventory on hand appears to be in good condition and ready for sale or use. Observation of items that appear to be in bad condition or are covered with dust or stored in an out-of-the-way place would suggest that the realizable value of inventory may be less than its cost, and recorded inventory should be written down. Finally, *examination* of forward purchase contracts for materials may indicate the need for disclosure of a long-term purchase commitment or unfavorable price changes on the purchase contract.

Examining documentary evidence of a prescribed processing control application is illustrated by selecting a purchase transaction from the database and tracing it to the supporting input documents. The documents might be a properly executed purchase order, receiving report, and payment voucher. The examination arrow from recorded accounting output to accounting input documents tests for the ownership of inventory and its cost for valuation. Observation shows existence, but does not show its pricing or that LJ Appliances has title to the goods. Examination of an invoice would provide evidence of ownership and pricing.

Reprocessing of inventory transactions is illustrated by the auditor's verification of pricing of inventory through looking up prices that were current at the time of processing and also recalculating ending inventory amounts on a FIFO or LIFO basis, as appropriate. As a part of reprocessing, the auditor would also check for completeness of information at the input stage as an indication that input controls are operating properly. Examination and observation of computer processing is another application of auditing procedures. These tasks validate the computer processing information by seeing that prescribed procedures are being followed in actual processing. Reprocessing of the pricing of inventory verifies the valuation of inventory through the proper application of a generally accepted accounting method.

Detailed Tests of Controls

The four labeled arrows between the four elements in Figure 6–2 illustrate detailed auditing procedures that directly assess the validity of the recorded amount for inventory (detailed balance tests). There are also three tests or procedures that auditors apply within information-world elements that indirectly verify the validity of inventory. These are drawn in Figure 6–2 as (unlabeled) arrows that begin and end at each of the three information-world elements. This type of test is known as a detailed test of controls.

The arrow from and to accounting input documents illustrates a detailed examination for consistency of recorded inventory purchase documents for evidence that prescribed internal control activities were applied for the particular document examined. For example, a payment voucher should be supported by the supplier's invoice, with an indication that it has been price tested and arithmetically verified; a receiving report; and perhaps a purchase order and evidence of approval by a department head. Existence of these documents properly completed does not guarantee that the recorded amount is correct. But it does give some assurance that the prescribed procedures were being applied during processing of transactions, and this indirectly increases confidence in the system and its output.

The unlabeled arrow beginning and ending with computer processing illustrates testing the program itself to see that the program correctly processes transactions as prescribed by the system design. As we will see in the next section, control tests of computer processing may involve several auditing procedures. Finally, the arrow from recorded output to recorded output represents examination of details of database output elements for consistency and completeness. This examination is analogous to data consistency analysis applied to aggregated data in analytical monitoring.

There are some control tests not marked by arrows in Figure 6–2. The auditor observes the real-world process of inventory counting by LJ Appliances personnel. In particular, the auditor observes the apparent care or seriousness with which employees are counting inventory, recording the amounts (preparing accounting documents for recording inventory on hand), and making sure that nothing is missed in the counting process. Similarly, the auditor can observe operation of data input and computer processing of transactions. Both of these activities provide indirect evidence about the internal control over recording of inventory. Direct substantive tests of balances in combination with the tests of controls and analytical procedures should give reasonable assurance that inventory is properly valued according to GAAP.

Inventory Counts and Observation

To illustrate detailed monitoring, let's be specific about the periodic physical counting of inventory for LJ Appliances. LJ Appliances' inventory includes many types of refrigerators and many other types of appliances at many locations. The counting task is not easy, and to assure accuracy, LJ's uses a systematic approach.

Under the supervision of the store manager, employees of each store make a complete count of all inventory on hand at their store at the end of each quarter. Since LJ Appliances sells a fixed schedule of products, the central accounting office prepares preprinted count sheets listing all the products that could be on hand at the location, but does not include quantities. Rather, it has a space for counts to be entered. Two pairs of workers form count teams that independently count the inventory quantities on hand and record their findings on the appropriate count sheets.

At the end of the counting process, the two sets of count sheets are compared item by item by the two count teams, any items with differences are recounted, and the correct amount is entered as the final count on one set of count sheets and the other set is discarded. The corrected count sheet is then scanned electronically and transmitted to the central accounting office inventory clerk *and* to the internal auditor. The internal auditor can then compare count sheet quantities from each store with central accounting's final processed and recorded quantities of inventory at each store. This test can reveal additions or omissions in the accounting records.

Each quarter, the internal auditor attends the quarter-end inventory counting process at a few stores on an unannounced basis. The internal auditor observes the count teams and whether they appear to be following the prescribed procedures, and also makes some test counts himself or herself. That is, the auditor selects some items from a copy of the preprinted count sheets, finds those items in the storeroom, and records his or her own counts. These counts are then compared to the corrected count sheets obtained by the internal auditor electronically and the inventory recorded by the inventory processing system.

Since the count teams work from the preprinted count sheets and attempt to locate the preprinted inventory types and count them, there is some risk of failing to find items that are on hand, and a value of zero is recorded by the count team. Also, if the inventory includes items that are not on the preprinted count sheets (perhaps because of a special purchase or a discontinuation of a line of goods), then the employees may not include them in their counts. As a test for completeness, the internal auditor observes a few product types in the storeroom; notes for each type its description, product number, and quantity; and then traces these counts to the final inventory record prepared. This is a test for completeness of ending inventory by determining in the real world what quantities *should be* recorded and tracing them into the accounting records to see whether they are recorded.

If the auditor making the surprise store visit is satisfied that count crews are taking their jobs seriously and the counts appear to be reliable, then he or she has increased confidence that the overall inventory will be validly recorded. For the stores not observed by the auditor, the auditor can compare the auditor's copy of the count sheets with those processed by the accounting department for completeness and for additions to quantities that were on hand at the count date.

AUDITING COMPUTER INPUT AND PROCESSING

With the general background of the previous section, we are now ready to look at detailed auditing of the four components of Figure 6–1. We begin with auditing of inputs and processing. Conceptually, the auditor either can audit around inputs and processing (focusing on the real world and the final output) or can audit the inputs and processes to reduce the cost of testing output by relying on the system. Neither of these approaches is likely to be economical by itself, but a combination is. However, it is useful to study them separately.

How can the auditor verify or validate that data input and computer processing are proper? The answer lies in validating the computer application software for processing, including what input the software will admit to processing. A theoretically possible approach to program or processing verification is for the auditor to examine the program code itself. This approach is akin to a mechanic disassembling a car engine to find out why it clunks or a physician opening the abdominal cavity to find out why the patient has a stomach ache. Both are theoretically possible, but it is usually economical to take less extreme and less costly measures to obtain indirect evidence for a diagnosis.

As a practical matter, the auditor has three alternatives for verifying programs. The first is study and evaluation of internal controls over application software design, testing, implementation, and operation and controls that protect the system from unauthorized changes. The auditor can then observe operation of the system and various computer applications such as sales, collections, and payroll processing. The auditor can inquire of computer and user personnel about system operation and can apply analytical procedures to computer processing activities. Analysis of computer operating statistics such as numbers of documents processed and downtime allow the auditor to assess risk of error or find a time when the system may have been compromised. This approach is sometimes called the *general controls* approach because it tests controls that apply to all computer applications. Tests of general computer controls in combination with detailed testing of output can lead to high confidence that the applications software must be proper.

In a second approach, an *application controls* approach, the auditor conducts what are called "outside tests" of the software for particular computer applications. Under this approach, the auditor conducts a stimulus–response test of the software either through using test data to test the program or by reprocessing actual transaction input data using software believed to be equivalent to the actual processing program. Figure 6–3 illustrates the test data and equivalent reprocessing approaches. In the first panel of Figure 6–3, the auditor develops input data to test particular features of the actual program. These will include valid data that should be accepted by the program as well as data that should violate input criteria specified for the program. For example, if the software is written not to accept transactions above $500, then the auditor's test data would include a transaction for, say, $600 to see whether the software will reject it from processing. Thus, the test data approach uses

FIGURE 6-3

Computer Processing Testing Procedures

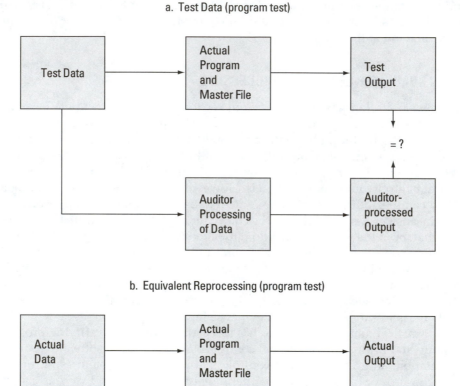

a. Test Data (program test)

b. Equivalent Reprocessing (program test)

data that the auditor develops to predict how the data *should* be processed by the program. The auditor then compares expected output given prescribed processing with that obtained from operating the actual program.

Some firms formalize the test data approach by creating a fictitious division or department in the computer system solely for the purpose of conducting test data applications on a continuing basis. The fictitious department processes fictitious transactions from the internal auditor with the applications programs used to process real transactions of the same type from actual departments. Thus, the payroll transactions for the fictitious "de-

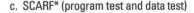

FIGURE 6-3

Computer Processing Testing Procedures (Continued)

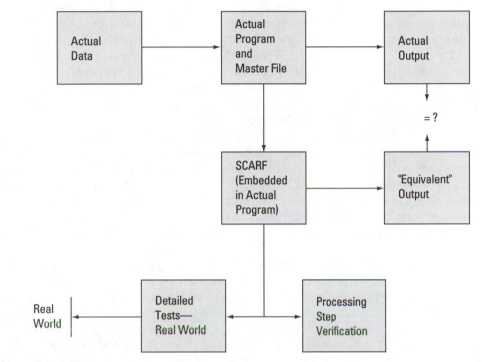

c. SCARF* (program test and data test)

*Systems Control Audit Review File.

partment 99" are processed with the same program that processes payroll for other departments. If the actual payroll program has been changed but the change was not documented, then the internal auditor will likely discover the change when transactions from department 99 result in output different from expected.

The other outside test is reprocessing of actual input data with a program believed to be equivalent to actual software. The equivalent program could be a copy of the software originally put into operation and updated by approved changes, or it could be based on the internal auditor's generalized audit software (see next section) to emulate, or mimic, essential features of the actual program. In applying the equivalent reprocessing approach, actual input data are stored, retrieved, and reprocessed using the equivalent program (see panel b.). If the output produced by the equivalent program is the same as the output produced during actual processing, then the auditor concludes that the actual program is valid.

Both types of outside tests suffer from the limitation that they will not be effective if there is a restricted variety of transactions in the input data. As examples, if the test data do not include the type of transaction or do not test the particular code segment that is in error or fraudulent, then the results will be as expected even though the program is invalid. Similarly, if the input for the time period selected does not include the erroneous account area or code section, then reprocessing actual data may appear to be correct even though the program is defective.

A third approach for program verification is not direct. Rather, it determines that the program is probably correct by verifying that the output is correct. Application of this method typically involves embedding in application software an audit routine known generically as SCARF (for Systems Control Audit Review File). SCARF selects transactions at the data processing stage, tags the transaction electronically, and then records related master file amounts necessary to process the item along with the processing step being executed and writes all the data onto the SCARF file for auditor follow-up (see panel c.).

Since transactions are selected during processing, the approach allows a test for completeness of records (i.e., transactions are not lost during processing of transactions), as well as their validity. Recording of related master file amounts is necessary to validate processing because the correctness of processing depends on the condition of other files at the instant at which a transaction is processed. For example, a credit sales entry made at 10:00 A.M. may be valid because the customer's account balance plus the sales amount was less than the maximum allowed as of 10:00 A.M., but a transaction of the same amount entered at 3:00 P.M. would be rejected. This is because by 3:00 P.M. the customer's updated master file balance plus the sales amount was greater than the customer's credit limit. In other words, the correct processing result depends on the account receivable balance and credit limit at the time of the entry. SCARF allows recreation of essential conditions to verify processing results.

Auditor follow-up of items recorded in a SCARF file can take any of several routes. First, he or she can determine the validity of transactions processing by comparing the final recorded amount with the components that make up that final balance (an information-world test). Second, the auditor can compare recorded amounts with real-world amounts by observation or inquiry of outsiders. Third, the auditor can validate the program by reviewing the processing steps recorded by SCARF and determining that they conform with the prescribed steps in the program. Thus, the SCARF approach provides a basis for several types of evidence resulting in increased assurance about the reported account balances and the system that produced them.

SCARF can tag transactions on a random basis, which serves as a test of completeness of processing and prevents errors from occurring. Or SCARF can be applied to a given class of transactions such as transactions that are especially large in amount, or transactions that arise when any of the controls have been manually overridden by the data entry clerk or other person entering a transaction. Transactions involving override are especially important to review because they indicate that the usual procedure embedded in the software has been bypassed and may have been bypassed inappropriately. Thus, the SCARF approach provides many benefits and is a powerful tool for management. A disadvantage of the SCARF approach is that advanced planning is required to incorporate it into application processing software.

AUDITING RECORDED ACCOUNTING OUTPUT

Detailed auditing of recorded accounting output requires that the auditor be able to select individual items from recorded accounting output. In a manual system, the auditor could observe the recorded output and manually apply the selection criteria. In an electronic environment, this approach is not possible since detailed visible output records do not exist. Therefore, the auditor must rely on electronic means for selecting items for detailed testing. This selection process and many other audit tasks are typically accomplished using generalized audit software, as discussed next.

Generalized Audit Software

In a computer-based processing environment, almost all auditing procedures are facilitated by the auditor's use of *generalized audit software*. Generalized audit software is a set of computer programs that can be adapted to conduct audit tasks on various types of data input as well as programs and computer processing tasks. It is used to *access* accounting data at the account balance level or at the input level, perform audit *processing* of the data, and *trace* and *compare* data within the accounting system. GAS can also be used to assist in *direct testing* of computer programs.

Six features are typically contained in generalized audit software (see Figure 6–4). Five features are applied to the inputs and outputs of the accounting system (that is, data and file-based), and the sixth is applied to the company's application software.

FIGURE 6 – 4

Generalized Audit Software

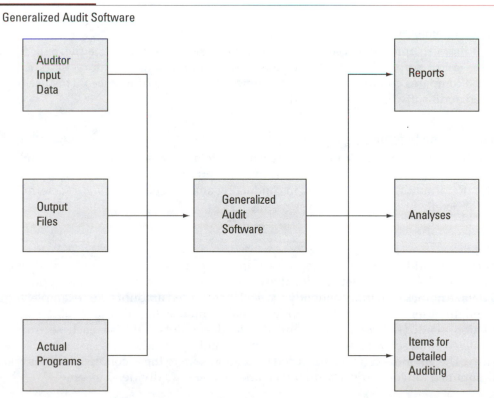

Select Items Based on Criteria

From an output file, generalized audit software can select items that have certain characteristics or combinations of characteristics. For example, the auditor may wish to select items that are especially large in amount, or items that have an unusual combination of amounts (for example, an inventory item for which there are several months of supply on hand), or items that have other unusual characteristics such as override of some of the ordinary processing (say, special approval by an executive).

Criteria-based selection allows the auditor to focus attention on items with unusual characteristics that may be especially risky and possibly misprocessed or fraudulent, or especially important because of their large size. Selected items can then be subjected to detailed auditing for substantive correctness through real-world observation, inquiry, or examination, or tests of the controls applied.

Select Items at Random

Generalized audit software can also select items in a random fashion. This approach is the opposite of selection based on criteria in that which items are selected is unpredictable. Random selection would not be economical for isolating risky or large items but is useful as a misstatement prevention tool. The idea is that if some items are selected for examination at random, then a would-be perpetrator of fraud cannot predict which item might be examined by the auditor, and thus will not be as likely to commit fraud. Random-based preventive selection also encourages honest employees to be careful in executing their duties.

Trace and Compare

The auditor can enter observed test counts or confirmed amounts into a file, and the generalized audit software traces the counts to the appropriate inventory or other asset records, compares counts to recorded amounts, and lists any differences. This use of generalized audit software conserves audit effort.

Summarize and Reformat Data

Generalized audit software can summarize files in total or by segment, and it can reformat data. For example, expenses can be arranged by department, product, expense type, or time period. Reformatting is often useful in conducting analytical monitoring to determine the need for detailed follow-up within segments.

Reprocess

Generalized audit software can reprocess transactions in several different ways. One has already been discussed—that of using it to emulate an application program to reprocess actual data. Another is to independently recalculate recorded amounts. For example, the auditor might observe marketable securities on hand and use the software to access from information vendors current prices and dividend amounts paid on each security. The generalized audit software would multiply prices and dividends times shares held for each security. The amounts can then be traced by the software to the accounting records and results summed for comparison with total market values and dividend income.

Evaluate the Program

Generalized audit software can also use an application program as input. An application program, set of access codes, or other element of the computer system is processed by analyzing it for content or for inconsistency of assigned duties. Some generalized audit software automatically generates flowcharts of program code. Thus, the auditor or systems analyst can visually review the logic of program code. This may assist in direct verification, or inside testing, of the actual computer code.

AUDIT SAMPLING CONCEPTS

Prior to widespread computer processing and incorporation of internal controls in software, external and internal auditors frequently relied on detailed tests using large audit samples of accounting data as the basis for conclusions about account balances. Without reliable controls, especially computer controls, extensive audit sampling was necessary to test the validity of output balances.

Computer processing using enterprise software changes things. It allows more reliable embedded controls in processing software, which can make information processing risk (IPR in Chapter 4) much lower than is typical for less automated systems. Also, improved analytical monitoring procedures are possible with integrated databases that can associate accounting data with related nonaccounting data. These developments make analytical monitoring more precise, reliable, and economical. Thus, extensive testing of details to determine the substantive validity of accounting output is no longer needed or economical.

Audit sampling of recorded items still has considerable value as a way of confirming conclusions reached from evaluating computer software and results from exceptions identified by analytical procedures. It is also useful as a prevention tool. Thus, audit sampling is important in deciding which, when, and how items should be selected for detailed testing.

Let's consider some overall concepts of audit sampling. This will show the relation of the amount of misstatement in an account balance that, if it exists, would be intolerable to management, to the audit effort required to limit to an acceptable level the risk of incorrectly accepting a materially misstated balance.

How Much Detailed Monitoring Is Enough?

Auditing of accounting numbers is too complex to be reduced to a single formula for required audit effort to acquire assurance. This is because accounting numbers involve several assertions, and the auditor has several sources of evidence about possible misstatement in the accounts. However, it is useful to consider a statistical sampling formula because such a formula will allow us to understand the relation among and between auditing effort required (characterized as the sample size, or the number of items to be audited in detail), the amount of misstatement that would be important or "material" to management, and the risk that the sample will (incorrectly) indicate the aggregate recorded balance is acceptable when, in fact, it is materially misstated. The relations are important because they help us understand the costs and benefits of additional auditing, how more auditing affects risk of material misstatement, and how materiality affects the required audit effort.

To illustrate the relations, let's reconsider Meena's Pearl Dock—the case from Chapter 1. In that problem, Meena was trying to decide whether to buy pearls from Nick, a seafaring man. Meena was naturally suspicious of Nick's trustworthiness, and we considered several ways in which she might obtain sufficient assurance that the bag of pearls did not contain more than 30 bad pearls out of the population of 1,000 in Nick's bag. Thus, 30 or 3 percent were the material magnitude and the material percentage, respectively, that were sufficiently important to Meena that, if the number exceeded 30 (or the rate exceeded 3 percent), then she did not wish to buy the pearls.

Suppose that Meena herself tests the pearls in Nick's bag by reaching in and selecting one pearl at random and tests the pearl. The pearl is tested as a "good" pearl. If Meena decides to accept the bag based on this favorable sample of size 1, then how much risk of incorrect acceptance would Meena face? Meena's risk can be expressed as the probability of observing one good pearl in a sample of one when the population (bag) contains 30 bad pearls. Mathematically, this probability is $1 - (30/1,000) = .97$. Thus, if Meena relies solely on the sample and accepts the sample as evidence that the bag is acceptable, she will have a 97 percent risk of incorrect acceptance if the bag actually contains exactly 30 bad pearls.

Meena then selects a second pearl for testing and it also tests as a "good" pearl. What is the probability of observing two good pearls in a sample of two if the bag contains 30 bad pearls? The answer (ignoring the fact that there are now only 999 pearls in the bag) is about $.97 \times .97$ or $.97^2$. The probability of two favorable pearls, each drawn independently from the population, is the product of their respective probabilities. The product is .94, or a slight reduction in risk, but risk is still very high. If Meena takes a third pearl and it is also a "good" pearl, then the risk drops to $.97^3$, or .91.

Suppose Meena continues to select pearls at random from the bag, and all that she selects test "good." One might ask what is the probability of selecting, say, 100 pearls at random and all testing out as good pearls if the bag actually contained 30 bad pearls. The answer is approximately $.97^{100}$. This probability is .048, or less than 5 percent risk, or 1 chance in 20, that Meena would be unlucky enough to test 100 good pearls in a sample of 100 when there are, in fact, 30 bad pearls in the bag of 1,000. Thus, if Meena is willing to accept 5 percent risk of incorrect acceptance of a "bad" bag, then selecting and observing the sample of 100 with no "bad" pearls would provide support for such a decision.

Now let's look at the formula and how it behaves. The numbers $.97^{100} = .048$ can be written in symbols as:

$$(1 - (M^*/N))^n = DR$$

where $M^* =$ a decision-relevant or material number of defective pearls for Meena, N is the population size, n is the number of pearls examined, and DR is the detection risk of obtaining a "pass" result from the sample (i.e., observing zero bad pearls) when the population contains M^* or more defects. What happens to the required audit effort (related to n) when M^* or DR is changed? For example, suppose Meena decides that she would not be satisfied if 15 or more of the pearls are bad, or decides she wishes to have a 2 percent detection risk of getting a "pass" result when the bag has 30 or more defective pearls?

Cutting M^* to 15 doubles the sample size required to 200, while reducing acceptable DR to 2 percent raises the required sample size to 130. Doing both raises it to 260. So audit effort required is rather sensitive to materiality and detection risk choices. Ideally, Meena would like to have a low risk of failing to detect any defects, but at some point the cost of defect detection is more than the expected losses due to accepting defects. Thus, a compromise or balance among M^*, DR, and n must be found.

Meena may have information about likely contents of the bag of pearls from sources other than sampling, and this information can reduce the sample size required. As we discussed in Chapter 1, Meena may have information about Nick's controls or about Nick's trustworthiness. For example, if Meena knows that Nick has been a reliable supplier in the past, then she may believe that the probability that this particular bag contains 30 or more defects is .20—without examining a single pearl. If so, then a much higher allowable risk of incorrect acceptance (DR) when relying on the sample outcome would be possible. To illustrate, if the allowable risk of incorrect acceptance from sampling is .25, then the required sample size is only 46. This shows that allowable risk from a test of details can be increased (and thus the amount of audit sampling effort reduced) to the extent that the auditor has more confidence from internal control or from analytical monitoring.

Which Items Should Be Audited?

Purely random selection of recorded items (every item has an equal chance of being audited) is useful for preventing misstatements. In particular, the auditor may select a few items at random to prevent errors or fraud from occurring in the future. The idea is that if employees know that some of their work may be "spot-tested," then they will be more careful in maintaining records day to day. Preventive sampling is much like the threat of a pop quiz as an incentive for students to be prepared for a given class. This is because a random selection cannot be predicted by the employee—it has no preset pattern.

For some purposes, random selection is not desirable because all recorded items in a population are not of equal importance to management or to the auditor. Some items are large in dollar value, and thus it is more important that they be recorded correctly. Other items are more risky per dollar (e.g., payroll entries are usually less risky than are entries for inventory valuation). Since all items are not of equal importance, auditors do not ordinarily follow a simple random sampling approach of selecting each recorded item with equal probability of selection.

In practice, auditors use a selection process that gives higher dollar value items or higher risk items increased probability of selection. For example, auditors may use generalized audit software to sort and reformat a population of expense items into groups based on recorded values. Historically, auditors have stratified a recorded population into items that are sufficiently large that auditors wish to take *no* chance of not including them in their audit, and those that are not important individually. Items with recorded values of greater than, say, $10,000, may be sampled 100 percent or selected with probability of 1.0. The remaining items are than sampled less than 100 percent. The auditor might then select, say, 10 percent of the items valued between $1,000 and $10,000 and only 1 percent of those less than $1,000.

When Should Sample Items Be Selected?

Figure 6–1 showed four possible points at which a sample of items could be selected for auditing—from real-world conditions, at input into the accounting process, during processing, or from the output databases. Each has advantages, but also limitations. The final balance (the recorded output file) is a natural point for selection if the auditor is concerned about overstatement of the recorded values. Therefore, the auditor might select at this point if he or she believes that the account in question is likely to be overstated. The auditor can find overstatements by auditing the recorded balance because the recorded balance *includes* the misstatement. That is, the overstated recorded value is equal to the true value plus the amount of overstatement ($Y_r = Y + M$, where M is the overstatement amount).

On the other hand, the recorded output file would be a poor place to sample for items *omitted* from the file. As an example, if the auditor is worried about omitted purchases, then sampling from the real-world population is a better sample selection point. Sampling inventory on hand and then searching for an accounting record of the liability for the purchase would be a way to search for unrecorded liabilities. Alternatively, the auditor might sample the recorded cash disbursements population for the following period, say, sample January's disbursements to see if they are paying invoices for goods received during the previous December. This sampling of January's disbursements for overstatement would detect an understatement of liabilities for the previous December. Thus, sampling from the real world or other records is an appropriate place to detect understatements due to omissions.

Selecting transactions at the input stage or during processing is effective in detecting omissions or deletions from processing. An item that was started into processing but for some reason was deleted would have a chance of appearing in a sample that was selected at the input stage or during processing, while there would be zero chance of including the deleted item in a sample selected from the final recorded values. Thus, we see that sampling strategy depends on the auditor's objective. One has to sample in the proper place and time to be effective. Embedding capabilities such as SCARF into application software applied day to day is often economical for audit sample selection.

What to Do with Sample Results?

When the auditor is using sample results as a test of the entire recorded balance, it will be necessary to project sample results to the population from which it was selected. For example, suppose the internal auditor selects 60 accounts from an accounts receivable file that contains 10,000 customer accounts and confirms their record balances by inquiry of customers. The sample results should be projected to the population of receivables. Let's assume that the auditor found two customer accounts with misstatements: one had a recorded value of $100, but an audited value of only $80, while the second had a recorded value of $40 and an audited value of $15. The total dollars of errors found are $45 in a sample of 60 items, or $.75 per account ($45/60). Projected misstatement for the total population that contains 10,000 customer accounts would be $.75 $\times$ 10,000 = $7,500. Thus, based on the sample, the most likely misstatement for the population is $7,500.

If allowable misstatement for total accounts receivable is, say, $25,000, then the point estimate of $7,500 is considerably below the allowable. However, because it is based on a sample, the point estimate could be higher or lower than the true total misstatement for the population. This is due to sample-to-sample variation and is called sampling error. The auditor must add to the point estimate an allowance for sample variation, or risk of sampling error. The allowance is comparable to the "reasonable range" in analytical monitoring. When using statistical sampling formulas, it is possible to quantify an upper limit on error that allows for sampling risk at a stated risk level. If statistical formulas are not used, then the auditor must quantify the sampling risk subjectively. Using either method, the allowance for sampling risk is larger if the sample size is small, and gets smaller as the sample size gets larger.[2]

If the sampled accounts were selected using a probability-proportionate-to-size (PPS) method (sometimes called "dollar unit sampling" in auditing, since each dollar of recorded value has an equal chance of being audited), then projection to the population is a projection of error *per dollar* rather than per account. If the sample above had been selected using dollar unit sampled, then the auditor would calculate misstatements per dollar unit sampled rather than per account sampling. So the misstatements in the sample would be $.20 = $20/100 and $.625 = $25/40. If the accounts receivable file had a total recorded value of $350,000 (or 350,000 dollar units), then projected misstatement would be

$$350,000 \times ((\$.20 + \$.625) / 60) = \$4,812.5$$

Thus, the projected misstatement for dollar unit selection is much lower than it is for physical unit sampling in this instance. Again, as was the case for physical unit sampling, statistical formulas have been developed by auditors to quantify the upper limit on misstatement or the reasonable range to allow for random variation due to sampling error.

AUDITING ACCOUNTING ALLOCATIONS AND ACCOUNTING ESTIMATES

Previous discussion in this chapter has focused on auditing of "hard numbers." Techniques for auditing accounting allocations and estimates are different since they tend to involve more judgments about the state of the world and allow for more flexible answers. In a sense, these judgments are less "auditable" or "verifiable" than are hard numbers, because people differ in their judgments.

For accounting allocations such as depreciation expense, the internal auditor can audit the recorded asset base in the same manner as the hard numbers are audited, but the allocation to time periods or to areas is more subjective. For example, a $100,000 asset may be depreciated using straight-line depreciation over a 10-year life and a salvage value of $10,000, which implies a $9,000-per-year depreciation charge. An internal auditor can easily recalculate the depreciation number, but is this number correct? It depends on the reasonableness of choices of useful life, the salvage value, and company policy about depreciation method.

Some companies prescribe policies for depreciation and little or no judgment is required by managers who apply the policies in the field. Absent such policies, however, managerial judgments enter into choices of method, useful life, and salvage value. The question for you as a top manager is, what should the internal auditor be instructed to do? Do you wish the internal auditor to "second-guess" choices of field management or apply a "reasonableness test," or something else? Most top managements follow a reasonableness test approach, and the auditor will consider depreciation in error only if it is clearly unreasonable in the circumstances. This means there is a certain degree of softness in the depreciation allocation since local managers have discretion to exercise accounting judgments.

Similarly, accounting estimates are "soft numbers" that have no single real-world referent. Accounting estimates such as the allowance for doubtful accounts, inventory valuation

---

2. If the auditor audits every item (a 100 percent audit, or $n = N$), then there is zero sampling error.

reserves, warranty liability estimates, and the related expenses are all estimates that require considerable judgment on the part of the preparer of financial information. These judgments can be biased upwardly or downwardly at the discretion of the party making the judgments. Again, the question is whose judgment do you wish to trust?

To illustrate, consider warranty liability, an important amount for many companies today. Warranty liability can be calculated in many ways, but the number realized in the real world will be known only in the distant future. The amount of warranty expense and accrued liability today is an estimate. The estimate could be shown to be clearly unreasonable if it were, say, $1,000,000 when most persons would agree that a reasonable amount might be between $5,000,000 and $10,000,000, but any number within that $5–10 million range could be considered reasonable even though the upper end of the range is 200 percent of the lower end. Thus, top management will be unable to get precision in accounting estimates of subordinate managers.

If local managers are allowed to use their judgments in determining the estimates, then they may bias the estimate to make their own performance look better. Yet, managers in the field are often in a better position than either the internal auditor or top management to know what the estimate should be. Without policy guidance, division managers may substantially change recorded divisional performance measures by padding their accounting estimates. The internal auditor may not be an effective tool in reducing this bias, unless he or she receives specific instructions from top management. Selecting trustworthy managers and maintaining a good control environment with communication of ethical values can mitigate the moral hazard faced by lower-level managers making such judgments.

This same problem of a range of accounting estimate values exists in reporting to outsiders, and we will address this issue in Chapters 8 and 9. The important thing to note for now is that the same vagueness of estimates is a problem in interpreting information within the company as well as reporting to outsiders.

INTEGRATING INFORMATION PROCESSING RISK AND MONITORING FAILURE RISK

We are now ready to consider the integration of risks of misstatement from internal control processes (IPR) and monitoring failure (MFR). Figure 6–5 diagrams the internal auditor's beliefs about possible accounting misstatement prior to application of monitoring procedures. This probability distribution is relatively flat and centered on a fairly large amount. That is, the internal auditor's prior beliefs are that fairly large misstatement is reasonably likely, and misstatement (overstatement of assets and earnings) greater than a decision-relevant or material amount (M^*) is reasonably high. There is also a fair level of risk of material understatement. These risk areas represent the premonitoring risk of material misstatement—the information processing risk (IPR) discussed in Chapter 4.

Monitoring procedures will identify areas of special risk, and analytical investigation and tests of details will isolate misstatements in recorded amounts. As misstatements are located, the internal auditor will direct accounting personnel to correct the recorded values. If no misstatements are found, then the auditor's confidence that total misstatement is small is increased, so that the distribution shifts to the left (toward zero) and the spread of the distribution is reduced. For those cases in which misstatements are found and corrections are recorded, the estimate of misstatement also goes toward zero with reduced spread. Either way, the final distribution is narrower and centered near zero, such that there

FIGURE 6–5

Aggregate Misstatement Distribution
(As Perceived by the Internal Auditor)

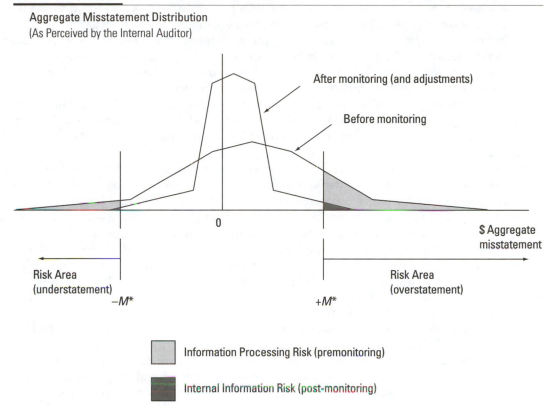

is little risk (little area under the curve beyond $\pm M^*$) that misstatement is material in either the positive or negative direction. The after-monitoring risk of material misstatement is the internal information risk (IIR = IPR × MFR), discussed in Chapter 4.

Thus, after all monitoring activities and any resulting adjustments in records and internal control process corrections, the internal auditor has a high level of assurance that any remaining misstatement is not material. With this level of assurance from the internal auditor, top management can rely on the accounting numbers and internal control processes to protect assets.

SUMMARY

Tests of details are the ultimate fallback procedure for determining whether potential for important misstatement identified as *possible* by study of internal control, or as *likely* by analytical monitoring is, in fact, a misstatement. Tests of details identify misstatements in particular recorded items and, thus, can lead to correction of individual items.

In addition to direct benefits of misstatement correction, detailed auditing procedures benefit management indirectly in at least two ways. One way is by identifying and correcting accounting *processes* that allowed errors to arise in the first place. A second is that by anticipating auditors' test of details, accounting workers will be more careful in their work and avoid the temptation to steal assets, thus preventing errors and fraud from taking place. This *anticipatory* effect of detailed monitoring can be quite important.

Improved computer controls and inclusion in computer programs of audit modules that operationalize auditing procedures such as a fictitious segment for test data and provision for a systems control audit review file add auditability to the software itself. Generalized audit software further enhances the auditor's ability to select transactions and perform automatically routine audit tasks. Computer assistance in both the processing software and generalized audit software allows the internal auditor to direct his or her efforts toward evaluating design of controls and using sophisticated analytical monitoring techniques.

Extensive (large sample) tests of details of final balances have become less necessary in recent years due to improved internal control and analytical monitoring procedures that are made possible by computer processing of accounting information and integrated databases. Tests of details remain important, however, as a tool for isolating actual misstatement and play a role in preventing small errors from becoming larger errors.

Combination of beliefs about the information processing risk (IPR) that material misstatement might occur in applying day-to-day internal controls with analytical monitoring and detailed monitoring (monitoring failure risk (MFR)) can lead to low internal information risk (IIR). As we saw in Chapter 4, internal information risk (IIR) is the product of IPR and MFR. The economical combination of these three sources of reliance (day-to-day processing controls, analytical monitoring, and detailed monitoring) is a design problem for top management. The stakes are high. Recorded accounting data containing material misstatement can lead to expensive decision errors. Also, poor accounting records increase the risk of loss of assets. Furthermore, as we will see in Chapters 11 and 12, public disclosure of materially misstated financial statements can lead to lawsuits and possible criminal actions against top management.

Top management should give careful consideration to the optimal mix of internal control and internal auditing as a means of informing top management about the firm. There is no economical alternative for obtaining reliable decision-making information and asset protection. A side benefit of better internal control and reliable monitoring by the internal auditor is that the cost of external audits used to inform others about the company can be obtained at lower costs (see Chapter 8).

CASE 6–1

JEFF'S DESIGNS, INC.

Jeff's Designs, Inc., produces automated window displays using neon light tubes. Jeff designs the basic products and then customizes them for particular customers. Receivables and inventory comprise the primary tangible assets of Jeff's, with receivables totaling $450,000 and inventory, $1,650,000.

Jeff's has outsourced internal auditing to Alex and Louis, CPAs. Outsourcing allows Jeff to concentrate on operations and rely on Alex and Louis's expertise for monitoring of day-to-day operations of internal control and quarterly financial statement audits. The quarterly audits are limited to sales and cost of sales, receivables, inventory, and accounts payable. The quarterly internal audits allow confirmation of conclusions about day-to-day operations of controls and provide more reliable quarterly information for Jeff's decision making.

The following paragraphs describe the condition of Jeff's accounts at the end of a recent quarter.

RECEIVABLES

Jeff's has 850 customer accounts, with five large accounts comprising $200,000. Lynn, the internal auditor assigned to Jeff's, believes an aggregate receivables error of $25,000 would be "intolerable." Lynn confirmed the five large accounts (finding and correcting a $20,000 overstatement) and decided to select a dollar unit sample from the 845 smaller accounts.

Lynn's audit manual shows that the required dollar unit sample size for the smaller accounts can range from 30 to 120, based on assessed information processing risk and other factors such as analytical monitoring results.

Lynn's control risk analysis indicates that Jeff's day-to-day control procedures are very reliable. Also, Lynn believes that, due to the high volume of customer transactions, it will be difficult to extend the quarter-end audit if the dollar unit sample indicates a problem with receivables. Lynn decided to confirm 30 dollar units from ending balances of the smaller accounts.

Required

Assume the role of Alex and Louis's outsourcing supervising partner and evaluate Lynn's choices and performance by considering the following:

- Does the sample size appear adequate?
- Assume that Lynn selects a sample of 30 dollar units and that the audit procedures indicate all sampled units are correct except for the following:
  1. A footing (addition) error in a customer's account with a book value of $500 has an audited value of only $400.

2. A customer claims that a $100 item was defective. The correspondence file indicates that Jeff's was notified a week prior to the confirmation date and a $50 credit was issued two weeks after the confirmation date.
3. One confirmation ($350 book value) was not returned, but Lynn has independently verified components of the account and believes it to be correct.
- Calculate *projected misstatement* for the population. What *receivables conclusion* should Lynn draw?

INVENTORY

A programming defect in Jeff's pricing program for inventory has caused a $19,000 average overstatement for each of seven items (in a population of 1,500 items). Also, Jeff's Designs' count teams omitted from ending inventory counts items costing $40,000 because they were located in a little-used room in the warehouse.

Required

Assume the role of Lynn's mentor and explain to her how

- She could use generalized audit software to detect the *overstatements*?
- A well-designed control system could prevent the *overstatements*?
- She might find the *understatement*?

CONCLUSIONS

Again, assume the role of the internal auditing outsourcing supervisor. What overall conclusions should be drawn about JDI's quarterly statements, underlying records, and day-to-day processing controls?

KEY WORDS

accounting uncertainties Possible losses (or gains) that at the financial statement date cannot be quantified as a point estimate, but have an effect on interpretation of financial statements because there are several outcomes that may arise in the future.

analysis   Analytical monitoring of accounting output, computer operating statistics, input relations, and reconciliation of related records (one of five basic auditing procedures).

application controls   Control activities programmed into software for particular computer applications such as sales, payroll, and disbursements.

completeness assertion   Financial statement assertions that all items that should be recorded under GAAP have been recorded (e.g., all liabilities and all expenses are recorded).

detailed control procedures   Control activities to prevent errors and fraud in individual items as they are being processed, and to detect and correct on a timely basis any error and fraud that does occur.

disclosure and presentation assertion   Assertions by management that financial statement numbers and informative disclosures are presented in a form that complies with GAAP.

equivalent reprocessing   Reprocessing of actual computer input data with software believed to be equivalent to that used to process the data and comparison of the two outputs.

examine   Visual or electronic inspection or reading of documents such as invoices, vouchers, and contracts, and tracing and comparing amounts within the accounting system.

existence (or occurrence) assertion   Assertion by management that recorded economic conditions, transactions, and events exist or occurred.

general controls   Computer controls over applications software design, testing, implementation, operation, change authorization, and data.

generalized audit software   Computer programs for auditors typically used to access computerized accounting data and to perform audit testing of the data.

hard numbers   Accounting numbers attached to physical and fiscal quantities of items that result from primary transactions or states such as revenues and cost of sales, and the related cash, accounts receivable, inventory, fixed asset additions, and accounts payable.

inquire (confirm)   Auditor questioning entity personnel about what they do or have done, and how they do it, and asking customers, suppliers, bankers, warehouse operators, and attorneys to confirm aspects of a recorded transaction.

observe   Auditor's visual examination of physical assets at a point in time, or business or accounting processes as they are taking place.

ownership (or obligations) assertion   Financial statement assertion that the entity owns, or has the right to use, the recorded asset, or has an obligation to pay or render service.

reprocess   Auditor reperformance of data processing, recalculation of allocations, or reperformance of internal control procedures.

Systems Control Audit Review File (SCARF)   Computer code embedded in an entity's general or application software that selects transactions during computer processing and records related master file amounts necessary for auditor reprocessing or detailed testing follow-up.

test data   Auditor-developed input data to test particular features of actual application software.

valuation assertion   Financial statement assertion by management that all items are valued according to GAAP.

7

CHAPTER

Informing Outsiders: Management Assertions and Independent Certification

- ◆ **H**ow can I lower my firm's costs of capital, production, selling, and distribution by sharing information?
- ◆ What must I do to have my assertions about my firm, its processes, and its prospects for the future certified as reliable?
- ◆ What characteristics should I seek in the external auditor who certifies my financial statement assertions?
- ◆ What will an external auditor ask of me as a member of top management?
- ◆ How can I minimize audit costs and increase audit value?

Previous chapters of this book have explored management's own development and use of relevant and reliable information to improve operation of the business, and to protect firm assets. This chapter begins a new section, entitled "Informing Others." In this chapter we explore how management can benefit from assembling and selectively sharing firm information relevant to those outside the business through certification of its declarations or *assertions* about the business. Chapters 8, 9, and 10 consider the external financial statement auditor's procedures, the financial statement auditor's report, and certification of nonfinancial statement assertions, respectively.

INFORMING OUTSIDERS THROUGH VOLUNTARY ASSERTIONS

Top management of a business entity is in a position to know a great deal about the firm. They have access to specific information about **past** financial transactions and relationships and **current** cash, receivables, inventories, and payables balances. And they know about **current nonfinancial** variables such as physical quantities underlying past operations and current position, order backlogs, and the status of business processes, research and development, product quality, contracts, supplier and customer characteristics, and employee qualifications and morale. Management also has information about **future prospects,** including research and development opportunities, markets, threats from competitors, threats from labor, and pending or threatened litigation as well as management's own plans for the firm's future.

Some outsiders are willing to compensate the firm for sharing relevant and reliable private information. Suppliers and workers will lower offering prices of their goods and services, customers will offer higher prices and longer term contracts, and debt capital suppliers will offer lower interest rates and more favorable lending terms. In a similar fashion, corporate directors, as representatives of stockholders, will offer more discretion and better compensation to top management if they are confident that they know about the actual state of the firm, the performance of management, and management's stewardship in safeguarding company assets.

Management's ability to benefit from information disclosure to outsiders is limited by three factors: (1) the need for a language or measurement rules to express information relevant to others, (2) management's interest in the subject matter of the information that they assert is properly displayed, and (3) laws, regulations, and competitive disadvantages regarding information disclosure. Independent assurance professionals such as CPAs in public practice can mitigate these limitations.

Independent Assurers and Certifiable Assertions

Measurement Criteria

An informational representation of real-world conditions requires the capability to objectively measure real-world conditions in a form that can be transmitted and displayed and then decoded by another party to form that party's mental image of real-world conditions. To have value for an outsider, the display must measure conditions in a way that the outsider finds relevant for making his or her decisions.

Figure 7–1 lists several types of assertions that management can make voluntarily to better inform outsiders. All of the items listed in Figure 7–1 reflect existing conditions that can be observed or assessed as of a point in time. For some there exist established criteria by which they can be measured. GAAP-based financial statements are one type of criterion and a certifiable set of assertions that can add value for management.

Financial statements based on GAAP as a language are not directly relevant to outsiders since they do not directly measure future prospects or the efficiency of past performance. However, they provide a standardized view of the firm that can become relevant when customized and compared to other information, including comparable information from other firms to "benchmark" and make judgments about relative past performance and inferences about prospects for the future.

Each of the assertions in Figure 7–1 can be certified by independent assurers. AICPA standards allow member CPAs to certify written assertions that are "capable of evaluation against reasonable criteria," and the assertion is "capable of reasonably consistent estimation or measurement using such criteria." Reasonable criteria can be established by a recognized body, such as the FASB or IASC, that define GAAP for public financial statements in the United States and internationally. Also, criteria can be stated as part of the assertion presentation itself if the criteria are sufficiently clear that a knowledgeable reader can understand them.

FIGURE 7–1

Examples of Firm-Specific Certifiable Assertions (and Related Measurement Criteria)

Financial:	
Statements of financial position, results of operations, and cash flows (historical financial statements)	(GAAP)
Market values and valuations of particular assets	(stated[1])
Forecasts of earnings, cash flows and resources based on management's plans and beliefs	(AICPA)
Process:	
Internal control quality	(COSO/CoCo/laws and regulations)
Business process quality	(ISO 9000)
Process efficiency (production, sales/distribution, administration)	(stated)
Nonfinancial:	
Customer satisfaction	(stated)
Employee satisfaction	(stated)
Supplier satisfaction	(stated)
Labor practices	(SA 8000)
Product quality	(stated)
Compliance with applicable laws and regulations	(laws and regulations)
Management's plans, strategies, and risk assessments	(GAAP/AICPA/ SEC/stated)

1. Measurement method (criteria) described and printed as part of the display of assertions.

Management as Information Source

Management as the source of information leads to concern by outside decision makers that management has been lazy or careless in applying measurement methods to prepare information. Also, management may have been unduly and unintentionally optimistic in making assumptions about asset lives, future prospects for collection of receivables, or the salability of inventory. Or management may have intentionally displayed false, misleading, or incomplete information that makes the firm and its prospects appear better than the actual real-world conditions (or worse than actual if management is negotiating a management buyout transaction). Because they know of management's interests in the information, outsiders will discount the information and raise the "price" at which they enter into a transaction with management.

Both accidental errors in preparation and unintentional or intentional bias in display of information provided by management can be mitigated by another party's investigation of the accuracy of the assertion. An independent party with a reputation for competence in measurement and trustworthiness in reporting his or her findings can improve an outsider's perception of information reliability by investigating the assertions, and attesting to the care and lack of bias in information display. An information assurer can add credibility by increasing the perceived reliability of management's information claims and assertions.

The added credibility can have value for management if the assurer's fee is less than the information user's resulting reduction in price protection discount.

Laws, Regulations, and Competitive Disadvantage of Disclosure

Top managements of public companies are required by law to disclose certain information about their firms, and the securities laws in some countries prohibit selective disclosure of some information (see Chapter 11). Beyond these constraints, disclosure of inside information that management possesses is neither prescribed or prohibited.

Assurance professionals can assist management in determining value-adding disclosures that comply with regulations such as SEC rules (see Chapter 11). They can also assure management that disclosures or data access by outsiders is limited. For example, in Chapter 1, Suzy's Discount Club provided George's Electronic Security, its supplier, access to Suzy's inventory and sales records for George's products by location, and benefited through George's lower prices and prompt service. But Suzy's did not want George's to have access to Suzy's cost, supply, and sales data for other product lines. Independent assurers can design, test, and evaluate internal control procedures that limit access to private information by unauthorized persons. These security evaluations require knowledge of information technology and internal controls, as well as human behavior and industrial espionage.

Some Examples of Value-Adding Certification of Management Assertions

Here are three examples of assertions and value-adding certification of compliance with measurement criteria: LJ Appliances' financial statements, Nike's labor practices, and US-Air's air safety procedures.

LJ Appliances' Earnings

Recall from Chapter 1 that Linda Jo, the owner of LJ Appliances, Inc., has high confidence in her internal controls and high confidence that her financial statements comply with GAAP in all important respects. Tim, the prospective buyer, believes that, in general, GAAP-based financial statements provide information relevant in determining an acceptable purchase price—Tim would be willing to pay eight times LJ's GAAP earnings if he were highly confident (say, 99 percent confident) that any earnings misstatement was less than an important (material) amount. But Tim discounts reported earnings that he believes might reasonably be overstated by $.50 or more. Tim deems $.50 to be too important to ignore, or material to his valuation calculation and buying decision.

LJ's (unaudited) earnings for the current year are $12, which would support a price of $96 (8 × $12). But, even though Linda Jo believes that the distribution of possible misstatement in these earnings is very peaked and centered on zero, Linda Jo also believes that Tim would assess possible misstatement as greater than zero, with a fairly wide spread or standard deviation. Tim's beliefs are based on his assessment of Linda Jo's possible carelessness in preparing information, bias in judgments, and self-interest in preparing the financial statements.

Figure 7–2 shows Linda Jo's beliefs about Tim's assessment of misstatement in unaudited earnings on the far right. The risk of material misstatement to Tim, the relative area

FIGURE 7-2

Linda Jo's Beliefs about Tim's Perceptions of Possible LJ Appliances, Inc., Earnings Overstatement

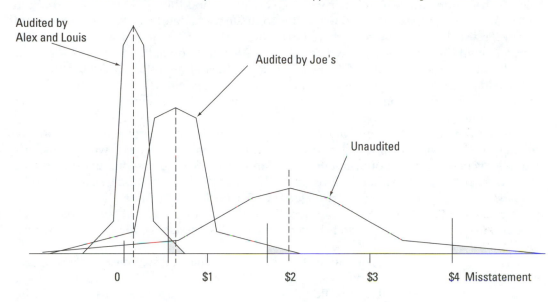

Note: Shaded areas represent negligible risk (say, 1 percent risk) to Tim for overstatement
of audited and unaudited earnings. For example, without an audit, Tim perceives
that there is negligible risk that earnings overstatement will equal or exceed $4.

to the right of $.50 under the "unaudited" distribution, is large, and there is nonnegligible (say, 1 percent) risk that the misstatement might be $4 or more. Linda Jo believes that without an independent audit, Tim would price protect himself by discounting unaudited earnings of $12 by $3.50 ($4.00 − $.50). This yields an offer price of $68 ($8.50 × 8), or a price-protection discount of $28 ($96 − $68).

Now let's consider the effects of an independent auditor's examination of Linda Jo's financial statement assertions. Two firms of auditors are available for hire by Linda Jo. Alex and Louis, CPAs, have an excellent reputation as competent and trustworthy accountants and auditors. The other audit firm, Joe's Auditing and Financial Services, LLC, has a well-regarded data processing service and tax advice business, but is not known for accounting and auditing expertise. Furthermore, Joe himself was a high school sweetheart of Linda Jo, and some members of the community believe that embers from that relationship remain.

Tim knows the reputations of Alex and Louis as well as Joe's, and Linda Jo knows that he will use his knowledge when evaluating the auditor's report on LJ Appliances' earnings. Linda Jo believes that Tim will discount reported earnings less if it is audited by Alex and Louis, other things equal, and Linda Jo expects audited earnings will be equal to $12 with either auditor because she believes that her pre-audit ("book") earnings are essentially error free.

The left and center distributions in Figure 7–2 show Linda Jo's beliefs about Tim's perceptions of possible misstatement after being audited by Alex and Louis or Joe's. The belief distributions differ as to their variance or spread and their closeness to zero. Both auditors *reduce imprecision* (related to auditor competence in detecting overstatement) and *relocate the distribution nearer zero* (related to auditor trustworthiness in correcting possible overstatement bias by Linda Jo). For an audit by Alex and Louis, the perceived misstatement distribution is centered on $.125, and the negligible risk area starts at $.50, while Joe's audit yields a distribution centered on $.625, with the negligible risk area starting at $1.75. The difference reflects the two auditors' reputations for professional competence and trustworthiness.

If Linda Jo correctly perceives Tim's beliefs, then the price protection discount for earnings of $12 after being audited by Alex and Louis is zero, because Tim would conclude that there is negligible risk of overstatement of more than $.50. Tim's offer price would be $96 ($12 × 8). On the other hand, earnings of $12 audited by Joe's would be discounted by $1.25 ($1.75 − $.50), and the offer price would be $86 ($10.75 × 8). Thus, the total discount for earnings of $12 will be $28 if unaudited, $10 if audited by Joe's, and zero if audited by Alex and Louis. Whether Linda Jo is better off with Alex and Louis, Joe's, or no audit depends on their audit fees.

This example illustrates the value of certification of financial statement assertions, but other information about LJ Appliances is also decision-relevant to Tim. He might raise the earnings multiple to 8.5 or 9 if he could be assured that Linda Jo's assertions about LJ's internal controls over transactions are credible. We will consider certification of internal controls and other possible value-adding assertions in Chapter 10. Management's statements about operating practices, in particular its treatment of workers, is an example of nonfinancial assertions whose credibility may be enhanced by independent certification and the need for relevant nonfinancial measurement criteria.

Nike's Labor Practices

In 1996, Nike, Inc., was embarrassed by allegations that it exploited, or was responsible for exploiting, workers in Asian shoe and clothing factories owned and operated by Nike's subcontractors. Thus, part of Nike's problems was due to the practices of firms it used to outsource production of shoes and clothing.

In an effort to clear its name, Nike engaged Andrew Young, former mayor of Atlanta, to investigate practices in 350 plants around the world. Young's report was only mildly critical of plant conditions. His conclusions were based in part on personal tours of plants and on-site interviews of workers through interpreters hired by Nike. While Mr. Young's integrity, trustworthiness, and record supporting human rights are well regarded, his professional qualifications as an investigator and his terms of employment argue against his certification being of value in assuring customers interested in human rights.

A confidential "investigation" report by Big Five accounting firm Ernst & Young (also hired by Nike) was less favorable to Nike and its labor practices in Vietnam. While the report stated that workers were paid at or above the legal minimum wage of $.19 per hour, it also revealed serious violations of labor and environmental laws.[1] Ernst & Young has professional

---

1. *Business Week,* December 1, 1997, p. 40.

qualifications as investigators and a worldwide reputation for objectivity and integrity. But measurement criteria relevant to outside decision makers were still problematic. For example, if $.19 per hour is viewed by Nike's customers as exploitative, then a certificate that minimum wages of $.19 are paid may not comfort those concerned with worker exploitation.

Criteria for fair and safe factories were established in early 1998 by the Council of Economic Priorities Accreditation Agency (CEPAA), an affiliate of a public service organization that monitors corporate social and environmental performances. The criteria, called Social Accountability 8000 (SA 8000), are similar to ISO standards for process quality. Human rights groups, labor, and several large CPA firms cooperated in developing the SA 8000 standard. According to the CEPAA, Avon Products plans to have its 17 factories SA 8000 certified, and Toys R Us will ask to see certificates from its 5,000 toy suppliers.[2]

CPA firms offer several advantages as certifiers of compliance with fair labor practices. CPAs have experience in examining processes to determine compliance with criteria, and they can acquire substantive knowledge of fair labor practices and SA 8000. However, in contrast to financial statement audits, for which CPAs as a group are a monopoly supplier, there are no restrictions on who can become a CEPAA-approved auditor. Thus, CPAs must compete on the basis of cost, effectiveness, and reputation for adding credibility to labor practice assertions.

USAir's Safety Procedures

Management's claims about product and process quality provide another example of value added by independent certification and the need for measurement criteria. After crashes of two of its jets in 1994, USAir, Inc., experienced a decline in passenger traffic as travelers were apprehensive about the safety of USAir's planes. A full-page advertisement in *The Wall Street Journal* (see Figure 7–3) announced two responses to assure travelers of the "validity and integrity" of USAir's operating standards. The airline hired a retired Air Force general to oversee safety practices, and it retained a respected airline consulting firm to conduct a "complete and independent audit of all our flight safety operations." One response provides day-to-day internal monitoring of safety, and the other outside point-in-time certification.

Four months after the *Wall Street Journal* advertisement, a report issued by the outside consulting firm (that received an audit certification fee of about $1 million) concluded that USAir was "in compliance with Federal Aviation Administration regulations and accepted airline operating . . . practices."[3] Thus, the audit confirmed compliance with legal minimums ("no laws or regulations are being broken") but gave no assurance of a higher level of safety such as "safer than the average airline."

The safety audit of USAir and the Nike report of Mr. Young are far from financial statement audits, but they exhibit essential aspects for certification to have value. Both Nike and USAir chose assurers who had unquestioned integrity, but only USAir insisted on professional competence. Also, both examinations required criteria by which real-world conditions could be evaluated, and while certificates of compliance with minimums set by laws and regulations may provide some comfort to others, independent certification of more relevant assertions requires development of objective measurement criteria.

---

2. "New Standards for Factory Audits Ready," *Public Accounting Report,* November 15, 1997, p. 4.

3. *The Wall Street Journal,* March 20, 1995, p. B-2.

FIGURE 7–3

USAir Advertisement

USAir

Dear Travelers:

On behalf of the 45,000 people of USAir, I would like to speak to you on a subject that is of vital importance to all of us—the safety of air travel in the United States.

We who are airline professionals know our system and our planes are safe. This is validated each and every day by federal regulators who fly with us, inspect our maintenance facilities and review our records.

To be certain that you share this conviction, I am announcing two important steps to assure you of the validity and integrity of our operating standards.

First, General Robert C. Oaks, a highly decorated command pilot and the former commander in chief of U.S. Air Forces in Europe, has agreed to oversee USAir's safety operations in the air and on the ground. He will report directly to me.

General Oaks is a proven dynamic leader of men and women who fly, maintain and support high-performance aircraft in a high-density, highly visible aviation environment. This is exactly the kind of environment in which we fly.

Second, I have asked one of the most respected groups of aviation experts in our country, PRC Aviation, to conduct a complete and independent audit of all of our flight safety operations.

Under the leadership of R. Dixon Speas, whose industry background in airline safety operations is unsurpassed, an expert team will go anywhere, ask any questions, and look at any records, manuals, bulletins or messages they think are germane to safety at USAir. There will be no limits to their inquiry.

In closing, let me say that we will not rest until each and every member of the flying public shares in the certainty of our commitment to be the safest of airlines.

Sincerely,

Seth E. Schofield
Chairman and Chief Executive Officer

Source: *The Wall Street Journal*, Wednesday, November 23, 1994, page A-7.

WHAT DO FINANCIAL STATEMENT AUDITS REQUIRE OF MANAGEMENT AND AUDITORS?

Other than paying the audit fee, what is required of a management that decides voluntarily to prepare and have audited GAAP-based financial statements? And what are the benefits, costs, and risks of serving as the external or independent auditor of financial statements?[4] The obligations of management and the auditor's stake in an audit can be assessed by examining a typical **engagement letter** that serves as a formal contract for the audit. The engagement letter is written by the auditor to the party hiring the auditor and the hiring party is asked to sign it. An engagement letter for the audit of LJ Appliances, Inc., is reproduced as Figure 7–4.

---

4. The auditor is in the business of selling professional services at a profit, even though there are professional aspects to auditing as well as a public responsibility, as we shall see in Chapters 11 and 12.

Alex and Louis, CPAs, L.L.P.

October 25, 1999

LJ Appliances, Inc.
Iowa City, IA

Dear Ms. Jo:

We will audit LJ Appliances, Inc.'s financial statements of the year ending December 31, 1999, for the purpose of expressing an opinion on the fairness with which they present, in all material respects, the financial position, results of operations, and cash flows in conformity with generally accepted accounting principles.

We will conduct our audit in accordance with generally accepted auditing standards. Those standards require that we obtain reasonable, rather than absolute, assurance that the financial statements are free of material misstatement, whether caused by error or fraud. Accordingly, a material misstatement may remain undetected. Also, an audit is not designed to detect error or fraud that is immaterial to the financial statements; therefore, the audit will not necessarily detect misstatements less than this materiality level that might exist due to error, fraudulent financial reporting, or misappropriation of assets. If, for any reason, we are unable to complete the audit or are unable to form or have not formed an opinion, we may decline to express an opinion or decline to issue a report as a result of the engagement.

While an audit includes obtaining an understanding of internal control sufficient to plan the audit and to determine the nature, timing, and extent of audit procedures to be performed, it is not designed to provide assurance on internal control or to identify reportable conditions. However, we are responsible for ensuring that the audit committee (or others with equivalent authority or responsibility) is aware of any reportable conditions that come to our attention.

The financial statements are the responsibility of LJ Appliances, Inc.'s management. Management is also responsible for (1) establishing and maintaining effective internal control over financial reports, (2) identifying and ensuring the company complies with the laws and regulations applicable to its activities, (3) making all financial records and

related information available to us, and (4) providing to us at the conclusion of the engagement a representation letter that, among other things, will confirm management's responsibility for the preparation of the financial statements in conformity with generally accepted accounting principles, the availability of financial records and related data, the completeness and availability of all minutes of the board and committee meetings, and, to the best of its knowledge and belief, the absence of fraud involving management or those employees who have a significant role in the entity's internal control.

Assistance to be supplied by your personnel, including the preparation of schedules and analyses of accounts, is described on a separate attachment. Timely completion of this work will facilitate the completion of our audit.

Our fees will be billed as work progresses and are based on the amount of time required at various levels of responsibility, plus actual out-of-pocket expenses. Invoices are payable upon presentation. We will notify you immediately of any circumstances we encounter that could significantly affect our initial estimate of total fees of $150,000.

If this letter correctly expresses your understanding, please sign the enclosed copy and return it to us.

We appreciate the opportunity to serve you.

Sincerely,

Partner's signature
Alex and Louis CPAs, L.L.P.

Accepted and agreed to:

_____
Client Representative's Signature

Title: _____

Date: _____

Auditor's Responsibilities

In the engagement letter, Alex and Louis, CPAs, agrees to conduct an audit of LJ's GAAP-based financial statements in accordance with generally accepted auditing standards (GAAS). By agreeing to apply GAAS, the firm of Alex and Louis becomes responsible for conducting an audit that is typical of the quality of audit that would be received from other reputable CPAs. The reference to LJ Appliances as both the client and the source of the financial statements indicates Alex and Louis's role as one of meeting LJ's needs for certification of its assertions, rather than as an investigator.

The engagement letter specifically limits Alex and Louis's responsibility to obtaining "reasonable but not absolute assurance" that the statements are free of material misstatement (reasonable assurance is the complement of "negligible risk"). It also reflects the limited scope of what an ordinary financial statement audit can do regarding detection of fraud or significant weaknesses in internal control. In particular, the letter states that the auditor cannot be expected to detect possible error, misappropriation of assets, or fraudulent reporting that is less than a "material" amount, and it warns that the audit will not provide even "reasonable assurance" that any serious weaknesses in internal control will be detected. Rather, the auditor will consider internal control only to the extent necessary to plan an adequate audit under GAAS. If LJ's management itself wants "reasonable assurance" about internal control, or if it wants to provide control assurance to Tim, then LJ's must separately contract to provide it. Alex and Louis, however, will inform LJ's management (but not outsiders such as Tim) about any important internal control weaknesses that the auditors might discover during the audit.

Some engagement letters discuss a special purpose for the audit or identify parties expected to rely on the audited financial statement (e.g., LJ's could identify the pending sale and even identify Tim as the prospective purchaser). Specificity as to purpose or user may extend the auditor's liability ex post, but also allows the auditor to plan for special risks ex ante. Engagement letters for audits of private companies in the United States sometimes state a limit or cap the auditor's liability to management, waive right to a jury trial, or prescribe use of arbitration or other nonlitigation dispute resolution mechanism in the event that there is a disagreement between the party signing the engagement letter (the client) and the audit firm.[5] These provisions may lower the auditor's expected total cost and, thus, produce lower-cost auditing for private company financial statements and for nonfinancial certifications for public companies (see Chapter 12).

Management's Responsibilities

The engagement letter outlines management's responsibilities, the most important of which is responsibility for the financial statement assertions themselves. Management must assume responsibility for financial statement presentation and assert in writing their belief that the statements comply with GAAP.

Management is responsible for internal control, compliance with applicable laws and regulations, and making all financial records and related information available to the auditor. Management also agrees to sign, at the end of the audit field work, a **representation**

---

5. Liability caps and alternative dispute resolution provisions are not applicable to financial statements of public companies and other entities regulated by the U.S. SEC.

letter that documents management's understanding of its primary responsibilities for the financial statements and its component assertions and management's beliefs about the absence of fraud. The representation letter is typically prepared by the auditor but printed on the client's stationery and signed by top management. Figure 7–5 is a representation letter from LJ's management.

By signing the representation letter, LJ's management acknowledges very specific responsibility for "hard" numbers (based on monetary units associated with individual transactions), allocations of transaction amounts across time or segments, and the judgments underlying accounting estimates and informative disclosures such as risks faced by the firm, as well as management's responsibilities to inform the auditor of certain matters. The representation letter is a legal document that can be used in defense of the auditor in lawsuits brought by top management itself that allege auditor negligence. It may also be used in defense of the auditor in lawsuits by third parties to show that management misrepresented to the auditor important facts, and thus may have impaired the audit of some amounts.

Having to sign a representation letter sometimes causes a corporate officer to reevaluate the justification for assertions or assumptions underlying the preparation of financial statements, or their completeness. For example, has management been overly optimistic in its estimates of reserves or allowances for incomplete transactions? Or it may bring to mind material current risks or threats for the near future that are not yet recorded in the accounting system but should be footnoted in the financial statements. Thus, requiring a signed representation letter can reduce the risk that the pre-audit financial statements are materially misstated due to management's carelessness or lack of diligence in their preparation.

As with USAir's operations data for an independent safety audit, management must make available to the auditor the basic accounting records supporting all financial statement amounts, including access to the databases and any underlying documents, whether electronic or paper. Also, management must allow access to company personnel for inquiries about operations, processes, and resulting balances, as well as access to certain nonoperating documents such as minutes of meetings of the board of directors and access to the entity's legal counsel. If access to these books and records, personnel, and legal counsel is denied, the auditor will react with a modified audit report that limits the assurance provided by the auditor (see Chapter 9). GAAP also requires that management acknowledge its responsibilities for the financial statements and internal control in its "management report" accompanying the financial statements and audit report.

Management Judgments (and Discretion)

In addition to maintenance of basic records of transactions and allocations, management also is responsible for making financial statement estimates and judgments. The subject matter of accounting estimates and judgments is the set of possible conditions that may occur (or become known) in the future.

Because of uncertainty, estimates and judgments are inherently imprecise. Historical financial statements, therefore, are inherently imprecise. Also, people differ in their knowledge, abilities, and incentives when making judgments. Frequently, given a defined set of facts and circumstances, reasonable persons will disagree on estimates and judgments and will draw different conclusions about what a GAAP-based presentation requires. These differences lead to honest differences of opinion, but also to bias of the results. Since no single answer can be established as correct, one must allow for such possible biases when interpreting estimates.

F I G U R E   7 – 5

Illustrative Representation Letter

LJ Appliances, Inc.

February 10, 2000
(Date of Auditor's Report)

To Alex and Louis, CPAs, LLP

We are providing this letter in connection with your audit of the financial statements of LJ Appliances, Inc., as of December 31, 1999, and for the year then ended for the purpose of expressing an opinion as to whether the financial statements present fairly, in all material respects, the financial position, results of operations, and cash flows of LJ Appliances, Inc., in conformity with generally accepted accounting principles. We confirm that we are responsible for the fair presentation in the financial statements of financial position, results of operations, and cash flows in conformity with generally accepted accounting principles.

Certain relations in this letter are described as being limited to matters that are material. Items are considered material, regardless of size, if they involve an omission or misstatement of accounting information that, in the list of surrounding circumstances, makes it probable that the judgment of a reasonable person relying on the information, would be changed or influenced by the omission or misstatement.

We confirm, to the best of our knowledge and belief, as of February 10, 2000, the following representations made to you during your audit.

1. The financial statements referred to above are fairly presented in conformity with generally accepted accounting principles.

2. We have made available to you all—
   a. Financial records and related data.
   b. Minutes of the meetings of stockholders, directors, and committees of directors, or summaries of actions of recent meetings for which minutes have not yet been prepared.

3. There have been no communications from regulatory agencies concerning noncompliance with or deficiencies in financial reporting practices.

4. There are no material transactions that have not been properly recorded in the accounting records underlying the financial statements.

5. There has been no—
   a. Fraud involving management or employees who have significant roles in internal control.
   b. Fraud involving others that could have a material effect on the financial statements.

6. The company has no plans or intentions that may materially affect the carrying value or classification of assets and liabilities.

7. The following have been properly recorded or disclosed in the financial statements:
   a. Related party transactions, including sales, purchases, loans, transfers, leasing arrangements, and guarantees, and amounts receivable from or payable to related parties.
   b. Guarantees, whether written or oral, under which the company is contingently liable.
   c. Significant estimates and material concentrations known to management that are required to be disclosed in accordance with the AICPA's Statement of Position 94-6, *Disclosure of Certain Significant Risks and Uncertainties.*

8. There are no—
   a. Violations or possible violations of laws or regulations whose effects should be considered for disclosure in the financial statements or as a basis for recording a loss contingency.
   b. Unasserted claims or assessments that our lawyer has advised us are probable of assertion and must be disclosed in accordance with Financial Accounting Standards Board (FASB) Statement No. 5, *Accounting for Contingencies.*
   c. Other liabilities or gain or loss contingencies that are required to be accrued or disclosed by Statement of Financial Accounting Standards No. 5.

9. The company has satisfactory title to all owned assets, and there are no liens or encumbrances on such assets nor has any asset been pledged.

10. The company has complied with all aspects of contractual agreements that would have a material effect on the financial statements in the event of noncompliance.

To the best of our knowledge and belief, no events have occurred subsequent to the balance-sheet date and through the date of this letter that would require adjustment to or disclosure in the aforementioned financial statements.

Jo Anne
Chief Financial Officer

Linda Jo
Chief Executive Officer

AstroGamas

As an example of management's discretion in exercising judgment in accounting, let's play the role of a member of top management of AstroGamas, Inc., in addressing an accounting issue that must be resolved to finalize financial statements for 1999.[6] Management's decision may have a significant impact on reported net income.

AstroGamas is a privately held developer and distributor of electronic games that has grown rapidly over the last three years. Its preliminary (unaudited) earnings before income taxes for 2000 are $3 million, on net revenues of $80 million with cost of sales of $36.7 million. For 1999, net income before taxes (NIBT), net revenues, and cost of sales were $5.8, $85, and $46 million, respectively.

Due to a recent downturn in the electronic game business, AstroGamas also faces uncertainty about future operations and about the valuation of ending inventory of its Trasher video game. Trasher is a mature game with slow sales for the last two months. As a result of high inventory quantities and slowing sales, the market value may be less than carrying cost and a writedown may be necessary.

AstroGamas's ending inventory includes $4 million in Trasher video games (500,000 units). Manufacturing cost is $8 per game, and normal wholesale prices range from $14 to $18. Retailers are reporting that Trasher is not selling, and management estimates that AstroGamas's customers are holding Trasher inventory of $7.5 to $12.5 million. While these sales were made with no right of return, some customers have threatened not to sell AstroGamas products unless some future concessions are made to compensate for keeping Trasher games.

There are several alternative actions available to management. Marketing personnel believe that the games could be sold domestically for between $5 and $8 per unit. This action might result in loss of up to $1.5 million [$3 per unit (cost of $8 minus market realization of $5) times 500,000 units]. Marketing also believes that the game might be sold offshore at a price of $8 to $9 per unit, thus avoiding a loss. Another alternative is to shrink-wrap Trasher with a new AstroGamas game, thus selling a package of two games—a new with an old—at a price greater than the total cost.

GAAP requires that inventory be accounted for in the 2000 financial statements at the lower of cost or market value. Does AstroGamas need to record an inventory write-down to reflect a lower market value? If so, how much?

Judgments of others who have considered the Trasher inventory issue differ about the appropriate income charge. Many say that $1.5 million of Trasher inventory should be written off, while others say that zero write-off is acceptable, and still others compromise at a $.75 million write-off. Judgments about market value (or net realizable value) today depend in part on how AstroGamas intends to use the games in the future. For example, if packaged with a new game and the pair is sold at a profit, then is there a loss on Trasher? Also, if Trasher is sold domestically at less than cost, it may anger existing retail customers who may demand that AstroGamas give concessions, or accept return of games that are still on retailers' shelves.

In addition to purely measurement considerations, management's judgment about Trasher may be influenced by another matter. The chief financial officer of AstroGamas is

---

6. AstroGamas is based on a case illustrating issues in accounting litigation prepared by the American Institute of CPAs for the National Law Institute.

in the process of renegotiating its long-term debt. Poor accounting earnings may adversely affect the outcome of the refinancing, and therefore management has an incentive to bias judgments to increase current earnings. Would (should) the pending debt renegotiations affect the judgments of AstroGamas management in making accounting estimates for their financial statements?

The AstroGamas situation shows some of the considerable discretion allowed management in preparing its financial statement assertions. Management is allowed to choose from many acceptable accounting methods, choose how to apply measurement criteria within a certain range, and even can choose the events that may determine the appropriate accounting under GAAP. For example, if AstroGamas's management shows plans to sell Trasher offshore, the auditor may conclude that market value exceeds cost.

What do you think an independent auditor with knowledge of these facts would conclude about acceptable accounting estimate magnitudes? Auditors with a reputation for objectivity would be expected to be more stringent in requiring adjustment or disclosure. But, other things equal, an investigating auditor hired by the bank renegotiating the debt might conclude that a $.75 million or $1.5 million charge to expense is appropriate, while a certifying auditor hired by AstroGamas's management might accept smaller, or even zero charges with, perhaps, footnote disclosure of uncertainty about future returned sales or allowances. Also, even an auditor hired by AstroGamas will tend to be stringent in requiring write-downs if the auditor believes that the company may fail in the future. Finally, because of the discretion allowed management, auditors are concerned with the integrity of management in exercising judgments about accounting (see "The Engagement Risk Approach," below).

Unfortunately, the future of the company depends on current financing, which in turn depends on the accounting chosen by AstroGamas's management and certified by their external auditor. Judgments are involved, and judgments depend on the facts of the situation, GAAP, the party making the judgment, and the interests and incentives of the parties involved. All of these factors should be considered when interpreting accounting estimates, disclosures, and the auditor's report (see Chapter 9).

WHAT DOES THE FINANCIAL STATEMENT AUDITOR DO?

Many outside-the-firm readers of audited financial statements believe that the auditor's report covers more than it does. While audited financial statements include management's assertions about a broad range of real-world conditions, there are omissions from the assertions. Also, while the auditor's certification is valuable, it has limits. Thus, it is important to know what the auditor certifies and what is not certified.

Auditors' Reports on Financial Statements

Annual reports by business entities are an important means of communicating information to stockholders, creditors, and other outsiders. The annual report typically contains an informal description of the company, its products, and operations. It also includes more formal financial highlights, management's report, and financial statements. Only the financial statements (including footnotes) are audited by the external auditor. The financial highlights and management report are read by the external auditor, who has a duty to note any material inconsistencies with the financial statements, but the management report and the financial highlights themselves are not audited.

An auditor's report on financial statements is based on the auditor's risk assessments and auditing procedures and expresses the auditor's opinion about compliance of the financial statements with GAAP measurement criteria. A standard audit report expresses the auditor's belief that the audit provides reasonable assurance (complement of "low risk") that the financial statement numbers are not misstated by a material amount.

Figure 7–6 presents a basic, generic "standard report" of the external auditor for LJ Appliances, Inc. For 1999, LJ's is a company with no material departures from GAAP criteria as to methods or misstatements, no accounting changes, no unusual uncertainties about its ability to continue as a going concern, and no items noted by the auditor for "emphasis." This report form is the most favorable audit report that can be issued. The report wording is standardized across auditors applying U.S. or international GAAS, and a report with any additional words indicates some reason for user concern (see Chapter 9). It is instructive to note the claims made in the audit report and to note claims that are not made.

The first (responsibilities) paragraph describes overall financial statement responsibilities of management and the auditor. The second (scope) paragraph describes what the

FIGURE 7–6

Auditor's Standard Report

Report of Independent Accountants

To LJ Appliances, Inc.

(*responsibilities*)
We have audited the accompanying balance sheet of LJ Appliances, Inc., as of December 31, 1999, and the related statements of income, retained earnings, and cash flows for the year then ended. These financial statements are the responsibility of the Company's management. Our responsibility is to express an opinion on these financial statements based on our audits.

(*scope*)
We conducted our audit in accordance with generally accepted auditing standards. Those standards require that we plan and perform the audit to obtain reasonable assurance about whether the financial statements are free of material misstatement. An audit includes examining, on a test basis, evidence supporting the amounts and disclosures in the financial statements. An audit also includes assessing the accounting principles used and significant estimates made by management, as well as evaluating the overall financial statement presentation. We believe that our audit provides a reasonable basis for our opinion.

(*opinion*)
In our opinion, the financial statements referred to above present fairly, in all material respects, the financial position of LJ Appliances, Inc., as of December 31, 1999, and the results of its operations and its cash flows for the year then ended in conformity with generally accepted accounting principles.

Alex and Louis, CPAs
Iowa City, Iowa
February 10, 2000

auditor has done by applying GAAS and the basis for "reasonable assurance" that the financial statements are free of "material misstatement." The audit also includes assessing the accounting principles used and significant estimates made by management. Thus, management's choice(s) of accounting methods are evaluated, and use of unacceptable accounting methods would be noted. Finally, the third (opinion) paragraph expresses the auditor's "unqualified" opinion that the financial statements conform to stated measurement and disclosure criteria. The criteria could be GAAP-based on U.S. or other national standards, international accounting standards, or another comprehensive basis of accounting, such as those of a regulatory body.

Not stated, but implicit in the auditor's standard report, is a presumption that informative disclosures in the financial statements are reasonably adequate. Also, under U.S. GAAP and GAAS, there is no mention of continued viability of LJ's by either management or the auditor. However, the omission of any reference to viability implies that the auditor believes that the firm will remain viable for at least the year following the financial statements' date. Finally, there is no mention of access to records, personnel, and data that the auditor considered necessary to conduct the audit. However, if access were restricted, the auditor's report would be modified as to scope and conclusions. So, as with access to safety operations granted by USAir, access to records, personnel, and data by independent auditors is unrestricted. Chapter 9 will interpret auditors' reports that are modified for uncertainty, unacceptable accounting, or an incomplete audit.

Note that the auditor's opinion relates only to the financial statement presentation and its compliance with GAAP criteria.[7] There is no mention of the relative efficiency of operations of the company or whether its strategies are adequate to maintain profit levels in the future. Rather, the only things "audited" are the numbers as measured by GAAP and informative disclosures necessary under GAAP. Thus, the amount of information that can be communicated by the audit report is limited.

Materiality and Reasonable Assurance

In a previous example, Tim, the prospective buyer of LJ Appliances, discounted the price offered if he believed that there was nonnegligible risk that earnings overstatement was $.50 or more. Because of Tim's beliefs, Linda Jo benefited by providing reasonable assurance that earnings were not overstated by more than $.50, but she would have no further gain for lower perceived overstatement. Thus, there are limits on the value of precision of LJ's audited financial statements.

For LJ's, the materiality of possible earnings overstatement and the risk that overstatement equals or exceeds materiality were based on what was relevant to Tim. Audits could be designed to meet the intended user's individual preferences. But this is impractical when there are multiple potential users with multiple objectives and preferences. As a result, the financial community comprised of financial statement preparers, users, auditors, and regulators have developed over time some rules of practice that provide rough quantification of amounts deemed material and risk levels deemed "negligible."

---

7. Additional disclosure rules apply to managements of public companies that are registered with the Securities and Exchange Commission. These requirements will be discussed in Chapter 11.

Materiality Defined

According to U.S. GAAS, financial statements are materially misstated "when they contain errors or irregularities whose effect, individually or in the aggregate, is important enough to cause them not to be presented in conformity with GAAP." Thus, guidelines for materiality in auditing standards are left to accounting authorities.

Accounting standards-setting bodies describe materiality in terms of the effect of a disclosure or correction on decisions of a generic financial statement user. In Statement of Financial Accounting Concepts No. 2, the FASB states that an omission or misstatement is material if

> in the light of surrounding circumstances, the magnitude of the item is such that it is probable that the judgment of a reasonable person relying on the report would have been changed or influenced by the inclusion or correction of the item [FASB, 1980, ¶ 132].

The SEC's Regulation S-X (Rule 1-02) is similar and focuses on matters "about which an average prudent investor ought reasonably to be informed." Any possible omission or error could be material to some decision maker in some circumstance. However, the definitions set limits based on "a reasonable person" in the FASB definition and the "average" prudent investor in the securities acts.

Quantitative limits on the misstatement magnitude deemed "material" are necessary for two reasons. First, omission or misstatement of extremely small magnitudes are inconsequential to external users of financial information for practical decision-making purposes—there is a limit to what has value for purposes of *disclosure*. Second, items that are to be considered for possible correction or disclosure must first be *discovered* by the auditor. As we saw in Chapter 6, the cost to discover possible errors or omissions increases rapidly as the size of the possible omission or error to be detected becomes small. Thus, the discovery aspect of materiality is important in limiting audit cost.

There are, of course, qualitative aspects to materiality as well as quantitative aspects. For example, a reasonable person's judgment about implications of an earnings misstatement of a given magnitude likely depends on "surrounding circumstances." Quantitatively immaterial accidental error or misappropriation fraud by management's employees may imply poor internal control, but intentional misrepresentation misstatement by management is likely to have greater implications.

Intentional misrepresentations reflect upon management's integrity and may lead to expected future legal actions against the company and penalties due to violation of the securities acts. Similarly, implications of an accounting error depend on its nature. An ending inventory count error's effect on cost of sales for this period will reverse itself during the next period as will a sales cutoff error. But failure to record current period purchases or underproviding for warranty costs will not cancel out during the next period.

Thus, disclosure of items that are quantitatively "immaterial" may be qualitatively "material." Auditing standards recognize the qualitative importance of disclosing some errors known to the auditor that may not be important quantitatively. However, auditing standards also warn that audits cannot be designed economically to *discover* small misstatements.[8]

---

8. SAS No. 47 (¶ 13) states, "Although the auditor should be alert for errors that could be qualitatively material, it ordinarily is not practical to design procedures to detect them."

Materiality in Practice

In practice, materiality standards are determined by what is "generally accepted." Several surveys have asked auditors, preparers, and users to assess the monetary amount deemed material in relation to a financial statement base such as revenues, total assets, or earnings. Most reacted in terms of earnings (net income before taxes (NIBT)), saying that an amount less than 5 percent of current earnings is immaterial while an amount greater than 10 percent of earnings is clearly material. As a first approximation then, 5 to 10 percent of NIBT is reasonable.[9]

While survey respondents typically think in terms of materiality as a percent of earnings, analyses of auditors' working papers indicate that auditors' documented judgments about materiality are more closely correlated with total revenues and with total assets than with NIBT. Furthermore, these analyses indicate that materiality as a percentage of total revenue, total assets, or NIBT declines as the size of the company increases. Since total revenues and total assets are close in magnitude for many companies, the materiality percentages are about the same. For growth companies and financial institutions, total assets are a more common base for assessing materiality.

For small companies (revenues of less than $100 million), materiality judgments typically range from about .75 percent of revenues or assets to about 1.5 percent, while for large companies (revenues of $1 billion or more), the range is from .3 percent to about .75 percent. These differences due to company size reflect several factors, including the auditor's reluctance to waive possible adjustments that are very large in dollar amount even though they are a small percent of total revenues, and the fact that precise audits for very small companies would be prohibitively expensive.

Total revenues or total assets as the base for materiality have three advantages over NIBT. First, total revenues and assets are less variable over time leading to a more stable scope of auditing.[10] Second, total revenues and assets differ less across companies that use different expense accounting methods. Third, total revenues are less subject to manipulation by management. For all three reasons, we will typically refer to materiality as a function of revenues or assets using the ranges discussed above. These considerations will be important in considering what level of disclosure one can expect to see in financial statements and will drive the scope or intensity of auditing required to discover errors of that magnitude.

Applying these quantitative guidelines to AstroGamas yields the following estimates of materiality. Since AstroGamas's revenues are less than $100 million, but near the upper end of the small-firm range, materiality of .8 percent of revenues is reasonable, or $640,000. Using 10 percent of current NIBT (unaudited) yields materiality of $300,000. However, this number would probably be adjusted by the auditor because the 1999 rate of earnings on

---

9. Note that 5–10 percent of earnings is much larger than what most managements would deem "non-negligible" or "important" for internal decision-making and control purposes. For example, employee theft of assets comprising 5 percent of earnings could be catastrophic. Thus, the precision required for reporting to outsiders is much looser than the precision required for internal control systems, and typically does not constrain management.

10. Since total revenues and assets are always positive, their use avoids the "near zero" problem of a fixed percentage rule on a very small base. For example, if NIBT for a firm with total assets of $100 million is, say, $1,000, then materiality would not reasonably be $100 or $50 since audit cost would be excessive. Also, if the same firm had a loss of $1,000, then a negative material amount is uninterpretable.

sales (3.75 percent) seems low for a video game company and is considerably lower than the rate for AstroGamas for 1998 (6.82 percent). Basing materiality on 10 percent of last year's earnings as more representative or "normal" yields a materiality estimate of $580,000. Thus, after adjustment, these two guidelines yield similar estimates of materiality. While results this close will not always be obtained, auditors often calculate materiality on several bases (e.g., assets, revenues, gross profit, and NIBT) before deciding on materiality for planning the audit to discover aggregate errors of a given size.

Auditors are reasonably consistent across firms in assessing materiality for both discovery and disclosure purposes. On the value-added side, an auditor who sets materiality too high would not detect important misstatements and the value of that auditor's report would decline. Materiality set too low would lead to excessive audit cost and price the auditor out of the market. Also, since an audit may be challenged in court ex post, auditors must be able to defend their decisions about materiality, audit risk, and auditing procedures applied as providing a reasonable basis for their conclusions. This means that other auditors must agree approximately with judgments made.

Reasonable Assurance in Practice

As with materiality, reasonable assurance doesn't have a mathematical expression. But its complement, "audit risk" (i.e., reasonable assurance = 1 − audit risk) can be assessed indirectly by data that the AICPA's Public Oversight Board maintains on alleged malpractice by its CPA members. These data suggest that about .5 percent of financial statements audited by auditors following GAAS may be materially misstated.

Taken together, these approximations of materiality and audit risk suggest that, given a standard audit report and a GAAS audit, the risk of misstatements exceeding about 1 percent of revenues of a small firm (or .5 percent of a large firm's revenues), is less than .01.

WHAT'S IN IT FOR THE AUDITOR?

What does an audit firm get from being the financial statement auditor for a client? One benefit is a substantial (and continuing) annual audit fee. Auditors also establish contact with CEOs, CFOs, and prominent directors of major corporations, and the nature of GAAP-based financial statements exposes auditors to the entire range of opportunities and risks faced by a business as well as its performance. This broad base of experience allows auditors to assess clients' needs for other assurance and consulting services that the audit firm might provide. Services range from advice on strategy, merger and acquisition transactions, and foreign investments, to more applied consulting about internal control design, reporting and design of performance measurement and risk assessment systems within the organization, and strategic and technical tax services.

The audit also exposes the auditor to substantial liability to management as well as to third-party users of financial statements. For privately held companies, this liability may be limited by contract between the auditor, the client, and specified third-party users. However, for companies issuing securities to the general public (public companies), the securities acts prohibit contracts that limit the auditor's liability to investors. The auditor also has some responsibilities for being what has been called a "public watchdog" of a public company (see Chapter 12). There is potential conflict between the auditor's role in "adding value" for management by certifying that its financial statement assertions comply with

GAAP and providing advice on information relevance and internal control with the auditor's responsibilities to inform outsiders of possibly inappropriate or illegal actions of management.

Because of these potentially conflicting responsibilities as auditor and information advisor, CPA/CA firms face a problem of deciding what should be their level of association with and scope of services for a client. Large fees from providing nonaudit services may cause third-party users of a company's financial statements to mistrust or devalue the CPA firm's work (and reputation) as its independent auditor. Thus, auditors and their clients must decide the optimal mix of auditor association with a particular client.

Regulators also have an interest in the relation of audit firms to their clients across the economy. This is because regulators, such as members of the SEC, are charged with protecting investors. Auditors who are not independent (for example, auditors who have an interest in financial statements other than their quality) may not protect investor's interests by assuring compliance with GAAP. Laws and private regulations governing auditor competence, as well as laws, regulations, and ethical rules regarding independence, will be explored in Chapter 12.

THE ENGAGEMENT RISK APPROACH

In reaction to legal liability to third parties, especially liability under the securities acts, Big Five CPA firms in the United States have each developed a risk-management approach called the **engagement risk model**.[11] Engagement risk is the overall risk of loss to a CPA firm from being associated with a business as its financial statement auditor. Loss to the CPA firm can be financial loss due to payment of damage claims to clients and financial statement users and legal defense costs, as well as loss of reputation from being sued or from being associated with unscrupulous (or defunct) clients.

The engagement risk model has three components: **audit risk** (AuR), **client business risk** (CBR), and **auditor's business risk** (ABR). AuR is the risk that the auditor will unknowingly certify that financial statements are free of material misstatement when, in fact, they are materially misstated; CBR is the risk of loss to the auditor because the auditor's client experiences declining performance (or even ceases to be a going concern) in the future; and ABR is the risk that the auditor will suffer damage to his or her reputation or pocketbook because of association with the client.

The three risks are partially overlapping, as diagrammed in Figure 7–7. Auditing procedures are directed toward AuR and limit it to a "negligible" level, and auditing procedures reduce CBR and ABR to some extent. For example, area 1 would include risk of accidental misstatement of hard numbers such as cash balances, cash wages paid, and accrued short-term liabilities. Area 2 would include future-oriented aspects of financial statements such as allowances for receivables and inventory valuation. Area 2 would also include the likelihood that the client may fail within the next year (cease to be a going concern). Both of these elements of area 2 reflect risk of a future decline in performance of the client. Similarly, area 4 reflects illegal client acts, such as violation of the U.S. Environmen-

---

11. See H. Huss and F. Jacobs, "Risk Containment: Exploring Auditor Decisions in the Engagement Process," *Auditing: A Journal of Practice and Theory*, Fall 1991, pp. 16–32; and AICPA, "Audit Risk Alert—1992" (1992).

FIGURE 7-7

The Auditor's Engagement Risk from Being Associated with an Entity as Its Financial Statement Auditor

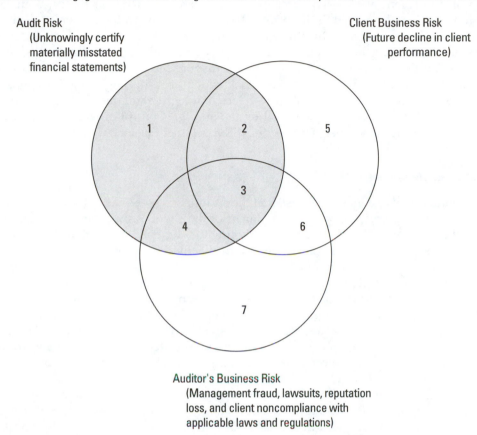

Audit Risk
(Unknowingly certify
materially misstated
financial statements)

Client Business Risk
(Future decline in client
performance)

Auditor's Business Risk
(Management fraud, lawsuits, reputation
loss, and client noncompliance with
applicable laws and regulations)

Note: GAAS and GAAP measurement and disclosure criteria apply to shaded areas 1, 2, 3, and 4 (see Chapters 8 and 9).

tal Protection Act, that may have a material effect on financial statements, and area 3 might include management fraud that materially misstates the current financial statements, affects future viability of the business, and violates the law.

But, as Figure 7–7 shows, some portions of CBR and ABR are not covered by GAAP and GAAS—they would exist even if the audited financial statements fully comply with GAAP and GAAS. Examples of risks in areas 5, 6, and 7 include risk of the auditor's financial or reputation loss due to significant decline in the client's future profitability even though the client remains viable (area 5), association with management engaged in unethical or illegal activities even though the acts don't materially misstate the financial statements (area 7), and declining client profitability due to management's or employees' immaterial unethical or illegal acts (area 6). Both CBR and ABR are due, in part, to the litigation environment in the United States and other common-law countries in the last quarter of the 20th century. They have become important since they may effectively be inseparable from financial statement defects or a defective audit.

The auditor faces heightened CBR when a company has declining profits or goes out of business soon after receiving an unqualified audit opinion. Such declines may cast doubts on the recent audit—shouldn't the auditor have known that the company was about to falter or fail, and didn't the auditor have a duty to warn the reader of this imminent failure? The auditor faces heightened ABR from mere association with an unscrupulous management, or when disputes between parties are likely (e.g., disgruntled stockholders attempting to take over the business or dispute the prudence or stewardship of management). CBR and ABR can interact—stockholders are especially vengeful against auditors when a company fails suddenly due to lack of integrity and outright fraudulent acts of management that were not discovered by the auditor. Control of engagement risk reflects all three of these risks beginning with ABR assessment (see Figure 7–8).

Auditor's Business Risk

The first component of engagement risk that the auditor assesses is ABR, the auditor's business risk of being associated with management of the client. As we have seen, top management has a great deal of discretion in designing the company and establishing the control environment and risk assessment and control activities, as well as information and communication and monitoring of business activities. All of these require judgment on the part of management, and judgments can lead to biases that may disguise or misrepresent real-world conditions. Also, management has discretion in replying to auditors' inquiries about business transactions, judgments, and strategies implicit in preparation of financial statements and the overall operation of a business. Finally, management may itself misappropriate assets or fraudulently misrepresent financial statements. Management fraud is often extremely difficult to detect, making the auditor especially vulnerable to unscrupulous managements.

As a primary line of defense against management fraud, auditors avoid ABR at the source (see Chapter 3). The auditor assesses management integrity as well as the overall business context in which the audit is to take place. This assessment is typically conducted before the client is accepted for an audit and reassessed at the beginning of an audit for a continuing client. Big Five audit firms sometimes hire private investigators to prepare background dossiers on top management and other parties before accepting an audit engagement. The assessment of management integrity continues throughout the audit as confirming (and especially disconfirming) evidence is discovered, and sometimes leads to resignation by the auditor. For example, in 1995, Coopers and Lybrand (merged to form PricewaterhouseCoopers in 1998) declined to be the auditor for a number of risky clients that would have brought in aggregate annual audit fees in excess of $22 million.[12] Also, Arthur Andersen resigned as auditor of Lloyd's of London due to its assessment of an unfavorable risk/reward relation for the insurance syndicate.[13]

---

12. E. MacDonald, "More Accounting Firms Are Dumping Risky Clients," *The Wall Street Journal,* June 30, 1997, p. A-2.
13. *Public Accounting Report,* November 15, 1997, p. 3.

F I G U R E   7 – 8

Engagement Risk Approach to Financial Statement Audits

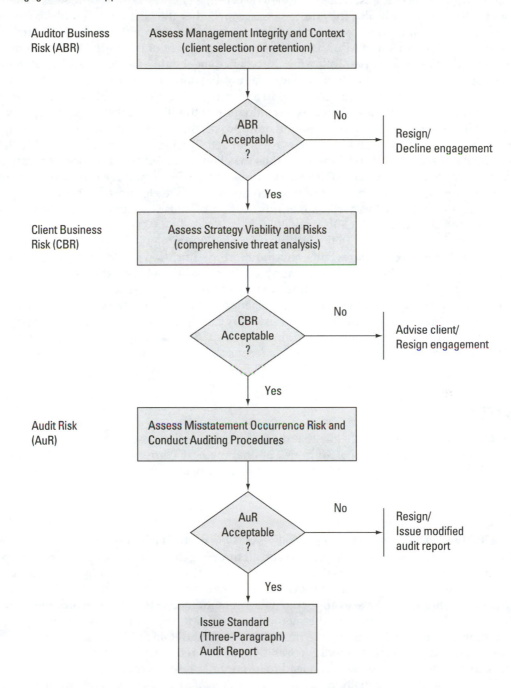

Client Business Risk

After deciding that ABR is sufficiently low to accept the client, the auditor assesses client business risk (CBR). Basically, the auditor assesses whether the client will be able to maintain its current position (i.e., assets, growth, profitability, and reputation) in the future. As we will see in Chapter 9, GAAP and GAAS require assessment of the ability of a client firm to remain in business for a year following the balance sheet date as a part of AuR, but there is no requirement that the auditor consider failure beyond one year or future profit declines. Thus, these latter risks are included in assessment of CBR and ABR, but not AuR.

The first step in CBR assessment is an evaluation of the client's business strategy. Does the client have a strategy that will maintain or improve its position into the future? Can the client continue to acquire goods and services and sell them at a reasonable profit? Is the company competitive within its industry (has the client adopted best practices, or does it have poor processes or practices)? This latter question has become increasingly important as information technology and worldwide competition have decreased reaction time to meet competitive threats, as well as the introduction of substitute products. Clients that aren't competitive have high CBR.

The auditor is interested in the viability of a client's strategy for several reasons. First, the auditor wishes to consider whether audit report modification is necessary. Second, the auditor knows that if the client has not adopted "best practices," then the client company may fail in the future and will not continue to provide an income stream to the auditor. The auditor may want to resign the audit engagement or advise the client on adoption of better practices as a means of adding to assurance service and consulting income. In addition to strategy viability assessment, the auditor assessing CBR also conducts a comprehensive business risk assessment of the client, considering all potential threats to continued profitability of the client.

Audit Risk

If ABR and CBR are sufficiently low that the audit firm decides to serve as auditor, the final step is assessment and control of audit risk of unknowingly certifying materially misstated financial statements. Auditing procedures to limit audit risk are the subject of Chapter 8.

Integration

AuR, CBR, and ABR are related in several ways. One particularly important interrelation is the effect that management integrity has on all three. As discussed throughout this chapter, management has great discretion in financial reporting as well as in operating an entity. Management can choose which transactions to enter, measurement methods to account for the transactions, and how to apply the measurement methods both as to judgments required and whether to misapply the methods chosen. Management's discretion exposes the auditor to risk of association since financial statement display of choices may be biased to portray management in a more favorable light. Discretionary choices in combination with even modest misstatements can lead to important biases in results.

Management's propensity to commit fraud is related to the underlying integrity of management and conditioned by its ability and motivation or incentive to do so. Prior in-

FIGURE 7-9

Five Common Conditions Accompanying Management Misrepresentation Fraud

1. Overstatement of revenues (including early recognition of revenues).
2. Understatement of expenses (including delayed recognition of expenses, nonrecognition of obsolescence or impairment, and accounting estimate manipulation).
3. Accounting method changes that increase current year earnings and net assets.
4. Declining business prospects for the industry (providing need for accounting manipulation to maintain earnings performance and trends).
5. Management compensation based on accounting performance measures (providing personal financial incentive for accounting manipulation and misstatement).

stances of management fraud show a high incidence of the five factors listed in Figure 7–9. The first two factors include choice of unacceptable accounting methods, but also result from accounting judgments in applying accounting estimates that are beyond a reasonable range. These choices and judgments are often jointly made. For example, for firms experiencing declines in actual performance, managements often recognize revenue earlier than is typical and delay expense recognition. Also, the same managements often make accounting method changes that increase currently reported net earnings and assets.

These judgment biases and discretionary choices are not violations of GAAP but are often accompanied by misapplication of GAAP that overstate revenues and understate expenses. They are also typically accompanied by motivational factors such as management compensation based on accounting performance and declining prospects within the client's industry.

Since the audit firm is associated with client management as well as its financial statements, the auditor should be aware of two things. First, indications of "pushing the envelope" on reasonable judgments in making accounting choices may reflect lack of integrity and the need to extend the audit to reduce heightened risk of fraud. Second, even if AuR can be limited to an acceptably low level, client business risk and auditor's business risk may make association with a client uneconomical or yield a poor risk/reward ratio.

SUMMARY

Top management has a great deal of information about a company, its processes, resources, and prospects for the future. Selectively sharing this information with outsiders can benefit management and its stockholders. Management's ability to make credible value-adding assertions about its beliefs about the company requires a language to express their beliefs and overcoming management's lack of credibility due to self-interest in the preparation and display of information.

Financial statements prepared using GAAP and audited by a reputable auditor applying GAAS can help resolve the information relevance and credibility problems for financial information about a firm. Management has primary responsibility for financial statements and assertions about the firm that are implicit in those statements. This legal obligation can lead to liability for assertions that are false. The benefit to management of having its financial statement assertions "certified" by a reputable independent auditor comes as a reduced price protection discount, or information risk premium required by capital suppliers and trading partners in dealing with the company. If the reduction is more than the auditor's fee, then management benefits.

Auditors are required by GAAS to obtain sufficient evidence to provide reasonable assurance that the financial statements are free of material misstatement. Audit fees can be reduced by management in various ways, including cooperating with the auditor, maintaining effective internal controls, and conveying to the auditor management's own integrity. This cost reduction is due to the fact that the auditor will face legal liability if the company fails or if material error exists in its financial statements. Litigation has also led auditors to evaluate client business risk and the auditor's business risk of association with the client. Auditors' assessments of business risks may lead to early identification of operating problems and improved client operations. On the other hand, it can lead to auditor resignation as the auditor avoids risks of client association.

Audit firms can also add credibility to nonhistorical financial statement assertions. Certification of these assertions requires reasonably objective measurement criteria and the ability to verify proper application of the criteria for an information display.

CASE 7

NORTHERN FRONTIER PARKS, INC.*

Northern Frontier Parks, Inc. (NFP), is a privately held company that operates a safari-style wildlife park in Montana. The NFP wildlife park is becoming a popular year-round tourist attraction, with the number of visitors increasing approximately 25 percent since the grand opening year in 1995. Similar to wildlife safari parks in Africa, visitors drive through NFP's 3,200-acre park, which is home to over 100 species of native animals, birds, and fish. Most of NFP's revenues are earned as park admission and hotel accommodation fees. Most expenditures relate to animal acquisition, feeding, and medical care and to hotel administration and operations.

Until late last year, NFP had been owned and managed by Cam Kramer, founder and chief executive officer (CEO). But Mr. Kramer died in January 2000 and his shares in the company were distributed to his family. No one in the Kramer family wants to manage the business, so the family will sell 100 percent of the NFP shares at the end of the current fiscal year to George Newton, the current acting CEO and chief financial officer (CFO) of NFP.

Because NFP is a private company, a market price for the shares is not available. Instead,

George has proposed that the purchase/sale price for the pending transaction be based on an agreed-upon multiple of net income for the year ended May 31, 2000, calculated using U.S. GAAP, and audited by Alex and Louis, CPAs, a medium-sized accounting firm. Alex and Louis provided an initial audit and other professional services beginning with the fiscal year ended May 30, 1999. In years prior to 1999, NFP's financial statements were prepared by the CFO without audit or review.

You are a partner in Olivia and Eleanor, CPAs, a trusted business advisor of Dorothy Benis, daughter of Cam and one of his heirs. Ms. Benis has invited you to present your evaluation of the prospective sale—especially the role of the audited financial statements. She may also ask that you independently apply auditing procedures to especially risky accounts or assertions.

To assist in preparing your evaluation, Ms. Benis has provided unaudited financial statements prepared by the CFO (Exhibit 1) and other

---

*Adapted with permission of the authors from an audit case "Instructional Case: Northern Frontier Parks," by F. Phillips and R. Martin, *Issues in Accounting Education*, November 1998, pp. 1005–18.

EXHIBIT 1

NORTHERN FRONTIERS PARKS, INC.
excerpts from the
Statements of Income and Retained Earnings
(thousands of dollars)

	Unaudited		Audited	
	April 30, 2000	Percent of Revenues	May 31, 1999	Percent of Revenues
Revenues:				
Park admission	$1,028	33.3	$1,120	33.9
Hotel rentals	1,907	61.7	2,080	63.0
Animal sales	156	5.0	102	3.1
	$3,091	100.0	$3,302	100.0
Hotel operating costs	$1,328	43.0	$1,451	43.9
Animal feed and care	992	32.1	1,129	34.2
Interest expense	198	6.4	96	2.9
Cost of animal sales	72	2.3	31	1.0
Depreciation and fence replacements	71	2.3	29	0.9
Restoration and other costs	162	5.2	10	0.3
	$2,823	91.3	$2,746	83.2
Income before income taxes	$ 268	8.7	$ 556	16.8
Income taxes	(80)	(2.6)	(167)	(5.0)
Net income	$ 188	6.1	$ 389	11.8
Dividends	(173)		(280)	
Retained earnings, beginning	257		148	
Retained earnings, end	$ 272		$ 257	

relevant information (Exhibit 2). Because today's date (May 5) precedes NFP's year-end (May 31), only 11 months of operations are included in NFP's income statement. Ms. Benis's discussions with the CFO indicate that, although the balances on the 12-month income statement will be larger, their relative percentage of revenues (as shown) are unlikely to change.

Required

a. As a partner in Olivia and Eleanor:

1. What advice would you give to Ms. Benis concerning the terms of sale, the business valuation relevance of the measurement criteria, the magnitude deemed to be material, and the audit to be conducted by Alex and Louis?

2. Which accounts do you believe have high pre-audit risk of material misstatement, and how would you audit those accounts if Ms. Benis asks you to conduct some additional auditing procedures?

b. Assume that you are the risk management partner for Alex and Louis. How would you rate auditor's business risk and client business risk for the NFP engagement?

E X H I B I T   1   (continued)

NORTHERN FRONTIERS PARKS, INC.
excerpts from the
Balance Sheet and Notes to the Financial Statements
(thousands of dollars)

	Unaudited	*Audited*
	April 30, 2000	**May 31, 1999**
Assets		
Cash	$ 244	$ 113
Hotel customer accounts receivable	403	460
Less: Allowance for doubtful accounts	(70)	(40)
Animal stock	659	714
Capital assets	1,956	1,942
Less: Accumulated amortization	(271)	(235)
	$2,921	$2,954
Liabilities		
Accounts payable	$ 537	$ 629
Accrued liabilities	308	155
Long-term debt	1,802	1,911
	$2,647	$2,695
Shareholders' Equity		
Share capital	$ 2	$ 2
Retained earnings	272	257
	$ 274	$ 259
	$2,921	$2,954

Significant Accounting Policies

Animal stock—In accordance with industry practice, the stock of animals is reported at the lower of cost or market value. Market values are estimated using current replacement costs.

Capital assets—Capital assets include land, fencing, hotel buildings, and equipment. Hotel buildings and equipment are amortized on a straight-line basis over their estimated useful lives. In 2000, the remaining estimated useful life of hotel buildings was reduced from 25 to 18 years. Land and fencing are not amortized.

Contingent liabilities—NFP does not routinely collect the scientific data needed to evaluate the ecological health of its parks, yet significant growth in visitors over the past five years is thought to be damaging park ecology. In 2000, NFP accrued a liability in the amount of $150 (thousand) for possible future environmental restoration costs that may be incurred as a result of deteriorating park ecology.

EXHIBIT 2

Other Client Information

Beginning the day NFP was founded, Mr. Kramer carefully controlled every aspect of NFP's operations, using his extensive knowledge of veterinary care, marketing, and federal laws and regulations. Mr. Kramer was respected by everyone—not only NFP's employees and customers, but also concerned environmental and animal-rights activists. On the financial side, Mr. Kramer worked closely with George to design and implement a strong accounting system. All purchases of animals for the parks were approved by Mr. Kramer; hotel profitability was reviewed on a monthly basis; and park admission revenues and cash receipts were compared daily to vehicle counts obtained from monitors installed at the admission gates. A perpetual inventory system was introduced to monitor quantities of animals.

George has described December 1999 as an unusually mild winter month and, accordingly, NFP was able to speed up replacement of fencing at substantial savings. Also, animal stock apparently survived the winter weather with greater success than usual. In fact, George mentioned that 30 newborn animals survived in 2000, as compared to only 20 in each of the prior three years. Many of these newborn animals were sold to private zoos and other animal parks in 2000; consequently, animal sales revenues have increased in the current year.

The growth in successful animal births also led George to reconsider the accounting policy used to record and update animal stock costs. The animal stock account primarily includes costs for adult animal purchases, although some birth-related medical care costs also are included. In the past, these animal costs were assigned to each individual animal using the specific identification inventory method. George found that method to be overly cumbersome, and decided to change to an average cost method in January 2000. Consequently, when newborn animals now are sold, the average cost of animal stock at the time of sale is used to determine the cost of animal sales to be expensed on the income statement.

KEY WORDS

audit risk (AuR) The risk that the auditor will unknowingly certify that financial statements are free of material misstatement when, in fact, they are materially misstated.

auditor business risk (ABR) The risk that the audit firm will suffer financial or reputation loss because of association with a client as its auditor.

certifiable assertions Written assertions that are capable of evaluation against reasonable measurement criteria.

client business risk (CBR) The risk of loss to the audit firm because the auditor's client experiences declining performance in the future.

engagement letter A letter written by the auditor to the party hiring the auditor specifying terms of the audit, signed by the hiring party, and serving as a formal contract for the audit.

engagement risk The overall risk of loss to a CPA firm, comprised of audit risk (AuR), client business risk (CBR), and auditor business risk (ABR), from being associated with a business as its financial statement auditor.

material amount (M*) The magnitude of misstatement that would make a financial statement (e.g., income statement) not in compliance with GAAP in all material (important) respects.

material misstatement The magnitude of a financial statement misstatement or omission that, in the light of surrounding circumstances, makes it probable that the judgment of a reasonable person (an average prudent investor) relying on the statement would be changed or influenced by correction of the misstatement or inclusion of the omission.

qualitatively material A misstatement or omission that is quantitatively immaterial, but because of its nature or surrounding circumstances has important implications for a decision maker.

reasonable assurance The complement of audit risk (i.e., reasonable assurance = 1 − audit risk).

representation letter A letter signed by top management documenting management's primary responsibility for all financial statement assertions, and management's beliefs about the absence of fraud and illegal acts.

standard auditor's report A three-paragraph audit report with standardized wording issued for an entity with no material departures from GAAP criteria, no accounting changes, no unusual uncertainties about its ability to continue as a going concern, and no items noted by the auditor for emphasis.

8

CHAPTER

Financial Statement Audits, Adjustments, and Disclosures

- ◆ **W**hat do auditors really do when conducting financial statement audits?
- ◆ What determines how much auditing they do?
- ◆ What must I disclose or publicly assert about my company?
- ◆ Where will the auditor give me the most discretion when certifying my financial statements?
- ◆ When will the auditor insist upon adjustments?

The first question is of only mild interest to most top managers, but we can't fully appreciate answers to the latter four without knowing the first. Economic self-interest and professional standards determine what the auditor does under an ordinary audit contract. Knowledge of the auditor's interests and professional standards will help you understand what is required of top management and the discretion or "wiggle room" allowed when issuing GAAP-based financial statements to outsiders. Understanding both will also help you decode the auditor's report when evaluating the financial statements of others.

We begin by discussing auditing standards and the audit risk model. This is followed by the audit adjustment process in determining acceptable amounts for audited financial statements and required disclosures.

THE ROLE OF GENERALLY ACCEPTED AUDITING STANDARDS

The auditor's contract with a client (see engagement letter, Chapter 7) typically specifies that the auditor will conduct an audit of management's financial statements by applying generally accepted auditing standards (GAAS) and will express a conclusion about the statements' conformity with generally accepted accounting principles (GAAP). These two sets of standards define the auditor's contractual obligations, and also underlie reporting requirements of the securities acts in the United States and many other countries.

GAAS describe the quality of performance typically rendered by professional auditors. While not specific about all procedures to be applied, GAAS express qualitatively the objectives to be achieved and judgments to be exercised. GAAS have the dual roles of providing (a) *ex ante* educational guidance to help auditors conduct a standard quality audit and (b) *ex post* enforcement guidance to help judges, juries and regulators resolve disputes about the quality of auditing services in legal actions against the auditor for breach of contract or malpractice and substandard performance.

GAAS are structured in the United States as 10 broad standards (see Figure 8–1).[1] The three general standards refer to two of the three conditions for value of independent certification studied in prior chapters. The technical training and proficiency of the auditor and exercise of due care in all aspects of the audit are related to auditor competence, while an

FIGURE 8–1

Generally Accepted Auditing Standards

General Standards

1. The audit is to be performed by a person or persons having adequate technical training and proficiency as an auditor.
2. In all matters relating to the assignment, an independence in mental attitude is to be maintained by the auditor or auditors.
3. Due professional care is to be exercised in the performance of the audit and the preparation of the report.

Standards of Fieldwork

1. The work is to be adequately planned and assistants, if any, are to be properly supervised.
2. A sufficient understanding of internal control is to be obtained to plan the audit and to determine the nature, timing, and extent of tests to be performed.
3. Sufficient competent evidential matter is to be obtained through inspection, observation, inquiries, and confirmations to afford a reasonable basis for an opinion regarding the financial statements under audit.

Standards of Reporting

1. The report shall state whether the financial statements are presented in accordance with generally accepted accounting principles.
2. The report shall identify those circumstances in which such principles have not been consistently observed in the current period in relation to the preceding period.
3. Informative disclosures in the financial statements are to be regarded as reasonably adequate unless otherwise stated in the report.
4. The report shall either contain an opinion regarding the financial statements, taken as a whole, or an assertion to the effect that an opinion cannot be expressed. When an overall opinion cannot be expressed, the reasons therefor should be stated. In all cases in which an auditor's name is associated with financial statements, the report should contain a clear-cut indication of the character of the auditor's work, if any, and the degree of responsibility the auditor is taking.

Source: AICPA, SAS No. 1, section 150.

---

1. Similar standards exist in other countries, and the basic principles underlie the International Standards on Auditing issued by the International Auditing Practices Committee of the International Federation of Accountants (IAF).

"independence of mental attitude" is an element of the auditor's integrity, objectivity, and trustworthiness.

Three standards of fieldwork define elements of a standard quality audit. The audit must be adequately planned and audit assistants properly supervised, and the auditor must understand internal control well enough to determine what audit evidence will be needed. The third fieldwork standard requires that the auditor obtain sufficient competent evidence to support an opinion on the fairness of financial statements. This means that the auditor must do whatever is necessary to reduce the after-audit risk of material misstatement to a "negligible" level.

The final four numbered auditing standards cover the auditor's report, with the first three relating to identification of measurement criteria (e.g., GAAP), consistency of measurement rules used across time periods, and the presumed adequacy of informative disclosures in audited financial statements receiving a standard audit report. The fourth requires that the auditor express an opinion on the financial statements taken as a whole, or explain why such an opinion cannot be expressed.

The reporting standards may seem tedious, but are necessary to prevent audit reports that seem adequate, yet avoid important issues. Under a *certification* contract, the certifying or "sell side" auditor is hired by the information source and has an incentive to please his or her employer, other things equal.[2] Ambiguous or incomplete report wording might please management in the short term but would lead to a decline in the value of audits in the long term. Strict audit reporting rules for GAAS encourage a certifying auditor to internalize the long-term as well as public interest aspects of the contract.

GAAS are supported by almost 90 Statements on Auditing Standards (or SASs) that provide interpretive guidance on how the 10 standards are to be applied. SASs are established and maintained in the United States by the auditors' professional trade association, the American Institute of Certified Public Accountants (AICPA) through its Auditing Standards Board. These privately set standards are then incorporated by reference into federal securities acts.[3] Historically, the primary impetus for issuing a SAS has been an auditor's failure to detect a previously unknown type of misstatement. As with GAAS in general, a SAS educates auditors about specific threats to audit quality and suggests auditing procedures that may mitigate the threats. SASs are also used to enforce sanctions on an auditor's substandard performance and increase user confidence in reliability of audited financial statements in general.

We will study the SASs related to audit planning, fieldwork, risk assessment, and auditing procedures in this chapter and the reporting SASs in Chapter 9.

THE AUDIT RISK MODEL

A primary SAS (SAS No. 47, AICPA, 1983), entitled "Audit Risk and Materiality in Conducting an Audit," outlines the role of audit risk and materiality in planning the audit to discover possible material misstatement and in evaluating audit findings to recommend

---

2. The same standards apply for an *investigation* type of audit contract but are less critical since the investigating ("buy side") auditor works for the decision maker.

3. In 1998, SASs interpreting the three general standards used three pages of text, while the three standards of fieldwork comprised approximately 280 pages, the first three standards of reporting about 30 pages, and the fourth 100 pages. Thus, procedural guidance on the basis for the auditor's opinion and expression of the opinion comprise about 92 percent of GAAS interpretations.

adjustments and express an opinion. SAS No. 47 defines **audit risk** (AuR) as "the risk that the auditor may unknowingly fail to appropriately modify his or her opinion on financial statements that are materially misstated" (para. 2).[4] Financial statements are **materially misstated** "when they contain misstatements whose effect, individually or in the aggregate, is important enough to cause them not to be presented fairly, in all material respects, in conformity with GAAP" (para. 4). It further states that "misstatements result from misapplications of GAAP, departure from fact, or omissions of necessary information," and that AuR is to be limited to an appropriately low level.

SAS No. 47 outlines a conceptual model for limiting audit risk through a combination of the auditor's assessments of the prior-to-audit risk that financial statements are materially misstated and auditing procedures designed to detect any material misstatement that might exist in unaudited financial statements. For audited financial statements to be materially misstated (e.g., individual or aggregate misstatements (M), such that $M \geq M^*$), two events must occur. First, material misstatement must exist in pre-audit recorded values and, second, the audit must fail to detect the misstatement(s).

The risk of the first event is called **occurrence risk** (denoted OR) and risk of the second is called **detection risk** (DR). Audit risk (AuR) faced by the auditor is about equal to the risk that an external-to-the-firm user may incorrectly rely on a standard auditor report when the financial statements are materially misstated. Either risk can be roughly approximated as the product of the individual risks of these two events. That is, AuR = OR × DR. Appendix A for this chapter elaborates on the risk approximation for both the external auditor and the external financial statement user.

Auditors assess OR and then design auditing procedures that yield DR sufficient for a risk product, AuR, that is "low." DR is varied inversely with assessed OR to keep the product low. For a given target AuR, DR can be high if OR is low, but DR must be low if OR is high. Auditing procedures with low DR—that is, little risk of failing to detect material misstatement when it exists—are more expensive to apply than are procedures with higher risk of failing to detect material misstatement.

Audit risk concepts apply to a multidimensional array of assertions (existence, ownership, valuation, completeness, and display/presentation) for each account comprising financial statements, but the audit risk model cannot be applied readily to the statements as a whole. Rather, audit firms apply it to component account balances and assertions individually and then aggregate results across accounts.

Collectively, the SAS No. 47 guidance on risk assessments and auditing procedures is often referred to as the **audit risk model.** The audit risk model is important to you as a top manager because (a) it shows primary cost drivers of audit fees that you must pay, (b) it underlies the value you receive for the audit fee, and (c) it is essential for understanding the risk that you take as a financial statement user in relying on audits, reviews, and compilations of another company's financial statements (see Chapters 9 and 10).

Relation to Engagement Risk

In Chapter 7, we discussed audit firms' use of the engagement risk approach to manage overall risk of being associated with an audit client. In applying the engagement risk ap-

---

4. Mathematically, audit risk is the complement of "reasonable assurance" mentioned in the auditor's report. That is, reasonable assurance = 1 − AuR, or reasonable assurance + AuR = 1.

proach, the auditor screens out prospective clients and reviews continuing clients for exceptional risk of litigation against the auditor or loss of reputation (auditor's business risk—ABR) and clients with exceptional risk of declining prospects in the future (client's business risk—CBR).

Audit risk (AuR) is a third element of engagement risk, and AuR is controllable by the auditor through risk assessments and auditing procedures. Client selection and retention policies and procedures allow the auditor to manage risks that arise irrespective of audit quality. Because auditing procedures cannot be 100 percent effective in eliminating CBR and ABR, client selection and retention policies and procedures are necessary to *avoid risk at its source.*

Audit Planning Overview

Application of the audit risk model begins after the auditor decides that ABR and CBR are low enough and the rewards from being the client's auditor are high enough to make the engagement attractive. Figure 8–2 diagrams components of the audit risk model approach to the control of audit risk.[5]

As shown in Figure 8–2, the auditor combines three sources of information—**pervasive factors risk, control failure risk,** and **book value risk** assessments—to yield an **occurrence risk** (OR) for each account and assertion. The auditor then plans and applies auditing procedures to provide sufficiently low **detection risk** (DR) to yield the target AuR for each account (and assertion). For accounts that do not "pass" the audit tests (e.g., substantial misstatements discovered or projected), the auditor will propose adjustments.

At the end of the audit, when the auditor is satisfied that each account (as adjusted) is reasonably stated, the auditor conducts a **final review** using analytical procedures similar to those applied in Chapter 5 to determine whether unexplained unusual relations exist in the audited values. This is the auditor's last chance to avoid certifying materially misstated financial statements, and it is also important as a legal defense because the auditor should have evidence to support the validity of any unusual or seemingly out-of-line account balances. Finally, if the auditor is satisfied that audit risk is sufficiently low, the auditor reviews ABR and CBR for any changes before signing the audit report and transmitting it to the client.

Occurrence Risk Assessment

Pervasive Factors Risk

OR assessments begin with the auditor's assessment of **pervasive factors risk.** Pervasive factors risk includes client viability threats, control environment weaknesses, motivation for misstatement or fraud by management or employees, industry and time specific factors, and weak general computer controls. These factors affect the risk of misstatement of the client's financial statements as a whole, as well as each individual account. Pervasive risk factors also affect interpretation of other risks for particular accounts.

---

5. The auditor's audit risk model is similar in form to management's internal information risk (IIR) model in Chapters 4–6. Both yield a posterior probability of misstatement and misappropriation, but they differ in that IIR measures reliability of the internal control process and the implicit reliability of information at any time, while AuR addresses reliability of information display at a particular point in time.

FIGURE 8–2

Audit Risk Model Components

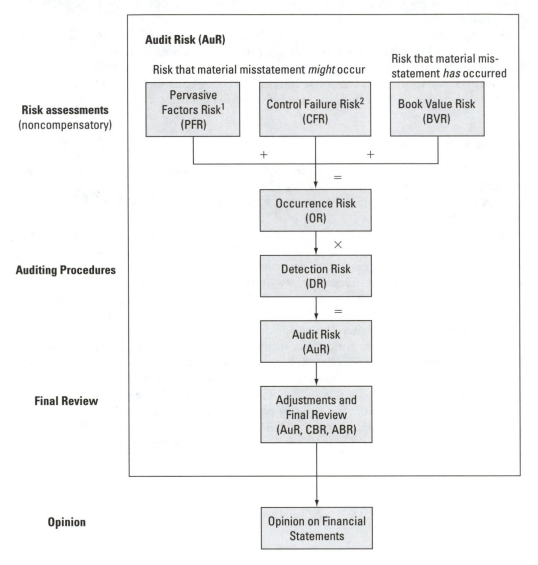

1. Pervasive risks: Process viability, management fraud, weak control environment, incentives to misstate,
   industry and time specific factors, and weak general (computer) controls.
2. Related to internal information risk (IIR) to management in Chapter 4.

One pervasive factor risk is the presence of client business process weaknesses, indicating risk of declining prospects for the client in the future (part of CBR). Even though the auditor initially decided that the client has an overall strategy sufficiently viable to serve as its financial statement auditor, the auditor evaluates component business processes to identify threats to business viability, key success factors, and reasonable expectations of "true" account balances. In other words, can the client's business processes support a viable and profitable business? If not, there may be an incentive to misrepresent.

A second pervasive risk is the client's overall control environment. In Chapter 4 we discussed the importance of the control environment from management's perspective as a means of facilitating other control activities. The external auditor must evaluate the control environment as an important condition for reliance on internal control to limit OR. Because a poor control environment affects other audit risk model components, the auditor must assess the attitude and awareness of top management toward control and how it is conveyed and applied throughout the organization. Adoption and enforcement of corporate conduct codes and prompt follow-up on any control exceptions by top management can raise the auditor's assessment of the control environment.

As previously discussed, management may have incentives to materially misstate financial statements. For example, management of a company that is under pressure to meet analysts' forecasts of earnings, is issuing new securities, or is renegotiating debt wants to report good earnings, even if the current year has disappointing results. Management compensation plans based on audited net income may provide similar incentives to overstate. Top management may also pressure lower-level management to report segment earnings that meet targets, and lower-level personnel may respond by misstating performance. Incentive conditions and pressures don't mean that pre-audit net income and assets are overstated or that management misrepresentation fraud exists, but they should increase the auditor's awareness of these possibilities. This is especially true for matters requiring judgment by top management, since management has both the incentive and the capability to overstate for personal gain.[6]

Some pervasive risks are specific to the industry, such as all tobacco firms facing consumer lawsuits, or to the time period, such as periods of recession. Also, an industry may face new competitors, labor problems, or introduction of new products. All of these factors increase the risk of accidental or intentional misstatement such as inadequate loss contingency accounting, obsolete inventory, and failure to remain a going concern.

A final pervasive factor risk is the quality of the client's general controls over computer processing of transactions. As discussed in Chapter 4, inadequate general computer controls may allow unauthorized changes in programmed application controls for particular transaction types that in turn lead to unreliable accounting and business processes. On the other hand, strong general controls allow reliance on programmed applications controls over processes.

Control Failure Risk

The pervasive control environment and general computer controls are part of the auditor's understanding of internal control. The understanding is the basis for satisfying the second

---

6. The auditor is also alert for indications of lack of management integrity and the possibility of fraud by management, especially financial misrepresentation fraud (related to ABR and AuR).

fieldwork standard of GAAS. Another part is the auditor's understanding and evaluation of less pervasive internal controls, including computer processing application controls over particular assets, liabilities, and classes of transactions such as sales, collections, payroll, purchasing, and disbursements.

The auditor typically assesses the risk of particular misstatements that might occur at the account level for each of the five assertions (existence, valuation, ownership, completeness, and display/presentation). Some auditors first assess the inherent risk that errors might arise in the accounting measurement process and then consider any controls, including monitoring, that would prevent or detect misstatements if they occur.

The auditor evaluates the design of controls, including separation of duties, for potential effectiveness. Application of prescribed controls is tested by observing the system in operation, making inquiries of personnel operating the system, and testing the inputs and outputs of processing (using techniques discussed in Chapters 4 and 6). Application of controls is also tested by evaluating the internal auditor's monitoring of internal control operations and protecting the system from unauthorized changes.

For internal control processes that are well designed and tested for effective operation, the auditor has increased confidence that control failure risk is low. Reliance on low inherent risk and effective controls is common for "hard numbers" resulting from routine sales, collection, payroll, procurement, and disbursement transactions. Reliance is less common for nonroutine accounting estimates that require significant expertise such as liability for actuarial losses or for lease capitalization values.

For some processes, the auditor may decide not to test internal control because he or she believes that controls are not reliable or that it would be more efficient to obtain assurance from direct testing of the account balances produced by the process. For these situations, the auditor usually relies on extensive tests of details of transactions and balances. Finally, the auditor considers the inherent limitations of internal control due to possible human failure, collusion, and override by a member of intermediate or top management.

Book Value Risk

Pervasive and control failure possibilities address the risk that misstatements *might occur.* What we will call "book value risk" is the risk that material misstatement *has occurred.* Since the prior-to-audit book values for the period being audited may be materially misstated, the auditor studies the book values for amounts or relationships that are unexpected. The auditor's knowledge of the client, its industry, and time period is used to form expectations of "true" account balances and ratios using analytical methods discussed in Chapter 5. Book values that are out of line with reasonable expectations indicate accounts with greater-than-normal material misstatement occurrence risk (OR) or pre-audit risk of misstatement.

Combining Occurrence Risks

Pervasive factors risk, control failure risk, and book value risk are combined into the auditor's assessment of the occurrence risk of significant misstatement in particular accounts and assertions. The three OR factors are approximately additive in their combination. This is because low risk for one factor does not compensate for high risk in another. So even if there are no pervasive risk factors and control failure risk is judged low, there may still be high OR if book values are out of line with reasonable expectations. For example, for a competitive business, a book value gross profit rate of 75 percent is unlikely to be correct and would suggest high OR, even if pervasive factors risk and control failure risk are low. Also, weak general controls over computer processing suggest high OR even with low control failure risk and book value risk.

To summarize, the occurrence risk that a prior-to-audit financial statement assertion is materially misstated can be approximated by the sum of the three risks:

$$OR = PFR + CFR + BVR$$

where PFR, CFR, and BVR refer to the respective risk components. Assessments of OR will vary across accounts and assertions depending on the levels of pervasive risk factors, internal control quality, and relationships among book values. We will see examples below.

Occurrence risk assessment is made by the external auditor in planning the audit of financial statements. Low OR allows the auditor to use auditing procedures with higher DR and thus lower audit cost. Since you as part of top management are central to the preparation of those statements, the risk that you might commit misrepresentation fraud or be lax in establishing and maintaining an effective control environment in your company may affect your auditor's assessment of OR.

To the extent you as a top manager can convince your external auditor that pervasive factors risks are negligible, that your internal control is reliable, and that out-of-line-with-expectations book values have a valid (nonmisstatement) explanation, your audit fees can be lower. Also, with better controls and control environment, you will have more reliable internal information (low IIR) and better asset protection day to day.

On the other hand, if the auditor assesses OR for an account to be high, then more extensive (and more costly) auditing procedures will be required and the auditor's fee will be higher. For accounts with very high OR assessments, the auditor may change approaches because the auditor believes that material misstatement *is* present and that adjustments *are* needed. For example, using the additive formula, calculated OR may exceed 1.0 (even though actual risk is limited to 1.0 or certainty of material misstatement). In such situations, the auditor may ask that your employees locate and correct misstatements prior to examination by the auditor or may increase the audit fee to allow an unusually detailed examination by the auditor.

Applying the Audit Risk Model to Limit Detection Risk

All large CPA/CA firms have developed software to assist with occurrence risk assessment and determination of auditing procedures required to economically limit detection risk to an acceptable level. The software is based on the audit risk model and operationalized by completing a risk identification, sourcing, sizing, and resolution (RISSAR) chart similar to those we studied in Chapter 3. In particular, the software assists the auditor in identifying sources of risk of material misstatement in each account and assertion, and possible causes of misstatement. After assessments of PFR, CFR, and BVR are entered, the software combines them into an overall judgment of occurrence risk for the source of misstatement. Then, the software suggests specific auditing procedures that would economically limit audit risk to a low level. The suggested auditing procedures may be analytical procedures or tests of details, and may be applied to test processes (e.g., sales, collections, purchases, disbursements) or to the year-end account balances.

LJ Appliances

Figure 8–3 illustrates an abbreviated account level RISSAR chart for the audit of LJ Appliances, Inc. As shown in Figure 8–3, Alex and Louis assess pervasive factors risk at a low level, and this level applies to all accounts. On the other hand, they assess control failure risk at the moderate level for cost of sales and the related inventory and accounts payable. This is because of control weakness observed in these processes. Finally, book value risk is assessed at the moderate level for Sales and Accounts Receivable as well as for cost of sales and inventory due to book values that were out of line with the auditor's expectations for the period.

Figure 8–3 shows the three OR factors combined in an approximately additive fashion, with OR ranging from low to high. For example, OR for Sales is assessed at the moderate level due to book values that are moderately out of line with expectations. Cost of sales is assessed at a high level due to moderate risk of control failure and moderately out-of-line book values.[7]

Based on the auditor's risk assessments and allowable misstatement for each account, the auditor decides the nature, extent, and timing of auditing procedures to apply to each. If OR is low, then the auditor may decide that analytical procedures will be sufficient. For accounts with intermediate levels of OR, the auditor may decide that some tests of details are required, but that the tests can be conducted before the balance sheet date. Thus, the auditor might observe inventory counting procedures on October 31 for a December 31 year-end firm and the results updated to year end using analytical procedures. Cheaper-to-apply analytical tests, reduced extent of testing, and flexible timing reduce the cost of obtaining sufficient competent audit evidence. On the other hand, if OR is high, then the auditor might decide that a substantial number or amount of recorded details should be audited and that the tests should be conducted as of the balance sheet date. Thus, DR can vary by the nature, extent, and timing of the auditing procedures applied. Again, low OR can lead to lower audit cost and fees.

The response side of the RISSAR chart shows the auditing procedures designed to yield detection risk that would limit AuR to a very low level. In particular, it shows a combination of auditing procedures for each account. For example, sales shows a moderate OR, and the auditor relies on a combination of tests of the sales processing system and analytical tests of year-end balances in combination with related tests of the ending recorded accounts receivable.

The combination of tests of processes (which are usually applied as the audit year progresses) plus year-end analytical tests of recorded Sales relative to other accounts and to nonfinancial information plus tests of details of accounts receivable is sufficient to yield low AuR for sales. In contrast, OR for cost of sales and OR for inventory are assessed at a high level and require that the auditor conduct year-end tests of details that have a low risk of *failing to detect* material misstatement (low DR) for these accounts.

---

7. Because the risk factor magnitudes can't be calculated precisely, most audit firms have scoring rules to classify risks as low, moderate, or high rather than stating probabilities. Also, their rules for combining risks are based upon weighting factors that tend to be either additive or multiplicative in nature.

F I G U R E 8 – 3

Abbreviated Account Level Misstatement
Risk Identification, Sourcing, Sizing, and Resolution (RISSAR) Chart for Audit of LJ Appliances, Inc.

Source	Size — Occurrence Risk (OR)				Response — Detection Risks (DR)						Final Review
	PFR	+ CFR	+ BVR	= OR	Tests of Processes (interim)[1]				Tests of Balances (year end)		Audit Risk (AuR)
Materially Misstated					Sales	Collections	Purchasing	Disbursements	Analysis	Details	
Sales[2]	L[3]	L	M	M	M				M	M[4]	VL
Cost of Sales	L	M	M	H			M		M	L[4]	VL
Cash	L	L	L	L		M			H	H	VL
Accounts Receivable	L	L	M	M	M	M			M	H	VL
Inventory	L	M	M	H			M		M	L	VL
Accounts Payable	L	M	L	M			M	M	M	M	VL

Typical auditing procedures for:

Tests of Processes
- **observation** of processes
- **inspection** of documents for evidence of processing and accuracy of processing
- **inquiry** of client personnel and outsiders to confirm processes
- **reprocessing** of selected transactions
- **analysis** of relationships of transactions with related transactions and nonfinancial measures

Analytical Test of Balances
- **analysis** of balances via
  - regression analysis and other relatively precise analytical procedures for expectations
  - detailed follow-up of large deviations from expectations

Detailed Tests of Balances
- **observation** of ending quantities on hand
- **inspection** of documents of purchase, receipt, sale, and shipment
- **inquiry** of outsiders to confirm balances
- **reprocessing** of transactions by tracing/comparing, verifying pricing, extension, summation

Final Review
- **analysis** of final balances for reasonableness given all results of the audit and all other information available

1. Tests of processes may be analytical or detailed and are typically the primary tests for income statement accounts. Tests of processes provide secondary evidence of the validity of the related balance sheet accounts at year end.

2. Some CPA firms partition account level analyses into the five assertions and identify particular misstatements that would lead to violation of each assertion. For example, a refrigerator delivered to a customer but no sale recorded would violate the completeness assertion for Sales and Accounts Receivable.

3. H, M, L, and VL indicate high, moderate, low, or very low risk of occurrence of material misstatement (OR) or risk of failure to detect material misstatement when it exists (DR). Audit program designs for DR are based on allowable DR for each test for each account or source of risk.

4. Detailed tests of balances evidence for Sales and Cost of Sales typically result from detailed tests of ending Accounts Receivable and from ending Inventory and Accounts Payable, respectively.

Finally, after a final review of the audited balances, the auditor concludes that there is very low risk of material misstatement in each of these important accounts. This conclusion of low AuR is a unique and important characteristic of audits applying GAAS. The conclusion applies to each account individually and to the aggregate over all accounts comprising the income statement or balance sheet. The auditor following GAAS will audit until he or she reaches a conclusion that there is low risk that undetected (and uncorrected) misstatements are material. As we will see in Chapter 10, other attest services by CPAs/CAs have varying levels of audit risk at the conclusion of an engagement.

Examples of OR Assessments and Audit Test Planning

Lincoln Savings and Loan

Lincoln Savings and Loan (LSL) was purchased in the early 1980s by American Continental Corporation, whose primary stockholder was Charles Keating.[8] LSL's major source of earnings became the purchase and resale of undeveloped land in Arizona. In some cases, LSL, in effect, also loaned the buyer the required down payment.

Initially, the strategy generated substantial profits, but by the mid-1980s, demand for real estate development had declined and future prospects for transactions in undeveloped land at then-current prices were not good. In particular, an analysis of Arizona housing starts and population growth projections during the mid-1980s would not support profitability of such a strategy in the future. These factors suggest high pervasive risks due to possible lack of business process viability, incentives to misstate (related to maintaining growth trends), and industry- and time-specific factors. Furthermore, while existence of revenue transactions may have been correctly recorded, future collectability of receivables (valuation) was suspect because of potential defaults by customers unable to develop the land or resell at a profit.

Other AuR, CBR, and ABR factors may also have been relevant. The prior auditor of LSL (Arthur Andersen) resigned because of a dispute between LSL management and federal regulators over applicability of accounting-based capital requirements that were constraining LSL's activities. Thus, there was motivation for management to misstate, increased legal risk to the auditor, and possible questions about management's integrity.

The LSL case is alleged to have cost U.S. taxpayers more than $2 billion to resolve, and its primary auditor, Ernst and Young, settled civil lawsuits for $63 million and settled with the Resolution Trust Corporation for about $40 million. More attention to pervasive factors risk, CBR, and ABR may have led to additional auditing procedures and detection of accounting misstatements, questions about business viability, and possibly the audit firm's resignation as LSL's auditor.

AstroGamas

AstroGamas (see Chapter 7) faced declining prospects for its Trasher game and was renegotiating its long-term debt, providing top management with an incentive to maintain recorded earnings as high as possible. This pervasive risk factor should make the AstroGamas

---

8. These details of the LSL case are derived from "Why Do Audits Fail?: Evidence from Lincoln Savings and Loan," by M. Erickson, B. Mayhew, and W. Felix, working paper, (September 26, 1997).

auditor more skeptical about management's accounting estimates as well as other numbers comprising earnings.

Financial ratios for AstroGamas provide a crude book value risk analysis based on last year's audited values as the expectation (see Figure 8–4). Sales have declined slightly, and inventory has increased substantially relative to cost of sales, receivables have increased relative to sales, and receivables have increased relative to payables. Even though cost of sales relative to sales has remained constant, the ratios show the weakening of the market for Trasher, as well as potentially increased risk of collectability of its receivables. The book value risk analysis also indicates an apparently high level of pre-audit ending inventory relative to cost of sales, suggesting that ending inventory may be overstated either due to excessive stock or to obsolete items. Furthermore, the declining receivables turnover may indicate customers are slow in paying their bills for Trasher purchases and the possibility of future sales returns of the Trasher game.

The auditor believes that control failure risk for receivables is low based on the routine nature of AstroGamas's revenue process with a clear revenue recognition point (the shipment of an order), good general controls over computer processing, strong computer application controls for recording sales transactions, and strong controls over collections. There is separation of duties for authorizing sales, billing of customers, and subsequent

FIGURE 8–4

Book Value Risk Assessment

ASTROGAMAS, INC.

Financial Statement Excerpts (in millions)

Account	1999 (audited)	2000 (unaudited)	Percent Change
Sales (net)	$85.0	$80.0	−5.9
Cost of Sales	39.0	36.7	−5.9
Net Income before Income Taxes	5.8	3.0	−48.3
Accounts Receivable (net)	14.0	24.0	71.4
Inventory	9.1	11.0	20.9
Accounts Payable	8.0	10.1	26.3
Total Assets	82.1	83.0	1.1

Simple Changes in Selected Ratios

Ratio	1999 (audited)	2000 (unaudited)	Percent Change
Sales/Sales last year	1.18	.94	−20.3
NIBT/NIBT last year	1.22	.52	−57.4
Total Assets/TA last year	1.08	1.01	−6.5
Cost of Sales/Sales	.54	.54	.0
Cost of Sales/Inventory	4.29	3.34	−22.1
Sales/Accounts Receivable	6.07	3.33	−45.1
Accounts Receivable/Accounts Payable	1.54	2.18	41.6

recording and processing of cash collections from customers. Overall, the auditor believes that OR for existence of recorded accounts receivable is small and therefore might rely on relatively few confirmations sent to customers to verify amounts owed.

In contrast to risk that recorded receivables don't exist, the auditor is likely to conclude that the bad debts valuation allowance needs special audit attention due to the pervasive and book value risk assessments. Management has discretion in preparing accounting estimates and the motivation to understate the allowance estimate because of the need to show profits to facilitate debt renegotiation. Also, low demand for the Trasher game suggests that increased auditor scrutiny of the sales returns policy and terms of sale is warranted. The auditor may conclude that the inventory existence assertion requires no extraordinary auditing, but lower-of-cost-or-market valuation requires careful assessment of salability and realizable values.

Pioneer Wholesale Lumber Co.

In applying auditing procedures for an audit of Pioneer Wholesale Lumber Co., Julie Jones uncovered conditions consistent with fraud risk factors identified in SAS No. 82 (AICPA, 1979), entitled "Consideration of Fraud in a Financial Statement Audit."[9] These conditions caused Julie to change her planned auditing procedures in response to the changed risk assessments. Julie's description of her unexpected experience follows (relations to the audit risk model are added in parentheses):

> Last year, my firm audited a privately owned lumber wholesaler with about $2.1 million in sales. The client had two locations in the state, one in town and a branch located in a city about 180 miles away. I stayed in town to do the audit at the main location, and sent a staff assistant to the branch for accounts receivable audit work. When the assistant returned after three days, I asked him if he had found anything. Because we were under time pressure, I was relieved when he replied he had not.
>
> As I reviewed the customer accounts and entries the assistant had selected for testing, I noticed an unusual one: a $90,000 credit to accounts receivable control, with an offset to the allowance for bad debts. The explanation read: "To adjust the general ledger to the accounts receivable trial balance at the branch." I asked the assistant why an adjustment that significant was necessary. He repeated the branch manager's explanation that the branch office had some collection problems with several long-time customers, and had eased credit terms and criteria to increase sales.
>
> When planning the audit (to determine allowable DR), I recognized that the manager dominated activities at the branch and could probably override internal controls (heightened pervasive risk and control failure risk). However, I did not worry when I first heard this since I was reasonably confident the company's remaining recorded receivables were collectible. Later that day, while reviewing the analytical procedures (book value risk assessment), I noticed that the accounts receivable write-off percentages at the branch were much higher than those of the main store. The assistant's work papers explained: "Per store manager, write-off and return policies were liberalized at the branch in order to attract customers in response to increased competition."

---

9. This discussion contains substantial quotes from an illustrative case entitled "Misappropriation of Assets" that appeared in A. Barnett, J. E. Brown, R. Fleming, and W. J. Read, "The CPA as Fraud-Buster," *Journal of Accountancy*, May 1998, pp. 69–73.

The next day I began to sense something was not right. While talking to the controller at the main store (auditor inquiry (DR)), I referred to the problems at the branch and said, "It appears the credit policy changes implemented earlier this year helped to attract new customers."

"Credit policy changes?" she said. "What are you talking about? The company is a wholesale distributor. Most of our customers are construction contractors. We have been very sensitive to the economic indicators in the industry, and the financial health of our customers. If anything, we have tightened credit." The branch manager's explanation, I learned, was incorrect.

With that, I was convinced something was wrong, so the audit team confirmed selected sales and cash receipts activity in the customers' accounts that looked suspicious (reducing DR). We also traced payments back and forth from the sub ledger to the general ledger. We found delays between the date customers said payments had been made and when they were recorded. We also found an unusually large number of write-off and allowance entries to the customer accounts.

It turned out the branch manager was stealing payments that customers had made on account. The manager was covering by writing off accounts, but with occasional errors. The errors increased the number of entries necessary to cover the theft, which is why the sub ledger did not agree with the general ledger and why the write-off rates were so much higher at the branch.

Julie detected the material misappropriation of assets by following the guidance in SAS No. 82. First, she noted presence of possible fraud risk factors or other conditions affecting her initial OR assessment. She was aware that duties for processing large amounts of cash at the branch were not adequately divided among individuals (control failure risk), that top management was not providing adequate oversight of branch activities (control environment, pervasive factor risk), and that the branch manager might override controls (pervasive factor risk). The combination of risk factors and the audit procedure results led to Julie's decision that the planned audit procedures were insufficient, so she extended them, leading her detection of material misstatement.

EVALUATING AUDIT RESULTS

After planning auditing procedures necessary to achieve the detection risk that will allow audit risk to be controlled at a low level, the auditor conducts the auditing procedures. The auditor applies analytical procedures by comparing recorded amounts with expectations based on the auditor's knowledge and expertise as an auditor and his or her specific knowledge of the client's industry and real-world conditions using the methods discussed in Chapter 5. The auditor also conducts tests of details of transactions and balances in a manner similar to that of the internal auditor in Chapter 6. The auditor then evaluates results at the account level and at the financial statement level.

Account Level Evaluation

Application of auditing procedures typically results in a "best estimate" or "most likely" amount of misstatement for the account (denoted $\hat{M}$). For accounts that are audited 100 percent such as the auditor's recalculation of depreciation expense, errors found are the same as likely misstatement. For accounts that are sampled, likely misstatement is based on projecting sample results to the population from which it was selected.

How much misstatement is allowable for each account or business segment? One approach is to judgmentally assess an intolerable magnitude of misstatement for each individual account as a first pass. For example, the auditor may believe that inventory misstated by more than $200,000 would not comply with GAAP, even though M^* for the statements as a whole is, say, $500,000. In addition, most audit firms have a systematic approach for audit planning that allocates materiality to accounts that are audited on a test basis. One Big Five firm simply divides M^* by 2 and audits each account to detect errors of $M^*/2$, irrespective of the book value of the account.[10] The smaller of the account level materiality judgment or a formula-based account level materiality is then used to plan the audit and evaluate results for the account.

The auditor then compares likely misstatement with account level materiality. If likely error is close to or exceeds account level materiality, then the auditor usually discusses the likely misstatement with client management. Management may decide to conduct its own investigation to determine the correct amounts, and the auditor typically reaudits the corrected amounts. If likely misstatement is near zero, the auditor typically considers the result as "pass" and ends the audit of that account.

Accounting Estimates

Accounting estimates present a particularly difficult area for auditors. Accounting estimates measure the effects of present and past conditions such as net realizable values of inventory and receivables, future costs to be incurred such as warranty costs, future income to be earned, and allocation of past transactions such as depreciation of fixed assets. All involve outcomes of future events that cannot be known at present. Accounting estimates also involve approximations of current conditions for which precise measurement is not cost effective.

To illustrate the magnitude of accounting estimates, consider the financial statements of Applied Materials, Inc., an information technology–based company. For 1997, Applied Materials had net sales of about $4 billion, net earnings of $500 million, and net assets of about $3.6 billion. Based on our guidelines for materiality, it is likely that M^* for Applied Materials is between $20 million and $40 million. Their balance sheet shows allowance for bad debts, inventory reserves, accumulated depreciation, and warranty and pension liabilities—all based on accounting estimates. These estimates totaled $787 million, or 22 percent of net assets, and contingent loss estimates totaled $214 million, or 6 percent of net assets. The total of accounting estimates ($787 million plus $214 million) is from 25 to 50 times materiality. The dollar magnitudes and percentages are large and cover a wide range of business transactions. While some estimates are routine in nature, others are difficult to estimate and involve considerable subjectivity.

By their nature, accounting estimates are based on assumptions and judgments. These judgments differ based on the information available, the context, and who is making the judgments. Since no single estimate can be defended against all possible alternatives, some flexibility is allowed by GAAP and GAAS. According to GAAS, the auditor should

---

10. Other firms use statistical concepts and allocate materiality based on the fraction of book value in a particular account to the total book value for accounts tested in the financial statement under audit. For example, if M^* is $500,000 and inventory comprises 25 percent of total assets to be tested, then account level materiality for inventory would be $500,000 \times (.25)^{1/2} = $250,000$.

review the assumptions made by management in determining its estimates and possibly test the calculations on which they are based. The auditor also considers whether an outside expert should be hired to assist the auditor in evaluating the estimate, such as an actuary to assess actuarial liability for pensions or other post-retirement benefits, or an engineer to assess the likely experience for warranty expenses.

Because no single estimate can be definitively defended, GAAS directs the auditor to determine a "reasonable" range for an accounting estimate. The question of "reasonableness" is an important one since GAAS states that "likely" misstatement for an accounting estimate is zero if book value is within the range. If the book value falls outside the "reasonable range," then only the difference between book value and the closest end of the range is counted as likely misstatement.

While defined in probabilistic terms, the term *reasonable* in many contexts means a 60 to 70 percent confidence interval. For example, suppose engineers have estimated warranty liability based on experience with warranty repairs. The point estimate of liability is $500,000 with a standard deviation of $125,000. A 68 percent confidence interval (i.e., ± 1 standard deviation) is from $375,000 to $625,000 and might seem "reasonable." Under GAAS, any amount from $375,000 through $625,000 would be considered misstatement free. A recorded value of $350,000 would be a likely misstatement of $25,000 since $350,000 is $25,000 beyond the nearest end of the reasonable range.

On the other hand, a 99.5 percent confidence interval would not be reasonable. A 99.5 percent confidence interval (± 3 standard deviations) would range from $125,000 to $875,000 and is almost certain to include the "true" amount. However, the endpoints are "unreasonable" in that recorded values of, say, $126,000 and $874,000 would be within the range but are substantially different from the most likely amount and are each relatively unlikely to be valid.

For many kinds of accounting estimates, expectations and standard deviations cannot be objectively calculated. For some estimates, even the form of the probability distribution is difficult to assess. This is especially the case for loss contingencies involving outcomes of lawsuits and catastrophic events. Accounting standards require accrual of estimated losses when the amounts are amenable to reasonable estimation. However, when confronted with this "booking" requirement, many managements and their advisors decide that a liability for loss was not estimable after all.[11] As we will see in Chapter 9, these loss contingencies still require disclosure to comply with GAAP.

Financial Statement Level Evaluation

At the conclusion of the audit, the auditor should have a high degree of belief that the financial statements are not materially misstated. And the auditor should be able to support that degree of belief with evidence that complies with GAAS and would be accepted by other auditors as reasonable under the circumstances. That is, other auditors should agree that the auditor's assessments of pervasive factors risk, control failure risk, and book value risk support a judgment that occurrence risks were properly assessed and that the subsequent steps that the auditor took in collecting sufficient competent evidential matter provided a reasonable

---

11. For a related example, see "Wickes Sets $11.2 Million for Liability on Carpeting, below Analysts' Estimates," *The Wall Street Journal*, August 26, 1987, p. 10.

basis for the auditor's expressed opinion. The auditor's mere belief is not sufficient to support a professional opinion.

SAS No. 47 requires that the auditor evaluate the risk that any misstatements remaining after recording adjustments exceed a material amount. This evaluation is required for each individual account as well as the aggregate of accounts comprising subtotals (such as gross profit, current assets, or current liabilities) or totals (net income or total assets). For example, if misstatement for an individual account exceeds account level materiality, then an adjustment is required for that account. An adjustment may be required if likely misstatement is less than account level materiality, but is sufficiently close that there is substantial risk that misstatement might exceed account level materiality. This same reasoning process is also applied at the financial statement level.

Since multiple (and individually immaterial) misstatements are sometimes offsetting, auditors often defer adjustment consideration until completion of the audit of all major accounts. Then, the auditor arrays likely misstatements for each account in the statements of income and financial position and makes a judgment about whether there is low risk that the aggregate of the misstatements equals or exceeds materiality (i.e., $\Sigma \hat{M} \geq M^*$).

Figure 8–5 diagrams the relation of occurrence risk assessment and auditing procedures to audit evidence, financial misstatement adjustments, and the auditor's report on the audited financial statements. As shown in Figure 8–5, a standard audit report expressing an opinion of reasonable assurance that the financial statements are free of material misstatement can result from book values that passed the audit tests without adjustment. Financial statements that initially fail the audit tests may receive a favorable audit report after correction of possible misstatements (audit differences) noted during the audit. Alternatively, when audit tests initially indicate audit differences, the auditor may choose to extend the audit to obtain more evidence and find evidence that supports the original values.

If management refuses to correct financial misstatements the auditor believes are material, the auditor may modify the audit report to indicate the possible misstatement (see Chapter 9). Alternatively, management may fire an auditor who plans to issue a modified audit report, or the auditor may resign from the audit engagement and not express an opinion on the financial statements.[12]

How Much Adjustment Is Enough?

According to auditing standards (SAS No. 47), the auditor should *not* certify financial statements as complying with GAAP in all material respects if there are likely misstatements (known misstatements or projected misstatements based on samples) that exceed materiality. Likely misstatements for individual accounts are each compared with materiality, and misstatements are aggregated across a financial statement (e.g., the income statement or balance sheet) and the aggregate compared with materiality. When likely misstatement(s) exceed materiality, the auditor should insist that the misstatements be adjusted to fall within the limits of materiality. If management refuses, then the auditor is to issue a qualified opinion (see Chapter 9) or resign from the engagement without issuing an audit report.

---

12. GAAS requires notification of an entity's audit committee of various problems encountered in an audit, including disagreements that might lead to resignation. For public companies, SEC regulations require notification of the SEC of auditor changes (see Chapter 11).

FIGURE 8−5

Auditing Procedures, Adjustments, and Audit Reports

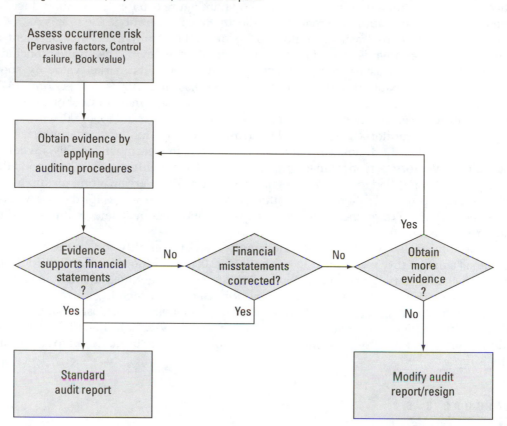

If the auditor's best estimate of aggregate misstatement is less than materiality, then the auditor should consider the risk that his or her estimates might be wrong due to imprecise analyses, imprecise judgments, or sampling error, as well as the risk that actual misstatements might exceed materiality. If the risk that misstatements might exceed materiality is more than, say, 1 percent, then the auditor should ask management to adjust the financial statements to reduce likely misstatement to an acceptable amount. Alternatively, the auditor might extend the audit to reduce uncertainty about the auditor's estimate of likely misstatement. Appendix B to this chapter shows graphically how adjustments are made for several fact situations.

To operationalize auditing standards for adjusting financial statements, some audit firms have adopted rules of thumb for deciding how much adjustment is enough. For example, some firms require adjustment of any account for which likely misstatement equals or exceeds 25 percent of materiality for the financial statement as a whole and adjustment of one or more accounts when aggregate likely misstatement for the income statement or balance sheet equals or exceeds 25 percent of materiality. These rules of thumb typically provide sufficient allowance for uncertainty in the auditor's estimates of likely misstatement.

Audit Difference Summary

To facilitate evaluation of audit differences for the overall audit, most auditors prepare a schedule of audit differences similar to that shown in Figure 8–6 for AstroGamas, Inc. The schedule reflects three audit differences for adjustment consideration. The first is AstroGamas's write-down of the Trasher inventory to the lower of cost or market—management asserts that no write-down is needed and recorded zero write-down. The auditor concludes that the cost of the Trasher ending inventory likely exceeds its market value by about $750,000, but a reasonable range for the cost is from $350,000 to $1,150,000. Therefore, GAAS (SAS No. 57) requires that the auditor consider likely understatement of Cost of Sales to be $350,000 (the difference between the recorded write-down of zero and $350,000, which is the closest end of the auditor's assessment of the reasonable range for the write-down).

The second audit difference is due to a cutoff error in December 31, 1999, inventory quantities. Inventory personnel inadvertently counted as inventory $45,000 of goods that had been sold and billed to customers as of December 31 but were awaiting pickup by the freight carrier. The third difference is a failure to record accrued wages for the last week of December. All three differences understate expenses and thus overstate earnings (and related net assets).

The total of likely misstatement does not exceed materiality for AstroGamas (AstroGamas's materiality was judged to be about $600,000), and the second and third differences are clearly not material individually. But aggregate likely misstatement is so large that the auditor is likely to conclude that some adjustment is needed to reduce the risk that misstatements might exceed $600,000. Also, likely understatement for Cost of Sales exceeds $M^*/2$, which implies that Cost of Sales (and ending inventory) may be materially misstated individually. So the auditor must either negotiate adjustments to be made or modify the auditor's report.

FIGURE 8–6

Audit Difference Summary

ASTROGAMAS, INC.
Income Statement
Year Ended December 31, 1999

| | Audit Differences | | |
| | | Adjustments | |
Account	Likely Misstatement, $\hat{M}$	Recorded	Not Recorded
Income Statement			
Cost of Sales			
Lower of cost or market	$350,000	$250,000	$100,000
Cutoff error	45,000	45,000	0
Accrued wages	35,000		35,000
Aggregate likely misstatement ($\Sigma\, \hat{M}$)	$430,000	$295,000	$135,000
Materiality (M^*)	$600,000		$600,000

The outcome of the negotiations, including the auditor's final conclusion about the valuation of the Trasher inventory, will depend on arguments raised by management and the auditor's final assessment of AuR, CBR, and ABR. Figure 8–6 assumes that AstroGamas's management decides to record $250,000 of the inventory write-down and to fully record the Cost of Sales cutoff error, but not to adjust for accrued wages. This leaves a likely overstatement of net income and assets of $135,000, which is less than 25 percent of materiality, and each account misstatement is individually less than 25 percent of materiality. With these adjustments recorded, the auditor believes that there is very low risk that actual misstatements remaining unrecorded exceed $600,000 and is willing to proceed toward a final review and possible issuance of a standard report for AstroGamas.

Final Review

After all planned auditing procedures have been conducted and adjustments negotiated and recorded, the partner in charge of the audit makes a final review of the financial statements. The partner considers the recorded amounts (as adjusted) in light of all that he or she knows about the firm. Analytical procedures are applied to final balances to identify any remaining unusual amounts or relationships. The auditor should have an explanation for any amounts that appear out of line with (revised) expectations. Seeking explanations may identify misstatements and prevent attesting to possibly misstated financial statements (and prevent future litigation and damage awards).

The ultimate outcome of auditor–client negotiation over adjustments depends on a number of factors, of course. In negotiating with the auditor, management must keep in mind these various factors. Being aggressive in negotiating can lead to more favorable accounting reports, but being too aggressive can cause the auditor to reconsider his or her decisions about CBR and ABR. Audit firms are well aware of their liability for materially misstated financial statements (part of AuR) and aware that future declines in stock price and revelation of management fraud will likely lead to lawsuits against the auditor (part of CBR and ABR) and higher judgments or settlements.

As discussed in Chapter 7, companies that have fraudulently misstated their financial statements have typically overstated revenues (and accelerated revenue recognition), understated expenses (and delayed expense recognition), changed accounting methods to increase net income and assets, experienced declining business prospects, and had management compensation plans based on accounting performance. In the final review, the auditor considers all five of these factors. Individually or in combination, they may suggest greatly increased CBR and ABR, leading to a tough negotiating stance by the auditor. At the extreme, the auditor may decide that ABR and CBR are sufficiently high that the audit firm should resign the audit engagement. This drastic action sometimes leads to large declines in stock price—don't push your auditor too far!

PRACTICAL CONSIDERATIONS REGARDING ADJUSTMENTS OF AUDIT DIFFERENCES

Incentives

The discussion above has characterized audit adjustments as part of a statistical process of applying GAAP and GAAS measurement rules. In the real world, behavioral tendencies and economic incentives of both management and the auditor, as well as the overall financial condition and future prospects for the client firm, have an effect.

Management typically is opposed to adjusting financial statements for several reasons. Since adjustments typically lower reported earnings, management is reluctant to make changes that will reduce its reported performance or reduce its apparent financial condition as measured by financial ratios. Management may also be committed to an earnings number because of information provided to financial analysts about prospective earnings, as well as press releases of preliminary earnings. Other things equal, management would prefer that audited earnings be consistent with analysts' forecasts, their own public forecasts, and any preliminary earnings releases. Differences may imply surprises, lack of good internal control, or lack of integrity on the part of management. Final earnings that are less than forecasts or preliminary announcements are sometimes severely punished in the stock market by stock price declines immediately following the release of final earnings amounts. For example, the stock price of Revlon Inc. fell 44 percent after management announced third quarter earnings of $.07 per share when analysts had forecasted $.73.[13]

Auditors would like to please client management, other things equal, to protect their future fees and earnings stream. Other things are *not* equal, however, when there is substantial risk that the auditor will violate GAAS or face future loss of reputation and legal damages from a client that overstates earnings in violation of GAAP or experiences financial declines. Thus, there is a tendency for client management and the auditor to negotiate proposed adjustments for audit differences that may equal or exceed materiality.

What Do You Get from a Financial Statement Audit?

Linda Jo (owner of LJ Appliances, Inc.) didn't fear an audit because she believed that her financial statements were essentially error free. For her, the decision to hire an auditor was simply a matter of comparing audit cost to the reduced risk premium or price protection discount demanded by the prospective buyer. But what about companies "on the average"? What does management get for its audit fee, and how is the information available to outsiders changed?

Audits do improve the quality of financial statements by reducing imprecision and bias in application of GAAP through the audit itself, and through anticipation of the audit by management and its employees. Studies of auditors' work papers across companies and across time indicate that for the typical audit, detected misstatements average from two to eight times M^*, in the direction of overstatement of earnings and assets.[14] Furthermore, while overstatements outnumber understatements and are larger in absolute magnitude, there are misstatements in both directions. Most material misstatements are adjusted by the client prior to issuing financial statements. As a result, both bias and imprecision are reduced.

Anticipation of an audit has several effects on the quality of pre-audit records. Management anticipates the audit by consulting with the auditor on how to account for routine matters such as revenue recognition and for significant transactions such as mergers and acquisitions, reorganizations, leases, and other long-term contracts and alliances (the CPA acts as an information originator). Management often improves its accounting system,

---

13. T. Parker-Pope, "How Revlon's Third-Quarter Results Got So Smudged," *The Wall Street Journal,* October 6, 1998, p. B-4.
14. For a summary, see W. Kinney and R. Martin, "Does Auditing Reduce Bias in Financial Reporting? A Review of Audit-Related Adjustment Studies," *Auditing: A Journal of Practice and Theory,* Spring 1994, pp. 149–56.

making it able to generate GAAP-quality reports, and improves the quality of internal control as a means of reducing the audit fee. These internal control improvements also lead to better information for day-to-day operating decisions by management and employees. Finally, management may benefit by the auditor's assessment of the firm's long-term viability and the competitiveness of its business processes.

Since management often installs better controls in anticipation of the audit, employees have less opportunity for fraud. Employees may also anticipate the audit by being more diligent in the conduct of their activities day to day. Some employees prone to theft may quit their jobs, and others will decide not to misappropriate company assets or misrepresent information because they believe that internal control (or the auditor) will detect their misdeeds.

Adjustments Waived

The effects of an audit are varied, and the resulting imprecision and bias reduction are not absolute or uniform. The booking of adjustments depends on a number of contextual factors. Work-paper analyses and experiments using audit partners and managers show that most potential adjustments are waived by auditors (i.e., not "booked" by the client).[15] Many of these are immaterial, but even those exceeding M^* are sometimes waived and are more likely to be waived if they are from subjective sources such as accounting estimates. This tendency to waive adjustments for errors in accounting estimates is understandable, given the imprecise nature of accounting estimates. However, it shows considerable "wiggle room" for management since an accounting estimate within a reasonable range is counted as error free under GAAS and the range itself could be large.

There have been no comprehensive studies of misstatements in accounting estimates. However, there is a comprehensive study of an important accounting estimate for property-casualty insurance companies—the amount of outstanding claim losses to be paid in the future (i.e., claim loss reserves). Researchers used regulatory reports required by state insurance commissioners to match accounting estimates with their eventual realization over the ensuing 10-year period.[16] They found accounting estimates of loss reserves were understated on average by five times M^* but with many materially overstated (the average absolute misstatement was about 16 times M^*). Since these amounts were subjected to estimation and testing by experts, it seems apparent that expertise alone is not sufficient to reduce misstatements to a negligible amount.

Public announcements of error corrections are rare, but those rare events reveal something about possible negotiations because they are disclosures of an extreme accounting failure—public release of materially misstated financial statements. Both the company and its (continuing) auditor would have preferred not to disclose such misstatements but chose

---

15. See C. Houghton, and J. Fogarty, "Inherent Risk," *Auditing: A Journal of Practice and Theory,* Spring 1991, pp. 1–21; R. Icerman and W. Hillison, "Disposition of Audit-Detected Errors: Some Evidence on Evaluative Materiality," *Auditing: A Journal of Practice and Theory,* Spring 1991, pp. 22–34; and A. Wright and S. Wright, "An Examination of Factors Affecting the Decision to Waive Audit Adjustments," *Journal of Accounting, Auditing and Finance,* Winter 1997, pp. 15–36.
16. K. Petroni and M. Beasley, "Errors in Accounting Estimates and Their Relation to Audit Firm Type," *Journal of Accounting Research,* Spring 1996, pp. 151–71.

to do so as the least costly alternative given the misstatement. In a study of 44 public companies correcting prior year's earnings, 93 percent were for overstatement of earnings and overstatements averaged 1.9 percent of recorded assets.[17]

In a study of 73 firms correcting previously publicly reported (but unaudited) quarterly earnings, researchers found that 62 percent of corrections of earnings were overstatements, 24 percent were understatements, and 14 percent netted to zero over the year (i.e., a timing difference).[18] The year-end announcements correcting previously reported quarterly earnings overstatements were noteworthy in that they were *preceded* by significant stock price declines, declining bond ratings, and litigation. These negative events did not precede the firms' correcting understatements or timing differences. It is as if the auditors or management decided to protect themselves by "coming clean" or perhaps the auditors audited more intensively due to the increased ABR and CBR of the clients experiencing hard times.

Management Discretion: The Case of IBM Corp.

How stringent are auditors in monitoring management's discretion in preparing financial statements? Consider the case of IBM management's accounting choices. In the mid- to late 1980s, IBM's strategy based on mainframe computers was faltering. One response of management was to change accounting practices. Two examples: Management began booking revenues when mainframes were shipped to dealers, even though dealers could return them without penalty, and it changed lease financing practices to allow recording of all revenue on a long-term computer lease when the lease was executed rather than as cash was received.[19]

The revenue process for mainframe computers is lengthy, and GAAP has no specific guidance for recording mainframe revenues. A very conservative practice would be recording a sale when the computer is installed in the ultimate user's offices and is properly functioning. Less conservative practices that might sometimes be justified are recording revenues when the computer arrives on customer premises or when the computer is shipped to a dealer for eventual sale. As IBM's troubles grew, the revenue-recognition point became less conservative.

Recording of income from leasing equipment under GAAP depends on whether the lease is an operating or a sales-type lease. Operating lease revenues are recorded as they are received, and sales-type lease revenues are recorded at lease execution. The FASB's rules for sales-leasing are extensive and require that the sum of lease payments plus the value of the computer at the end of the lease total at least 90 percent of the computer's cost at execution. IBM began purchasing insurance that guaranteed a value of the computer at the end of lease that achieved the 90 percent hurdle. Purchase of the insurance allowed IBM to record revenues earlier than would have been possible otherwise.

---

17. M. DeFond and J. Jiambalvo, "Incidence and Circumstances of Accounting Errors," *The Accounting Review*, July 1991, pp. 643–55.
18. W. Kinney and L. McDaniel, "Characteristics of Firms Correcting Previously Reported Quarterly Earnings," *Journal of Accounting and Economics*, February 1989, pp. 71–93.
19. See M. Miller and L. Berton, "Softer Numbers—as IBM's Woes Grew, Its Accounting Tactics Got Less Conservative," *The Wall Street Journal*, April 7, 1993, p. A-1.

Neither of these activities violate GAAP, and the formal accounting changes were disclosed in financial statement footnotes. However, the amounts were large and delayed financial statement recognition of the financial difficulties of the company.

Will Your Auditor "Turn in" You or Your Employees?

The external auditor is not trained to make a legal determination of violations of law and has no special responsibility for enforcement of laws regarding client activities. The auditor has a responsibility to plan the audit to detect material fraud by client employees or management, and a responsibility to consider illegal acts by clients that may have a material effect on financial statements. The auditor also has an obligation to report to an appropriate level of higher management or the audit committee any audit findings suggesting that significant illegal acts might have occurred.

Under GAAS, the auditor has an obligation as part of a financial statement audit engagement to communicate several matters to the audit committee of the board of directors (and auditor distribution of any such written report is restricted to the audit committee). The auditor is to report

- The auditor's responsibilities under GAAS, and limits of those responsibilities.
- Significant internal control weaknesses, fraud, and illegal acts detected during the course of the audit.
- The basis for significant accounting policies chosen and accounting estimates made by management.
- Likely misstatements and potential adjustments arising during the audit.
- Disagreements with management over accounting principles and audit scope matters.

For private companies, the auditor's responsibilities for these disclosures end with the report to the audit committee. For public companies regulated by the SEC, the auditor has additional obligations to inform the SEC of certain matters if the audit committee does not forward the auditor's concerns to the SEC within one business day (see Chapter 11).

SUMMARY

The external auditor assesses pervasive factors, control failure, and book value risks and applies auditing procedures to detect material departures of financial statements from GAAP. GAAS guides the sufficiency of evidence to obtain reasonable assurance, or low risk, of unknowingly certifying financial statements that are materially misstated. These two sets of standards (GAAP and GAAS) define obligations of client management, guide the auditor's work, and define the rights of outside users of financial statements.

After planned auditing procedures are conducted, aggregate likely misstatements are compared with financial statement materiality and misstatements of individual accounts are compared with account level materiality. If there is low risk that likely misstatement(s) equal or exceed materiality and footnote disclosures comply with GAAP, then the auditor can issue a three-paragraph standard audit report. If at the end of the audit there is unacceptably high risk that the financial statements are materially misstated, then before signing a standard report the auditor will ask the client to correct the financial statements through adjustments or additional disclosures.

Auditor and client management incentives affect the final outcome of the audit process as potential adjustments and footnote disclosures are discussed and negotiated. Within the limits of GAAP and GAAS, the auditor is likely to accommodate the client, other things equal. The auditor is less likely to accommodate the client when there are large misstatements, misstatements are "hard numbers" (rather than allocations or estimates), or the auditor believes that the client has a high risk of poor prospects in the future or that the auditor faces high risk of litigation or loss of reputation.

APPENDIX A

Audit Risk for Financial Statement Users

Audit risk to the auditor (AuR) and the risk to the financial statement user of relying on materially misstated financial statements are slightly different. Risk to the user is the risk that audited financial statements receiving a standard (unqualified) audit opinion are, in fact, materially misstated. This risk is slightly smaller than AuR.

To illustrate the difference, let's apply the audit risk model—AuR = OR × DR—to a single asset account. Component recorded elements (book values) for the account are either correctly recorded or are fictitious, and the aggregate recorded asset balance contains either zero fictitious elements ($M = 0$) or a material amount of fictitious elements ($M = M^*$). OR is the risk that the aggregate prior-to-audit book value is materially misstated. DR is the risk that auditing procedures will fail to indicate or detect material misstatement when it exists. Stated differently, DR is the probability that a materially misstated account will "pass" the auditor's misstatement detection tests.

Figure A diagrams the possible misstatement of book value ($M = 0, M = M^*$), possible results of audit tests (pass audit tests, fail audit tests), and their possible outcomes and probabilities. For the first two outcomes, audit tests are passed and the auditor's decision is to accept the book values without adjustment or correction. But the two outcomes differ as to the presence of misstatements. For the first, $M = 0$, and the accept decision is correct. For the second, $M = M^*$, and the accept decision by the auditor is incorrect. The third outcome (M^*, fail audit tests) is a correct reject decision. It typically leads to management's correction of the book values before the auditor agrees to issue a favorable audit report.

The auditor's (audit) risk in accepting book values that have *passed* the audit tests can be seen in Figure A as OR × DR / (OR × DR + (1 − OR × 1). This is because, given the "pass audit test" outcome, the auditor doesn't know whether the book values contain zero misstatement or are materially misstated. The auditor's audit risk is the risk that the second outcome (M^*, pass audit tests) has occurred, rather than the (0, pass audit tests) outcome. For the "fail audit test" result, the auditor requires correction of the misstatement before issuing a favorable audit report on the account.

In Figure A, all audits will result in a standard unqualified audit report either because the audit test results were favorable or, if the audit results were unfavorable, the account was corrected. The outside-the-firm financial statement user's risk of relying (incorrectly) on materially misstated financial statements that receive a favorable auditor's report can be seen in Figure A as OR × DR divided by 1.0, which is the sum of the probabilities of all outcomes or simply OR × DR. This is because the outside user of audited financial statements will *not* know whether the audit tests were passed and therefore no adjustments recorded, or the audit tests were failed and management has corrected the material misstatement that was detected by the auditor.

For a given level of OR and DR, the user's AuR = OR × DR is slightly larger than the auditor's AuR = OR × DR / (OR × DR + (1 − OR) × 1). The difference is very small for low OR and larger for high OR. Stated another way, suppose an auditor uses the auditor's AuR formula to plan allowable DR for a given OR to achieve AuR of, say, .01. The resulting

DR will yield AuR for the user of slightly less than .01. Thus, the user's AuR = OR × DR formula provides an upper limit on audit risk for both. Because it is a simple and reasonable approximation of risk for both parties, AuR = OR × DR is used in our discussions of AuR and risk to users.

FIGURE A

Audit Test Results and Audit Outcomes

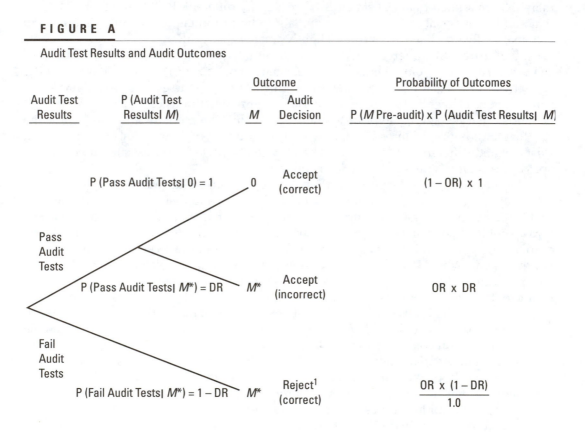

1. When the auditor rejects financial statements as possibly materially misstated, they are typically corrected, and the auditor gives a standard report. If the statements are not corrected, then the auditor gives a modified audit report that indicates the nature and likely amount of misstatement (see Chapter 9).

APPENDIX B

How Much Adjustment Is Enough—in Pictures

Figure B, panel a, diagrams the auditor's after-audit probability distribution or beliefs about the possible magnitudes of misstatement in audited earnings taken as a whole. This diagram is an abstract integration of multidimensional beliefs about individual components and is illustrative rather than a description that can be mathematically calculated. However, the diagram is useful in understanding the concepts in SAS No. 47 and the audit risk model.

Panel a shows a typical posterior distribution of the auditor's beliefs. Distribution A is centered near zero (denoted $\hat{M}_A$ for "likely" misstatement), with very little of the distribution to the right of M^*, which denotes material overstatement, or to the left of $-M^*$. This posterior distribution might be obtained for a client with little pre-audit misstatement or after adjustment for a client with material misstatements. Distribution B (panel b) is also centered on $\hat{M}_A$, but with more spread—there is considerable risk that misstatement equals or exceeds M^* (or is less than or equal to $-M^*$). For B, the auditor is rather uncertain about possible misstatement and needs to reduce the uncertainty by obtaining more evidence. Distribution C (panel c) shows the posterior distribution for a client with material overstatement likely, and it is "more likely than not" that overstatement exceeds M^*. The auditor would not be able to give a standard report for a company in situation C without

FIGURE B

Auditor's Post-Audit Beliefs about Possible Earnings Misstatement

a. Typical post-audit beliefs

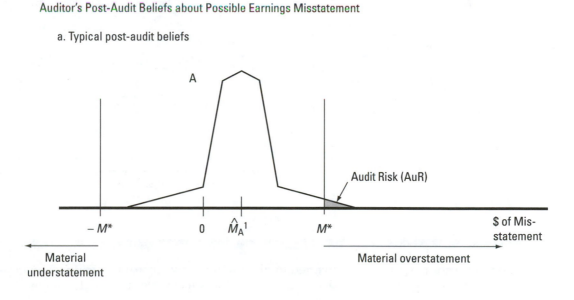

1. $\hat{M}_A$ = likely misstatement for typical audit beliefs (distribution A).

FIGURE B (Continued)

Auditor's Post-Audit Beliefs about Possible Earnings Misstatement

b. Inadequate evidence

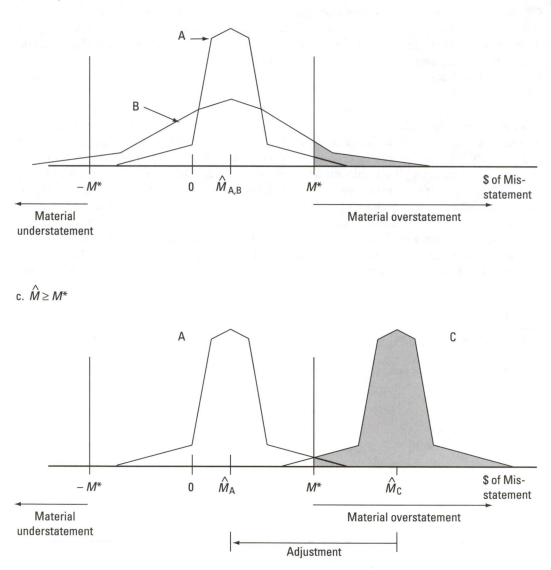

c. $\hat{M} \geq M^*$

adjustment. Distribution C can be converted to distribution A by recording an adjustment of $\hat{M}_C - \hat{M}_A$. Adjusting the recorded balance to $\hat{M}_A$ reduces likely misstatement to an immaterial amount.

Distribution D in panel d shows an intermediate case with $\hat{M}_D < M^*$, but there is nontrivial risk (area to the right of M^*) that misstatement exceeds M^*. For case D, there are two

FIGURE B (Continued)

Auditor's Post-Audit Beliefs about Possible Earnings Misstatement

d. High risk of $M \geq M^*$

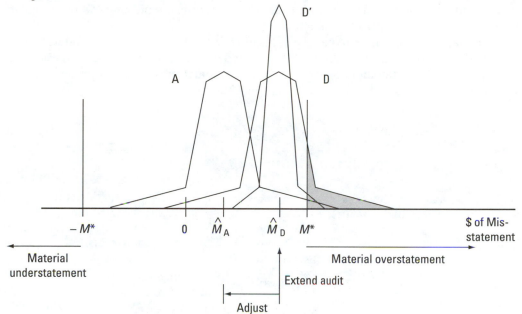

e. High risk of $M \leq -M^*$

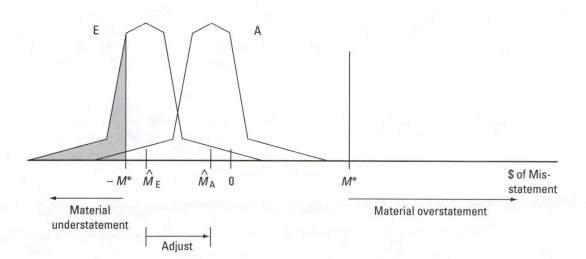

possible solutions. One is to book an adjustment of $\hat{M}_D - \hat{M}_A$ to convert distribution D to distribution A. Alternatively, the auditor could audit more to increase his or her belief that misstatement does not exceed materiality, and the peaked distribution (D′) might become the after-audit distribution. While the alternative is possible, it is not often pursued in practice because obtaining virtual certainty that the amounts are not materially misstated entails greatly increased audit costs.

Finally, Distribution E in panel e of Figure B indicates sufficient understatement to require adjustment to raise the amount of reported earnings. While these situations are less common than overstatement of earnings, they are sometimes the appropriate risk—for example, in the Northern Frontier Parks case in Chapter 7.

CASE 8

PRECISION VISION CORPORATION

Precision Vision Corporation (PVC) is a Canadian firm that sells high-quality glass lenses to individual eye-wear customers by mail order. For 2000, recorded revenue was $1,950,000 and total assets were $1,550,000, while gross profit was $950,000 and net earnings were $550,000. PVC wants to expand to the United States, and to do so is seeking a substantial bank loan in the United States. To enhance the credibility of its financial statements (as part of the loan application), PVC has hired a prominent CA firm, Eleanor and Olivia, to audit its 2000 financial statements using U.S. GAAS. PVC wants to show the best earnings and financial position possible to maximize its loan prospects.

The Eleanor and Olivia audit of PVC reveals the following items for consideration:

a. Eleanor and Olivia selected an essentially random sample of 80 accounts from the approximately 8,000 customer receivables. The total book value of PVC receivables is $525,000 and Eleanor and Olivia believe that errors totaling $10,000 would be "intolerable" for receivables. They found that two sampled accounts were in error—a $500 account had an audited value of $300 and a $15 account had an audited value of $3.

b. The beginning inventory was understated by $2,500 due to an audit adjustment for the prior year that had been waived in 1999 as immaterial. The current audit covered about 20 percent of

PVC's ending inventory ($810,000 book value) and revealed 35 errors. Some errors were overstatements and some were understatements, but over all items, the net was $125 overstatement.

c. A change in the accounting for depreciation reduced depreciation expense by $8,000 from what it would have been using the 1999 method.

d. Warranty expense is shown as $50,000 and the Eleanor and Olivia auditor believes that it should be $75,000, but that a range of $65,000–$80,000 could be defended.

e. An error in prepaid insurance resulted in an overstatement of insurance expense of $1,000.

Assume the role of Eleanor and Olivia as the auditor of PVC to recreate the auditor's thought process in aggregating audit results, proposing adjustments, and discussing results with management.

a. Prepare a schedule of "likely misstatements" in the 2000 PVC income statement using U.S. GAAS.

b. Calculate a rough estimate of materiality for overall earnings of PVC and compare it to aggregate "likely misstatement" as defined in SAS No. 47. What would be an "acceptable" audited earnings number for PVC?

c. What adjustments would you propose for PVC's statements? Will PVC management accept them? How would you respond if they won't? What amount of misstatement is likely to remain in PVC's audited financials, and what are the implications for a banker who will evaluate PVC's loan application?

KEY WORDS

audit difference summary   A schedule of (audit) differences between recorded values and the misstatement-free GAAP amount aggregated for the overall audit for adjustment consideration.

audit risk model (AuR)   Approximation of audit risk (AuR) as the product of material misstatement occurrence risk (OR) and risk that auditing procedures will fail to detect any material misstatement (DR): $AuR = OR \times DR$.

book value risk (BVR)   The risk that material misstatement has occurred based on the auditor's comparison of pre-audit recorded values with the auditor's expectations of their values.

control failure risk (CFR)   The risk that material misstatement might arise in the accounting measurement process and controls would fail to detect the misstatement.

detection risk (DR)   The risk that auditing procedures fail to detect material misstatement(s) that exist in pre-audit recorded values.

final review   Auditor consideration of the recorded amounts (as adjusted) in light of all knowledge about the firm after all planned auditing procedures have been conducted and audit adjustments negotiated and recorded.

generally accepted auditing standards (GAAS)   Ten characteristics, codified by the AICPA and recognized by the SEC, that describe the quality of performance typically rendered by professional auditors in conducting financial statement audits.

occurrence risk (OR)   The approximately additive risk ($OR = PFR + CFR + BVR$), comprised of pervasive factors risk (PFR), control failure risk (CFR), and book value risk (BVR), that material misstatement exists in a pre-audit financial statement assertion.

pervasive factors risk (PFR)   Factors that affect the risk of pre-audit misstatement of more than one account, such as client viability threats, control environment weaknesses, motivation for misstatement or fraud by management or employees, industry and time-specific factors, and general computer control weaknesses.

9

CHAPTER

Auditors' Reports and Their Interpretation

◆ **W**hat types of companies voluntarily change accounting methods, or correct previously reported financial statements?

◆ What are the consequences if my auditor issues a modified auditor's report?

◆ Should my interpretation of an auditor's report be affected by who hired the auditor?

◆ What do external auditors know that they won't tell financial statement readers?

◆ What important messages are hidden in the auditor's words and financial statement footnotes?

All of these questions involve interpretation of audited financial statements and the auditor's report on those statements. The statements and report result from the complex interaction of GAAP, GAAS, and the incentives, strategies, and reputations of management and the auditor. They cannot be properly interpreted without considering each of these factors.

In Chapters 7 and 8 we considered management's responsibilities for financial statement numbers under a typical audit contract. This chapter outlines GAAP-based risk disclosures required of management and the structure of required audit report modifications for audits under GAAS. It also considers the effect of the certification contract and incentives on the auditor's behavior. The concepts discussed apply both to voluntary reporting under GAAP and GAAS and to regulatory reporting (discussed in Chapter 11).

FINANCIAL STATEMENT ASSERTIONS/DISCLOSURES AND AUDIT REPORT MODIFICATION

In a typical certification-type audit contract, the auditor's client is the management or directors of the company preparing financial statements. Acting on their own or on behalf of stockholders, management hires an audit firm to certify that the statements comply with

GAAP. Management and/or the directors want to inform outsiders of the favorable characteristics of the firm in order to reduce the risk premium or price protection discount demanded by outsiders in doing business with the firm. Alternatively (or perhaps additionally), the client may simply wish to comply with contractual or regulatory requirements as discussed in Chapter 11.

Because management is responsible for both the real-world condition of the firm and preparing information about the firm, it has a stake in the information that may conflict with the interests of an outside user of the information. Due to this conflict, an auditor's certification of compliance with GAAP can add value for management if outside financial statement users believe that it adds credibility (reliability) to the statements. Users' perceptions depend on the auditor's reputation for applying GAAS and trustworthiness in reporting conclusions—even if the conclusions are unfavorable to the management hiring the auditor.

Management asserts that its financial statements represent real-world conditions of the firm as measured by GAAP. For example, the assertions include the existence, valuation, ownership, completeness, and disclosure/display of each asset balance—according to GAAP. "According to GAAP" means that the measurement methods are generally accepted and are applicable to the circumstances. It also means that misapplication of accounting methods (if any) results in misstatements of less than a material amount (M^*), both individually and in the aggregate. GAAP specify methods of measurement of real-world conditions and provide for disclosure of conditions that cannot be measured in financial statement numbers such as loss contingencies and possible business failure. GAAP (and GAAS) limit the ability of management (and an auditor hired by management) to paint a more favorable picture of real-world conditions than exists. But GAAP and GAAS are also inherently imprecise, and discretion left to management can lead to a wide range of allowable net income and asset values.

GAAS provide criteria for the auditor's reporting on adverse or unusual conditions that are not (or cannot be) addressed by adjusting financial statement amounts. The auditor is required to modify the standard audit report when (a) the financial statements depart materially from GAAP, (b) the scope of auditing procedures applied is less than GAAS requires, or (c) unusual circumstances exist such as potential business failure, or accounting method changes.

As discussed in Chapter 7, the three-paragraph standard audit report is the most favorable report that can be given. Management prefers a standard report, and the auditor would like to please management to the extent possible. Because of these preferences, when a modified audit report *is* issued, it almost always contains or implies important information, and is usually of more consequence than literal interpretation of its wording would suggest.

FINANCIAL STATEMENT FOOTNOTE DISCLOSURE CRITERIA

As part of its financial reporting responsibilities, management is required to prepare informative financial statement footnote disclosures about the firm as well as its financial measurements. Included are disclosures of accounting policies, contract terms, transactions with related parties controlled by (or controlling) the entity, accounting changes, and loss contingencies and other uncertainties.

Single-number measures of asset or liability values may not adequately represent the range of possible conditions that have occurred, or may occur or change in the near future. While risk is less subject to quantification than amounts of inventory on hand or cash wages paid, risk information is necessary to interpret the real-world condition of a firm as measured by GAAP financial statements. In recent years, disclosures of risks and loss contingencies have become more important. This is due, in part, to the speed with which conditions change.

In the United States, disclosures by management of risks and uncertainties that must accompany GAAP-based financial statements come from the FASB, the AICPA, and, for public companies, the SEC. Management is required to make assertions about or disclose loss contingencies, certain aspects of accounting estimates, the nature of operations, and vulnerability to certain concentrations. Management is not required to assert that the company has the capability to remain in business for the foreseeable future without outside intervention or assistance (i.e., that the business is a "going concern"). However, as we shall see, the auditor may require footnote disclosure of substantial doubt about going-concern status.

FASB

SFAS No. 5, entitled "Accounting for Contingencies" (FASB, 1975), and FASB Interpretation No. 14, "Reasonable Estimation of the Amount of a Loss" (FASB, 1976), define GAAP for contingencies. Contingencies are defined as "an existing condition, situation, or set of circumstances involving uncertainty as to possible gain or loss to an enterprise that will ultimately be resolved when one or more future events occur or fail to occur" (para. 1). Thus, a contingency involves future events that *cannot* be known as of the financial statement date.

Loss contingencies are to be quantified and recorded in financial statement numbers if it is "probable" that a material loss has been incurred as of the financial statement date and the amount of loss can be reasonably estimated. If the probability of a material loss is greater than "remote" but cannot be reasonably estimated, then disclosure of the possible loss in a financial statement footnote is required for a GAAP presentation.

SFAS No. 5 and Interpretation No. 14 apply to all types of loss contingencies, including those related to litigation, both pending and threatened. Litigation contingencies present a particularly difficult problem for disclosure since they involve an adversarial relation with another party and complex legal matters that are beyond the expertise of the auditor. For example, client counsel doesn't want to prejudice its legal case by making negative predictions about possible settlements or outcomes at trial. Because of the complex relations and the technical nature of litigation-related contingencies, financial statement disclosure of such matters is regulated by a special set of rules for auditors and client counsel. This set of procedures was negotiated by their respective trade associations (AICPA and the American Bar Association) and requires that client counsel provide the auditor with a representation letter that describes all litigation, legal claims against the firm (both asserted and unasserted), and assessments known to the counsel that require disclosure under GAAP (i.e., that may involve material loss as defined in SFAS No. 5).

Risk of adverse outcomes is not often quantifiable in objective terms such as numerical probabilities. To deal with this difficulty, subjective probability phrases have been used to characterize ranges of probabilities. SFAS No. 5 defines an event as "probable" if it is "likely" to occur, "reasonably possible" if it is more than remote but less than likely, and "remote" if its likelihood of occurrence is "slight." Interpretation of the terms remote, reasonably possible, and probable is important because they determine the required accounting disclosures and the auditor's report modification response. But what do they mean? Unfortunately, the terms have different meanings in different contexts and in the same contexts across different parties.

Surveys of auditors, investors, bankers, and managers have determined broad borderlines for the phrases in terms of probabilities. These parties typically view the borderline between remote and reasonably possible as about .2 in probability, and the borderline between reasonably possible and probable as about .7, with considerable variation around these borders across individuals and contexts. So a loss with a probability of less than about .2 would be deemed remote and not require footnote disclosure. But if the probability of a material loss is greater than about .2, then at least footnote description is required by GAAP. If material loss is about .7 or greater and is reasonably estimable, then GAAP requires recording of the estimated loss amount.

Auditors as a group tend to view the threshold values lower than do managers, with financial statement users in between the two.[1] Thus, management may dispute the auditor's assessment of the threshold value for applying SFAS No. 5. For example, management and the auditor may agree that the probability of loss of a material amount is, say, "7 chances in 10," but disagree about whether the possible loss is "probable" and thus requires recording it in current financial statements. Auditors also judge thresholds higher for clients that are in sound financial condition with good prospect for the future than they do for clients with poor prospects and poor current conditions.[2] Thus, the auditor might decide that a client with poor prospects must disclose a possibly material loss that has a .2 probability, but not require footnote disclosure for a .2 probability material loss for a client with excellent prospects.

To apply the risk measurement concepts of SFAS No. 5, the auditor must evaluate the probability that a possible loss will equal or exceed a material amount. Figure 9–1 shows some possibilities under several probability distributions. All three distributions in Figure 9–1 have an expected loss equal to 1.5 times materiality ($1.5 \times M^*$).

In case a, which might represent the future warranty cost distribution, the point estimate of loss is $1.5 \times M^*$, with a "bell-shaped" distribution of possible values around that best estimate and well over half the distribution to the right of M^*. While the accounting for warranty expense is an accounting estimate, it is also possible to consider warranties as a loss contingency. Applying SFAS No. 5 and Interpretation No. 14 would lead to a conclusion that the amount of loss in case a is reasonably estimable and that the point estimate, or at least the lower end of a reasonable range of possible future expenditures, for warranty services should be recorded as a current expense. For example, a 68 percent confidence interval ($\pm$ one standard deviation for a normal distribution) might be considered a "reasonable range" for expense measurement. This would imply that an expense and liability of at least M^* should be recorded to comply with GAAP.

1. J. Reimers, "Additional Evidence on the Need for Disclosure Reports," *Accounting Horizons,* March 1992, pp. 36–41.
2. K. Hackenbrack and M. Nelson, "Auditors' Incentives and Their Application of Financial Accounting Standards," *The Accounting Review,* January 1996, pp. 43–60.

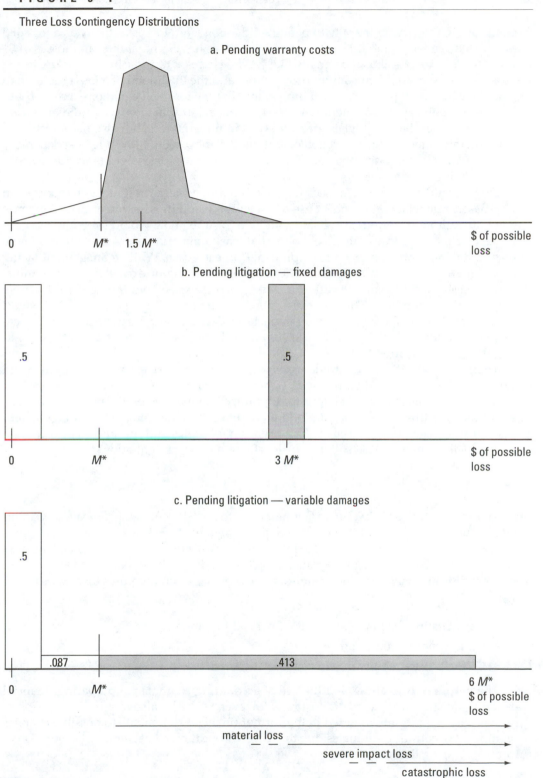

FIGURE 9–1

Three Loss Contingency Distributions

a. Pending warranty costs

0   M*   1.5 M* $ of possible loss

b. Pending litigation — fixed damages

.5   .5

0   M*   3 M* $ of possible loss

c. Pending litigation — variable damages

.5   .087   .413

0   M*   6 M*
$ of possible loss

material loss

severe impact loss

catastrophic loss

In case b, which might apply to pending litigation, zero loss is as likely as a loss of 3 $\times$ M^*, with no other possibilities. For case c, a zero loss has .5 probability, and losses of \$1 through 6 $\times$ M^* are possible and equally likely. While cases a, b, and c have equal expected losses, they differ as to the maximum possible loss and the likelihood of a loss greater than or equal to M^*. Case a has the highest probability that the loss will equal or exceed M^* but the lowest probability that it might have a severe or catastrophic impact on the operation of the entity. Case c has the highest probability of immaterial loss, but also has substantial risk of possibly catastrophic impact on operations (see next section). While the probability distribution of possible losses may be important, GAAP provides no guidance for describing the probability distribution.

How would you expect to see these loss contingencies in Figure 9–1 reported in GAAP-based financial statements? Case a is likely to result in adjustment of the expense and liability amounts, while cases b and c are not. Cases b and c would probably result in footnote disclosures because the likelihood of at least a material loss is more than remote but less than common assessments of "probable" in each case. While management facing case c might argue that the .413 probability of a loss equaling or exceeding M^* is remote, thus not requiring disclosure, the auditor is likely to disagree about the need for footnote disclosure by management. This is because there is a .25 probability of a loss of $3M^*$ to $6M^*$. The latter might be considered a severe impact or even catastrophic impact loss. The reasonable possibility of catastrophic impact loss would be considered by the auditor in evaluating disclosure required by GAAP.

There is no specific GAAP guidance as to how different risk exposures in cases b and c should be described. Rather, financial statement footnote descriptions are matters for sometimes heated negotiation between the auditor, client management, and client counsel. The auditor may threaten to issue a modified audit opinion and negotiate for adjustment or additional disclosure by the client. The resulting footnotes and/or audit report contain considerable information that still may be less benign than it might appear.

AICPA

The Accounting Standards Executive Committee of the AICPA (AcSEC) has issued accounting disclosure guidance in addition to that required by the FASB. The additional disclosures of risks and uncertainties are intended to provide early warning of possible financial setbacks over the coming year. Statement of Position (SOP) 94-6 (AICPA, 1994), entitled "Disclosure of Certain Significant Risks and Uncertainties," is part of GAAP and requires disclosure of

- The nature of business operations.
- Use of estimates in preparation of financial statements.
- Certain significant estimates.
- Current vulnerability due to concentrations.

The nature of operations and the use of accounting estimates in preparing financial statements are straightforward disclosures. However, SOP 94-6 also requires discussion of the sensitivity of amounts reported in the current financial statements to possible changes in significant accounting estimates due to changed conditions that might arise in the near future (i.e., during the next year).

Disclosure of vulnerability to concentrations applies to concentration of customers and concentration of suppliers. Thus, a company that is a captive supplier would require disclosure, as would a company that has one or a few primary customers (e.g., George's Electronic Security would be required to disclose that its sales are to a single customer, but not its suppliers). Management is also required to scale the magnitude of possible adverse effects of the concentration on operations by categorizing the impact as "material," a "severe impact," or a "catastrophic" impact. A "severe" impact has significant and financially disruptive impact on normal operations of the entity. Catastrophic impact is not specifically defined, but might include ceasing operations or insolvency.

SEC

Under Regulation S-X, the Securities and Exchange Commission requires disclosure of the nature of a registrant's operations, risks and uncertainties, and other matters in a section of Form 10-K filings called "Management Discussion and Analysis." These requirements, which do not apply to privately held companies, will be discussed in Chapter 11.

Knowledge of the disclosure requirements of the FASB, AICPA, and SEC is essential for you as a top manager because it determines your reporting responsibilities and defines conditions necessary for you to avoid an auditor's qualified opinion or modified report. Knowledge of these requirements will also facilitate your interpretation of the audited financial statements of other companies.

THE RULES FOR AUDIT REPORT MODIFICATIONS

As we saw in Chapter 7, the auditor issues a three-paragraph standard audit report, including an unqualified opinion paragraph, under the three "standard" conditions: (a) audit evidence obtained is sufficient to satisfy GAAS, (b) financial statements comply with GAAP in all material respects, and (c) no unusual uncertainties or relationships are present. The auditor's report is modified when there are important departures from the standard conditions or when the auditor decides modification is in his or her best interest. Modification always implies a warning for you as a financial statement user to be careful interpreting the statements and evaluating what they mean in forming a mental image of the real-world condition of the firm.

The four standards of reporting in GAAS (Chapter 7) underlie three broad departures from the three-paragraph standard audit report. Figure 9–2 diagrams these three branches beginning with a standard report issued under standard conditions. As shown in Figure 9–2, audit report modification is required *only* when there are "material" or greater departures from standard conditions. Less than material departures do not require audit report modification. For example, immaterial departures from GAAP need not be noted by the auditor.

Auditing Defects

In some cases, the auditor may be unable to obtain sufficient audit evidence for an opinion. A common example of this auditing defect is an initial audit in which the auditor is hired after the balance sheet date. Even with good internal control, the auditor may be unable to

FIGURE 9-2

Audit Reports under Various Circumstances

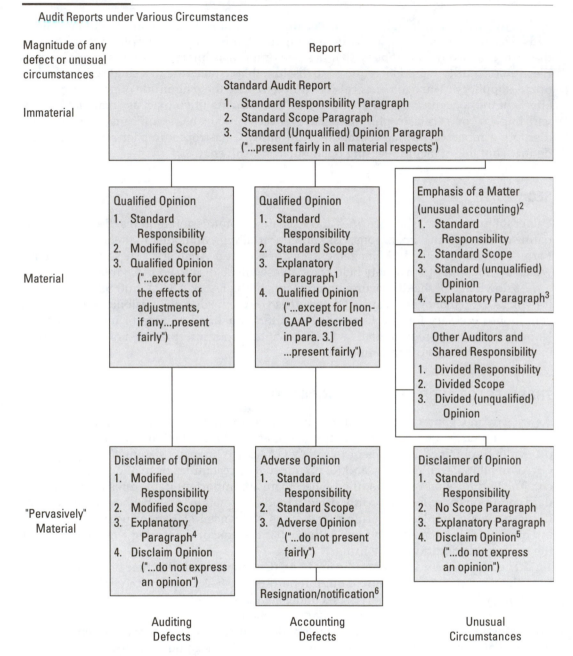

1. Describes GAAP departure and monetary effect.
2. Emphasis of a matter: going concern, related parties, accounting method change, justified GAAP departure, omission of GAAP-required supplemental information, other.
3. Usually references a financial statement footnote.
4. Paragraph explaining lack of sufficient evidence to express an opinion.
5. Possible for going-concern situations.
6. Auditor resignation may indicate serious unresolved accounting issues or illegal client acts.

verify material quantities of inventory on hand at the balance sheet date, and without sufficient evidence to support the ending inventory balance, the auditor cannot verify cost of goods sold. In other cases, evidence may not exist because of inadequate accounting records, weak internal control, or a natural catastrophe that destroyed essential records.

An important special case of inability to obtain sufficient audit evidence arises when client management restricts the scope of an audit. For example, a client may not allow the auditor to confirm receivables with customers, may refuse access to inventory for observation, may not allow the auditor to read minutes of directors' meetings, or may refuse to furnish a representation letter from the client's legal counsel. It is conceptually possible for the auditor to conduct alternative auditing procedures to obtain evidence in these situations. However, GAAS place a very high burden of proof on the auditor in such circumstances. The practical result is that the auditor must issue a disclaimer of an opinion (i.e., disclaim or express no opinion on the financial statements). The threat of this outcome is usually sufficient to convince management to remove the restrictions and allow the auditor unrestricted access.

In the presence of material auditing defects other than client-imposed audit scope restrictions, the auditor's standard report is modified in several ways. First, the standard scope paragraph is modified to indicate that the auditor did not conduct the usual procedures. Second, the auditor may add an explanatory paragraph providing details of the departure. Third, the opinion paragraph is modified for the auditing defect by inserting the qualifying language

> In our opinion, except for the effects of such adjustments, if any, as might have been determined necessary had we been able to examine evidence regarding [the restricted accounts] the financial statements present fairly, . . .

This expression of a conclusion on everything except for certain items (for which there is nonexpression of a conclusion) is called a *qualified opinion*, and so are opinions modified because of accounting defects.

In the presence of *pervasively material* auditing defects, the auditor is unable to express an opinion on the statements taken as a whole because of the limited scope audit. A pervasively material defect might be several income statement and balance sheet accounts for which the auditor could not obtain evidence and misstatements could be material, or it could be a single set of very important related accounts such as sales and accounts receivable or cost of sales and inventory. In these circumstances, the auditor modifies all three paragraphs. The first is modified to state that the auditor was "engaged to audit" the financial statements. It *does not* contain the statement "we have audited" or a statement of the auditor's responsibility. The scope paragraph is modified to describe the limited nature of the auditor's procedures, and the auditor adds a paragraph after the second paragraph stating that the scope of the audit was not sufficient to warrant expressing an opinion.

The opinion paragraph, sometimes called a *disclaimer* of opinion, is modified to state ". . . we do not express an opinion on these financial statements." Furthermore, the auditor is prohibited from expressing an opinion on those parts of the statements that were audited. Thus, the auditor can't give a "piecemeal" opinion that would tend to contradict or overshadow the overall disclaimer of opinion, and the auditor is even prohibited from listing procedures that were conducted.[3]

---

3. These restrictions on the auditor's ability to communicate do not apply to limited engagements in which there are restrictions on report distribution, such as agreed-upon procedures engagements (see Chapter 10).

Accounting Defects

Now that we have discussed auditing defects that lead to inadequate evidence for an auditor to form a conclusion about GAAP compliance, let's consider accounting defects. Accounting defects arise when sufficient evidence is obtained, but the auditor concludes that there is a material departure from GAAP. Financial statements may be materially misstated through monetary amounts, use of unacceptable accounting measurements methods, or misleading disclosures or omissions.

In the presence of material accounting defects, the auditor makes two modifications to the standard report. After the standard scope paragraph, a paragraph is added explaining the departure from GAAP and its monetary effect (if determinable). For omitted information or other inadequate disclosure, the auditor includes the omitted information in the new paragraph. Then, the opinion paragraph is qualified for the accounting defect by inserting the phrase "except for the effects of [misstated items, disclosures, or omissions] as discussed in the preceding paragraph, the financial statements present fairly in all material respects . . ."

Audit opinions qualified for departures from GAAP exist for private companies in the United States, and for public and private companies in the United Kingdom and some other countries. However, with rare exceptions, an SEC registrant is not permitted to file with the SEC financial statements accompanied by an auditor's report containing a GAAP qualification. Since the SEC has the power to suspend trading of securities of companies that do not comply with this rule, GAAP departures for public companies are extremely rare. The main exception is for regulated companies that follow regulatory accounting principles, even though they do not comply with GAAP.

When several accounts do not follow GAAP, the auditor may conclude that a qualified opinion is not sufficient to alert readers. In these cases, the auditor can give an adverse opinion, modifying the opinion paragraph to state that the financial statements "do not present fairly." As with qualified opinions, adverse opinions are not allowed for SEC registrants and are also extremely rare for private companies. However, the threat of an adverse opinion can lead management to comply with GAAP.[4] When faced with the prospect of receiving an adverse opinion due to pervasively material accounting defects, managements typically choose voluntarily to comply with GAAP by making necessary corrections and disclosures. Alternatively, management may dismiss the auditor before the audit report is issued. Dismissal of the auditor by an SEC registrant requires notification of the SEC (see Chapter 11).

The auditor of a client refusing to make adjustments or disclosures required for GAAP-based financial statements should consider management's possible motivation for refusing. The auditor may question management's integrity and may decide to resign from the engagement rather than be associated with a client that is likely to have high CBR or ABR. The auditor may also decide to resign if management does not respond promptly to deal with illegal acts that have been discovered during the audit, or for any other reason that the auditor chooses.

---

4. Some managements have asked auditors simply to disclaim an opinion, rather than issue an adverse opinion. Such a switch would violate GAAS, since the auditor *has* an opinion!

Unusual Circumstances

Material accounting and auditing defects are potentially important to financial statement users but are rare in practice, at least for public companies. For example, departures from GAAP occur for less than .5 percent of the approximately 4,000 public companies on the National Automated Accounting Reporting System (NAARS) file in recent years, and audit scope limitations occur for less than .15 percent. This is due in part to the effect of SEC rules for registrants. On the other hand, about 35 percent of all audit reports contain modified language for what we will call "unusual circumstances." These modifications are not to the opinion—all express an unqualified opinion—and all are "full scope" audits. They simply announce an unusual circumstance or circumstances regarding the financial statements or the audit.

As to frequency of occurrences, the most common unusual circumstance leading to an audit report modification affected about 10 to 50 percent of all audit reports, depending on the year. The modification is for inconsistent application of GAAP and is issued when a company changes accounting methods from one year to the next. The second most frequent modification is for "substantial doubt" about the ability of the company to remain a going concern. Substantial doubt modifications apply to about 5 percent of NAARS firms in the 1990s. Reliance on auditors other than those of the CPA/CA firm signing the audit report accompanying the financial statements arises for about 3 percent of audit reports, and disclaimers occur in less than .2 percent.

Emphasis of a Matter

With the exception of reports modified because other auditors conducted part of the audit, unusual circumstances result in a standard audit report plus an explanatory paragraph referencing a matter of potential importance to the financial statement user. Typically, fourth paragraphs reference a financial statement footnote prepared by client management. We will refer to all of these "fourth paragraph" reports as "emphasis of a matter" reports. They are required to reference management's financial statement footnotes on accounting changes having a material effect and for going-concern problems. They are optional for referring to other matters such as footnotes about presence of related-party transactions.

Accounting Changes

Accounting method changes affect comparability of measured performance over time. Some accounting changes are mandated when the method prescribed by an accounting authority changes and a company must adapt its statements. In other cases, a company voluntarily changes accounting methods, and some critics suspect that managements change accounting methods to influence currently reported earnings.

U.S. GAAP require that management disclose in the financial statement footnotes the nature and quantitative impact of any accounting changes that have a material monetary effect. GAAS require that a fourth paragraph referencing the accounting change footnote be added to the auditor's report. Also, when assumptions that underlie an accounting estimate are changed, a footnote reference and an explanatory paragraph may result if the change is deemed sufficient to affect the comparability of numbers from year to year. For example, a change from a 25-year life to a 10-year life (or the reverse) for calculating depreciation on fixed assets might mislead users if not disclosed.

Finally, auditors in the United States are required to evaluate the new accounting method, and *qualify* the audit report for a GAAP exception if the auditor disagrees with the justification for an accounting change or does not believe that the new method is "preferable" to the old. Such exceptions are rare, in part because many accounting method choices are somewhat arbitrary. Preferability judgments are inherently subjective and difficult to disprove.

Going-Concern Assumption

Perhaps the most important single circumstance that outsiders would like to know about a company is whether it has the ability to remain in operation for the foreseeable future. International accounting standards state that "when management is aware . . . of material uncertainties related to events or conditions which cast significant doubt upon the enterprise's ability to continue as a going concern, those uncertainties shall be disclosed" (IAS, 1997, p. 1). The auditor can then test management's assertion by applying auditing procedures to see whether it is justified in the circumstances.

Financial statements under U.S. GAAP are prepared under the assumption that a company "is a going concern and will continue in the operation for the foreseeable future." If this assumption is not justified, then a basis of accounting other than GAAP-based accrual accounting is appropriate. Managements applying U.S. GAAP are not required to assert that they will be able to remain a going concern for the foreseeable future. Yet, many lawsuits against auditors and managements have been based on a claim that the auditor *should have* warned readers of the future decline of a company. As a result, U.S. GAAS requires that the auditor consider whether there is substantial doubt that a company can remain a going concern.

Despite its importance to users, U.S. GAAS requires no unique auditing procedures directed toward assessing a company's ability to remain a going concern. Rather, the auditor is instructed to consider all the evidence obtained in the conduct of the audit to evaluate whether the evidence obtained for other audit purposes indicates "substantial doubt" about the company's ability to remain a going concern in the 12 months following the balance sheet date.[5] Figure 9–3 lists conditions and events that SAS No. 59 (AICPA, 1988) lists as indicators of substantial doubt about the going-concern assumption.

If substantial doubt may exist, the auditor is to inquire of management about its plans for avoiding solvency problems. Management may convince the auditor that it has plans that will allow it to remain a going concern. For example, a company appearing to have a severe near-term cash-flow problem may show the auditor a bank line of credit that will cover the shortage. If the auditor is not satisfied that the company has plans that give it a high probability of remaining in business, then the auditor should (a) require the client to describe conditions surrounding this "substantial doubt about going-concern status" in a financial statement footnote and (b) add a fourth paragraph referencing the substantial-doubt footnote, and using the words "substantial doubt" in the paragraph.[6] Thus, the fi-

---

5. Survey results indicate that auditors and bankers believe that the substantial doubt range starts at a probability of about .6 (see L. Ponemon and K. Raghunandan, "What Is Substantial Doubt?" *Accounting Horizons,* June 1994, pp. 44–54).

6. The auditor may also disclaim an opinion (i.e., not express an opinion) because of doubt about going-concern status. This form of reporting may be appropriate when the substantial doubt calls into question the usefulness of most of the accounting display.

F I G U R E   9 – 3

Conditions and Events That May Indicate *Substantial Doubt* about an Entity's Ability to Remain a Going Concern

- *Negative trends*—for example, recurring operating losses, working capital deficiencies, negative cash flows from operating activities, adverse key financial ratios.
- *Other indications of possible financial difficulties*—for example, default on loan or similar agreements, arrearages in dividends, denial of usual trade credit from suppliers, restructuring of debt, noncompliance with statutory capital requirements, need to seek new sources or methods of financing or to dispose of substantial assets.
- *Internal matters*—for example, work stoppages or other labor difficulties, substantial dependence on the success of a particular project, uneconomic long-term commitments, need to significantly revise operations.
- *External matters that have occurred*—for example, legal proceedings, legislation, or similar matters that might jeopardize an entity's ability to operate; loss of a key franchise, license, or patent; loss of a principal customer or supplier; uninsured catastrophe such as drought, earthquake, or flood.

Source: SAS No. 59 (AICPA, 1988), para. 6.

nancial statement reader is warned about the assumption violation and the precarious prospects of the company as well. Figure 9–4 diagrams the steps in the auditor's decision.

The paragraphs presented in Figure 9–5 appeared in the 1996 annual report of Trans World Airlines, Inc., a major U.S.-based airline. The auditor's report is a standard three-paragraph report accompanied by two additional paragraphs that reference an accounting change and a going-concern footnote. The stern wording of the footnote and audit report would seem to identify serious risks faced by TWA. The standard report also makes it clear that TWA management's accounting choices are deemed acceptable.

For some companies, challenge by the auditor of the going-concern assumption can lead to a favorable outcome because it alerts management to the potential difficulty and allows management to take corrective actions on a timely basis. For example, management may arrange for additional financing or for other reorganization activities that will eliminate the doubt. In other cases, management already is aware of the doubt and has taken all preventive actions possible. The auditor's concern may lead to demise of the firm because outsiders will be informed of the nature and extent of the company's problem. Lenders may decide to call in debt, and trade creditors may demand payment or cease doing business with a company with a going-concern modification. Management's problem is compounded if outsiders realize that, due to the auditor's business risk, modification is more likely when the auditor believes that the company will fail in the future. Thus, a first-time going-concern modification itself may have a negative impact on a firm's future prospects.

Emphasis of Other Matters

Auditors can also add voluntarily a fourth audit report paragraph discussing anything that they wish. These paragraphs provide "emphasis of a matter" and call attention to some aspect of the client's financial statements or condition. The paragraphs are not qualifications about GAAP or expression of doubt about the condition of the business, but indicate a

FIGURE 9–4

Going-Concern Auditing and Reporting—U.S. GAAS

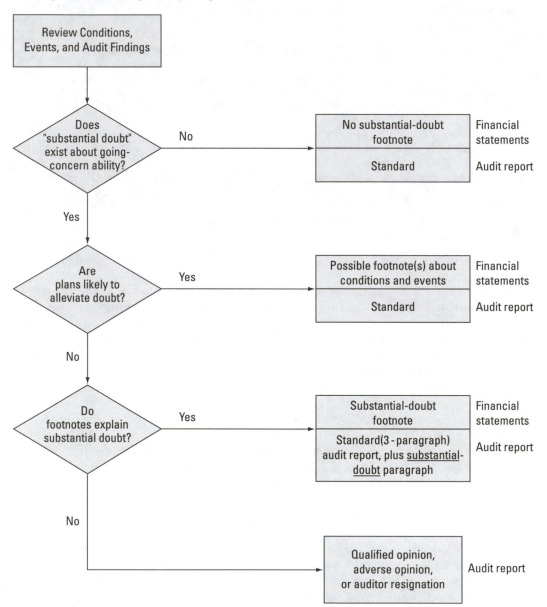

FIGURE 9–5

Trans World Airlines, Inc., and Subsidiaries Annual Report Excerpts

Fiscal Year Ended December 31, 1996

A. Auditor's Report

[standard three-paragraph auditor's report]

As discussed in Note 3 to the consolidated financial statements, the consolidated financial statements reflect the application of Fresh Start Reporting as of September 1, 1995, and, therefore, are not comparable in all respects to the consolidated financial statements for periods prior to such date.

The accompanying consolidated financial statements have been prepared assuming that Trans World Airlines, Inc., and subsidiaries will continue as a going concern. The company's recurring losses from operations and its limited sources of additional liquidity raise substantial doubt about the entity's ability to continue as a going concern. Management's plans in regard to these matters are described in Note 1. The consolidated financial statements do not include any adjustments that might result from the outcome of this uncertainty.

KPMG Peat Marwick, L.L.P.

Kansas City, Missouri
March 24, 1997

B. Notes to Consolidated Financial Statements

1. FINANCIAL CONDITION AND LIQUIDITY:

[. . .]

The accompanying consolidated financial statements have been prepared on a going-concern basis, which assumes continuity of operations and realization of assets and liquidation of liabilities in the ordinary course of business. The Company remains highly leveraged and substantially all of TWA's assets are and will likely remain subject to various liens and security interest, and many of its loan agreements contain mandatory prepayment provisions in the event that the assets are sold. Accordingly, management expects that TWA will not be able to rely in any significant degree, on the proceeds from sales of assets to fund operations and that TWA may have limited sources of additional liquidity other than cash generated by operations. The Company's ability to improve its financial position and meet its financial obligations will depend upon a variety of factors including: significantly improved operating results, favorable domestic and international air fare pricing environments, absence of adverse general economic conditions, more effective economic cost controls and efficiencies, and the Company's ability to attract new capital and maintain adequate liquidity. No assurance can be given that the Company will be successful in generating the operating results or attracting new capital required for future viability.

special risk for the reader such as particularly important loss contingencies or concentrations. The audit report emphasis may reduce the auditor's risk exposures.

The most commonly emphasized matter is presence of a related party with which the firm conducts transactions. Related-party transactions are not unethical or illegal, but they are different from other accounting transactions. Accrual accounting assumes that transactions with those outside a business are conducted at arm's length, with each party free to bargain transaction terms including the exchange price at which the transaction is valued. Since each party is acting in his or her own interests, the exchange price should be objective and reflect the conditions of the transaction. In cases where one party is controlled by the other party or exercises considerable influence over its financial and operating decisions, prices may not have these properties. GAAP require that certain material related-party transactions and amounts be noted and quantified in financial statements.

Under U.S. GAAS, the auditor may choose to emphasize the extent of related-party transactions by an audit report reference to the client's footnote detailing related-party transactions. In the absence of such a footnote, however, the auditor should qualify the opinion for the lack of adequate disclosure of material related-party transactions.

Other Independent Auditors

For many multinational and multisegment companies, more than one audit firm is hired to conduct audits of particular segments of the business. Companies operating in several industries may have been merged into a conglomerate with auditors of some segments remaining unchanged, or may take advantage of another auditing firm's strengths in certain countries or industries. Laws in some countries require that local subsidiaries of foreign parent firms be audited by locally domiciled audit firms. Also, some audit committees hire more than one audit firm and rotate their assignments to obtain fresh insights and increase auditors' independence of management. In all situations, one auditor is designated to be the principal auditor, who takes responsibility for the statements of the company as a whole and whose name appears on the audit report that accompanies the audited financial statements.

In many cases, the use of an independent audit firm other than the firm signing the audit report for part of an audit is not known to outsiders since the audit report is a standard three-paragraph report that makes no mention of the other auditor, or auditors. The standard report is issued because management does not wish to call attention to the use of more than one auditor. It is issued if the principal auditor (a) agrees to take responsibility for the other auditor's work as it relates to the principal auditor's opinion on the statements as a whole and (b) agrees not to modify the audit report by mentioning the other auditor. The principal auditor would likely agree to a "no reference" standard audit report if the portion audited by the other auditor is not material to the combined statements, or if the other auditor is a firm associated with the auditor or has been hired by the principal auditor to assist in the work. Also, even though the principal auditor did not hire the other auditor, there may be no mention if steps are taken to coordinate the audits so that the principal auditor is fully satisfied with the other auditor's work.

In other cases (comprising about 3 percent of the NAARS file), the principal auditor does not agree to take responsibility and makes reference to the work of the other auditor. For example, the auditor may decide to make reference because of the relative size or importance of the other auditor's portion of the audits. Whether or not the auditor decides to make reference to the work of another auditor, he or she must make inquiries to assess the other auditor's professional reputation and take appropriate steps to coordinate the audits.

For example, care would be taken to prevent the same inventory items appearing on the inventory counts of a French parent and a Belgian subsidiary of the same company, as would be the case if a single audit firm conducted the audits of both companies.

When the principal auditor decides to make reference to the work of another auditor (or auditors), the other auditor is not identified. The scope paragraph of the principal auditor's report is modified to indicate the other auditor's responsibilities, including percentages of total assets and total earnings audited by the other auditor. The second and third paragraphs of the principal auditor's report are modified to indicate that part of the basis for both is the report of the other auditors. Thus, the reader is informed that another auditor did a portion of the work and that the principal auditor is not taking full responsibility for that portion of the opinion.

Figure 9–6 presents the divided responsibility, scope, and opinion audit report of Deloitte and Touche on the financial statements of The Boeing Company for 1995, 1996, and

FIGURE 9–6

Independent Auditors' Report

Board of Directors and Shareholders, The Boeing Company:

We have audited the accompanying consolidated statements of financial position of The Boeing Company and subsidiaries as of December 31, 1997 and 1996, and the related statements of operations and cash flows for each of the three years in the period ended December 31, 1997. These financial statements are the responsibility of the Company's management. Our responsibility is to express an opinion on the financial statements based on our audits. The consolidated financial statements give retroactive effect to the merger of The Boeing Company and McDonnell Douglas Corporation, which has been accounted for as a pooling of interests as described in Note 2 to the consolidated financial statements. We did not audit the statement of financial position of McDonnell Douglas Corporation as of December 31, 1996, or the related statements of operations and cash flows for the years ended December 31, 1996 and 1995, which statements reflect total assets of $11,631,000,000 as of December 31, 1996, and total revenues of $13,834,000,000 and $14,332,000,000 for the years ended December 31, 1996 and 1995, respectively. Those statements were audited by other auditors whose report has been furnished to us, and our opinion, insofar as it relates to the amounts included for McDonnell Douglas Corporation for 1996 and 1995, is based solely on the report of such other auditors.

We conducted our audits in accordance with generally accepted auditing standards. Those standards require that we plan and perform the audit to obtain reasonable assurance about whether the financial statements are free of material misstatement. An audit includes examining, on a test basis, evidence supporting the amounts and disclosures in the financial statements. An audit also includes assessing the accounting principles used and significant estimates made by management, as well as evaluating the overall financial statement presentation. We believe that our audits and the report of the other auditors provide a reasonable basis for our opinion.

In our opinion, based on our audits and the report of the other auditors, the consolidated financial statements referred to above present fairly, in all material respects, the financial position of The Boeing Company and subsidiaries as of December 31, 1997 and 1996, and the results of their operations and their cash flows for each of the three years in the period ended December 31, 1997, in conformity with generally accepted accounting principles.

Deloitte & Touche LLP
Seattle, Washington
January 27, 1998

1997. The 1995 and 1996 statements for Boeing are presented to reflect retroactively the merger of Boeing with McDonnell Douglas Corporation on August 1, 1997. Ernst and Young had been the auditor of McDonnell Douglas, and Deloitte and Touche continues to be auditor for the new Boeing. Note that the scope of the audit of Deloitte and Touche is not limited, and the opinion is not qualified. But Deloitte and Touche does mention the work of another (unnamed) auditor and does not take responsibility for the work of another auditor. They could have issued a standard audit report with no mention of the other auditor, but they did not. Deloitte and Touche must have had substantial reasons for being unwilling to take full responsibility for the work of the other auditor for 1995 and 1996. Boeing management may have decided that the extra audit effort required for Deloitte and Touche to be willing to take full responsibility and not to mention the other auditor's work and issue a standard audit report was not worth its incremental cost.

What does it all mean? The divided scope, divided responsibility audit report referencing another auditor does not mention any reason for concern, but the reader may have reason for concern because of the inferences of the extra words. This is because, other things equal, the client would prefer a standard report and the auditor would like to accommodate the client. The presence of the extra words in the principal auditor's report indicates sufficient concerns about the work of the other auditor to insist upon a report form not preferred by the client. Perhaps the client was not willing to pay for sufficient audit coordination. Or perhaps the auditor does not have full confidence about the portion audited by the other auditor, or is simply not willing to bear the risks for the overall audit.[7] The possible causes of the divided scope, divided responsibility, and divided opinion report warrant some consideration by an outside user of the financial statements.

EMPIRICAL RESULTS: AUDIT REPORT MODIFICATIONS

Accounting Changes

What kinds of companies make accounting changes and under what conditions? In a large-scale study of almost 7,000 voluntary and mandatory accounting changes made by publicly traded companies over the 1969–88 time period, researchers found several patterns to accounting changes.[8] First, they found that frequencies of voluntary and mandated accounting changes were about equal. Of the voluntary accounting changes, about 40 percent were for changes from FIFO to LIFO inventory accounting, with the others spread over various categories. The mandated changes had the average effect of increasing earnings by about 13 percent. The voluntary changes increased earnings by 14 percent for non-LIFO changes, but changes to LIFO reduced earnings by 55 percent on the average.

Voluntarily made revenue-increasing changes outnumbered revenue-decreasing changes by about 2 to 1, and expense-recognition decreases outnumbered expense-recognition increases by about 2 to 1. The voluntary changes do not appear to be made at random. Furthermore, the researchers found that compared to a randomly selected sample of control firms, EPS growth for the income-increasing change firms was significantly less than the EPS growth for the con-

---

7. For legal, ethical, and reputational reasons, an auditor who has reason not to have confidence in the competence or independence of the other auditor would not likely agree to serve as principal auditor, even if reference to the other auditor is made in the audit report.

8. M. Pincus and C. Wasley, "The Incidence of Accounting Changes and Characteristics of Firms Making Accounting Changes," *Accounting Horizons*, June 1994, pp. 1–24.

trol sample for both the year before the change and the year of the change, while for the income-decreasing companies there was no significant difference.

Thus, companies voluntarily making income-increasing accounting changes appear to be experiencing financial difficulties, and may be using accounting changes to improve the reported performance of their firm (at least in the short run). An astute reader of audited financial statements would note the effect of voluntary income-increasing accounting changes and consider management's possible motivations for the changes.

Unusual Conditions

Evidence on the correlation of auditor behavior and stock prices has been provided in several empirical studies relating auditors' report modifications calling attention to loss contingencies when a company's prospects have recently been declining (e.g., low stock returns), other things equal.[9] Also, auditors' report modifications for loss contingencies have been associated with significant increases in bond risk premiums (in the neighborhood of 50 basis points).[10]

The consequences of audit report modification are generally negative, although they sometimes have little pricing effect. When audit report modifications provide first-time mention of an event or condition information rather than confirmation of existing conditions, the stock price reaction to the announcement is negative, and sometimes very negative. When modified audit reports merely confirm conditions about which the market is already aware, there is little price reaction. Stock price reactions that are observed may be due to the auditor's implicit message that the client's plans to remove going-concern doubt may not be successful or to information that indicates poor quality of controls in the client company. Both of these factors have implications for future profitability of the firm.

For management's announcements of accounting problems and the extreme form of auditor action, resignation from the audit, stock price declines can be very negative. For example, the price of Premier Lazer Systems, Inc., dropped 48 percent in reaction to announcement of accounting problems and the resignation of Ernst and Young.[11] Similarly, the price of National Auto Credit, Inc., fell 70 percent after Deloitte and Touche resigned the audit, the CEO and CFO took leaves of absence, and the company announced that loan-loss reserves (an accounting estimate) would be substantially increased.[12]

THE AUDITOR'S REPORTING INCENTIVES AND DECISION MODEL

The CPA/CA hired by client management to certify its financial statement assertions is not indifferent to his or her client's success. Successful clients generate a stream of future audit and other attestation fees for voluntarily informing outsiders and for certifying compliance

9. N. Dopuch, R. W. Holthausen, and R. W. Leftwich, "Predicting Audit Qualifications with Financial and Market Variables," *The Accounting Review,* July 1987, pp. 431–54.

10. I. R. Backmon and D. W. Vickrey, "An Empirical Examination of the Relationship between Bond Risk Premiums and Loss Contingency Disclosures," *Journal of Accounting, Auditing, and Finance,* Spring 1997, pp. 179–98.

11. R. L. Rundle, "Ernst and Young Quits as Outside Auditor for Premier Lazer, Citing Disagreements," *The Wall Street Journal* (interactive edition), May 26, 1998.

12. "Auditor Doubts Raise Questions," *Public Accounting Report,* March 15, 1998, p. 4.

with laws and regulations. Successful clients are also a source of fees for other assurance services that improve the quality of information for management's internal decision making and other consulting services not involving information improvement. These interests in a client's success provide incentives for the auditor to please client management by allowing them flexibility in preparing financial statements and disclosures.

On the other hand, to add credibility to management's financial statements, the auditor must be strict in enforcing GAAP rules. While there is a range of discretion for an auditor's reporting, there are limits to how far they can go. Because of the peculiar nature of certification contracts, each audit firm must maintain its reputation for competence in detecting misstatements, and for trustworthiness in reporting any defects in its clients' assertions. Also, CPA/CA firms must maintain their reputations as a group if the industry is to remain viable (see Chapter 12).

A CPA firm's reputation is the basis for adding value through perceptions of outside financial statement users, and it may provide a barrier to entry to the profession.[13] A firm's reputation for integrity and objectivity may also add value for other (nonfinancial statement audit) CPA services for which CPAs don't have a government-authorized franchise. In addition to individual CPA firm incentives, CPAs as a group have established an ethical code (see Chapter 12) and standards of fieldwork and reporting to facilitate education of auditors on requirements for GAAS-based audits, as well as enforcement to discipline substandard auditors. These standards of reporting also apply to regulated reports required by law.

An auditor hired by an outsider to audit financial statement compliance with GAAP (an "investigation" contract) may also apply GAAS reporting rules but does not face the same incentive problem with respect to disclosures faced by a "certifying" auditor. This is because the investigating auditor naturally represents interests of the user that hired the auditor. Also, an auditor hired only to certify GAAP compliance to meet regulatory requirements faces an environment more like that of an investigator. That is, if the client does not use the audit to reduce price protection discounts from investors and others and does not hire the audit firm for any nonaudit services, then the auditor will focus on avoiding sanctions of the auditor by regulatory authorities. Such an auditor will be more strict in applying GAAP, other things equal.

Analysis of the effects of incentives in real-world "certification" audits in the United States is difficult because audits of pubic companies are required for regulatory purposes. Under laws of various states, CPAs licensed to practice in that state are the only suppliers of financial statement audits made available to those outside the firm. U.S. federal law imposes some public reporting duty on auditors hired by public companies. But voluntary actions by auditors also have an effect since audits would also exist in the absence of a regulatory requirement because they reduce the cost of capital and other transactions costs for companies. And, in contrast to some countries, providing nonaudit services to audit clients is not prohibited in the United States and is a substantial source of income for audit firms.

---

13. *The Economist* (January 31, 1998, p. 20) cites the substantial reputations of (then) Big Six auditing firms as a barrier to entry that should be considered by regulators in evaluating whether the six should be allowed to merge to four or five. Ernst and Young and KPMG Peat Marwick later dropped their planned merger and the Price Waterhouse and Coopers and Lybrand merger was approved by regulators.

The Auditor's Reporting Decision Model

The GAAS-prescribed form and wording of the auditor's report on GAAP-based financial statements is primarily a function of the real-world financial conditions of the client. But the report will also reflect the auditor's own interests in the client, as well as the auditor's knowledge, skills, and utility function. Figure 9–7 diagrams a decision model incorporating these factors and their relation to the auditor's reporting decision. The auditor's decision is whether to issue a standard audit report, to require financial statement adjustment or disclosure before issuing a standard report, or to modify the audit report.

Auditors apply the reporting decision model in Figure 9–7 from top to bottom to choose the report form that maximizes the auditor's utility. You as a user of the audited financial statements prepared by others can use the auditor's report and reverse the process going from bottom to top to decode or infer the real-world condition of the entity. Modifications to the standard audit report may tell you something directly about application of GAAP, or indirectly about the auditor's assessments of client business risk or the auditor's business risk. Both types of information can aid your understanding of the auditor's report on financial statements of other companies.

As shown in Figure 9–7, a primary input to the auditor's reporting decision model is the real-world condition of the client, and in particular the three risks comprising the auditor's engagement risk. Some of the conditions are related to audit risk (AuR) based on the financial statements; some to the auditor's assessment of client business risk (CBR), auditor business risk (ABR), and the economic potential of the client for the auditor; and some to professional regulations and audit firm strategy and values. The GAAP-relevant and going-concern-relevant portions dictate auditing procedures to be applied, and non-GAAP portions of CBR and ABR affect the auditor's personal observations about the company. Each of these factors may have an impact on the auditor's mental image or beliefs about the client's real-world conditions.

The auditor combines this mental image or beliefs about the client's conditions with his or her knowledge and skills in decision making and the auditor's utility function to make a decision to require adjustment, disclosure, or audit report modification. Knowledge and skills include knowledge of GAAP and GAAS criteria, as well as legal and contractual duties, audit firm operating policies and practices, and codes of behavior.

The auditor's utility function specifies how the auditor values his or her association with the auditing firm and the profession, and personal reputation for objectivity, integrity, and independence. These values determine whether the auditor will be willing to sacrifice long-term reputation for short-term gain in the form of higher compensation from a particular client. Auditing firms monitor employees for unacceptable personal and professional behavior and values, design compensation systems that reward desired behaviors by auditors, and provide assistance through training, performance reviews, codes of behavior, and procedures manuals. They also apply quality control procedures such as review by another partner before an audit report is released and periodic after-the-fact reviews by auditors from other firms (called peer reviews).

The auditor as a self-interested economic being naturally considers the CBR, ABR, and client fee potential or risk/reward factors. In particular, other things equal (i.e., for the same AuR circumstances), the auditor will be more likely to require adjustments to financial statements or disclosures of negative conditions, modification of the audit report, or resignation for clients with higher CBR, higher ABR, or lower potential for future fees.

Auditor's Reporting Decision Model

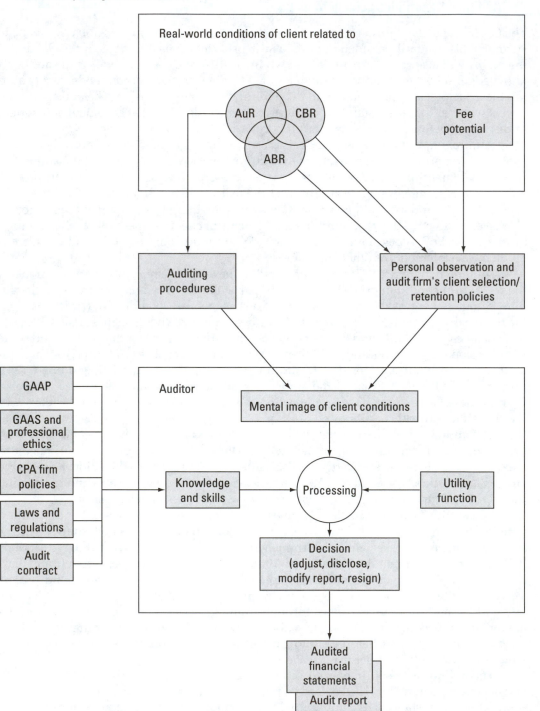

The behavior of auditors dealing with going-concern situations has led some critics to charge that auditors are like those who roam the field after a battle making sure that the wounded are dead. On the other hand, for a client in a strong financial position with good prospects for the future and thus little chance that the financial statements will be challenged, the auditor is less likely to require adjustment or additional disclosures of negative conditions, and may even raise the magnitude of misstatement or omission judged to be material.

Any reporting biases of a certifying auditor are less for those CPA firms with good reputations. Your creditors and trading partners know this. You should consider reputation in choosing an auditor to certify your assertions. You should also consider the context and potential for bias when interpreting reports of others. In some situations, you may want to hire an auditor to investigate on your behalf through a full audit, a review, or agreed-upon procedures to reduce the bias (see Chapter 10).

SUMMARY

The auditor's report on audited financial statements is the result of complex interaction between the real-world conditions of the client firm and professional standards, characteristics of the auditor and audit firm, and client-specific risk/reward incentives for the auditor. Proper interpretation of the auditor's report form requires consideration of the various factors. Other things equal, a modified auditor's report is more likely the greater the violation of GAAP criteria, the poorer the client's condition, the higher the quality of the auditor, and the lower the risk/reward ratio from association with the client as perceived by the auditor.

Audit report modifications are made for important departures from auditing standards, accounting standards, and the presence of unusual circumstances. The auditing departures are regulated by GAAS, accounting departures are regulated by GAAP, and unusual circumstances are affected by various factors including GAAS and GAAP, as well as the auditor's perceived risk/reward ratio. Material audit scope restrictions result in a modified report and a qualified opinion (no opinion) for the accounts for which audit evidence was not obtained. Material accounting deficiencies lead to a qualified opinion stating which accounts are not fairly presented.

Accounting changes, doubt about the going-concern assumption, and the use of other auditors to conduct part of the audit comprise the most common types of unusual circumstances leading to audit report modification for public companies. The auditor may also choose to modify the report without qualifying the opinion, by adding a fourth paragraph that emphasizes a matter or refers to some unusual aspect of the financial statements or condition of the client firm.

All audit report modifications warrant attention since they affect interpretation of the audited financial statements. With the possible exception of a change in accounting method to a newly mandated accounting method, all audit report modifications have potentially important negative implications. All detract from the financial statement representations because they indicate some degree of auditor concern with the financial statements or the condition of the firm. Since professional standards do not fully determine the auditor's reporting behavior, interpretation of audit reports is useful in revealing more information than the auditor states in his or her report.

CASE 9

WORLD WIDE ACQUISITIONS, INC. (NUDGE, NUDGE/WINK, WINK)

World Wide Acquisitions, Inc. (WWA), is a Swiss firm that specializes in acquiring businesses around the world. Located in Zurich, analysts at World Wide rely on GAAP-based financial statements and auditors to provide some information prior to their acquisitions. They believe that auditors know a great deal about a company, its operations, and its viability. They also believe that the auditors "know more than they tell" and want to make sure that they understand the "nudges and winks" through which auditors communicate.

They have hired you to advise them on the interpretation of audit reports under U.S. GAAS. Your job is to reverse the encoding process to "present the message" in auditors' reports and their clients' financial statements.

Presented below are several questions related to acquisitions that WWA is considering. Each case describes a company, its financial statements, and related audit report language. In each case, you are asked to interpret what the report means, giving any likely hidden message as well as the stated message. Some of the cases are guided by questions that World Wide analysts have asked. For these cases, to the extent possible, you should be specific in answering the question raised.

The official answers to most of these questions are contained in the AICPA's Statements on Auditing Standards. However, rather than merely applying criteria of the standards, you are to take the result of application of the standard and reverse the process, consider any likely client–auditor negotiations, and infer the underlying state of the firm. That is, you must take a user's perspective in determining what the audit report means.

Present your findings as a report for WWA analysts.

Case A

A Company's audit report is a standard three-paragraph report except for the following. At the end of the first paragraph the following was added:

> . . . We did not audit the financial statements of J Company, a wholly owned subsidiary, which statements reflect total assets and revenues constituting 20 percent and 22 percent, respectively, of the related consolidated totals. Those statements were audited by other auditors whose report has been furnished to us, and our opinion, insofar as it relates to the amounts included for J Company, is based solely on the report of the other auditors.

The second paragraph was standard, and the third paragraph is as follows:

> In our opinion, based on our audit and the report of the other auditors, the consolidated financial statements referred to above present fairly, in all material respects, the financial position of A Company at December 31, 1999, and the results of its operations and its cash flows for the year then ended in conformity with generally accepted accounting principles.

The WWA analysts are puzzled by the "splitting" of the auditor's report and wonder if there is some problem with the audit. Should WWA be cautious? Should they discount the auditor's report regarding J, or should they treat this the same as if it had been a standard report with the usual three paragraphs?

Case B

B Company has WWA analysts especially perplexed. Footnote X indicates some "going concern" or "future viability" problems at B Company, but it also indicates management's plans that are expected to alleviate the conditions. Furthermore, the auditor's report is a standard three-paragraph report with the following paragraph added at the end:

> The accompanying financial statements have been prepared assuming that the Company will continue as a going concern. As discussed in

Note X to the financial statements, the Company has suffered recurring losses from operations and has a net capital deficiency that raise substantial doubt about its ability to continue as a going concern. Management's plans in regard to these matters are also described in Note X. The financial statements do not include any adjustments that might result from the outcome of this uncertainty.

The WWA personnel find the report noninformative as to what the auditor believes about the company's prospects. Give what help you can in interpreting the auditor's report, including an assessment of the likelihood of, say, bankruptcy over the next 12 months. Does the auditor believe that management's plans will be successful?

Case C

C Company is a 51 percent owned U.S. subsidiary of a Dutch conglomerate. During the year, C Company has changed its accounting method in an apparently straightforward fashion. Yet, after standard first and second paragraphs, the auditor's report has been modified by the following language:

As disclosed in Note X to the financial statements, the Company adopted, in 1999, the first-in, first-out method of accounting for its inventories, whereas it previously used the last-in, first-out method. Although use of the first-in, first-out method is in conformity with generally accepted accounting principles, in our opinion the Company has not provided reasonable justification for making this change as required by generally accepted accounting principles.

In our opinion, except for the change in accounting principle discussed in the preceding paragraph, the financial statements referred to above present fairly, in all material respects, the financial position of X Company as of December 31, 1998 and 1999, and the results of its operations and its cash flows for the years then ended in conformity with generally accepted accounting principles.

WWA personnel are puzzled about these paragraphs. The change appears to be to an acceptable method of accounting and its earnings appear fairly stated. Yet, the change is "flagged" by this lack of justification. The Swiss are unfamiliar with the concept of "justification." Is this a serious problem or is the language just "American boilerplate"?

Case D

D Company received a standard three-paragraph audit report with the additional paragraph inserted:

As discussed in Note X to the financial statements, the Company changed its method of computing depreciation in 1999.

WWA personnel have noted that a similar company (D' Company) made the same accounting change of a similar magnitude and with a similar footnote. But D' Company received no such fourth paragraph. Should these two companies be interpreted the same or is there "a hidden message" here?

Case E

E Company has transactions with a "related party" that have been documented in a footnote to the financial statements. Furthermore, the auditor of E Company has inserted a fourth paragraph into a standard audit report. The fourth paragraph says "As noted in footnote X, E Company has significant transactions with a related party." WWA wants to know the importance of this fourth paragraph and whether it should affect their consideration of the company.

Case F

F Company received a standard three-paragraph auditor's report. WWA personnel want to know whether the auditor found any important problems during the audit (resulting in major adjustments) and what they think of F's internal controls. They also want to know how the auditors evaluate F's accounting choices—were they "aggressive"? Furthermore, is there anything on the horizon that should cause WWA to be wary of the future of Company F?

As to the "uncertainties" footnote, WWA personnel are curious about whether the auditor believes that an unrecorded possible loss exceeding a material amount is probable. Finally, WWA would like to know how the auditor would warn them if F is taking excessive risks or is being operated imprudently. Can you help them?

KEY WORDS

accounting change   Accounting methods or the way that they are applied differs from the prior accounting period.

accounting defect   A material departure from GAAP due to materially misstated monetary amounts, use of unacceptable accounting methods, misleading disclosures, or omissions.

adverse opinion   An audit report opinion paragraph stating that the financial statements are not presented fairly in accordance with GAAP.

auditing defect   Exists when the auditor is unable to obtain sufficient audit evidence for an opinion as required by GAAS.

contingency   An existing condition, situation, or set of circumstances involving uncertainty as to possible gain or loss that will ultimately be resolved when one or more future events occur or fail to occur.

disclaimer of opinion   An auditor's report that expresses no opinion on a financial statement's compliance with GAAP.

emphasis of a matter   Fourth paragraph of auditor's report that calls attention to some aspect of the client's financial statements or condition.

going concern   An entity that is, for at least the next 12 months, able to continue in business and meet its financial obligations as they come due with funds from operations.

going-concern assumption   A basic assumption underlying use of accrual accounting under GAAP.

going-concern modification   Addition of a fourth paragraph to an auditor's report, containing the words "substantial doubt" and referencing a financial statement footnote disclosing doubt about whether the entity is a going concern.

qualified opinion (material accounting defects)   An audit opinion paragraph qualified by inserting the phrase "except for the effects of [misstated items, disclosures, or omissions] as discussed in the preceding paragraph, the financial statements present fairly in all material respects."

qualified opinion (material auditing defects)   An audit opinion paragraph qualified by inserting the phrase "except for the effects of such adjustments, if any, as might have been determined necessary had we been able to examine evidence regarding [the restricted accounts], the financial statements present fairly in all material respects."

related-party transaction   A transaction with an outside party that controls or is controlled by the entity, or that exercises considerable influence over its financial and operating decisions.

substantial doubt   The minimum probability that an entity will fail to be a going concern (typically, probability = .5–.7), for which GAAP and GAAS require footnote disclosure and audit report modification.

10 CHAPTER

Other Certification, Investigation, and Origination Assurance Services

- ◆ **W**hat process certifications and other nonfinancial statement certifications can add value for my firm?
- ◆ How can I use "limited distribution certifications" to add value?
- ◆ How should I interpret examination, review, and agreed-upon procedures reports on assertions by managers of other firms?
- ◆ Should I hire CPAs to provide nonmandated assurance services?
- ◆ Should I outsource internal auditing, information design, and information processing?

All five questions address the economics of improved information for decision making using independent assurance services other than financial statement audits. None of the services is mandated, and none has officially established criteria for measurement and disclosure.[1] In all cases, the value of assurance services depends on the existence of decision-relevant criteria and the perceived competence and trustworthiness of the assuror.

The chapter begins with consideration of a variety of financial and nonfinancial assertions and certification services followed by an analysis of lower-cost and higher-risk assurance services. Finally, we evaluate the use of independent assurance professionals for investigations and origination of information, information system design, and context improvement services.

---

1. Some financial institutions are required by regulations to obtain independent certification of compliance of their internal control with prescribed criteria. There are other requirements for some industries. However, there is no general requirement for certification of internal control.

BACKGROUND CONCEPTS

We've seen in prior chapters that management can benefit by disclosing private information perceived by outside parties as decision relevant, competently prepared, and reliably displayed. We've also seen how independent assurance professionals with good reputations for competence and trustworthiness can add value by adding credibility to information prepared by management.

GAAP criteria applied to historical financial statements are one important and comprehensive type of assertion and information disclosure by management. However, there are many other things that outsiders would like to know about a company beyond its condition as measured by GAAP-based financial statements, or more detailed than a GAAP presentation. For example, historical financial statements provide stockholders a measure of how well the company has done and the risks inherent in the current environment. But historical financial statements do not directly address whether the company could suddenly fail because of unreliable information or systems, or its assets could be stolen by employees or by outsiders in the near future.[2] Stockholders and the directors, as well as management, would like to have *process* assurance that the internal control is reliable in protecting assets of the firm and provides relevant and reliable information for internal decision making.

As we have seen, the external auditor may or may not evaluate strength of internal control when certifying financial statements. In particular, the auditor may decide that it is more economical to audit the details of financial statements than the process that produced them. In effect, the auditor can determine the reliability of an entity's financial statements for a particular period by auditing its transactions and balances rather than auditing the process that produced them. As a result, two companies may produce the same financial statements and both may receive a standard audit report, but they may have different risks of failure due to internal control weaknesses.

To illustrate differences between process versus output or condition certification, suppose you are about to board a flight from Dallas–Ft. Worth to Denver and are worried because weather reports indicate difficult flying conditions. Airline A provides you with an audit report certifying that A's plane has just flown successfully from Detroit to Dallas, that the flight was smooth, arrival was on time, and no safety problems were encountered. The aircraft from airline B has also just arrived from Detroit, and airline B's management provides an audit report certifying that all on-board sensors monitoring aircraft conditions and external conditions were operating properly, and reliably displayed their measurements on cockpit dials and meters. Also, the pilot and crew followed FAA and airline-specified operating procedures. Which auditor's report would be more useful to you in making your decision about your flight to Denver under unknown conditions? For an upcoming flight, most people value process and instantaneous measurement assurance more than past outcome and measurement assurance. The same is true for business processes and outcomes.

Other nonhistorical financial statement assertions that management might want to make to outsiders to reduce information asymmetry include security of transactions with customers on the World Wide Web, forward-looking information (e.g., forecasted financial

---

2. As an example, Oxford Health Plans, Inc., experienced a near failure due to inadequate data processing for billing and claims payment for its rapidly expanding managed-care business (*The Wall Street Journal*, November 16, 1997, p. A3).

statements), business process quality, compliance with laws and regulations, and quality of products and services offered by the firm. Because of their long-standing reputations for competence in auditing historical financial statements and their reputations for trustworthiness in reporting on financial statements, CPA firms may have a competitive advantage for adding credibility to other types of assertions by management.

Attestation Standards

In its role as CPAs' trade association, the AICPA has established 11 *attestation standards* and a set of related Statements on Standards for Attestation Engagements that generalize GAAS concepts for nonfinancial statement assertions and add specific standards for some specialized services.[3] The AICPA has several interests in providing attestation standards. It wants to promote the value of being a CPA by providing educational guidance to its members on how to produce high-quality services, as well as guidance to enforce sanctions against poorly performing members. Also, by providing quality control over new services, compliance with these standards will not erode the traditional reputation of CPAs for financial statement audits that assure reliability.

CPAs have also leveraged their reputations to serve as the source of information and information systems designs. CPAs may be able to expand their services and income by offering "branded" information services that produce relevant and reliable information, thus adding to the value of being a CPA. Figure 10–1 displays a sample of attestation services offered by CPAs, as well as selected services for which the CPA is the source of information.

NONFINANCIAL STATEMENT CERTIFICATIONS

This section elaborates on three types of nonfinancial statement certification that have potential for broad application for the future and one whose future is cloudy, at least for general distribution to unknown third parties. Internal control certification can add assurance about internal information relevance and reliability and asset protection for management, directors, and creditors. CPA WebTrust[SM] certificates assure customers of a business about assertions of World Wide Web transaction security and order processing reliability. Also, certificates of compliance with regulations and practice quality codes can assure customers and others. On the other hand, certification of forward-looking information for outsiders has produced, to date, insurmountable litigation problems for all CPA firms.

Internal Control

Management would like assurance that its internal control is well designed to meet its objectives and is operating effectively. Directors who oversee management, as well as stockholders and other outsiders, would also like to have such assurance. Management can obtain assurance from a variety of sources including hiring internal auditors to evaluate controls and monitor details of transactions processing.

---

3. Financial statement audits are a subset of attestation services. Therefore, GAAS is encompassed by Attestation Standards, with adaptation of the 11 standards for peculiarities of financial statement audits.

FIGURE 10-1

Selected Assurance Services

Certification and Investigation (Attestation Services)

Financial:

  Annual financial statements

  Quarterly financial statements

  Pro forma financial statements

  Prospective financial statements (forecasts and projections)

  Financial statement elements

  Supplementary financial information for regulatory requirements

  Outsourced internal auditing

Nonfinancial:

  Internal control compliance with COSO standards or stated criteria

  Process compliance with ISO 9000

  Labor and safety compliance with Social Accountability 8000 (CEPAA)

  Compliance with contract terms

  Product quality compliance with stated criteria

  Association for Investment Management and Research (AIMR) standards for investment management
    performance

  Ethical behavior of employees

Assurer as Information Source

Outsourced accounting processing

System design (e.g., internal control, performance measures, compensation plans, tax planning,
  information processing, electronic commerce, risk monitoring)

System implementation

Risk assessments

Performance measurement and benchmarking against best practices, competition

Preparation of databases (trade association members' performance [Moss Adams], semiconductor
  industry book-to-bill ratio [PricewaterhouseCoopers])

Supervision of balloting (labor union elections, Academy Awards)

Performance measurement and direct reporting of results (Canadian Post delivery [Ernst & Young])

Internal auditors can also provide some assurance to directors whose audit committee may meet periodically with the internal auditors. But even under the best of conditions, it is difficult for an internal auditor to be objective about evaluating and reporting to the audit committee the performance of his or her own top management. Also, stockholders and other outsiders have no opportunity to meet with internal auditors, yet would like to know whether the company has adequate systems to identify and mitigate risks on a timely basis, including risks that company assets will be stolen. These factors lead to a demand for internal control evaluation by independent assurers from outside the firm.

CPA firms offer several advantages as the provider of internal control process certification. As financial statement auditors, they have experience auditing results of internal control, and, as information originators and advisors, they have experience designing internal control processes. Thus, they have subject matter expertise and are also perceived as trustworthy by outsiders. These natural advantages can also have related disadvantages, however, due to association with audited financial statements, since some may question whether an external auditor can objectively evaluate reliability of internal controls designed by employees of the auditor's firm. We'll consider these and related independence questions in Chapter 12.

How should a favorable report on internal control be interpreted? Does it mean that there have been no internal control process failures in the past? Does it mean that material internal control failure in the future is impossible? An aircraft "auditor's" certificate that aircraft controls are working properly at a point in time does not mean that they will not break down in the future, or that they will be effective if extremely rare or previously unknown flight conditions occur. Yet, new conditions or internal control breakdowns involving substantial loss to management or to outside users who relied on an internal control certificate may lead to lawsuits against the auditor for failure to conduct a proper process audit.

Independently certified internal control reports have been increasing in frequency over time, but are not common. As internal control has become increasingly automated, and as improved information systems and global competition have shortened the time allowable for reaction to changed business conditions, internal control quality has become much more important to a business. Independent certification of the adequacy of internal control design and current operation in preventing theft, as well as in monitoring risk and providing reliable operating performance measures, has become increasingly valuable to management and to outsiders evaluating management and assessing risk. In the future, after-the-fact performance measures and risk assessments will be relatively less important and point-in-time measurements more important. Thus, it is worthwhile to consider certification of internal control reports in more depth.

Reports on Internal Control

Internal control examination reports by independent auditors can either "stand alone" or result from a financial audit. Stand-alone reports require management's assertion about internal control in either a management report to which the auditor's examination report is attached or in a representation letter to the auditor. If the internal control assertion is only in a representation letter, then distribution of the auditor's examination report is restricted to management, other insiders, and regulators.

A standard examination report for a stand-alone certification of management's internal control over financial reporting assertions under AICPA standards for examination (comparable to GAAS for audits) parallels the auditor's standard report on financial statements. An internal control report typically refers to COSO criteria as the standard on which it is evaluated (comparable to compliance with GAAP for financial statement audits). Figure 10–2 shows an auditor's stand-alone internal control examination report that is parallel to a standard auditor's report on financial statements.

While the auditor's examination report has many features that parallel the auditor's report on financial statements, there are important differences. One noteworthy feature of the auditor's internal control examination report is that it is as of a point-in-time—the balance sheet date. The auditor does not take a position about the adequacy of control before that date, such as during the period of the financial statements, or after. In fact, the opinion warns that the auditor's conclusion as of the date of the financial statements may not apply

FIGURE 10–2

Independent Accountant's Report on Internal Control over Financial Reporting

---

Report of Independent Accountants

To LJ Appliances, Inc.

[Introductory paragraph]

We have examined management's assertion that LJ Appliances, Inc., maintained effective internal control over financial reporting as of December 31, 1999, included in the accompanying Management Report.

[Scope paragraph]

Our examination was made in accordance with standards established by the American Institute of Certified Public Accountants and, accordingly, included obtaining an understanding of the internal control over financial reporting, testing and evaluating the design and operating effectiveness of the internal control, and such other procedures as we considered necessary in the circumstances. We believe that our examination provides a reasonable basis for our opinion.

[Inherent limitations paragraph]

Because of inherent limitations in any internal control, misstatements due to error or fraud may occur and not be detected. Also, projections of any evaluation of the internal control over financial reporting to future periods are subject to the risk that the internal control may become inadequate because of changes in conditions, or that the degree of compliance with the policies or procedures may deteriorate.

[Opinion paragraph]

In our opinion, management's assertion that LJ Appliances, Inc., maintained effective internal control over financial reporting as of December 31, 1999, is fairly stated, in all material respects, based upon criteria established in *Internal Control—Integrated Framework* issued by the Committee of Sponsoring Organizations of the Threadway Commission (COSO).

Alex and Louis, CPAs
Iowa City, Iowa
February 10, 2000

---

after that time because of changed conditions in the external environment or deterioration in the implementation of controls. Also, there is a paragraph explaining inherent limitations of any internal control. Thus, it should be clear to readers that the effectiveness of future operations or future design adequacy is not being certified.

A second type of report on internal control arises as a by-product of the audit of financial statements. Distribution of this type of report is restricted to management and others within the entity. Figure 10–3 shows such a report for a retired workers' association and a response by management. As the report indicates, the financial statement audit was not designed to detect all possibly material internal control weaknesses, and thus can't provide positive assurance about them. However, the report does give negative assurance—even though the audit was not to evaluate internal control, no material internal control weaknesses were noted in conducting the financial statement audit.

FIGURE 10-3

Internal Control Reports as Part of a Financial Statement Audit

Report of Independent Accountants

March 21, 1992

To the Executive Board
The National Association of Retired Federal Employees

In planning and performing our audit of the financial statements of The National Association of Retired Federal Employees (NARFE) for the year ended December 31, 1991, we considered its internal control structure in order to determine our auditing procedures for the purpose of expressing our opinion on the financial statements and not to provide assurance on the internal control structure. Our consideration of the internal control structure would not necessarily disclose all matters in the internal control structure that might be material weaknesses under standards established by the American Institute of Certified Public Accountants. A material weakness is a condition in which the design or operation of the specific internal control structure elements do not reduce to a relatively low level the risk that errors or irregularities in amounts that would be material in relation to the financial statements being audited may occur and not be detected within a timely period by employees in the normal course of performing their assigned functions. However, we noted no matters involving the internal control structure and its operation that we consider to be material weaknesses as defined above.

During our recently completed and prior year audits, we did become aware of certain matters that we believe would be of interest to management. These matters have been discussed with appropriate management personnel. These matters along with our related recommendations are included in the attached report:

Part I—Recommendations to management to improve internal accounting controls and administrative efficiency which were developed during the current year.

Part II—Status of recommendations developed during the prior year's audit.

This report is intended solely for the information and use of the Executive Board, management, and others within the organization.

Price Waterhouse

Management's Response

The following are responses to the Price Waterhouse Report of Independent Accountants:

1. Include a Statement of Cash Flows with the Annual Audited Financial Statements.

Currently, generally accepted accounting principles do not require not-for-profit organizations such as NARFE to prepare a Statement of Cash Flows. However, the Federal Accounting Standards Board has recommended that the requirement be extended to not-for-profit-groups. In anticipation of this change, NARFE will present this financial statement with its annual audited financial statements in 1993.

2. Reevaluate the Existing Procurement and Cash Disbursement Procedures.

To improve the efficiency of the procurement and cash disbursement functions, management has appointed an internal committee to evaluate the current process and make recommendations to the National Officers for appropriate changes.

Harold Price
National President
Chief Executive Officer

Carolyn A. LeeDecker
Chief Operating Officer

Source: "Price Waterhouse Recommendations to Management," *Retirement Life*, September 1992, pp. 31–32.

The report also notes two *reportable conditions* that should be of interest to management. Reportable conditions are "matters coming to the auditor's attention that, in his judgment, should be communicated to the audit committee because they represent significant deficiencies in the design or operation of the internal control structure, which could adversely affect" management's ability to produce GAAP-based financial statements (AICPA, SAS No. 60, 1988, para. .02). The last paragraph of the auditor's report to the association's executive board notes that it is intended solely for those within the organization. The executive board apparently decided to publish in the association's magazine the report and responses of management as a means of communicating to its membership that management had been diligent in correcting internal control defects noted by the auditor.

The Figure 10–3 example shows one value-adding use of internal control reports by management. Independent certification of management's stewardship or diligence in carrying out duties can be valuable to management in reporting to outsiders in public reports and also in limited distribution reports to association members, boards of directors, and regulatory agencies. Reports to directors and regulatory agencies are an especially attractive form of reporting because they involve limited liability on the part of the assurer, and therefore lower the CPA's "attestor" business risk from being associated with the entity as an attestor, and can be obtained at lower cost.

Is it necessary for auditors to report to outsiders internal control weaknesses and risk exposure found in an audit? Reporting to outsiders a firm's internal control weaknesses and special risks or strategy weaknesses might unnecessarily damage stockholders. For example, when the auditor communicates reportable conditions regarding internal control weaknesses to management, management often takes corrective actions or concludes that the risk is cost justified. Absent any exposure to loss contingencies or risk exposures that are required to be disclosed under GAAP, it is difficult to see how outsiders can use or benefit from public disclosure of such information.

An effective solution may be for auditors to report these sensitive matters to the firm's directors, who can understand detailed reports about conditions and controls and are able to take follow-up action to correct deficiencies. Stockholders benefit from this reporting by external auditors even though they do not receive the information. Stockholders benefit because they now have assurance that those who need to know about the defects in order to take action on behalf of the stockholders are so informed, and exposure of sensitive information to competitors is avoided. Similar arguments apply to reports to regulators.

CPA WebTrust^SM

The World Wide Web offers opportunities for substantial reductions in the cost of accessing customers and conducting business transactions. Individual consumers can themselves search Web sites for lowest cost service on a world-wide basis. However, the openness of the World Wide Web also causes consumers (retail customers) to have concerns about security of their credit card and other information that might be divulged when using the Internet for business transactions. Consumers are also concerned about the reliability of delivery, service, and sales return assertions of a remote seller.

The AICPA has branded a new service, designated CPA WebTrust, that leverages the CPA's traditional reputation for expertise in business assurance and control by licensing use of a logo. The CPA examines a Web page of a client and allows those satisfying certain criteria to display a CPA WebTrust seal and a VeriSign trademark (see Figure 10–4). The CPA's examination covers business practices disclosure, transaction integrity, and information protection. Thus, the customer is assured of how long it takes the client to fulfill an order, order confirmation practices, and use of appropriate technology to encrypt private customer information.

Presence of the seal (equivalent to a standard auditor's report on financial statements) should increase the customer's confidence that they can deal with the company on a confidential basis and receive a stated level of service. From the CPA's perspective, the examination is like other examinations, but it is focused on reliability of process control over time rather than being a point-in-time statement of condition. The seal is easy to copy for a Web site display but is backed up by a secure site of CPA-certified businesses maintained by VeriSign, Inc. A customer wishing to verify that use of the CPA WebTrust logo is backed by an examination can click the logo, which is linked to a VeriSign Web page that confirms the company's status as a proper recipient of the seal (see www.cpawebtrust.org).

CPAs and the AICPA have competition for Web site certification. For example, the National Computer Security Association also certifies Web site security at a fee of $8,500 per Web server. Whether CPAs will win a major portion of the Web site certification business depends on whether the CPA's traditional reputation for competence and trustworthiness can be transferred to this new area. Other suppliers may have more technical competence in electronic commerce but less name recognition for assurance. Success also depends on technological developments in encryption that may reduce security concerns by consumers. CPA WebTrust focuses on more than technical matters, however. CPAs take a "value for users" approach that addresses users' concerns for relevant information about order processing and delivery as well as security matters. This approach may be beyond the expertise of technically oriented computer companies.

Compliance with Laws, Regulations, and Accepted Practices

The latter quarter of the 20th century has brought increasing use of regulations and codes of acceptable practices. These have taken the form of laws and regulations by regulatory agencies, as well as concerns of consumers about labor practices in the United States and

FIGURE 10–4

CPA WebTrust[SM] Web Site Seal

Source: R. Koreto, "In CPAs We Trust," *Journal of Accountancy*, December 1997, p. 62.

around the world, and corporate citizenship involving compliance with environmental laws and ethical behavior in general. Many regulations for internal control in U.S. financial institutions resulted from the savings and loan failures in the 1980s.

CPA firms are perceived to have expertise in determining compliance with a set of prescribed criteria and either possess or can obtain expertise in the subject-matter area of an assertion. Thus, CPAs are natural providers of compliance-with-criteria certification services. A CPA's standard examination report on a client's assertion that it complies with stated laws and regulations parallels an auditor's report on financial statements, including an opinion that assertions are "fairly presented in all material respects." There is one exception—the scope paragraph includes: "Our examination does not provide a legal determination on the Company's compliance with specified requirements." This is because the auditor is not an attorney and does not possess the expertise to determine compliance with all requirements specified by law.

Certification-of-compliance assertions provide a hybrid situation regarding value added. Compliance certification may be required by law and regulation, or by contract, and thus adds value by enabling transactions. Compliance certification may also add further value to a company by in effect "advertising" compliance with laws and regulations as well as voluntary good practices (e.g., safety at USAir and fair labor practices of Nike (see Chapter 7)). Thus, the certifier's reputation may or may not be important for determining value added for the assertion's preparer.

Forward-Looking Information

Many outside parties such as prospective stockholders and other investors would like to know management's forecasts for earnings and balance sheets. In some cases management would benefit by disclosure of their forecasts and, to the extent possible, would benefit further by having these forecasts certified by an independent expert. CPAs are allowed to be associated with management's "best estimate" forecasts of financial statements. In particular, CPAs can certify that prospective financial statements have followed AICPA's standards for presentation of prospective financial statements and are arithmetically correct and that the assumptions on which forecasted financial statements are based are "reasonable."

In the early 1980s, auditors' examinations of forecasted financial statements as part of an investment promotion package were reasonably common for oil-drilling ventures in Louisiana, Oklahoma, and Texas and nationwide for real estate developments based on then favorable tax treatments. Due to an unforeseen decline in oil prices and overbuilding stimulated by the liberal tax code in the first half of the 1980s, many promoters declared bankruptcy and forecast users sued the auditors of forecast information. By the late 1980s, auditors' legal costs including settlements and judgments paid plus attorneys' fees exceeded total revenues from their examinations of financial statement forecasts. Thus, major CPA firms dropped from their service offerings examinations of prospective financial statements for general distribution to third parties.

Auditor association with prospective financial information continues for limited distribution reports, including projections of expected results conditional on particular assumptions, such as "worse case scenarios" or hypothetical facts, continues to be useful in information settings involving management and a *particular* outside party. The auditor's liability for association with these forecasts and projections can be limited to certain matters by contract because distribution of the auditor's report is limited to the contracting parties. Thus, the auditor's expertise is used in reducing the information asymmetry, but with limited liability for the auditor.

CERTIFICATION RISK LEVELS

Most of the certification services discussed so far have been at the *examination* level. For examinations, the auditor (attestor) obtains a sufficient basis for low "attest" risk of undiscovered important defects in management's assertions.[4] Misstatement detection procedures applied in an examination are chosen by the attestor, and the attestor must obtain enough evidence to warrant a conclusion of low risk (i.e., examinations are "required conclusions" engagements).

In some situations, low attest risk may not be worth the cost of obtaining it. For example, management may be considering acquiring a company and does not wish to take the time or pay the cost of a full audit of the acquiree's financial statements. However, it may be cost effective and timely to engage a CPA to conduct a limited investigation involving analytical procedures and inquiries of management of the firm to be acquired. This level of service is called a *review.*

AICPA standards and IASC standards define four types of auditor association with assertions of management: examinations, reviews, agreed-upon procedures engagements, and compilations. The latter three types of engagements could be called "required procedures" engagements since the auditor agrees to apply stated procedures in the case of reviews and compilations and procedures agreed-upon by management and the stated user of management's assertions for agreed-upon procedures engagements.

For attestation report users, there is a very important distinction between examinations positing that the auditor came to the "required conclusion" that there is low (attest) risk that the assertion is materially misstated and "required procedures" positing only that the procedures be applied and that the auditor report his or her findings. The distinction is the level and variability of the *user's risk* in relying on the attestor's report. For example, in a financial statement audit (an examination-type engagement), the user's level of risk in relying on an attestation report with no exceptions is very low, and thus not subject to much variation. For reviews and agreed-upon procedures engagements, occurrence risk is not assessed, and attest risk will vary depending on the effectiveness of the stated or chosen procedures and the occurrence risk for material misstatement.

Because of the increased risk to the assertion user, agreed-upon procedure reports state that distribution (and the auditor's responsibility) is limited to the contracting parties (the information preparer and the information user). For a compilation, the "auditor" does not assess occurrence risk and does not apply auditing procedures. Rather, the auditor merely places client-supplied information into a prescribed form such as GAAP-based financial statements. Figure 10–5 summarizes the major requirements of the four levels of attestor association including required conclusions versus required procedures, who sets the procedures, and the attest report distribution limits, if any.

---

4. Attest, attestation, and attestor are used to denote generalization of financial statement auditing activities to other types of written assertions of one party to be used by another. Independent attest services improve the quality of written information for decision making by improving users' perceptions of its reliability.

FIGURE 10−5

Assembly Levels

Level of Service	Procedures/ Conclusions	Occurrence Risk (OR)	Detection Risk (DR)	User's Risk Level[1]	Opinion Form	Distribution
Examinations (e.g., audits of financial statements)	Conclude low risk of material misstatement	Assessed	Varies inversely with assessed OR	Low	Positive assurance	General (no restrictions)
Reviews (historical and pro forma financial statements)	Analytical procedures and inquiry	Not assessed	Moderate	Low to moderate	Negative assurance	General (no restrictions)
Agreed-upon procedures	Procedures agreed upon by preparer and user	Not assessed	Varies with criteria and procedures agreed upon	Low to very high	Findings (negative assurance prohibited)	Limited to preparer and user agreeing to procedures
Compilations	Assembly and formatting	Not assessed	Very high	Low to very high	No assurance expressed	General[2]

1. Risk to the user that an assertion accompanied by a favorable attest report is materially misstated.

2. Distribution of prospective financial statement compilations using hypothetical assumptions is limited to insiders.

Reviews of Financial Statements

An audit is the highest level of attest service for financial statements. An audit is an examination-type engagement for which the independent auditor obtains sufficient evidence to provide "reasonable assurance" that the statements are not materially misstated. The auditor's opinion is based on the auditor's assessment of pervasive risk factors, an understanding of the client's internal control, and pre-audit risk assessments based on book-value analysis that determine an overall occurrence risk. The occurrence risk then is reduced to a low level of audit risk by the conduct of auditing procedures to detect material misstatements, if any. The auditor's audit opinion expresses "positive assurance" in that it states the auditor's conclusion of belief, based on audit results, that the financial statements are not materially misstated.

Two other levels of auditor association with financial statements are possible. One level, review, utilizes only analytical procedures and inquiries of management as the basis for the auditor's conclusions. There is no study and evaluation of internal control, no required consideration of pervasive risk factors, and no requirement that the auditor apply auditing procedures to reduce audit (or "attest") risk to a low level. Rather, the auditor merely conducts the required procedures of inquiry of management and analytical procedures, and then follows up on any exceptions noted by these procedures. If there are no exceptions, then the auditor proceeds with a report expressing his or her conclusions.

The form of assurance in a review report has been called *negative assurance* since it expresses no opinion (i.e., it disclaims an audit opinion) and the auditor is allowed to report only a conclusion that "nothing came to our attention" that suggests the statements are materially misstated. Figure 10–6 presents a review report of LJ Appliances' financial statements for the first quarter of 2000.

Auditing procedures for review services are limited to inquiries of management about operations and financial statements of the business and analytical procedures applied to

FIGURE 10–6

Auditor's Interim Financial Statement Review Report

To: LJ Appliances, Inc.

We have reviewed the accompanying Balance Sheet and Income Statement of LJ Appliances, Inc., as of March 31, 2000, and for the three-month period then ended. These financial statements are the responsibility of the company's management.

We conducted our review in accordance with standards established by the American Institute of Certified Public Accountants. A review of interim financial information consists principally of applying analytical procedures to financial data and making inquiries of persons responsible for financial and accounting matters. It is substantially less in scope than an audit conducted in accordance with generally accepted auditing standards, the objective of which is the expression of an opinion regarding the financial statements taken as a whole. Accordingly, we do not express such an opinion.

Based on our review, we are not aware of any material modifications that should be made to the accompanying financial statements for them to be in conformity with generally accepted accounting principles.

supporting data. There is no evaluation of internal control and no detailed testing of supporting data. Therefore, the attestation risk for reviewed financial statements varies depending on the detection risk (DR) for inquiry and analytical procedures and the actual occurrence risk (OR) for material misstatement. To illustrate, Figure 10–7 presents calculations of AuR and RvR (review risk) for two companies—one with OR = .2 and the other with OR = .7. AuR is calculated using the simplified audit risk model (AuR = OR × DR) and a target audit risk (AuR* = .02). Allowable detection risk for an audit is calculated using the planning formula: DR* = AuR* / OR, and DR for a review is fixed at .4. DR is fixed for reviews because, although auditors will follow up on exceptions noted by analytical procedures and inquiries of management, these identification and follow-up procedures will often fail to indicate an exception even though material misstatement exists.

As shown in Figure 10–7, the user's risk of material misstatement is .08 or .28 when relying on reviews since the audit procedures were fixed and OR varies. For audits the user's risk is constant at the target AuR* = .02 (since auditing procedures and the resulting DR* vary depending on OR). A problem arises for the user because the user has no way of knowing whether occurrence risk is .2 or .7, and thus whether the resulting RvR is .08 or .28. In an audit examination, the auditor assesses and/OR conducts more auditing procedures for Company A than for Company B resulting in AuR of .02 in either case. For a review, RvR could be .08 or .28, depending on OR. Thus, as an outside user of reviewed assertions, you will face varying information risk. You should "price protect" yourself accordingly by discounting reviewed information more.

The attestor's certification report for review services reflects this limited involvement. Figure 10–6 showed a review report for interim financial statements of a public company. Note that the auditor's procedures are described, an audit opinion is disclaimed, and the conclusion is in the form of negative assurance, rather than a positive assurance. That is, the auditor states he or she is "not aware of any material modifications that should be

FIGURE 10–7

User's Attestation Risk of Incorrect Reliance on Materially Misstated Financial Statements
User's Audit Risk vs. User's Review Risk

Company A—Low Occurrence Risk (OR = .2)	Company B—High Occurrence Risk (OR = .7)
Audit Risk (AuR)	Audit Risk (AuR)
DR* = AuR* / OR	DR* = .02 / .7
= .02 / .20	= .0286
= .10	
AuR* = OR × DR*	AuR = .7 × .0286
= .2 × .1	= .02
= .02	
Review Risk (RvR)	Review Risk (RvR)
RvR = OR × DR	RvR = .4 × .7
= .2 × .4	= .28
= .08	

Note: Target audit risk (AuR*) is .02 for both Company A and Company B. DR is fixed at .4 for reviews.

made," rather than a positive opinion that the statements are "fairly presented in conformity with GAAP."

Compilation of Financial Statements

To compile financial statements, the CPA (we won't call the assurer an auditor since no auditing procedures are conducted for a compilation) takes data from the client and arranges it in proper form for GAAP-based financial statements. The CPA's procedures entail merely reading the available information to put it into the proper form. Only if the data appear to be in error upon reading would the CPA have responsibility to correct any amounts or disclosures on compiled financial statements.

The CPA's report on a compilation expressly denies an opinion (provides no assurance), but the CPA still has association with the statements and has some responsibility (although the responsibility is limited to what a reasonable auditor would have noted by merely assembling and reading the financial statements). The service is primarily that of putting unaudited financial amounts into GAAP form.

Agreed-Upon Procedures

Agreed-upon procedures engagements are increasingly common but are limited in their scope. They are limited as to the nature of the assertions being made, the procedures applied, and the expression of conclusions of the auditor. For example, agreed-upon procedures reports might relate to the quantities of a certain type of inventory on hand at a given date rather than the cost or market valuation of inventory on that date or inventory valuation as a component of GAAP-based financial statements. Auditor certification of particular elements can be obtained at much lower cost than an examination and can add value when specific elements are critical to management and the outside party.

For an agreed-upon procedures engagement, the party that is the source of the information and the user must agree upon measurement criteria for the assertions and the procedures to be applied by the auditor. The auditor then applies the agreed-upon procedures to the assertions and reports his or her findings. The auditor's report merely lists the findings from carrying out the procedures. If proper application of the agreed-upon procedures turns out not to have been adequate to detect something of concern to one of the parties to the agreement, then this prior agreement of the parties as to procedures to be applied should protect the auditor against legal claims by either party.

A user of an agreed-upon procedures report should be aware of the limitations of the prescribed procedures. If ineffective procedures are chosen, then the result will not be reliable even though the procedures were applied as stated and no exceptions were found. Thus, the user may take considerable risk in relying on an agreed-upon procedures report. Expertise must be used in specifying procedures to be applied prior to the engagement.

Figure 10–8 shows a standard agreed-upon procedures report. This report is noteworthy in that it is addressed to both parties rather than just the party hiring the auditor and it specifically denies a representation regarding the sufficiency of the procedures for any purpose (sufficiency is clearly the responsibility of the agreeing parties). Also, there is a sometimes lengthy paragraph describing the procedures and findings, standard language

FIGURE 10-8

Independent Auditor's Report on Applying Agreed-Upon Procedures

To the Audit Committees and Managements of ABC Inc. and XYZ Fund:

We have performed the procedures enumerated below, which were agreed to by the audit committees and managements of ABC Inc. and XYZ Fund, solely to assist you in evaluating the accompanying Statement of Investment Performance Statistics of XYZ Fund (prepared in accordance with the criteria specified therein) for the year ended December 31, 1999. This agreed-upon procedures engagement was performed in accordance with standards established by the American Institute of Certified Public Accountants. The sufficiency of these procedures is solely the responsibility of the specified users of the report.

Consequently, we make no representation regarding the sufficiency of the procedures described below either for the purpose for which this report has been requested or for any other purpose.

[*Include paragraphs to enumerate procedures and findings.*]

We were not engaged to, and did not, perform an examination, the objective of which would be the expression of an opinion on the accompanying Statement of Investment Performance Statistics of XYZ Fund. Accordingly, we do not express such an opinion. Had we performed additional procedures, other matters might have come to our attention that would have been reported to you.

This report is intended solely for the use of the audit committees and managements of ABC Inc. and XYZ Fund, and should not be used by those who have not agreed to the procedures and taken responsibility for the sufficiency of the procedures for their purposes.

Source: AICPA, *Statement on Standards for Attestation Engagements*, No. 4, Agreed-Upon Procedures Engagements, 1995, para. 3.

disclaiming an examination opinion, and a statement limiting the use of the report to the specified (agreeing) parties. While this type of engagement has limited usefulness, it can be obtained at very low cost and can provide assurance about decision-relevant matters that are discoverable by the stated and agreed-upon procedures.

THE CPA AS INVESTIGATOR AND INFORMATION SOURCE

The discussion so far has considered the CPA as a certifier of assertions of one party to another. As we saw in Chapter 1, independent assurance professionals can also serve as investigators hired by the user of information prepared by others to validate its reliability or as the source of information itself. In this section, we consider how the nature of the employment contract for the assurer, in particular a CPA, changes the risks and benefits of assurance services.

Investigations

Auditors hired by management to certify management's assertions have value for management only to the extent that the user of the certified assertions believes that the measurement criteria used are decision relevant and that the auditor is competent to detect defects and trustworthy enough to report defects in presentation or display. In hiring a certifying auditor, then, management has an incentive to choose an auditor with a reputation that will be known and recognized by the outsider users.

In an investigation-type contract, the auditor is hired by the party using the auditor's report. For example, management of a firm considering acquiring another firm may hire an auditor to independently examine some aspect of the firm to be acquired. The other firm agrees to the examination because the information assurance provided to the prospective acquirer will facilitate successful completion of the transaction. In an investigation contract, the user (client) can choose an auditor with a good reputation and can specify criteria that the auditor is to apply in conducting his or her investigation. Investigation-type contracts have an advantage for the auditor in that his or her liability to the user is limited by the contract itself. Thus, the auditor's fee can be lower.

Auditors as investigators can audit financial statements and issue audit reports that are identical to certification reports. Auditors can also be instructed to observe things not covered by GAAP, to conduct special investigations of certain accounts or certain transactions, or to investigate in detail for possible fraud. This is possible because management can specify measurement criteria to be used as well as the extent of auditing to be conducted in an investigation. Third-party users in a certification engagement ordinarily do not have these choices available because they can't instruct the certifying auditor.

Internal auditors are hired by management to assist management. In a sense, internal auditors can be viewed by management as independent assurance professionals in that they are independent of the information preparer or party being investigated (or, at least, can be independent, depending on organization structure). Those responsible for maintenance of basic accounting records may also be considered by management to be independent of the subject matter of the information.

In the 1990s, companies experimented with outsourcing noncore processes and services as a means of exploiting their unique advantage through core processes. Noncore services are "hired out" to outside suppliers. Internal auditing and basic accounting record maintenance are not core processes for the overwhelming majority of companies. Therefore, they are natural candidates for outsourcing consideration. An outside firm such as a CPA firm can offer cost savings and may enhance value to management because auditing and accounting services are core processes for CPA firms. CPA firms have competence in business measurement and basic accounting functions as well as experience with controls and a reputation for trustworthiness in reporting.

Outsourcing Internal Auditing

When CPA firms are hired to conduct internal auditing for a company, the CPA typically hires the existing internal audit staff of the client. These staff members become employees of the CPA firm, and receive training and supervision from the CPA firm, but continue to conduct internal audits of their old employer. Some of these internal auditors work for more than one client, but others are "dedicated" to a particular client, thus having a great deal of specialized knowledge of that client.

The potential for specialized audit training across many clients is a cost advantage for CPAs in maintaining technical competence of internal auditors, but what about their loyalties to their employer? The outsourced internal auditor works for the CPA, but also for a client. Professional success for the outsourced internal auditor may depend more on pleasing the CPA firm than pleasing the client management. This split loyalty may have negative implications for you as management of the client firm. On the other hand, audit committees (and compensation committees) may feel more fully informed about management because the outsourced internal auditor is more independent of management than is an internal auditor who is a career employee of management.

Some managements as well as some directors and regulators are concerned about the independence of the external auditor when internal auditing has been outsourced to the firm's external auditor. These parties are concerned that the external auditor will overrely on the internal auditor's work and not provide an independent or objective "second look" at the operations of the company. The disadvantage of not having an independent second look is balanced at least in part by the fact that the external auditor can now rely more on the internal auditor because of increased confidence in the internal audit staff's training and competence, as well as increased ability to plan and coordinate audits with employees of the CPA firm. The optimal balance is one to be decided by the management and directors of the firm, after considering the effect on outsiders' perceptions of auditor independence.

One group of outsiders, accounting and securities regulators, is concerned about aggregate marketplace perceptions of independence. To allay regulators' concerns, the AICPA has issued ethical interpretations that constrain internal audit outsourcing for audit clients of CPA firms. The AICPA rules allow the CPA firm to serve as auditor and internal auditor only if the internal auditor has no management decision-making functions (see Chapter 12). Management determines the scope of outsourced internal audit activities, evaluates its results, and evaluates the adequacy of procedures performed. Also, management must designate an individual within the client company (typically a member of top management) to be responsible for the internal audit function.

Assurer as Information Source

Outsourcing Accounting Processing

Many firms have decided to outsource the operation of their accounting function. Some of these companies are very large and the contracts involve substantial resources. For example, one of the first contracts was between Andersen Consulting and LTV with $350 million in professional fees to operate the accounting system of LTV for a 10-year period. An annual fee of $35 million is at least 10 times the likely audit fee for LTV. More recently, Shell Oil and Ernst and Young have entered into a joint venture to supply accounting services to Shell itself (Shell is not an audit client of Ernst and Young). Non-CPAs, in particular large companies such as EDS, also provide outsourcing services for accounting.

Outsourcing of accounting services has clear implications for external auditor independence. AICPA rules allow an auditor to provide some bookkeeping services and still serve as an independent auditor. However, SEC rules prohibit the auditor from providing bookkeeping services. Thus, a CPA firm that provides accounting processing for a publicly traded entity cannot serve as its external auditor. In one case, a Big Five auditor resigned the audit engagement with a fee of less than $50,000 per year to provide accounting and systems services with fees of $300,000 to $400,000 per year. The client expects to save $50,000 to $100,000 in consulting fees it would have otherwise paid.[5]

---

5. "In with Outsourcing, out with Audit," *Public Accounting Report,* April 15, 1996, p. 4.

Other Assurance Services

CPA firms possess substantial expertise in accounting, internal control, information technology, plus industry knowledge and legal, cultural, and business operations knowledge on a worldwide basis. While no one person possesses all of these skills, the firm can assemble teams that provide all of these services on an integrated basis as needed by a client. Thus, the CPA firm can offer a competence advantage and cost advantage (see Chapter 2).

What other advantages, if any, do CPAs offer to you as manager of a large corporation? To answer this question, you must consider what other characteristics a CPA brings—in particular, a reputation for providing relevant, competent, and trustworthy advice, especially for matters involving measurement. When you propose a restructuring of your business or a major new venture to the board of directors, is it more likely to be accepted if you have been advised by a CPA firm? The answer is not always clear. For services that are related to accounting and auditing, finance, measurement, and compliance, directors are likely to value more highly the advice of a CPA firm. For services that are far from accounting and auditing, the reputation of the auditor or providing relevant, competent, and trustworthy advice is less clear, but may exist.

According to one study, Big Six CPA firms (premerger of Price Waterhouse and Coopers and Lybrand) and Andersen Consulting comprised 7 of the 11 largest management consultancies and accounted for 22.6 percent of aggregate management consulting revenues of $73 billion worldwide in 1997.[6] Management consulting also accounted for 46 percent of the firms' total revenues. The study found that CPA firms benefit from their combination of information technology implementation and operations management expertise and their ability to deliver "one-stop shopping" for multiple services. They also benefit from an increased focus on corporate accountability, as well as the presence of their personnel as providers of outsourced services who are able to identify additional problems that can be addressed by the firms.

The ability of CPA firms to leverage the essence of their traditional reputations for their core processes has dictated the product offerings that large CPA firms have developed. While large CPA firms offer a wide variety of services, including general management consulting services, there is a pattern to their choices that can be tied to their core process reputations. Most CPA firm services improve the quality of information for decision making, and most are applied so as to maintain independence. That is, most services are assurance services, whether improving information (or context) relevance or reliability.

SUMMARY

Many business situations involve parties who would like to do business with each other but are reluctant to do so because of asymmetry of information. One party has better information about relevant real-world conditions than does the other. The costs of engaging in a business transaction can be reduced if the party with more information can (a) develop or obtain measurement rules that can provide decision-relevant displays representing real-world condi-

---

6. "The Global Management Consulting Market: Key Data, Forecasts and Trends for 1998," by Kennedy Research Group of Fitzwilliam, NH, and firm data from *Public Accounting Report* as summarized in "Big Six Grab 23% Share of Global MCS Market," *Public Accounting Report,* January 31, 1998, pp. 1 and 5.

tions and (b) have the information display certified by someone perceived by the other party as possessing competence and trustworthiness in certification.

Audits of GAAP-based financial statements conducted by CPAs following GAAS are one example of value-adding certification that reduces the information asymmetry between parties who would like to do business with each other. There are many others, and you as management are limited only by your ability to develop relevant measurement rules that are reasonably objective and to attract a certifier with a good reputation. Certification of business processes such as manufacturing quality, internal control, and forward-looking information provides examples of value-adding possibilities. Assurance about these real-world conditions to your customers, suppliers, and workers, as well as stockholders, potential stockholders, and members of your board of directors, can add value for you.

Examinations of management's assertions provide users the lowest risk of important departures from the established or stated measurement criteria. Examinations, such as financial statement audits, require sufficient evidence to support a conclusion of low risk of important information defects. Since examinations are costly and the added precision or reduced information risk is not always worth the extra cost, lower levels of assurance can be purchased. A review of assertions is limited to required applications of analytical procedures and inquiry of management. Also, agreed-upon procedures (agreed-upon by the information preparer and user) can be applied to particular assertions. Agreed-upon procedures engagements result in a statement of findings of the auditor, rather than an opinion about the assertions. For both of the required-procedures type of engagements (reviews and agreed-upon procedures engagements), the user of the information bears the risk that the required procedures fail to detect a material or important defect in the assertions. For examinations, the auditor is required to have an adequate basis for his or her conclusion of low risk of important assertion defects; thus procedures failure risk is taken on by the auditor.

Finally, auditing firms have leveraged their reputation for knowledge of relevant information measurements, competence in conducting analyses and investigations, and trustworthiness (independence, integrity, and objectivity) in reporting defects by providing other information improvement services such as design of information systems, analysis of proposed transactions, and even outsourcing of functions such as internal auditing and operation of accounting systems. These services may offer an advantage to you as management due, in part, to the reputation of the CPA firms with outside parties.

CASE 10

JOSE'S FINANCE CORPORATION

Jose's Finance Cooperative makes loans to small businesses. In the past, Jose has not required independent assurers' association with financial statements of loan applicants. However, Jose has found that although all applicants always report earnings and assets sufficiently high to warrant a loan, about 50 percent of the successful loan applicants have net earnings and net assets that are materially overstated. The problem is that Jose can't tell which are overstated at the time the loan decisions are made!

Aracely, the new financial officer at Jose's, has recommended that all statements be accompanied by a report from an auditing firm. She says that three levels of association are possible—audits, reviews, and compilations. The procedures and risks are as follows:

Audits: Auditors assess a client's "prior-to-audit risk" (denoted OR for "occurrence risk") of aggregate misstatement $M \geq M^*$, and then apply auditing procedures (related to detection risk (DR)) to yield audit risk (AuR*) = .01 risk of failure to detect material misstatement when it exists.

Reviews: "Reviewers" do not assess OR, and they apply only analytical procedures and inquiry of management. For review procedures, DR = .4.

Compilations: "Compilers" use the applicant's unaudited records and merely tabulate financial statements in proper form. Only the most obvious misstatements and other departures from GAAP will be noticed by an accountant compiling financial statements. For compilations, P ("pass" compile "test" | $M \geq M^*$) = .98—the compiler will almost certainly not notice material misstatement when it exists.

For simplicity, assume that all prospective borrowers' "true earnings" and reported earnings take on only one of two possible values. True earnings are either "high" or "low," where "low" is lower than "high" by M^*.

Jose decides to require auditing firm association with all loan applicants' financial statements. He also decides to offer a 2 percent discount from the usual interest rate if an applicant submits audited financial statements and a 1 percent discount for reviewed statements. Jose charges a "default risk" premium of 50 basis points (.5 percent) for applicants with "low" earnings reports.

Audit firm fees for auditing, review, and compilation services are approximately:

$15,000 for audits of clients with bad controls.

$10,000 for audits of clients with good controls.

$3,000 for reviews.

$1,000 for compilations.

You are the financial advisor to a prospective borrower from Jose's. Your client's loan application is for $1,000,000. You believe that your client's pervasive factors risks and book value risks are low and controls are "good" (OR = .2), and an auditor will be able to correctly assess OR. Your client's pre-audit earnings are "high."

Required

a. Which level of service would you recommend that your client acquire and why? (Hint: calculate the risk that (a) your client's pre-audit earnings are materially overstated, and (b) the risk that the auditor will detect the overstatement and require a downward correction (see Chapter 8, Appendix A). Then calculate expected gain or loss through net interest cost savings).

b. How would your recommendation change if you believed that
- Your client's pervasive factors risks and book value risks are moderate and controls are "bad" (OR = .8)?
- Your client's OR will be assessed at OR = .2, but you know that earnings are overstated by M^* (i.e., your client's "true" earnings are "low")?

c. Be prepared to answer the following questions, if asked by your client:
- What do your analyses in parts *a* and *b* tell you about self-selection of audit firm services?
- Who benefits from financial statement certification and who pays its cost?
- Who bears the risk of audit, review, or compilation failure to detect/correct material misstatement?

KEY WORDS

agreed-upon procedures engagement An attest engagement in which the party that is the source of information and the user agree upon procedures to be applied by the auditor.

compilation engagement An engagement in which the assurer arranges, without review or audit, data from the client in proper form for GAAP-based financial statements.

CPA WebTrust An AICPA-branded certification service, certifying that a client's Web page security and performance assertions satisfy criteria to display a CPA WebTrust seal.

examination engagement An attest engagement in which the auditor (attestor) obtains a sufficient basis for low audit (attest) risk of undiscovered material defects in management's assertion.

generally accepted attestation standards (GAAtS) Eleven characteristics that generalize the concepts of GAAS for nonfinancial statement assertions.

negative assurance Form of attest conclusion that disclaims an opinion, but reports a conclusion that "nothing came to our attention" that suggests the statements (assertions) are materially misstated.

positive assurance Form of examination conclusion that expresses an affirmative conclusion that the assertions are free of important (material) misstatement.

reportable (internal control) conditions Significant deficiencies in the design or operation of internal control discovered by the auditor conducting a financial statement audit.

review engagement An attest engagement in which the auditor (attestor) conducts an investigation of financial statement assertions by applying analytical procedures and inquiries of management and expresses negative assurance that the statements are free of material misstatement.

Statements on Auditing Standards Official interpretations of the 10 components of GAAS prepared by the AICPA's Auditing Standards Board.

11
CHAPTER

Regulatory Reporting and Disclosure from Management's Perspective

- ◆ **W**hat disclosures and reports are required of a public company in the United States?
- ◆ Will my auditor "turn me in"?
- ◆ What must I do (and not do) as a manager of a public company?
- ◆ How do regulated audit and accounting reports differ across national borders?
- ◆ What should I look for in evaluating auditors' reports from other countries?

All of these questions from top management relate to mandated reports and public disclosures required by laws and regulations of various jurisdictions. The mandates are part of the costs of raising capital in certain public markets. Collectively, they comprise an important determinant of how companies are organized and operate.

This chapter begins the last section of the book, which addresses the demand for assurance services to interpret regulated reports and to show compliance with laws and regulations. We start by reviewing requirements of the Securities and Exchange Commission (SEC) of the United States and the cost and benefits of public registration versus remaining private. This is followed by comparison with standards and practices in other large industrialized countries.

THE U.S. SECURITIES AND EXCHANGE COMMISSION

The SEC, an independent government agency created in 1934 by an act of Congress, is the primary securities and accounting disclosure regulatory authority in the United States. It administers the Securities Act of 1933 and the Securities Exchange Act of 1934 as well as other subsequent acts.

The 1933 act was designed to protect the investing public from misrepresentation of information, manipulation of stock prices, and other fraudulent practices surrounding the initial public offering (IPO), distribution, and sale of securities. The 1933 act requires registration of securities with the SEC prior to their sale to the general public. The registration process includes disclosure of financial and other information through a registration statement with a prospectus and financial statements audited by an independent accountant (auditor).

The 1934 act addresses disclosures for trading of previously issued securities. The 1934 act covers dissemination of financial and other information for securities traded on national exchanges and over-the-counter markets in the United States. Under the 1934 act, these companies must register the securities and file certain reports with the SEC on a continuing basis. There are exemptions from the registration process for small companies and certain foreign private issuers.

Both the 1933 act and the 1934 act are intended to protect investors by requiring disclosure of certain information about securities. Detailed descriptions of the business and audited annual and reviewed quarterly financial statements are required at the initial registration, and periodically thereafter. Also, the acts require disclosure of additional information as significant events occur.

In addition to disclosures, the 1934 act requires that corporate "insiders," registrant's directors and officers, and principal owners (beneficial owners of 10 percent or more) of the registrant's equity securities disclose their holdings of equity securities and changes in their holdings on a timely basis. These parties are also prohibited from trading that exploits private information that they hold as "insiders," and some trading gains of these parties are subject to recapture by the corporation. All of these features are designed to protect "outsider" investors and potential investors and facilitate capital formation by providing a "level playing field" for all investors through the disclosure process. The securities acts also prohibit certain trading practices that manipulate stock prices.

The SEC does not prohibit sale of speculative or risky securities but requires disclosure of risks and financial and other information about the firm and its prospects. Passing the review of an IPO registration statement by the SEC staff for a particular security does not imply approval. In fact, every prospectus contains a statement that the securities have *not* been approved or disapproved by the SEC. However, the staff of the SEC may differentially review disclosures of companies that are speculative and may refuse to allow the registration document to become effective (thus not allowing security sales) until questionable matters are resolved. For example, the SEC staff may delay the effective date by questioning the accounting treatment of certain items. Thus, sale of the securities will be barred until the registrant clarifies or corrects the matter.

In addition to disclosure of financial information and restrictions on management's actions, registration with the SEC also subjects management to an internal control requirement and exposes management to the possibility that the external auditor will report securities acts violations by management and/or the company to the SEC.

The internal control provisions originated with the Foreign Corrupt Practices Act of 1977 and specify that registrants will maintain adequate (cost-effective) internal controls over transactions. Wording of the internal control requirements follows that of U.S. GAAS. Firms meeting COSO standards for internal control discussed in Chapters 4 and 10 should be in compliance with SEC requirements.

The Private Securities Litigation Reform Act (PSLRA) of 1995 altered private litigation under federal securities acts (see Chapter 12), but several of its provisions also affect the external auditor and management behavior. Specifically, auditors of SEC registrants are required to apply procedures designed to provide reasonable assurance of detecting fraud, illegal acts, and related-party transactions that have a direct and material effect on financial statements. Also, the auditor must evaluate whether there is substantial doubt about the ability of a registrant to remain a going concern for the next fiscal year. Thus, the PSLRA codifies into federal law requirements existing in U.S. GAAS.

The illegal acts section of the PSLRA (section 10A) provides that, when the external auditor concludes it is likely that fraud or illegal acts by management or its employees materially misstate the financial statements, the auditor must report the acts to the registrant's audit committee or board of directors. If the audit committee or board fails to take timely and appropriate remedial action and the auditor decides that he or she must resign from the audit or issue a qualified or adverse audit opinion, then the auditor is to report to the SEC within one business day. Furthermore, the PSLRA prohibits private legal actions against auditors making such reports to the SEC and has penalties for the audit firm that fails to notify the SEC when it is warranted. Thus, top management of public companies may be "turned in" to federal authorities by the independent auditor that they hired to certify their financial statements.

Accounting, Auditing, and Disclosure Standards

The SEC has the authority to prescribe auditing and independence standards for auditors and accounting methods to be used by publicly traded companies in preparation of financial statements. In practice, the SEC has generally not specified accounting practices or auditing procedures. Rather, it has allowed private standard-setting bodies (for example, the FASB, the AICPA's Auditing Standards Board, and the Independence Standards Board (see Figure 11–1)) to determine such methods and procedures. The SEC occasionally overrules or overrides these provisions, however.

FIGURE 11–1

Private-Sector Financial Reporting Standards and Oversight by SEC

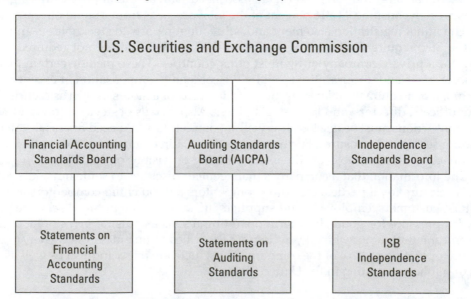

The SEC's Regulation S-X prescribes the form and content for financial statements filed with the SEC. Regulation S-X covers annual reports (part of Form 10-K) and quarterly financial statements (Form 10-Q). The SEC issues Financial Reporting Releases (FRRs) and Accounting and Auditing Enforcement Releases (AAERs) to communicate its positions on accounting matters and the auditing of financial statements. AAERs document the SEC's findings in enforcement actions against registrants and auditors. While AAER cases often involve auditor and client conditions that are extreme or otherwise exceptional, they give an indication of matters that the SEC finds in violation of its rules and standards of the profession.

Regulation S-K was adopted in 1977 to standardize nonfinancial statement disclosures in SEC filings. For example, S-K governs content of Management Discussion and Analysis (MD&A) disclosures about how the firm is managed and explanation of its financial condition, results of operations, liquidity, capital needs, and its risks, sensitivities, and concentrations of suppliers and customers.

"Going Public"

Public sale of securities and registration with the SEC allow a business to raise substantial capital and to share risks of ownership with many other investors. Registration with the SEC and listing on public exchanges make it easier for the owner of a business to borrow money by using issued and outstanding securities with an established market value as collateral, and may facilitate expansion through business combinations involving mergers and acquisitions. The securities allow negotiations without using the company's cash, since the value of the company can be demonstrated through the public markets. The liquidity of shares also makes the company's stock more attractive to investors and its stock options more attractive in retaining key employees.

On the other hand, "going public" has substantial disadvantages in addition to the expense of the registration process and expenses of capital issuance such as the fees of the investment bankers, auditors, and others associated with an initial public offering. These expenses often consume 9 to 16 percent of the total proceeds from a small offering.

The initial registration statement and subsequent reports to stockholders and filings with the SEC require disclosure of aspects of the business that are not required by U.S. GAAP for a private company or by most other countries. These include certain plans for the future, risks and uncertainties faced by the company, compensation of executives and directors, major contracts, related parties, and interests of insiders as well as security holdings of officers, directors, and large stockholders. Also, details of stock options and related party transactions must be disclosed, as well as complete GAAP-based financial statements including segment disclosures. Furthermore, officers, directors, and primary stockholders of equity securities are subject to the insider trading provisions of the 1934 act.

The information that a company's management discloses to some outsiders may require disclosure to all parties, including competitors and potential competitors as well as creditors, customers, employees, and suppliers. In addition, the public disclosure process increases pressure for good short-term operating results as outside investors look to the company for profitability. Finally, by issuing securities to outsiders the owner/manager may lose operating control of the company. Thus, there are many indirect as well as direct costs to public registration in the United States.

Principal Forms

Form 10-K

Form 10-K is the primary annual report form for commercial and industrial businesses. It is required by the 1934 Securities Exchange Act for periodic reports of securities registered either through IPO or listing on a national exchange. Form 10-K is to be filed at the SEC within 90 days after the close of the fiscal year covered by the report. Almost all companies file Form 10-K within two days before the latest possible date, although companies experiencing financial difficulties often file later than the deadline date.[1]

In addition to descriptive material about the business, and its financial statements and supplementary data, Form 10-K requires "Management's Discussion and Analysis" (MD&A) of financial conditions and results of operations. These latter disclosures go beyond the requirements of generally accepted accounting principles. The balance sheets, statements of income, cash flows, stockholders' equity, and financial statement schedules are audited by an independent accountant qualified to practice under the SEC's rules. Other elements of a 10-K such as MD&A are read by the auditor for inconsistency with the audited financial statements, but are not audited. Form 10-K also requires an annual report to the stockholders.

Form 10-Q

Registrants are required to file quarterly reports using Form 10-Q within 45 days after the end of each of the first three quarters of a fiscal year. Form 10-Q contains two parts, a financial report and a special events report. Financial information includes quarterly financial statements and MD&A for results of operations for the quarter. In addition, other information is disclosed on Form 10-Q, including legal proceedings, changes in securities, changes in capitalization of the firm, and status of matters previously reported to the SEC on Form 8-K (see below).

Quarterly financial statements are not required to be audited by an independent accountant, but reviews (see Chapter 10) by an independent accountant are required. However, these reviews may be conducted "after the fact." That is, either the auditor can review the quarterly statements contemporaneously (before issuance to the public and filing with the SEC) or the first three quarters can be reviewed all at once at the end of the fiscal year. Companies choosing contemporaneous reviews tend to be firms with higher agency costs, but less than 8 percent publicly report timely reviews.[2] All Big Five audit firms require contemporaneous quarterly reviews of their clients' interim financial statements as a risk mitigation tool to lower their own auditor's business risk (ABR).

Form 8-K

When certain specific events occur, disclosure is required on Form 8-K. These events include acquisition or disposition of significant assets, sale of equity securities, bankruptcy or receivership, changes in control of the registrant, or resignations of directors. Events also

---

1. The filing of Form 10-K is typically from 30 to 60 days after the release of a company's annual report to stockholders and analysts.
2. M. Ettredge, D. Simon, D. Smith, and M. Stone, "Why Do Companies Purchase Timely Quarterly Reviews?" *Journal of Accounting and Economics*, September 1994, pp. 131–55.

include accounting matters such as changes in the external audit firm, accounting disagreements with the auditor, and changes in previously released financial statements or fiscal year. Form 8-K is required to be filed within 15 days for these events, with the exception of a change in audit firm, which must be reported within 5 days. Thus, the SEC (and investors) must be informed of significant events on a relatively timely basis.

Provisions for disclosure of disputes with the external auditor regarding accounting matters are particularly important. Disclosure of disagreements with the outside auditor may specify differences of opinion about compliance with GAAP. Disagreements may also be indicative of nonaccounting problems within the company so significant that the auditor questions the client business risk and/or the auditor's business risk-versus-reward trade-off. Thus, the auditor may be willing to risk losing a client because of substantial risks that may go beyond application of GAAP.

The auditor is allowed to respond to the SEC regarding the validity of the client's characterization of the disagreement in the 8-K. Formal studies of the content of 8-K filings and the auditor's response suggest that many disagreements are minor, with excessive audit fees a frequently cited reason, but the 8-K's may not disclose the full extent of disagreements. In the presence of disagreement, the auditor may prefer to disassociate from the client, and the auditor may not require full disclosure of the extent of disagreement. This is especially true for matters for which positions were not fully determined prior to replacing the auditor.

In the early 1990s, many resignations of auditors (or firing of auditors by management) were followed shortly thereafter by the appointment of another well-qualified auditor. The AICPA has recently changed required communications between the auditor being replaced and the successor auditor (SAS No. 84). These rules are intended to increase the successor auditor's knowledge of the client, which in turn may encourage client management not to disagree with their present auditors on matters involving accounting principle.

Studies of Form 8-K filings show substantial differences between registrants announcing auditor resignations and those announcing auditor changes for reasons other than auditor resignations. One finds that registrants whose auditors resigned from the audit engagement were much smaller than those that had an auditor change for other than resignation, and they had higher debt, lower current ratios, lower return on assets, and higher stock price volatility.[3] Also, the firms experiencing auditor resignation were more likely *not* to retain a Big Five auditor as the successor. Furthermore, while auditor change is not typically accompanied by significant stock price changes, for the firms whose auditors resign, stock returns (adjusted for firm-specific risk) average -3.11 percent in the three-day period surrounding the 8-K filing and -16.1 percent in the year preceding resignation. Each of these factors may indicate that the resigning auditor is reducing auditor business risk by disassociating from these clients.

Form S-1

Form S-1 is the principal form for registration of securities under the Securities Act of 1933. It includes many provisions for disclosure of information about a company, including financial statements following GAAP and audited by an independent auditor. The require-

---

3. S. Shu, "An Empirical Examination of Auditor Resignations," working paper, University of Rochester, December 1998.

ments of S-1 for IPOs and their application in practice are very technical and beyond the scope of this book. The SEC imposes substantial liability for the issuers and technical experts such as the underwriter (investment banker), attorneys, and the certifying auditor. The technical experts must exercise "due diligence" (a legal standard of duty) in determining that management's representations are truthful. Liability for auditors as well as for management will be explored in Chapter 12.

Form 20-F

Foreign private issuers of securities can register with the SEC by filing Form 20-F under either Item 17 or Item 18. Both Item 17 and Item 18 allow use of non U.S. GAAP, but both require reconciliation of results with U.S. GAAP. As with other registrants, these foreign private issuers must disclose certain information describing the business and selected financial data. Disclosures required for Item 17 filings of Form 20-F are much less than is required for Item 18 or Form 10-K filings, but Item 17 firms cannot issue new securities in the United States. The financial data required are less extensive than those required on Form 10-K, but the requirements for disclosure for MD&A are similar.[4]

"No Form"—Rule 144A

Regulation D of the SEC exempts from registration certain sales of securities. One important exemption is securities of foreign private issuers under Rule 144A. Rule 144A allows sale of securities to qualified institutional buyers (such as banks, insurance companies, investment companies, and savings and loans) without registration with the SEC. After a two-year holding period, these securities may be resold in public markets, but have an initial exemption from the registration process.

The objective of Rule 144A is to increase the flow of capital by allowing qualified institutional buyers to freely trade these unregistered securities. Qualified institutional buyers are presumed to have the knowledge and expertise necessary to interpret the risks that they incur in investing in such securities. Also, these buyers are able to negotiate privately with the issuers for additional information or disclosures.

While securities issued under Rule 144A do not require that the issuer be an SEC registrant or file financial statements with the SEC, the rule does provide for certain information to be provided to the buyer. This required information includes a statement of the nature of the issuer's business and its products and its most recent balance sheet and income statements for the three most recent years. Foreign issuers may use GAAP from their domicile country (they need not follow or provide reconciliations to U.S. GAAP). Also, the financial statements may be audited using whatever auditor or auditing standards are agreed to by the parties.

LISTING REQUIREMENTS OF U.S. STOCK EXCHANGES

The New York Stock Exchange and the National Association of Securities Dealers Automated Quotation system (NASDAQ) comprise the major listing alternatives for companies whose securities are traded in the United States. Each has size requirements for net worth

---

4. Item 18 filings of Form 20-F are more comparable to Form 10-K.

and requirements on the numbers of stockholders and publicly held shares. Also, each requires that all listed companies have an audit committee comprised of a minimum of two outside (independent) members of the company's board of directors.

Directors have a fiduciary duty to oversee corporate activities on behalf of the stockholders. They also have substantial legal liability for proper conduct of their duty to monitor the performance of top management. The directors' duties for public companies include oversight of financial reporting and auditors' association with financial reporting. Figure 11–2 diagrams the relation of the board of directors to the auditor, management, and stockholders in a certification contract situation that is typical for public companies in the United States. Figure 11–2 shows consultation, review, and communication links between the board and the external auditor. These links are described in detail below.

Not shown in Figure 11–2 is typical membership of a board of directors. The chairman or chairwoman of the board of directors is often the chief executive officer of the company, and other officers are also often members. Other board members are sometimes relatives of corporate officers or are associated with major customers or suppliers of the firm. Since these board members have interests that may sometimes conflict with those of the stockholders, some modification of the consultation, review, and communication structure is necessary to protect the interests of the stockholders. That is, there may be an "independence of judgment" problem with some directors. An audit committee comprised of directors who have no such interests is one way to approach the problem.

Independent directors have recently been defined as members of the board of directors who "have no relationship to the corporation that might interfere with the exercise of their independence from management or the corporation."[5] For example, independence might be questioned for a director who is an employee of the corporation, who has significant contracts with the corporation, whose spouse is an officer of the corporation, or who is an executive of another entity for which any of the corporation's officers serve on its compensation committee.

Independent Directors

Independent ("outside") directors can add credibility for the company in the investment community through their business experience and technical competence. They can provide a sounding board for management's ideas and increase the perception of integrity of corporate affairs by lending their own reputations in overseeing the affairs of the company.

Independent directors are not part of management itself so that they will be perceived as more credible in overseeing management than would directors who are part of management. Independent directors rarely hold a major block of stock in a company that they direct. This is due, in part, to U.S. securities laws prohibiting trading on inside information by managers and directors, as well as provisions for recapture of trading profits for such parties.

Some have argued that the lack of significant equity interest in the company's success leads to less attention to the affairs of a corporation, and this lack of incentive to exercise

---

5. Blue Ribbon Committee on Improving the Effectiveness of Corporate Audit Committees, *Report and Recommendations of the Blue Ribbon Committee on Improving the Effectiveness of Corporate Audit Committees,* 1999.

FIGURE 11–2

Director's Roles in Certification for Public Companies

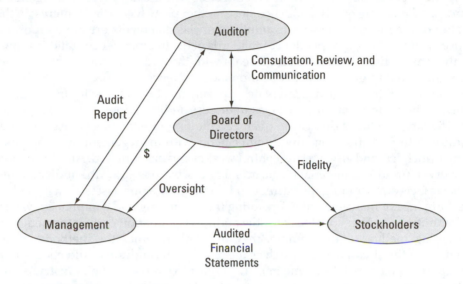

active oversight impairs the ability of the board to take timely action to discipline or remove ineffective management or take action on internal control.[6] In other words, the active involvement of a board of directors with substantial financial interests in the corporation will lead to more effective monitoring of the affairs of management, more attention to long-term problems within the corporation, and more attention to strategy. U.S. capital markets may suffer from the lack of commitment by directors and from passive investors who merely trade their stocks and diversify their risks rather than long-term investors committed to success for a particular corporation.

Audit Committees

Since outside directors are not part of management, they are frequently called upon to serve as members of the audit committee of the corporation. As audit committee members, they have the duty to formally retain external auditors and meet with the auditors on a periodic basis to discuss the audit and the auditor's findings, including any fraud, illegal acts, or significant internal control weaknesses noted by the auditor during conduct of the financial statement audit. In many companies, the audit committee also meets with the internal auditor, and the internal auditor may have a direct link or contact with the chairman of the audit committee.

An audit committee comprised of outside directors is not required by the SEC, but the New York Stock Exchange and NASDAQ require them, with the former requiring that all

---

6. M. Jensen, "The Modern Industrial Revolution, Exit, and the Failure of Internal Control Systems," *Journal of Financial Economics*, July 1993, pp. 831–80.

members be outside directors and the latter requiring that the majority of the committee be outside directors. An audit committee comprised of outside directors provides a communication link between outside auditors and directors who are not part of management. This structure has a measure of independence since neither party has a direct interest in the subject matter of the information—for example, financial statements are not a report on performance of either. Also, Independence Standards of the Independence Standards Board requires that the auditor disclose to and discuss with the audit committee, all relationships with the client that might reasonably bear on independence.

Audit committees in the United States typically meet with the external auditor to discuss the planned annual audit, as well as to discuss audit findings after the audit is completed. The latter includes discussion of any accounting misstatements discovered during the audit and their disposition, any disagreements with management over matters of accounting principles, and any internal control weaknesses encountered. Also to be discussed is discovery of fraud and material illegal acts. The discussions allow the audit committee to know basic facts surrounding the current audit and allow some assessment of the attitude and performance of management in operating the accounting and compliance systems.

Committee members often ask for the auditor's evaluation of management's choices of accounting methods. For example, they may ask whether the methods chosen are "preferable" in the circumstances (such as the one that the auditor would choose if the auditor prepared the financial statements), are "typical" of those of the industry, or perhaps indicate an "aggressive" stance by management that recognizes revenues at an earlier point than do other firms. They may also ask for clarification of the logic for accounting estimates that have questionable bases.[7] Knowledge of the auditor's independent judgments of management's behavior about these matters is valuable to a director overseeing corporate affairs on behalf of stockholders.

In concept, these private meetings of the external auditor and the audit committee allow expression of auditor judgments about the "quality" or appropriateness of accounting measurement within the GAAP framework. In practice, it is not clear that auditors feel free to discuss fully any concerns that they have. There are several reasons for this. The most basic is that auditors' primary contact with the registrant is through top management, and management can influence the board of directors and the audit committee in making auditor retention decisions. Also, an open working relationship with top management encourages free disclosure of information to the auditor. This contact facilitates an effective and efficient audit. Management would be less willing to have open discussion with an auditor who reports minor infractions to the audit committee.

Officers of one corporation often serve as audit committee members of another, and vice versa; in many corporations, the board chairperson also serves as CEO. These relationships may impair objective oversight through the independent audit committee mechanism. Also, there may be associations among and between management and the audit committee that are not apparent in the typical organization chart. In particular, the board

---

7. The Blue Ribbon Committee on Improving the Effectiveness of Corporate Audit Committees has recommended that the auditor be required to discuss with the audit committee the auditor's judgments about the "quality" of accounting principles applied by management.

FIGURE 11–3

Typical Auditor Communication Links for Public Companies in the United States

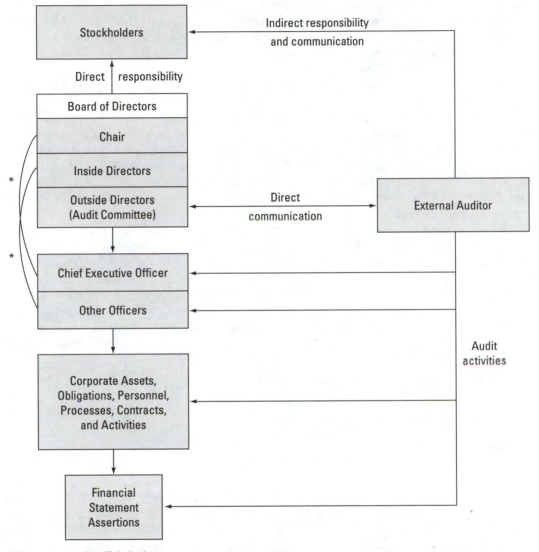

*Same person sometimes fills both roles.

chair may also be the CEO and other officers may be board members (see Figure 11–3). Finally, audit committee members are involved with company affairs for perhaps 8 to 12 working days per year, while the CEO and CFO are involved all year. It is unclear that external auditors can fully reveal their own judgments about full-time management to a part-time audit committee with whom they have little contact.

Empirical Results

Since you as a member of top management are a source of information about your own firm, you would like to know whether the presence of outside directors and an outside audit committee may affect your ability to make credible representations to the public. Also, since your firm invests in other corporations, you would like to know whether outside directors and an audit committee comprised of outside directors should substantially increase your confidence in the assertions of another company and its management. Are they at least associated with reduced fraud by management and reliability of financial information issued by firms?

Two important archival research studies document positive differential performance of companies with substantial differences in corporate control, including audit committees comprised of outside directors. Both studies were conducted during the period before audit committees were required by NASDAQ, both use firms committing financial statement fraud or earnings manipulations and subjected to SEC Accounting and Auditing Enforcement Actions (AAERs) in the 1980s, and both selected a sample comprised of non-AAER firms of similar size and industry.[8]

Firms accused of financial statement fraud by the SEC (either falsified financial statements or management misappropriation of assets) had a smaller percentage of audit committees (41 percent versus 63 percent), a smaller percentage of board seats held by outside directors (50 percent versus 65 percent), outside directors that had served less time as outside directors (3.8 years versus 6.6 years), and a higher percentage share of stock ownership (12 percent versus 5.4 percent of outstanding shares).[9]

In another study of corporate control and AAERs, researchers found a relation between earnings manipulation and the firms' internal governance structures.[10] In particular, firms manipulating earnings were more likely to

* Have boards of directors dominated by management.
* Have a CEO who also chairs the board.
* Have a CEO who founded the firm.

They were less likely to

* Have an audit committee.
* Have an outside (nonmanagement) holder of a major block of stock.

The researchers also found that firms manipulating earnings experienced an 11 percent stock price drop after the manipulations were made public by the SEC.

Both of these studies rely on comparisons of firms that were subjects of AAERs versus those that weren't, and may not be representative of a broad cross-section of firms. For example, AAER firms are small on average, and the SEC may have focused regulatory at-

---

8. Audit committees were not required by NASDAQ until 1987.
9. M. Beasley, "An Empirical Analysis of the Relation between Board of Directors Composition and Financial Statement Fraud," *The Accounting Review,* October 1996, pp. 443–65.
10. P. Dechow, R. Sloan, and A. Sweeney, "Causes and Consequences of Earnings Manipulation: An Analysis of Firms Subject to Enforcement Actions by the SEC," *Contemporary Accounting Research,* Spring 1996, pp. 1–36.

tention on firms without audit committees. Also, whether outside directors cause more reliable reporting or more reliable firms simply choose to have more outside directors can't be determined from the available archival data. However, both studies are consistent with the view that outsiders participating in corporate governance may yield substantial benefits to other stockholders through improved control and oversight.

CAPITAL FORMATION AND MANDATED REPORTING ENVIRONMENTS

Two distinctive capital formation and related mandated financial reporting environments have emerged in industrialized countries. One of these has been characterized as the British-American (B-A) accounting model and the other the Continental model.[11] Other characterizations refer to the former as "micro" and the latter as "macro" based on the objectives of financial reporting as meeting investor needs for firm-specific investment information or government needs for policy matters.[12] We will refer to the environments as B-A and Continental for convenience.

The two environments differ as to their basic legal systems and the way in which capital is raised, as well as the roles of reporting to investors, accounting criteria, and the role of independent auditors. Figure 11–4 summarizes the primary differences.

As shown in Figure 11–4, the legal systems of the two capital formation environments differ, with a common-law tradition in English-speaking countries based on cases that developed over time where one party claimed wrongdoing by another. In Continental model countries, laws tend to proscribe certain behaviors by legislative action rather than by experiences in courts.

Capital markets differ, with B-A environments characterized by many investors holding small portions of stock and unable as individuals to demand information from the firm. On the other hand, in Continental environment countries, investments are made by large banks (Germany), the government (France), or other corporations (Japan). These parties are able to obtain information directly from the firm either through seats on the board of directors, by contract, or by law. Total capitalization of stock markets also differs substantially. Based on 1993 figures, total capitalization is 61 percent of gross domestic product in the United States, 143 percent in the United Kingdom, 62 percent in Japan, and only 27 percent in Germany.[13]

Differences in capital formation environments have led to different roles for mandated public reporting, with firms in B-A countries using GAAP designed to provide useful information to investors unable to demand it on their own. The U.S. securities acts require such disclosures to reduce information asymmetry and facilitate capital formation, but GAAP itself is determined by the private sector. On the other hand, reporting requirements in Continental model countries are more likely to be prescribed in detail by the government or tax authorities to protect the interests of banks or the government. These differences extend to the liability of auditors for failure to detect material misstatement. In

---

11. G. Mueller, H. Gernon, and G. Meeks, *Accounting an International Perspective*, 4th ed. (Burr Ridge, IL: Richard D. Irwin, 1997), chapter 1.

12. For example, C. Nobes and R. Parker, *Comparative International Accounting* (New York: Prentice Hall, 1995), chapter 4.

13. *The Wall Street Journal*, May 12, 1994, p. 11.

FIGURE 11-4

Financial Reporting Environments around the World

Characteristic	British-American (e.g., U.S., U.K., Canada, Australia)	Continental (e.g., France, Germany, Italy, Japan)
Legal system	Common law (permissive except when prohibited)	Code law (prescriptive)
Capital markets[1]	Broad, many investors, users unable to demand information from firm	Narrow, few investors, users able to demand information from firm
Role of public reporting	For investors, to lower cost of capital/to "level the playing field"	For government or to protect banks' interests
Accounting criteria:		
Set by	Common agreement in private sector	Government (on tax or policy objectives)
Guidance	Broad principles/fairness as the objective	Specific rules/meeting rules is enough
Asset valuation	Conservative	Very conservative
Disclosure required	Extensive	Limited
Frequency of reports	Quarterly	Annually or semi-annually
Time lag for reports	31–60 days	90–120 days
Liability for auditors	High (to facilitate level field/right to know)	Low (meet statutory duties)
Corporate governance	Board seats held by management and independent (nonmanagement) directors not holding large equity positions	Board seats held by bankers and persons representing other companies holding large equity positions

[1] Six percent of German adults own stock versus 35 percent in United States and 20 percent in United Kingdom; five largest German banks own 15 percent of publicly listed shares and have proxies for 20 percent more (*The Wall Street Journal*, May 12, 1994, p. 11).

particular, liability for auditors in B-A countries tends to be higher, in part, because of the legal tradition and in part because the information is of more relevance and consequence in B-A countries.

Figure 11–5 shows a standard audit report in the United Kingdom. This report shares many characteristics with the U.S. reports, with a "true and fair view" being the equivalent of "fairly presents." The principal exception appears to be its reference to the Companies Act of 1985 as a source of measurement criteria. However, the Companies Act incorporates by reference the accounting guidance of the Institute of Chartered Accountants of England and Wales' Accounting Standards Board (a private accounting standards-setting body).

Figure 11–6 shows a standard report in Germany. In contrast to the U.K. and U.S. reports, it references compliance with German legal provisions rather than a body of accounting principles intended to provide useful information to investors.

FIGURE 11–5

U.K. Standard Unmodified Audit Report

REPORT OF THE AUDITORS TO THE MEMBERS OF THE BRITISH PETROLEUM COMPANY p.l.c.

We have audited the accounts on pages 28 to 50, which have been prepared under the historical cost convention and on the basis of the accounting policies set out on pages 28 and 29. We have also audited the information specified for audit by the London Stock Exchange which is set out on pages 59 to 61 in the Report of the Remuneration Committee.

RESPECTIVE RESPONSIBILITIES OF DIRECTORS AND AUDITORS

As described above, the company's directors are responsible for the preparation of the accounts. It is our responsibility to form an independent opinion, based on our audit, on those accounts and to report our opinion to you.

BASIS OF OPINION

We conducted our audit in accordance with Auditing Standards issued by the Auditing Practices Board. An audit includes examination, on a test basis, of evidence relevant to the amounts and disclosures in the accounts. It also includes an assessment of the significant estimates and judgments made by the directors in the preparation of the accounts and of whether the accounting policies are appropriate to the group's circumstances, consistently applied and adequately disclosed.

We planned and performed our audit so as to obtain all the information and explanations which we considered necessary in order to provide us with sufficient evidence to give reasonable assurance that the accounts are free from material misstatements, whether caused by fraud or other irregularity or error. In forming our opinion we also evaluated the overall adequacy of the presentation of information in the accounts.

OPINION

In our opinion the accounts give a true and fair view of the state of affairs of the company and of the group as at 31 December 1997 and of the profit of the group for the year then ended and have been properly prepared in accordance with the Companies Act of 1985.

Ernst & Young,
Chartered Accountants
Registered Auditor
London
10 February 1998

Finally, corporate governance tends to differ along the same capital formation environment lines. In particular, corporate board seats in the United States tend to be held by officers of public corporations and by prominent outsiders who are typically not major investors who hold substantial interests in the firm and do not represent investors with substantial interests. Major institutions such as pension funds may even avoid representation on a board for fear of being subjected to insider-trading provisions of the securities acts. In Continental environment countries, board seats tend to be held by major investors such as banks and representatives of other corporations holding large blocks of stock. These differences in governance have implications for corporate control as well as disclosure. As an example of the latter, there may be less need for public disclosure in Continental model countries because major investors have access to information via their own representatives on the board.

FIGURE 11–6

German Standard Unmodified Audit Report

Berlin and Munich, November 25, 1997
Seimens Aktiengesellschaft
The Managing Board

Report of independent auditors

The consolidated financial statements, which we have audited in accordance with professional standards, comply with the German legal provisions. With due regard to the generally accepted accounting principles, the consolidated financial statements present a true and fair view of the Siemens group's assets, liabilities, financial position and earnings. The content of the Management's discussion and analysis is consistent with the consolidated financial statements.

Munich, December 3, 1997

KPMG Deutsche Treuhand-Gesellschaft
Wirtschaftsprüfungsgesellschaft

Professor Dr. Havermann   Dr. Hoyos
Wirtschaftsprüfer   Wirtschaftsprüfer
                (independent auditors)

Empirical Results

Research comparing financial statements and accompanying disclosures from companies around the world show substantial differences. There are differences in accounting and disclosure policies within countries where all firms are following the local GAAP criteria, as well as across countries making disclosures in a particular environment (such as foreign companies making disclosures in the United States under U.S. securities laws).

The following paragraphs review accounting practices across countries, followed by going-concern disclosure differences across countries and disclosures of foreign companies registering with the U.S. SEC.

Accounting Practices across Borders

In a recent study that matched 40 firms each from France, Germany, Japan, the United Kingdom, and the United States, researchers compared accounting policy disclosures, certain historical financial reporting such as segment disclosures, and forward-looking information.[14] All five countries require disclosure of accounting policies, but accounting standards vary as to their application in practice. For example, all 40 U.K. and U.S. firms provided cash-flow statements, in contrast to only 5 German, 18 French, and 17 Japanese firms. Also, while it is not clear whether all 40 firms in each country had "reportable" segments (under segment-reporting rules of each country), the extent of reporting of segment revenues, profits, and assets differs substantially among capital-formation environments. Segment results were reported by 34 U.K. and 25 U.S. firms, but by only 12 French, 1 German, and no Japanese firms.

---

14. C. Frost and K. Ramin, "Corporate Financial Disclosure: A Global Assessment," in *International Accounting and Finance Handbook,* 2nd ed., ed. F. Choi (New York: John Wiley & Sons, 1997), chapter 18.

As to reporting forward-looking information, more than half of the U.S. firms disclosed forecasts of capital expenditures, with very few disclosures in other countries. However, more than half of the German firms forecast future earnings and sales, with nine or less in the other countries. Fear of investor litigation for earnings forecasts that are not realized may have led to fewer earnings forecasts by U.S. firms. Only two Japanese firms had forecasts of either type.

These differences in disclosure across borders reflect the public availability of more information in B-A model countries on the average than exists in Continental model countries. There are also differences in the frequency of reporting, the timeliness of disclosures to the public, and regulatory filings (British-American model companies disclose more and do it more frequently and earlier). The lack of information available to outsiders has been suggested as a factor in delaying recognition of the financial difficulties of some Japanese firms in late 1997 and Metallegesellschaft AG in Germany in 1993.[15]

Going-Concern Disclosures across Borders

As discussed in Chapter 9, going-concern disclosures in financial statement footnotes and audit reports are an official way of recognizing "substantial doubt" about a firm's ability to remain in business for the foreseeable future. Going-concern disclosures allow communication of uncertainties as of the balance sheet date that affect the interpretation of accounting numbers. Financial statement readers in any country would benefit from going-concern disclosures when there is substantial doubt about a firm's ability to continue as a viable business.

Are "official" going-concern disclosures in financial statements and audit reports comparable across borders? Should they be? Maybe not. For example, for a given level of financial or operating difficulty, firms in Continental model environments might be expected to be less likely to fail than in B-A environment countries. This is because the government, primary stockholders, or creditors (e.g., major banks) are expected to provide additional capital or refinancing in the presence of financial difficulty. On the other hand, B-A environment firms might fail under the same degree of financial difficulty.

A recent study selected firms whose 12-month stock returns were in the lowest-performing quartile (bottom 25 percent) of stocks listed on their respective exchanges in France (30 firms) and Germany (31 firms). These firms were then matched by size and industry to firms in the United States also performing in the bottom quartile.[16] The researcher compared (a) officially prescribed disclosure standards for GAAP- and GAAS-based audited financial statements in each country, (b) official going-concern disclosures in the sample firms' actual audited financial statements, and (c) newspaper stories, financial statement footnotes, and other "unofficial" discussion of factors that professional standards mention as being related to going-concern status. For example, these factors include change in debt ratings, refinancing of debt, changes of management, selling of business units, legal difficulties, reorganization, take-over attempts, and bankruptcy.

---

15. G. Whitney, "Frankfurt Banks Concentrate Power: Market Fairness, Cost-Effectiveness Worry Outsiders," *The Wall Street Journal*, May 12, 1997, p. B-11.
16. R. Martin, "Going-Concern Uncertainty Disclosures and Conditions: A Comparison of French, German, and U.S. Practices," working paper, Michigan State University, 1999.

The officially prescribed going-concern disclosure rules under GAAP and GAAS in France and Germany are essentially equivalent to U.S. standards discussed in Chapter 9. Since the disclosure rules are comparable and the samples of firms were from the lowest-performing quartiles of their respective stock exchanges, one might expect comparable "official" going-concern disclosure rates of publicly available audited financial statements and comparable rates of the less-formal newspaper articles and other discussion of the presence of going-concern factors.

Figure 11–7 summarizes the disclosure results. The U.S. firms were selected to match each French and German firm by industry and size based on 1989 sales, and Figure 11–7 shows the firms to be of similar size across countries. There was only one "official" going-concern disclosure in France and Germany over the five-year period (1987 to 1991), while there were 11 in the United States. If the criteria for disclosure and auditor reporting of "substantial doubt" about the ability of firms to remain a going concern are essentially the same and the firms in the sample are experiencing similar levels of financial difficulty, then the differences in "official" disclosure rates may imply one of two alternatives. Either auditors in the United States are more stringent than those in France and Germany or the probabilities of ceasing to be a going concern are higher in the United States.

To try to find out which explanation is correct, the researcher scanned the financial press, financial statement footnotes, and other sources searching for indication of the presence of going-concern factors for the firms in the sample. Figure 11–7 shows some differences in frequency of discussion of debt-related factors across countries. Debt-related factors are more frequent in the United States, in part because there is relatively less debt issued to the public in France and Germany. However, the frequencies of discussion of nondebt-related going-concern factors are statistically indistinguishable across environments. Thus, the risk of corporate failure may simply be lower for the French and German firms.

FIGURE 11–7

Going-Concern Reporting in France, Germany, and the United States[1]

Firms Selected from Bottom Quartile Stock Price Performers in Each Country for 1989

	France (N=30)	Germany (N=31)	U.S. Firm Matches for	
			France (N=30)	Germany (N=31)
Median sales (fiscal year 1989)	$1,869	$1,449	$1,880	$1,313
"Official" going-concern disclosure in financial statement footnotes and audit reports (1987–1991)	1	0	4	7
Going-concern "factors" in financial press and financial statement footnotes (1987–1991)				
Debt-related	3	3	23	26
Not debt-related	41	57	70	63[2]

1. R. Martin, "Going-Concern Uncertainly Disclosures and Conditions: A Comparison of French, German, and U.S. Practices," working paper, Michigan State University, 1999.

2. Difference between France and United States is statistically significant, but differences between Germany and the U.S. and between France and Germany combined versus U.S. are not statistically significant at the .10 level (one-tailed).

To summarize, the results cited above are consistent with firms in the two capital formation environments being approximately equal in the financial difficulties that they experience, but are reported differently through audited financial statements. The financial statement disclosure differences may be attributable to real differences across countries in the probability of failure to remain a going concern rather than differences in disclosure rules or criteria. Thus, harmonization of GAAP and GAAS criteria across borders may not eliminate differences in reporting, and the same "official" report in audited financial statements may have different implications. Also, independent assurance professionals at multinational CPA firms may improve information quality and context for their clients by interpreting the meaning of financial statements and audit reports of firms from other countries.

Foreign Firms Disclosures in the United States

Researchers have compared financial statement disclosure content, frequency, and timing of foreign registrants in the United States with similar U.S.-domiciled registrants. As an example, one study selected foreign registrants trading on American stock exchanges for the calendar year 1990 and matched these firms by size and industry to U.S. firms.[17] A total of 156 foreign firms were selected. Revenues of the foreign and U.S. firms averaged $7 billion and $6.8 billion respectively, with two countries substantially different—16 Japanese firms averaged $26 billion in revenues and 21 firms from Israel averaged $135 million. Figure 11–8 summarizes financial reporting and disclosures in SEC filings of these companies.

As shown in Figure 11–8, foreign registrants filing Form 10-K parallel the U.S. comparison firms in their disclosure practices, while Form 20-F users file their annual reports later, file one interim report rather than three, and disclose annual earnings in the media later. Furthermore, 76 of the foreign firms did not disclose either or both industry or geographic segment information about revenues, operating profits, or identifiable assets. Some of these firms supply partial segment information, and some were exempt by the SEC (the 16 Japanese firms) and some were exempt because of their filing status (filing Form 20-F under item 17).[18]

Thus, we see that U.S.-domiciled firms disclose more information to investors (and their competitors), and disclose it more often and on a more timely basis. Foreign registrants avoid any competitive disadvantage of disclosure as well as the cost of obtaining information for disclosure. Whether these savings are compensated by higher costs of capital is not known at present. However, differences in disclosure and their related costs are a source of concern to managements of U.S. firms because the differences place U.S. firms at a competitive disadvantage.

As international borders have become more transparent and barriers to listing on foreign exchanges have fallen, it has become unclear whether companies are better off raising capital in regulated foreign markets or domestically. Also, the power of a regulatory body such as the SEC to impose comprehensive and detailed disclosure requirements has become more tenuous. Since firms can raise capital across borders via the Internet, the power of particular regulatory bodies is reduced.

---

17. See C. Frost and W. Kinney, "Disclosure Choices of Foreign Registrants in the United States," *Journal of Accounting Research,* Spring 1996, pp. 67–84.
18. Japanese firms are allowed by the SEC to file financial statements using Form 20-F without disclosing profits by segment. This was an accommodation allowed to attract Japanese firms to the U.S. capital markets. Firms from other countries filing Form 20-F and U.S. firms filing Form 10-K are required to disclose segment profits.

FIGURE 11–8

Frequency and Timing of Financial Reports and Media Disclosures
Fiscal Years Ending July 1, 1990, through June 30, 1991

	Foreign Firms Trading on NYSE, ASE, or NASDAQ				U.S. Comparison Firms
	Form 20-F			All Foreign Firms (N=156)	Form 10-K (N=156)
	Form 10-K (N=30)	Item 18 (N=88)	Item 17 (N=37)		
Annual reports					
Mean lag[1]	85.1	160.6	173.5	153.2	86.0
Interim reports					
Mean number per firm	3.0	1.2	1.4	1.9	3.0
Mean lag[1]	44.9	58.2	81.4	54.6	43.1
Media disclosures of annual earnings					
Mean lag[2]	47.5	72.3	78.5	70.1	43.4

See Frost, C., and W. Kinney, "Disclosure Choices of Foreign Registrants in the United States," *Journal of Accounting Research,* Spring 1996, pp. 67–84.

1. Calendar days between filing date and fiscal period end.

2. Calendar days between disclosure issuance date and fiscal period end.

The net value of disclosure of real-world conditions following recognized measurement criteria and certified by independent assurance professionals remains an open question. One way of assessing the value of particular accounting criteria and auditing standards is through analysis of Rule 144A offerings in the United States by private foreign companies. In this environment, the buyer and seller of securities can agree on the disclosure combination that maximizes value.

SUMMARY

Compliance with laws and regulations creates several demands by management for assurance services. Regulations require certain disclosures, certification of compliance of those disclosures with established measurement criteria, restrictions of actions of management, and provision for corporate governance. Stock exchanges have similar and additional requirements for listing on an organized exchange. While both types of requirements many improve the quality of information for outside decision makers and thus lower the cost of capital, they also impose substantial costs on management through the direct cost of preparing information, restricting actions, and providing information to competitors.

The U.S. securities acts require that companies issuing stock or trading on U.S. exchanges periodically file GAAP-based financial statements and other disclosures with the SEC, comply with trading restrictions by management, and file notice of "significant events" on a timely basis. Some of these filings must be certified by an independent auditor. Furthermore, financial and other information must be made available to all market participants, and insider trading on private information is prohibited.

Regulations and disclosure requirements differ across borders, but tend to follow patterns based on two capital formation environments. The British-American environment tends to promote a "level playing field" across investors through required public disclosure, with accounting reports providing information useful for investors who, as individuals, cannot demand information from the company. Even though there is seeming similarity of disclosure rules across environments, there are substantial differences in the observed disclosures across environments. The observed differences may reflect real differences in the underlying conditions of firms, or they may not. Thus, there may be need for an assurance professional's services to improve information context by interpreting for their clients standardized financial information across borders and capital market environments.

CASE 11

IT'S THE (SECURITIES) LAW

The U.S. securities acts are designed to facilitate capital formation and investor protection by providing for disclosure of certain firm-specific information and requiring certain assurances from outside experts. SEC registrants are allowed to raise capital from investors in any state. This privilege has some costs to registrants. What's a manager to do?

PART I

Part I explores some of the disclosure requirements of the securities acts for U.S.-domiciled registrants. It follows the format of a traditional true/false exam with correction or clarification of false statements. All of the statements have an element of truth to them so that they are not completely false—yet it is important to know what makes them true.

For each situation, indicate whether the U.S. securities acts require the action by officers of an SEC registrant. If the statement is not true, then offer a correction or clarification that would make it true. Also, where possible, indicate the SEC forms or regulations that are applicable.

a. File, within 90 days of the close of the fiscal year, financial statements that comply with generally accepted accounting principles and are audited by a firm of CPAs following generally

accepted auditing standards (these statements must be manually signed by principal officers).

b. File, within 45 days of the close of a fiscal quarter, interim financial statements that comply with generally accepted accounting principles and have been reviewed by a firm of CPAs following generally accepted auditing standards.

c. Notify the SEC, within 15 days, of any changes of management, resignation of directors or auditors, loss of a major customer, changes of accounting methods, or fraud discovered by the company.

d. Obtain SEC staff approval of any changes in the auditor of record.

e. Maintain an audit committee comprised of at least three members of the board of directors who are not a part of management and who are not shareholders effectively holding 10 percent or more of the registrant's stock.

f. Maintain a well-designed and effectively operated system of internal accounting controls, report to stockholders at least annually on the firm's internal controls, and obtain an independent accountant's report on these internal control assertions.

g. Disclose risks and uncertainties, as well as major customers, concentrations of risk, and key factors on which future profitability depend (these assertions are not required to be audited).

h. Cease personal trades and trading on insider information in the registrant's securities (also applies to beneficial owners of 10 percent or more of registrant's equity securities).

PART II

Part II considers foreign-domiciled registrants with the SEC. As indicated in our readings, foreign-domiciled firms are allowed to meet lower disclosure requirements than are similar firms domiciled in the United States. These accommodations are claimed to increase the alternatives available to U.S. investors through increased numbers of foreign registrants by reducing foreign firms' cost of compliance with U.S. disclosure requirements.

Here are some questions about the nature and effect of the accommodations, and their desirability.

a. What disclosure alternatives are allowed foreign firms wishing to enter U.S. capital markets and what are the disadvantages of using the "limited disclosure" forms?

b. What is the apparent effect of the accommodations on the amount and timeliness of financial disclosures of foreign registrants?

c. Do foreign earnings seem to be "less informative" than earnings of U.S.-domiciled firms? What are the implications of your answer for "investor protection"?

d. If you were CFO of a U.S.-domiciled multinational conglomerate, would you consider the accommodations to be an unfair advantage for foreign firms with which you must compete?

e. Overall, should the United States suspend the accommodations and require 10-K levels of disclosure for all registrants in the United States?

KEY WORDS

audit committees   A committee of board of directors members (typically directors who are not part of management) that oversee external auditing activities on behalf of stockholders.

British-American (B-A) accounting model   An accounting model, commonly applied in English-speaking countries, characterized by accounting methods chosen to meet information demands of investors who are unable individually to demand information from the firm.

Continental accounting model   An accounting model, commonly applied in non-English-speaking countries, characterized by accounting methods chosen to meet the information demands of large banks, the government, or other corporations.

Form 8-K   Form required by the SEC whenever certain specific events occur.

Form 10-K   The primary annual financial report form required for registrants by the SEC under the Securities Exchange Act of 1934.

Form 10-Q   Quarterly financial reports required for registrants by the SEC.

Form 20-F   Annual financial report form required by the SEC for certain foreign private issuers of securities listed on U.S. stock exchanges.

Form S-1   The primary financial report form required by the SEC for initial registration of securities under the Securities Act of 1933.

independent directors   Members of a corporation's board of directors who have no relationship to the corporation that might interfere with the exercise of their independence from management or the corporation.

management discussion and analysis (MD&A)   Registrant management disclosures required by the SEC about how the firm is managed and explanation of its financial condition, results of operations, liquidity, capital needs, and its risks, sensitivities, and concentrations of suppliers and customers.

NASDAQ National Association of Securities Dealers Automated Quotation system.

Private Securities Litigation Reform Act (PSLRA) of 1995 Requires auditors of SEC registrants to apply procedures designed to detect material fraud, illegal acts, and related-party transactions and to evaluate the registrant's ability to remain a going concern.

Regulation S-K Governs registrant's nonfinancial statement disclosures in SEC filings, including content of Management Discussion and Analysis (MD&A) disclosures.

Regulation S-X Prescribes the form and content of (annual and interim) financial statements filed with the SEC.

Rule 144A Allows sale of securities to qualified institutional buyers (such as banks, insurance companies, investment companies, and savings and loans) without registration with the SEC.

Securities Act of 1933 Requires registration of securities with the SEC and disclosure of financial and other information through a registration statement containing a prospectus and financial statements audited by an independent accountant (auditor) prior to their sale to the general public.

Securities Exchange Act of 1934 Requires registration with the SEC and disclosure of financial and other information on a continuing basis for securities traded on national exchanges and over-the-counter markets in the United States.

C H A P T E R

Legal and Ethical Responsibilities in Public Reporting

- ◆ **C**an stockholders, regulators, or my auditor sue me?
- ◆ How does the auditor's dual role as "value enhancer" and "public watchdog" affect me as a manager or director?
- ◆ Under what conditions can I expect to collect damages from my auditor or another firm's auditor?
- ◆ Are legal damages from auditors likely to indemnify me?
- ◆ Do auditors' professional ethics affect the benefits and costs of audits?

All of these questions address legal responsibilities and prescribed codes of behavior related to audited financial information. The answers affect the costs and benefits of audits as a means of informing you and protecting assets, informing others, and showing compliance with mandated disclosures.

We begin with a brief review of the responsibilities of directors and management, followed by auditors' liability under U.S. common law as well as statutory law in the U.S. securities acts. Empirical results of litigation against auditors and management follow, including who got sued, for what, and with what result. We end with the roles of CPAs' reputations and professional ethics.

BAD OUTCOMES, BAD DECISIONS, OR BAD AUDITS?

In real-world situations, it is sometimes difficult to separate the effects of a defective audit from defective information prepared by management, or to separate the effects of defective audited information from bad decisions and outcomes that may have been unpredictable given the information potentially available at the time of a decision.

To illustrate, assume that Tim buys 100 percent of the stock in LJ Appliances, paying $9,600,000 ($96 per share × 100,000 shares). The price offered by Tim is based on audited earnings of $12 per share as certified by Alex and Louis, CPAs, and an earnings multiple of 8. Four months after the financial statement date (three months after the purchase), LJ Appliances closes its doors and seeks court protection in order to liquidate its assets. LJ experienced a huge decline in revenues due to greatly increased sales of major appliances by competitors via the Internet. The value of Tim's LJ Appliances shares is uncertain but is estimated to be less than $1,000,000.

Tim believes that LJ's financial statements didn't comply with GAAP because they did not adequately disclose the threat of Internet sales and LJ's resulting inability to remain a going concern. Furthermore, Tim believes that Linda Jo knew or should have known of the threat and that financial statement disclosure was inadequate. He also believes that a proper audit by Alex and Louis would have uncovered the threat and required that Linda Jo add cautionary language in the footnotes, and that Alex and Louis's audit report should have had a "substantial doubt" paragraph to warn him about the going-concern problem.

Were the financial statements bad (i.e., not in compliance with GAAP)? Did Linda Jo know that the statements were bad? Would a proper (GAAS-based) audit have detected and disclosed the going-concern problem? Did Alex and Louis follow GAAS? Alternatively, did Tim simply make a bad decision based on the best information available, or make a good decision with a bad outcome? Or was Tim at fault for not being sufficiently responsive to changed environmental conditions after he bought LJ's stock?

Tim is considering a lawsuit against Linda Jo and Alex and Louis, CPAs. His prospects for success through litigation depend on a number of important factors. Some are questions of fact (what Linda Jo knew, whether Tim was partially responsible, and the apparent quality of the audit). Other factors are applicable reporting criteria and auditing standards (GAAP and GAAS), applicable law (common law of contracts or torts versus securities law such as the Securities Act of 1933 or the Securities and Exchange Act of 1934 in the United States), whether Linda Jo has assets with which to pay damages, and which party is responsible for paying litigation costs of the winning party at trial. We won't resolve this particular case, but we will consider many of these factors in the discussion below.

RESPONSIBILITIES OF MANAGEMENT AND DIRECTORS

Corporate officers and directors have a legal duty to act in the interests of the stockholders of a corporation. This duty includes diligence in managing the corporation efficiently and effectively, protecting its assets and position, and complying with applicable laws and regulations such as those encompassing financial reporting under the securities acts. The latter responsibility is evidenced by the signatures of the CEO, CFO and all directors on Form 10-K for SEC registrants.

Liability of officers and directors under the U.S. securities acts is substantial. It includes both civil and criminal liability for fraudulent, materially misstated, or misleading information in registration statements and annual reports filed with the SEC, as well as liability for not maintaining adequate internal control.

Risk Mitigation by Management and Directors

Management and directors can limit litigation loss exposure from suits by stockholders and third-party users of financial and other information by using the approach outlined in

Chapter 3. They can avoid risk at the source, transfer or share risk, and limit its potential effects by risk mitigation procedures.

Management is in a position to provide for reliable and timely information to outsiders and for compliance with laws and regulations. It can do this by direct actions and by delegating responsibilities for designing and implementing internal control day to day. Management can also limit risk by hiring internal auditors to monitor internal controls applied by others. Finally, they can hire external independent assurance professionals to advise them about disclosure requirements and timing of disclosures, and to assess risks, design risk containment activities, and evaluate performance of systems in place.

The reports of internal and external auditors can reduce the risk of poor information for decision making and can provide protection for stockholders even if distribution of the external auditor's report is limited to management and perhaps the directors. This is because those who are in a position to interpret and evaluate the report can take remedial actions as appropriate. Evaluations of risk and risk mitigation systems by outside experts also provide a basis for a "due diligence" defense of management's conduct since they may demonstrate a good faith effort to comply with regulations.[1]

Directors exercise oversight of management and corporate affairs on behalf of stockholders. Directors are unable to take an active role in observing management of the corporation or corporate affairs. But they can rely on reports of independent assurance professionals about the state of the firm and its processes. One means for obtaining such assurance on financial reporting requirements is through an audit committee comprised of independent directors (see Chapter 11). Also, directors can obtain some assurance from internal auditors who periodically report to and meet with the audit committee or its chair. Finally, directors and corporate officers can be protected by directors and officers insurance and by corporate indemnification from losses. These means of mitigating risks are discussed next.

Internal Auditors

In some corporations, the internal auditor is assigned to report to the CEO, and some have direct access to the audit committee. The same practical communication difficulties mentioned above for external auditors apply even more to the internal auditors. This is because the internal auditor is an employee of the firm, and necessarily has more interest in the information subject matter than does the external auditor because the internal auditor ultimately succeeds in the firm by pleasing top management of the client firm.

An internal auditor who discovers significant misdeeds by top management is in a difficult position. "Turning in" his or her boss to the board, or, in some circumstances, to governmental authorities, is required by job description, the ethics code of the Institute of Internal Auditors (an internal auditor trade association), and law. However, there may be a significant penalty to an internal auditor who does so, whatever the facts of the situation. Some auditors prefer resigning their jobs to the burden of documenting the case against top management, and the possible failure to adequately communicate and establish the case. For this reason, audit committee scrutiny of internal auditor resignations is important.

---

1. For some examples, see M. Kessel, "A Shield for Directors," *Financial Times*, September 30, 1997, p. 12.

Internal Audit Outsourcing

Internal audit services that are outsourced to a CPA firm, and especially the entity's external audit firm, present an interesting case for independence from top management. An internal auditor employed by the external auditor may personally feel more free to report his or her reservations to either the audit committee or CPA firm employer because of the separation of employment from management. On the other hand, top management will be more reluctant to fully involve the outsourced internal auditor in all aspects of corporate affairs because of split loyalties of the outsourced internal auditor. The widespread practice of internal audit outsourcing to a firm's external auditor is too recent to know the net result for control efficiency and effectiveness.

The legal obligations, relationships, and behavioral tendencies among and between the audit committee and outside and internal auditors should be kept in mind in evaluating control over investments that your firm makes in others, and when you serve as a director for another firm. The presence of a formal audit mechanism does not necessarily mean that the mechanism is functioning. Also, internal auditing practices differ substantially across firms and cultures.

In some firms, internal auditors are career employees who conduct audits of financial reports and controls. In other firms, the internal auditor has broader responsibilities and conducts audits of business operations rather than financial details. The latter type of auditor is typically a manager who serves as internal auditor for a limited time, lending expertise to particular aspects of business operations and learning about the affairs of the firm. Then this type of internal audit returns to a line management position.

In the British-American accounting model countries, internal auditors are more likely to report to the audit committee, while in Continental model countries, they are more likely to report to the CEO. In a large sample survey of corporations, researchers found that the internal auditor reports to the audit committee chair (CEO) in about 38 percent (21 percent) of corporations in Australia, Canada, United Kingdom, and United States, while in France, Italy, and Japan, the rates are 0 percent (70 percent).[2] Thus, the effectiveness of internal auditors as a monitor acting on behalf of stockholders may vary substantially across borders.

Directors and Officers Insurance

Directors and officers face the risk of lawsuits from stockholders who claim that they have not performed their duties regarding stockholders' interests. Because of these personal risks, many corporations purchase insurance to indemnify directors and officers from loss. Such indemnification is often necessary to encourage qualified persons to serve as a director. This is particularly true for independent or outside directors who are asked to serve on compensation committees and audit committees.

While insurance is often necessary, it is not without limits and problems. As to limits, insurance contracts exclude fraudulent acts by directors and officers, and typically exclude initial public offerings. As to problems, presence of directors and officers insurance has been shown to be highly correlated with the incidence of class actions against corporations.

---

2. P. Burnaby, N. Powell, and S. Strickland, "Internal Auditing Internationally: Another Step Toward Global Harmonization," *Internal Auditing*, Winter 1994, pp. 38–53.

In effect, the presence of insurance to pay damages acts as a necessary condition for some lawsuits against the corporation.[3]

RESPONSIBILITIES OF AUDITORS

External auditors have prescribed duties and responsibilities for financial misstatements under private audit contracts (see the engagement letter in Chapter 7) that lead to liability to the client and to some third-party users of audited financial statements. In addition, under the securities acts, the auditor can be liable for client information misstatements to third-party purchasers of initial public offerings of securities, to purchasers of securities in the secondary market, and to fines and criminal charges by regulators.

Auditors cannot be expected to act as guarantors or insurers of information or future outcomes. External audits based on audit fees that for large firms average $200 per $1 million in revenues can't guarantee future revenues, earnings, or assets. Rather, their work provides reasonable assurance about the reliability of historical and some forward-looking information with respect to stated measurement criteria. The auditors may be held liable for substandard performance of the work that the auditor agreed to conduct, however. The auditor is also liable for his or her own fraudulent acts.

The auditor's liability for attestation services (examinations, reviews, and agreed-upon procedures) is governed in the United States and most other English-speaking countries by the common law of contracts and torts, as well as by statutory law such as the securities acts, as specified by legislative actions and interpretations by regulators. The latter imposes what have been called "public watchdog" duties on the auditor (i.e., the auditor acts as if he or she were working for outside investors and creditors as well as potential investors and creditors, rather than working for the client that hired the auditor to certify its financial statements). The auditor's duty, legal penalties, and burdens of proof vary across these types of law, the type of engagement, and the party suing the auditor.

Common-Law Liability

Investigation Contract

Assume that Mamie, the owner/manager of Mamie's Pie Frontier (Case 4), hires an auditor to audit (investigate) her own financial statements as a means of evaluating her information system and controls. Since the audit report is for Mamie's own use rather than use by outsiders, Mamie and the auditor can specify the magnitude of possible misstatement the audit is designed to detect, and the risk that the audit will fail to detect that magnitude if it exists.

Before hiring the auditor, Mamie and the auditor discuss the possible gains from "discovery" of GAAP-based earnings misstatements of a given magnitude against the cost of conducting the auditor's investigation and the risk of misstatement of that magnitude or more. In particular, they discuss materiality (M^*) and target audit risk (AuR^*) for the audit. They balance the expected costs of decision errors from using imprecise or erroneous

---

3. J. Alexander, "Do the Merits Matter? A Study of Settlements in Securities Class Actions," *Stanford Law Review* 43 (February 1991), pp. 497–598.

financial information against the cost of increased audit effort to obtain more precision using lower M* or lower AuR* to plan the audit.[4]

Figure 12–1 is a conceptual diagram of the relations underlying the cost–benefit analysis for the extent of auditing. Figure 12–1, panel A, shows that the expected loss due to GAAP-based information misstatement declines as the auditor's investigation cost increases. The minimum total cost (min_A = the minimum of the sum of expected losses from unreliable information plus the auditor's fee) occurs at audit effort level = AE*. At the AE* level of audit effort, Mamie will receive the maximum net benefit from an audit investigation. Therefore, she signs a contract with the auditor to conduct an audit specifying a dollar amount for M* and AuR* that implies AE* units of audit effort. The auditor then conducts the examination and reports his or her findings.

Let's assume that the auditor fails to detect a fraudulently inflated invoice and supplier kickback scheme perpetrated by Willie, the baking manager. The amount of the fraud during the audit period was $600,000, and another $400,000 was lost by the time Mamie discovered the fraud.

Mamie believes that a proper audit comprised of AE* units of audit effort would have discovered the fraud, and that the auditor did not follow one or more of the 10 generally accepted auditing standards. For example, the auditor did not properly plan and supervise the audit, obtain sufficient evidence, exercise due professional care, or properly report findings. She then sues the auditor for breach of the audit contract. Should the auditor be required to pay damages to Mamie, and, if so, in what amount?

One way for a court to assign damages for an audit failure is a "negligence rule" that holds the auditor responsible for breaching the audit contract. The auditor promised to deliver AE* level of service, and if the auditor actually delivers less than AE*, then the auditor reimburses Mamie for the resulting actual loss suffered. However, if the auditor conducts an examination equal to or greater than AE*, the auditor would pay zero damages, since the auditor fulfilled contract terms. A "negligence rule" has the desirable feature of encouraging the auditor to fulfill his or her contract, since the auditor's expected total cost is the sum of the auditor's cost of examination plus the expected costs of legal damages.

Figure 12–1, panel B, shows expected costs to the auditor under negligence rule liability to the client. The bold lines in panel B trace the results of negligence rule liability and show the auditor's total expected cost as a function of AE. Under a negligence rule, the auditor must pay actual losses if the auditor performs less than the amount of auditing agreed to in the audit contract (i.e., actual audit effort is less than AE*). The expected loss is the sum of each possible user loss amount weighted by the probability of each amount of loss. The auditor's expected loss (damages) equals the user's expected loss from unreliable GAAP-based information in Figure 12–1, panel A. However, if the auditor performs at a level of audit effort equal to or exceeding AE*, then the auditor will have zero liability for damages.

In Figure 12–1, panel B, the auditor's total expected costs under a negligence liability rule is represented by the bold line that has a discontinuity at AE*. If the auditor examines at or above the AE* level, then the auditor's total cost is min_B. If the auditor examines less than the contracted AE*, then he or she faces considerable expected damages that raise cost

---

4. As we saw in Chapter 7, materiality (M*) and audit risk (AuR*) in combination determine the approximate audit effort (AE*) required (AE* = f(M*, AuR* | audit technology)).

FIGURE 12–1

User's and Auditor's Expected Costs under Negligence Rule Liability
Panel A. User's Expected Costs

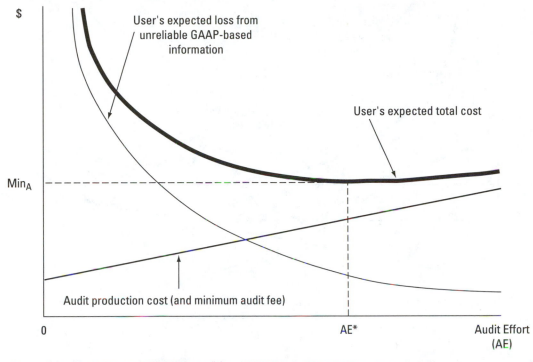

Min_A = user's minimum expected total cost (minimum audit fee + expected loss from unreliable information I audit of AE)
AE^* = optimal amount of audit effort

substantially. If the auditor conducts an investigation greater than AE^*, then audit production costs and the auditor's total expected cost will rise. In concept, the auditor could charge a higher fee for audit effort greater than AE^*. In practice, competition will limit the audit fee to the minimum if the contract calls for a standard quality (GAAS-based) audit and the auditor isn't able to differentiate his or her audit.[5]

Under negligence rule liability, the auditor will likely be held responsible for Mamie's losses if she can show

  a. Financial losses were suffered.

  b. The losses were due to reliance on materially misstated financial statements.

  c. The auditor failed to comply with the audit contract.

Mamie satisfies requirement *a* since she has suffered $1,000,000 in fraud losses, but as to causation (requirement *b*), only the $400,000 could have been caused by a defective audit

---

5. Figure 12–1 ignores cost of litigation, including attorney's fees, and the cost of determining AE^* and actual AE.

FIGURE 12-1   *(continued)*

User's and Auditor's Expected Costs under Negligence Rule Liability
Panel B. Auditor's Expected Costs

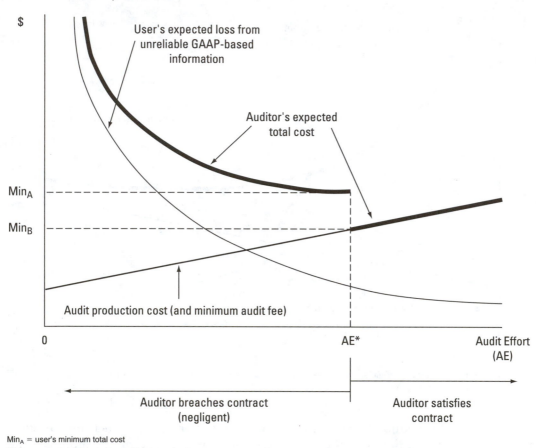

Min$_A$ = user's minimum total cost
Min$_B$ = auditor's minimum expected total cost (audit production cost + expected litigation awards I audit of AE) = minimum audit fee
AE* = contract amount of audit effort

since fraud totaling $600,000 occurred prior to the audit. If she can show that less than AE* audit effort was expended, then she can satisfy requirement *c* and will likely be awarded $400,000 in damages from the auditor.

In their defense, the audit firm will try to show that the statements complied with GAAP, and/or that the audit complied with GAAS, or, in this case, that the AE* effort level was expended. Determining compliance with GAAP and GAAS typically requires the use of expert witnesses such as CPAs employed by other CPA firms, retired CPAs, and professors of accounting and other areas of business. These experts testify as to their judgments about what GAAP and GAAS require in the particular circumstances, and the performance of the auditor in meeting those requirements. Experts supporting a particular position are typically hired and paid by the plaintiff or the defendant for their time to prepare and present their testimony. For example, an expert witness for the defense may give testimony that he or she believes that GAAS was followed, and that other competent auditors applying GAAS would also have failed to detect the fraud.

The audit firm may also attempt to prove that Mamie relied on factors other than the misstated financial statements in making her decisions. Finally, the auditor may attempt to show that any damages that Mamie suffered were not due to reliance on the audited financial statements, but rather were caused by other factors, or that she contributed to her own losses by mismanagement (i.e., Mamie was contributorily negligent).

Certification Contract

A certifying auditor typically contracts with a client firm to conduct an audit following GAAS to express an opinion on the client's assertions that its financial statements comply with GAAP. The resulting audited financial statements may be used by third parties. However, third parties that are not named in the contract ("ordinary" third parties) cannot sue the auditor for breach of contract under contract law, since they were not party to the contract.

Under common law, some third parties are said to be "third-party beneficiaries" of the audit contract. Such a party is either named in or can be inferred from the contract as a potential user of the financial statements, and therefore one to whom the auditor owes some duty to perform in accordance with GAAS.

Third-party beneficiaries typically have the same rights under contract law as the client has. This means that they must prove negligence by the auditor, but need not prove that the auditor was "grossly" negligent. Negligence may be the auditor's failure to follow GAAS, or the failure to perform at the level expected from a competent auditor. Gross negligence in auditing is a "reckless" disregard for auditing standards that is deemed by the law to be equivalent to the auditor defrauding financial statement users.

Another possibility for the plaintiff case is to show that the auditor knew of the defect in the financial statements (sometimes called "scienter"), and thus participated in defrauding the financial statement user. Fraud or gross negligence by the auditor is rare, and either is usually very difficult to prove at trial. Therefore, if your firm plans to rely on the report of an auditor hired by another firm (perhaps a potential business acquisition), it is important to have your firm's name specified in an audit contract when you expect to rely on the audit results, even though you are not a direct party to the contract.

Tort Law

Auditors hired by management to certify its financial statement assertions to third-party users have no contract with possibly numerous third-party users of audited statements, so breach of contract provisions do not apply. However, third parties can be damaged by the auditor's negligence in not meeting contractual duties.

Tort law has developed over time and allows noncontracting parties damaged by defective audited statements to sue the auditor for gross negligence, or fraud. Thus, auditors are liable to their clients for negligence (performing at less than the GAAS level), to third-party users of financial statements when they have performed much less than GAAS (were guilty of gross negligence—a reckless disregard for duties), or to either for auditor fraud.

Some lawsuits are filed even though there may be little chance of winning at trial. Rather, the plaintiff hopes to induce a settlement. Such lawsuits are especially likely under class actions led by attorneys who are compensated on a contingent-fee basis—third-party users have nothing to lose and the possibility of some gain. The result is excessive production of rather frivolous cases relative to that which would prevail if the third parties bore some of the cost of litigation that fails.

Allegations of defective audited financial statements can lead to litigation against both the preparer of the financial statements and the auditor since both may have erred in their representations. Furthermore, the common law in a particular jurisdiction may include "joint and several" liability for sharing of losses caused by defective audited financial statements. Under joint and several liability, the plaintiff is entitled to collect the entire damages suffered from *all* parties that are at fault, or from *any* party that is at fault, irrespective of the proportion of loss caused by that defendant.

For example, suppose that a court determines that a $1,000,000 loss was caused by improper reporting by management and an audit that failed to detect the misstatement. As we saw in Chapter 9, material misstatement by management is a necessary condition for materially misstated audited financial statements, and therefore the auditor can't be 100 percent responsible. Assume that the court determines that, based on the facts presented, management was 90 percent responsible for the loss and that the auditor was 10 percent responsible. Under proportionate liability, the auditor would be liable for only $100,000. Under joint and several liability, the auditor could be liable for 100 percent of the loss, or $1,000,000, and plaintiffs could choose to sue the auditor for the full amount.

Joint and several liability presents grave difficulties for auditors since the client and client management may both be insolvent. Thus, any damage payments must come from the auditor alone. Federal securities acts also impose joint and several liability in some circumstances. As a result, the prospect of full recovery from the auditor may encourage initiating lawsuits that would not be economical to pursue if the auditor could be held liable for only the portion of losses caused by the auditor's behavior.

Statutory Law—Securities Acts Liability

As we have seen, the U.S. securities acts impose substantial liability on management of firms issuing securities to the public, as well as to their auditors and other experts associated with issues of securities. Management has liability for false and misleading statements, including those made in financial statements, and for differential disclosure, as well as forward-looking information.

Under the 1933 act, auditors have extreme risks for IPOs due to the fact that the burden of proof shifts. Stockholders purchasing an initial public offering of securities need to show only that financial statement assertions were misleading. They need not show that they relied on the audited financial statements or that the audit was defective. Rather, the auditor can reduce his or her liability for misleading financial statements by showing that the stockholder (plaintiff) relied on something other than the statements and that reliance caused the loss, and by proving that the audit itself complied with GAAS. Thus, the auditor has a substantial burden under the 1933 act.

Under the 1934 act, the auditor's liability is similar to that under the common law. The Private Securities Litigation Reform Act of 1995 changed the auditor's liability and the liability of management in important ways. First, the act replaced joint and several liability with proportionate liability for the auditor to most investors (certain small investors are still covered by joint and several liability), providing that the auditor can show that he or she was not aware of the defects and did not intend to deceive investors. Under the act, auditors are responsible only for that portion of a plaintiff's loss that was "caused by" the auditor's substandard performance, and auditors are rarely 100 percent responsible for misstated financial statements of their audit clients.[6] Also, as mentioned in Chapter 11, there are some circumstances for which the auditor may be required to report management's unlawful actions to the SEC.

Also, the 1995 act provides a "safe harbor" for management making forecasts about future plans and events. The safe harbor encourages management to disclose forward-looking information that might benefit investors by providing exemption from suits if the information turns out to be incorrect. Management is required to make its forecasts in good faith and to provide adequate warning about the limitations and uncertainties surrounding the forecasts. That is, to qualify for safe-harbor protection, the forecast must be accompanied by language that "bespeaks caution" in interpreting the forecast. Figure 12–2 presents an example of such language.

Audit Litigation Costs

Allegations of auditor malpractice lead to substantial legal costs for both the plaintiff and the defendant. To be successful, the plaintiff must show that the AE was less than AE*, and AE* must be determined by reference to the audit contract or to GAAS. Determination of actual AE is made difficult because the audit may comprise several thousand hours of effort. And testimony must be presented to a lay jury (and perhaps a judge) unfamiliar with auditing and with many aspects of business. Thus, the litigation process can be difficult, time consuming, highly uncertain as to outcome, and expensive.

FIGURE 12–2

Example of "Bespeaks Caution" Language in Management Discussion and Analysis on Form 10-K

Excerpt from ITI Technologies, Inc., Annual Report on Form 10-K, December 31, 1997, Part II.

Item 7. MANAGEMENT'S DISCUSSION AND ANALYSIS OF FINANCIAL CONDITION AND RESULTS OF OPERATIONS

When used in this discussion, the words "believes," "anticipates" and similar expressions are intended to identify forward-looking statements. Such statements are subject to certain risks and uncertainties which could cause actual results to differ materially from those projected. Readers are cautioned not to place undue reliance on these forward-looking statements which speak only as of the date hereof. The Company undertakes no obligation to publish revised forward-looking statements to reflect events or circumstances after the date hereof or to reflect the occurrence of unanticipated events. Readers are also urged to carefully review and consider the various disclosures made by the Company, which attempt to advise interested parties of the factors which affect the Company's business, not only in this report, but also in the Company's periodic reports on Forms 10-Q and 8-K filed with the Commission.

6. At least one court has held an audit firm 100 percent responsible because it provided poor advice to a client on how to account for a transaction under GAAP.

Malpractice allegations are further complicated by possible class actions in which stockholders as a group sue the auditor. The group may have been assembled by an attorney who represents the class, and who is compensated on a fee that is contingent on winning the lawsuit or settling out of court. The class action attorney bears all costs of the litigation and typically receives 25 to 40 percent of any settlement or damages awarded. Some attorneys specialize in securities class action suits that frequently include claims against management as well as auditors. One source estimates that more than 70 percent of class action suits against auditors are filed by one of eight particular law firms.

It is difficult to obtain reliable estimates of the cost and benefits of litigation against auditors. However, the large accounting firms recently estimated these costs and benefits.[7] From their estimates, the typical damages claim against auditors in federal securities act violations was about $85 million, and the average cost to defend against these cases is about $3.5 million. The same source says that the average resolution of these cases from damage awards at trial and pretrial settlements is about $3 million. From other sources, it has been estimated that the average cost for an audit firm to take litigation through trial is about $1.25 million.

While these figures are not based on the same cases, and may be biased given their source, they suggest several things. First, damaged investors are not made whole by the litigation process. The average compensation to plaintiffs through settlements and damages awarded at trial is far less than the damage claimed. Second, the costs of litigation are substantial, especially for the auditor. These costs of legal defense as well as the cost of damages awarded must be borne in the long run by those hiring the auditor. This implies that financial statement preparers and their shareholders have a substantial interest in lessening the cost of litigation. Third, these aggregate numbers suggest that opportunistic attorneys may be able to induce settlements against auditors by offering to settle for a modest amount. Settlement saves defense costs for the auditor and allows coverage of the plaintiff's attorney's costs for litigation plus some recovery of losses even for cases that are unlikely to succeed at trial (low merit cases).

Since all of these costs affect the total cost of assurance and, thus, the cost of doing business, you as top manager have an interest in limiting the cost of securities litigation. You can do this through support for favorable laws, as well as alternative means of limiting costs through alternative assurance contracts including provision for alternative dispute resolution.

External Auditors' Response to Litigation

In the early 1990s, large CPA firms' "practice protection" costs rose substantially in the United States. The out-of-pocket costs of legal liability insurance, attorneys fees, settlements, and damage awards net of insurance reimbursements summed to about 19 percent of accounting and auditing revenues of Big Five CPA firms in the United States. This level of liability-related costs is extremely high and threatened the continued existence of financial statement audits as a line of business.

---

7. Arthur Andersen, Coopers & Lybrand, Deloitte & Touche, Ernst & Young, KPMG Peat Marwick, and Price Waterhouse, "Statement of Position," *The Liability Crisis in the United States: Impact on the Accounting Profession* (New York: Arthur Andersen, Coopers & Lybrand, Deloitte & Touche, Ernst & Young, KPMG Peat Marwick, and Price Waterhouse, 1992).

The large CPA firms reacted in a number of ways. First, as individual firms, they began avoiding risk at the source (as in Chapter 3) by applying the engagement risk model of Chapter 7. They screened prospective clients for high client business risk (CBR) and high auditor business risk (ABR) including evaluation of management integrity and prospects for continued profitable operations of clients. Existing clients were also reviewed, and auditors resigned from clients with excessive CBR and ABR.

Second, auditors mitigated risks by altering auditing procedures to focus on the strategic viability of their clients, which reduced the client business risk of future declining profits, as well as going-concern problems. Third, auditors explored other ways of limiting risk through the audit contract (engagement letter). As examples, some auditors of private companies include in the audit contract (engagement letter) a limit on legal liability (typically a multiple of the audit fee). Others include a provision for arbitration of any disputes involving the audit rather than a legal proceeding and still others add an agreement from management not to sue the auditor in court.

In addition, many auditors wrote assurance contracts as agreed-upon-procedures engagements rather than as examinations. The agreed-upon-procedures form has the advantage of limiting an auditor's responsibility to application of procedures agreed upon by the parties to the contract. CPA firms also reorganized as limited liability partnerships (LLPs) to protect most partners' personal assets from malpractice judgments against the audit firm.

As a collective action, audit firms joined with various businesses and consumer interest groups and began a lobbying effort with the U.S. Congress to reform securities litigation laws. These efforts culminated in 1995 with passage of the Private Securities Litigation Reform Act (PSLRA). This act had the effect of providing proportionate liability for auditors to most third-party users when the auditor has no knowledge of any material fraud or defect in financial statements. The PSLRA also removed auditors from coverage of the Racketeer Influenced Corrupt Organizations Act and its potential for trebled damage awards to plaintiffs when there are no criminal convictions. It also increased stockholder's control over class action attorneys, making some suits more difficult to bring to trial. The act's original proposal of the "English rule" that would have required losing plaintiffs to pay the defendant's legal costs failed to pass.

Some provisions of the PSLRA have been extended to provide similar restrictions on liability imposed in securities legislation by state governments. Auditors have also lobbied state legislatures for strict privity of contract legislation limiting auditors' liability to those that are a party to the audit contract.

EMPIRICAL RESULTS IN LITIGATION

Auditors as a Source of Indemnification

Can auditors be viewed as a viable source from which investment losses can be recovered? To examine this question, researchers have evaluated lawsuits against the largest CPA firms for a period of more than 30 years.[8] Also, the (then Big Six) accounting firms studied litigation against their firms under the securities acts as part of their basis for recommending

---

8. Professor Z. Palmrose has prepared a database of cases from 1960–1995. See Z. Palmrose, *Empirical Research on Auditor Litigation: Considerations and Data* (Sarasota, FL: American Accounting Association, 1999).

securities litigation reform. The latter research found that between 40 and 50 percent of all lawsuits against large CPA firms resulted in either pretrial dismissal of the case against the auditor (summary judgments) or settlement, with the auditors making no payments to the plaintiffs. Thus, nearly half of these cases against auditors might be judged to have been without substantial merit for a court claim.

Defending against these nonmeritorious claims is not cheap. The Big Six data show that these summary judgments and zero payment cases for Securities Exchange Act of 1934 claims took an average of 3.7 years to resolve, which, at an estimated cost of $1 million per year per lawsuit, yields $3.7 million to defend against the claims. Summary judgments took even longer, with an average of 4.3 years to summary judgment.

Analysis of payment data available for the Palmrose database lawsuits reveals that in only 8 percent of lawsuits against officers, directors, and professional advisors such as underwriters and auditors did the auditors contribute more than 50 percent of the settlement and pay more than $5 million to plaintiffs.[9] Thus, auditors are not a major source of indemnification for damaged investors. While some individual settlements have been large, the large settlements must be considered against the large number of audits conducted each year, which number in the tens of thousands (including more than 10,000 public companies).

As we studied in prior chapters, the audit is concerned primarily with audit risk (AuR), but the self-interested auditor will also consider client business risk (CBR) and the auditor's business risk (ABR) when making decisions about acceptance and retention of an audit client. Client bankruptcy is one source of CBR, and client fraud is an element of ABR. Also, client bankruptcy may be due to fraud by either employees (the company was stolen) or firm management.

Some believe that lawsuits by stockholders begin with a large decline in stock prices due to client bankruptcy or announcement of fraud. These losses then lead to claims that the auditor knew or should have known about the impending bankruptcy and/or fraud. Thus, the damaged investors may sue the auditor claiming malpractice.

The Palmrose database of about 1,200 lawsuits indicates that about 35 percent were against auditors involved in a bankrupt or failing client. However, in related research, a sample of about 650 public companies that declared bankruptcy between 1972 and 1992 indicated that less than 20 percent of these bankrupt firms had litigation against their auditors.[10] The larger bankrupt clients were more likely to be involved in litigation than the smaller—median assets for firms with auditor litigation were $244 million, compared to $39 million for those without litigation. Furthermore, suits against auditors preceded filing of bankruptcy papers in 55 percent of the bankrupt-client sample. Thus, more often than not, lawsuits against auditors precede bankruptcy.

The bankrupt-public-companies sample with private lawsuits against auditors was divided into those involving client fraud and those that did not. Thirty-eight percent of the auditor lawsuit cases showed evidence of client fraud such as SEC enforcement actions

---

9. See Z. Palmrose, "The Joint and Several vs. Proportionate Liability Debate: An Empirical Investigation of Audit-Related Litigation," *The Stanford Journal of Law, Business & Finance*, Fall 1994, pp. 53–72; and Z. Palmrose, "Who Got Sued," *Journal of Accountancy*, March 1997, pp. 67–69.

10. J. Carcello and Z. Palmrose, "Auditor Litigation and Modified Reporting on Bankrupt Clients," *Journal of Accounting Research* supplement, 1994, pp. 1–29.

against the companies or management. Only 1 percent of the nonauditor lawsuit cases had SEC enforcement actions against the company or management. The ability of auditors to avoid litigation by audit report modification for going-concern uncertainties is mixed but difficult to assess because suits often involve several audit periods. For example, plaintiffs argue that "substantial doubt" warnings should have been issued in years prior to the year preceding bankruptcy.

Litigation against Management and Directors

In addition to securities litigation against auditors, management also faces legal liability for false and misleading claims made in the financial reporting process. One recent study analyzed litigation against auditors as well as management and directors associated with the SEC's AAER actions over the 1982–1995 time period.[11] Figure 12–3 summarizes the findings.

As shown in Figure 12–3, some AAERs result in no litigation against either management, directors, or the auditor of companies cited, while others result in litigation against the auditor as well as management or directors, and still other litigation results in action against management or directors, but not against the auditor.

Several patterns can be noted in the data. First, management is more likely to be the subject of lawsuits by private parties (as opposed to SEC-initiated suits) for companies that are larger, are NYSE listed, and have a defect in their interim statements (as opposed to year-end statements). Auditors are more likely to be included in litigation when the fraud covers more years, the firm is bankrupt, or the firm is an IPO (although the IPO itself wasn't necessarily the subject of litigation). Stock price declines around the release of fraudulent financial statements are more likely to be large for those involving litigation against the auditor and others, indicating a potential "deep pockets" effect of corporate assets and liability insurance, and the potential for economic gain from a lawsuit. Furthermore, private actions against auditors or others are rare for those cases with SEC actions against the auditor or others that are accompanied by little price change, and thus less financial loss to investors.

CODES OF PROFESSIONAL CONDUCT

In Chapter 1, we learned of the importance of an auditor's reputation for competence and careful conduct of examinations and trustworthiness in reporting his or her conclusions. In Chapter 7, we learned that the typical audit contract (engagement letter) specifies that the auditor applies generally accepted auditing standards, and, in Chapter 8, we learned that GAAS specifies that the auditor be competent in all areas of the engagement and that he or she plan the audit properly, supervise any assistants, and exercise due professional care in the conduct of the audit. Auditing standards also require that the auditor be "independent." Then, in Chapter 11, we saw that the securities acts also require independence for the auditor as well as competence. Thus, there are economic incentives for individual auditors to maintain a reputation for competence and independence as well as contractual and legal regulations that require the same thing.

---

11. S. Bonner, Z. Palmrose, and S. Young, "The Effects of Frequent and Fictitious Frauds on Auditor Litigation: An Analysis of SEC Accounting and Auditing Enforcement Releases," *The Accounting Review,* October 1998, pp. 503–32.

FIGURE 12 – 3

Private Litigation Related to AAER Actions by the SEC
(1982–1995)

	Total Sample (n=261)	No Litigation (110)	Litigation[1]	
			Auditors (98)	Others (53)
Total assets (in millions)	$2,817	$1,419	$1,977	$7,273
Years of fraud	2.06	1.93	2.39	1.74
NYSE listed	21%	9%	25%	40%
Bankrupt	26%	6%	54%	17%
IPO	35%	27%	46%	30%
Big Six auditor	60%	38%	75%	77%
Interim statements only	17%	15%	9%	34%
Frequent categories:				
Fictitious or overvalued revenues or assets	39%	36%	50%	26%
Premature revenue recognition	33%	32%	40%	23%
Overvalued assets and undervalued expenses/liabilities	38%	30%	45%	43%
Omitted or improper disclosures	40%	33%	42%	51%
Stock price change[2] (twelve mo. around financial statement date)	−24%	2%	−40%	−29%
Size of fraud:[3]				
Amount (in millions)	$12	$7	$12	$22
Percent of net income after taxes	192%	288%	175%	67%

Source: S. Bonner, Z. Palmrose, and S. Young, "Fraud Type and Auditor Litigation: An Analysis of SEC Accounting and Auditing Enforcement Releases," *The Accounting Review,* October 1998, pp. 503–32.

1. "Auditors" comprises suits against auditors, but others may have been included. "Others" is litigation against directors, officers, and others, but auditors were not sued.

2. Reduced sample: n's = 114, 36, 47, 31.

3. Reduced sample: n's = 108, 39, 50, 19.

One might ask why additional incentives beyond these contractual and legal regulations are necessary. One reason is to protect the value of the reputation of the profession as a whole, thus benefiting its individual members. The AICPA in the United States, the Canadian Institute of Chartered Accounts (CICA) in Canada, and similar professional organizations throughout the world have codes of professional conduct (or professional ethics) that proscribe certain behaviors by members of these private professional organizations or trade associations. Historically, these codes of behavior may have been useful in signaling the quality of performance of association members. That is, membership in the association allowed a presumption of ethical behavior, including competence and trustworthiness in professional matters.

In the present market, dominated by five international CPA firms conducting audits of more than 90 percent of all public companies, the value of professionwide codes of pro-

FIGURE 12-4

AICPA Code of Professional Conduct Rules

	Independence, Integrity, and Objectivity
Rule 101	Independence (proscribes (for attest clients) stock ownership in client, material indirect financial interest in a client such as loans or debt, and management functions performed by the CPA firm)
102	Integrity and Objectivity (proscribes subordination of CPA's judgment, knowingly misrepresenting facts, and conflicts of interest)
	General Standards Accounting Principles
201	General Standards (requires professional competence, due professional care, planning and supervision, and sufficient relevant data for all CPA services)
202	Compliance with Standards (requires CPA to follow established auditing, tax, and consulting standards as applicable)
203	Accounting Principles (technical standard regarding fairness of GAAP in a particular circumstance)
	Responsibilities to Clients
301	Confidential Client Information (proscribes CPA's disclosure of client's private information except in court or other specified situations)
302	Contingent Fees (proscribes for attest tax return clients fees based on CPA's findings)
	Responsibilities to Colleagues (no current rules)
	Other Responsibilities and Practices
501	Acts Discreditable (proscribes acts that discredit CPAs)
502	Advertising and Other Forms of Solicitation (proscribes illegal forms)
503	Commissions and Referral Fees (proscribed for attest clients)
505	Form of Organization and Name (proscribes illegal forms)

fessional conduct is reduced. This is because each of these large firms may have more at stake in maintaining their firm's reputation than that of the profession as a whole. They also have more stringent internal policies and codes of behavior to develop, maintain, and monitor their reputations.

Even though the codes of conduct may duplicate contractual and legal requirements and other incentives, it is useful to study their content to understand the nature of professional memberships and the behavior of CPAs. The code of professional conduct (CPC) in the AICPA is organized around four sets of rules or prohibitions (proscriptions) of behavior. The Rules of Behavior are reproduced in Figure 12–4.

As might be expected, the CPC includes rules on independence and objectivity (section 100) and rules on professional competence and standards (section 200). It also includes responsibilities to clients (Rules 301 and 302) and other responsibilities and practices (Rules 501, 502, 503, and 505). Given the importance of assurance services, including third parties' reliance on CPA certifications, it is not surprising that most of the rules can be related to the auditor's reputation for competence and trustworthiness. Also, note that except for independence-related rules (independence [Rule 101], contingent fees [Rule 302], and commission and referral fees [Rule 503]), the CPC applies to all CPA services.

Competence

Rule 201 requires that the CPA comply with general standards of professional competence, due professional care, planning and supervision, and sufficient relevant data for an engagement whether it is for attestation, tax, or consulting services. Rule 202 specifies that the auditor is to comply with standards for these particular kinds of services, such as GAAS and other attest standards, and tax and consulting services standards. Rule 203 relates to a special case of GAAP application.

Rule 301 requires that CPAs maintain confidentiality of client information obtained in assurance, attest, tax, and consulting engagements. There are two exceptions: Financial information required to be disclosed to satisfy GAAP or GAAS is exempt from Rule 301, and CPAs must comply with requests from legal authorities and certain investigative bodies. Rule 301 may also be interpreted as affecting competence of evidence. Clients who have confidence that the auditor will not disclose private information about the company to outsiders, including competitors, will be more likely to provide information necessary for conducting an audit than will those who do not have such confidence. Thus, the rule has the effect of increasing the availability of information to the auditor, which will allow formation of a more complete opinion.

Trustworthiness

CPC Rules 101,102, 302, and 503 relate to independence and the perception of independence by users. Rule 101 states that the auditor is to be independent in fact and appearance, while Rule 102 expresses the same concepts in terms of integrity and objectivity. Rule 102 is expressed in terms of honesty and lack of subordination of judgment or conflicts of interests. Independence applies only to attest clients of CPAs, but integrity and objectivity apply to all professional services of CPA firms.

Rule 101 lists and proscribes auditor/client relationships and behaviors that are presumed to indicate a lack of auditor independence. For example, audit firm partners cannot own even a single share of stock in an audit client and cannot hold a material amount of debt of an audit client. These financial interest restrictions also apply to some CPA firm staff members, such as those working on the audit, and to certain family members. Also, auditors can't make managerial decisions for an audit client. In addition to CPC rules and similar rules of the SEC, individual CPA firms have guidelines that attempt to insulate CPAs from the effects of dependence on particular clients. These guidelines encourage objectivity of auditor judgments about client assertions.

Rule 302, prohibiting contingent fees for services to attest clients, specifically relates to compensation incentives of the auditor. In particular, the auditor should not have incentives that might bias his or her conclusions in order to obtain higher compensation such as a profit share based on audited net income. Similarly, compensation by commissions earned only if a CPA's recommendation is accepted by a client could lead to lack of objectivity in making product recommendations to clients, and in evaluating results. Commissions are allowed for services to non attest clients.

Other Conduct Rules and History

The ethics rules not related to independence or competence prohibit acts by CPAs that are discreditable to the profession (Rule 501), advertising that is illegal (Rule 502), and illegal organization forms for a CPA firm (Rule 505). These proscriptions apply to illegal and reprehensible acts and are mere shells of proscriptions in the 1970s.

The AICPA Code of Professional Conduct has changed substantially over time. In 1970, there were 21 prohibitions of behaviors; at present there are only 11. All rules that were withdrawn possibly violated federal antitrust laws. The withdrawn rules prohibited all advertising, competitive bidding for engagements, solicitation of clients of other CPAs, and other actions that provided barriers to entry of others into the profession (these included all 400-numbered rules). The profession had justified these prohibitions of behaviors as being in the public interest, but they were withdrawn in the late 1970s and 1980s rather than face legal challenges by the federal government that the rules illegally restricted competition for professional services. Other professions such as pharmacists, engineers, and physicians, also withdrew rules that had similar effects.

On the other hand, the rules on independence and competence have increased in number since 1970 and provide more guidance on avoiding conflicts of interest that might affect integrity and objectivity. Thus, we see that CPAs as a group have maintained the rules regarding the core values, while deleting those that were strictly in the self-interest of CPAs.

Historically, Rule 505 on organization and name limited CPAs to a partnership form of organization. This form might be interpreted as increasing perceptions of independence since each partner could be liable for the acts of other partners, thus increasing monitoring by partners. In the early 1990s, large CPA firms lobbied to change state laws to allow limited liability partnerships (LLPs) for CPA practices. The LLP organization form protects personal assets of partners not involved in a litigated engagement. All states now allow limited liability forms of CPA firm organization that protect personal assets of CPAs who were not involved with an audit failure that leads to a CPA firm's bankruptcy.[12]

Alternatives and Issues in Independence

There are several open issues regarding auditor independence. As noted above, one issue is whether independence and the objectives to be achieved should be defined. Historically, regulatory authorities and the AICPA have listed certain relationships between the auditor and client as violating independence or the appearance of independence from attest (auditing) clients. An alternative is to define objectives to be met and to allow exercise of judgment in particular contexts.

Assurance services as defined by the AICPA include independence in the definition (assurance services are independent professional services that improve the quality of information, or its context, for decision makers). The AICPA's Special Committee on Assurance Services (SCAS) defined assurance independence as

> an absence of interests that create an unacceptable risk of bias with respect to the quality or context of information that is the subject of an assurance engagement. (AICPA, 1996)

---

12. Auditors are protected financially through professional liability insurance carried by CPA firms.

According to this definition, the assurer would not be independent if he or she had a relation to the **information** that the assurer is certifying, investigating, or originating. This is in contrast to being independent of the **preparer** of the information such as an audit client.

Since auditing is an assurance service, the definition could apply to the audit as well. Many believe that the definition could replace the numerous and rather tedious proscriptions that comprise the AICPA and SEC regulations. For example, for an attest engagement such as an audit, ownership of a substantial amount of equity shares might create an interest that creates an unacceptable risk of bias with respect to the amount of net income or assets and thus be proscribed, even though ownership of a single share might not.

The SCAS independence definition also applies to other assurance engagements such as origination of information: decision relevance advice, risk assessments by CPAs, transactions advice, and designs for improving information systematically. For example, a CPA might be biased in the advice that he or she gives about a computer system if he or she receives a commission on sale if the client buys the recommended system. The test for the SCAS-based definition of independence approach would be an assessment of whether there is an absence of interests that create an unacceptable risk of bias, rather than whether a pre-set proscribed relationship exists.

A system of independence monitoring based on the SCAS definition would require that the assurer assess independence in each situation, or apply a set of guidelines that give guidance for the situation. These guidelines might originate at the profession-wide level, such as the AICPA, or at the firm level. The audit firm level has the advantage of being adaptable to the needs of a particular audit firm. In particular, it can be incorporated into their partner compensation scheme. For example, the future of a local audit partner of a large CPA firm could be dependent upon pleasing management of an important client at the office level even though the client is immaterial to the audit firm worldwide. If the partner in charge of the audit is compensated based on the pool of profits audit-firmwide, then the threat to independence (or biased judgment) for a particular client may be less than if partners are compensated based on clients in their office or those that they manage. Also, firms can avoid penalizing partners who "fire" (or are fired by) clients that pose unacceptable client business risk or auditor's business risk to the audit firm.

Since CPAs and CPA firms depend on independence as a hallmark of their profession and one of their core assets, many believe that CPAs should be allowed to regulate their own independence. CPA firms could compete on the quality of their independence reputation (based on quality of firm guidelines) in the marketplace. Those with better reputations for independence could command a higher fee because their opinions lead to lower price protection discounts. In 1997, the Independence Standards Board in the United States received a proposal from the AICPA for such a self-regulatory approach.

The SEC has considered alternatives to the present system of information certification by independent auditors hired by management and communicating with audit committees as a means of protecting investors. Alternatives include prohibition of nonaudit services to audit clients, government appointment of auditors, government auditors, forced rotation of audit firm, and audit firm displacement only by cause. Other countries have some of these alternatives in place, but each has significant costs associated with their possible benefits. The SEC has also considered the effects of nonaudit services on investors' perceptions of auditor independence. At one time, in the 1980s, the SEC required disclosure of the proportion of total fees paid to the audit firm that were from nonaudit services such as tax and other assurance and consulting services. The SEC decided that such disclosures were not cost-effective.

Finally, the management hiring an auditor is also interested in users' perceptions of auditor independence and the appearance of independence. This is because if the auditor is believed not to be independent by outside users, then the auditor's report will not be trusted and will not add value for management. Similarly, management is interested in the reputation of the auditor to add credibility to its assertions when reporting to the audit committee. Here are three independence issues of interest to top management:

- Should an outside auditor who quits the audit firm be allowed to go to work for his or her audit clients?
- Should outside auditors be allowed to be the *internal* auditor or supply accounting services to their audit clients (i.e., be outsourced)?
- Should auditors or audit firms be rotated by client or audit firm policy or by law?

All three questions affect the degree of actual and perceived independence of the auditor and the level of control exercised by management. Auditors are often hired by their audit clients to staff financial management, controller, and internal auditor positions because of their knowledge of the firm and their professional expertise. Such hiring lowers the cost of training for clients, but may also cast doubt on the independence of the auditor for two reasons. First, the new employee may have compromised his or her independence prior to obtaining the new position. Second, outsiders may perceive that the new financial manager will know of the audit plan or personnel of their former employer, thus increasing the risk that the auditor will fail to detect and correct misstatements.

In the United States, external audit firms have been hired to conduct internal auditing services for their audit clients. Frequently, the external auditor hires the former internal auditors and these personnel audit their former employer. The client receives the benefit of the external audit firm's training and expertise, as well as the inherent assurance about internal audit quality. Outsourcing internal auditing allows client management to concentrate on its core processes (which do not include internal auditing). Some companies have hired audit firms to operate their accounting processing and reporting systems. According to SEC rules, the record-keeping function cannot be outsourced to the registrant's external auditor. Therefore, potential for CPA firms to be providers of accounting outsourcing for public company clients is restricted.

Some managements and directors believe that internal control effectiveness is increased if they change their outside audit firms on a periodic basis such as every three to five years. Some multinationals rotate auditors of divisions or segments on such a schedule. Rotation provides a "fresh look" at operations and prevents long-term segment manager/auditor relationships from developing that might compromise the independence of the auditor. The cost of such rotation is the additional cost of first-year audits and potentially the cost of an "other auditor" audit report on consolidated operations.

SUMMARY

Auditors have substantial incentives to maintain their core reputations as providers of valuable services through their expertise in measurement, care and competence in applying their expertise, and trustworthiness in reporting results. These reputations are maintained through audit firm policies as well as through the standards and ethical codes of professional organizations.

Maintenance of the reputation of auditors and particularly the auditor of your firm is important in maximizing the value of the auditor's certifications. These reputations may also be useful to you as top management in reporting to directors the advice that you sought and actions taken, and in reporting to you when auditors investigate activities of others.

Auditors as well as top management face substantial liability when they fail to perform according to the law and to expectations of others. Auditors face substantial legal liability to third parties for financial statements that are materially misstated as well as for failure to discover material fraud by management, or for failing to warn investors about companies that suddenly cease to exist. Management can limit risk by acquiring advice on compliance with laws and regulations, and by hiring competent independent assurance professionals to assist with implementation.

Since auditors cannot limit all sources of risk, they have adopted a multifaceted engagement risk-based strategy for dealing with risk. The strategy includes more careful client selection and retention policies (limiting exposure to risk at the source), improved audit methods to reduce audit risk economically, and adopted contractual mechanisms to transfer risk or share risk with management through alternative dispute resolution and liability limits. Auditors have also changed risk through sponsoring legislation to limit auditors' liability.

CASE 12

LONG-GONE CORP. SHAREHOLDERS V. ALEX AND LOUIS, CPAS

A group of stockholders believes that its members have suffered damages of $85 million from their recent purchase of the stock of Long-Gone Corp. They relied on financial statements (audited by Alex and Louis) that may have been misleading. They are considering filing a lawsuit against Alex and Louis. They have discussed the case with attorneys at Ketchem, Knapp, Ng (KKN) of San Diego. The attorneys believe that the case against the auditors is a fairly weak one, with a probability of winning a favorable verdict at trial (P) of only .1, and if the stockholders prevail at trial, they believe that the judgment (J) will be $42.5 million, or one-half of the amount of claimed damages. Furthermore, the attorneys estimate that the total cost to take the case to a verdict at trial (C_p) will be $1.25 million. The stockholder group will bear all legal costs and will receive all of any settlement or damages awarded.

Attorneys for Alex and Louis have the same perceptions of the probability that the stockholder group will win at trial, and the same belief as to damages to be awarded if the plaintiffs win. Their estimated costs to defend the case through a verdict trial (C_d) is $3.5 million. This cost includes attorney's fees and other out-of-pocket costs of litigation. It does not include the cost of partners' time to testify, nor the emotional and other costs of a disrupted practice.

SCENARIO A—JOINT AND SEVERAL LIABILITY

Joint and several liability for damages applies and is relevant in this case, because the other potential defendants to a lawsuit are unable to pay any damages. The officers of Long-Gone Corp. are personally bankrupt, and Long-Gone Corp. is now in receivership and is unlikely to have any funds available for stockholders. Thus, the plaintiffs' only hope for damages is through the auditors. Under joint and several liability, Alex and Louis could be liable for the entire $42.5 million judgment. To focus on the effects of legal structure, assume that costs to settle the case are negligible for both parties.

The decision tree (Exhibit 1) shows calculation of the expected value to the stockholder group of taking the Long-Gone case against Alex and Louis to a verdict at trial.

a. Would the stockholder group likely file a suit under joint and several liability for the auditor?

b. If the suit is filed, what settlement would the stockholders require to put them in the same expected value position as would taking the case to trial and verdict?

c. If the suit is filed, what is the maximum settlement offer that Alex and Louis would make, and would this case be settled?

d. Suppose that stockholders decide not to sue, but KKN offers to take the case on a contingent-fee basis. KKN would bear all costs of the litigation and receive 35 percent of any judgment or settlement as their fee. How might this change the decision of the stockholder group?

SCENARIO B—PROPORTIONATE LIABILITY

Now assume that proportionate liability for damages applies—the auditor is potentially liable only for that proportion of loss "caused by" the auditor. In the case of Long-Gone Corp., both parties believe that the auditor is responsible for at most 20 percent of the damages suffered by the plaintiffs ($R = .2$), and a judge or jury will likely share their belief. Therefore, under proportionate liability, the auditors would pay 20 percent of any judgment.

a. Calculate the expected value to the stockholder group of taking the case to verdict under proportionate liability.

EXHIBIT 1

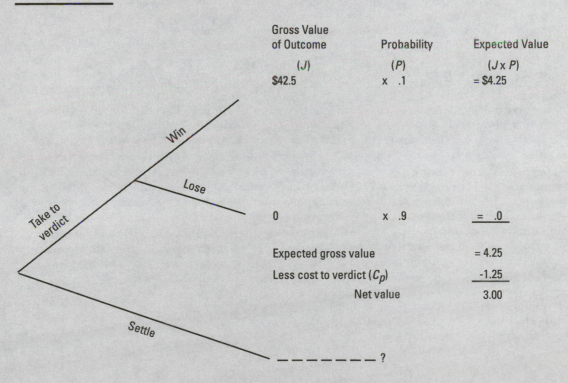

	Gross Value of Outcome	Probability	Expected Value
	(J)	(P)	$(J \times P)$
Win	$42.5	x .1	= $4.25
Lose	0	x .9	= .0
	Expected gross value		= 4.25
	Less cost to verdict (C_p)		-1.25
	Net value		3.00

Take to verdict

Settle — — — — — — ?

b. Would the case be taken to verdict under proportionate liability? Would the stockholders be likely to file the suit hoping to induce a settlement?

c. Suppose that the attorneys from KKN indicate to Alex and Louis a willingness to accept a settlement offer of $3.0 million. Should Alex and Louis pursue this settlement? What compensation would the damaged stockholder plaintiffs receive if the case is settled for $3 million?

d. Do the merits of the case against the auditor matter under proportionate liability? Would proportionate liability make the auditor less careful in conducting an audit under GAAS?

SCENARIO C—ENGLISH RULE COST SHARING

Now suppose that the legal cost-sharing rules are different—the "English Rule" applies. Under the English Rule, the losing plaintiff must reimburse the winner for the winner's cost of the litigation. For example, the plaintiff must pay the defendant C_d when the verdict is for the defendant, and when the plaintiff prevails, the plaintiff's legal costs (C_p) are added to the judgment paid by the defendant.

How would the English Rule affect the desirability of bringing suit, defending to verdict, or eliciting a settlement offer for the Long Gone stockholder group?

PUBLIC POLICY

Taking the perspective of what is good for society as a whole, give your thoughts on the following questions related to the audit of Long-Gone Corp.

Does joint and several liability for damage assignment provide an adequate remedy for the damaged stockholders of Long-Gone?

How would the recent litigation reform passed by the U.S. Congress affect the Long-Gone case?

How do generally accepted auditing standards interact with the legal environment in concept and in practice?

What should be public policy regarding auditors who perform at a level less than is expected of them, or less than they contract to provide?

KEY WORDS

assurer independence An absence of interests that create an unacceptable risk of bias with respect to the quality or context of information that is the subject of an assurance engagement.

auditor independence rules Proscribe certain auditor/client relationships and behaviors that define a lack of independence, including audit firm partners or close relatives owning stock in an audit client, and partners holding a material amount of audit client debt or making managerial decisions for an audit client.

codes of professional conduct Rules that proscribe certain behaviors by members of private professional organizations or trade associations, such as the AICPA and the Canadian Institute of Chartered Accounts (CICA).

contributory negligence A legal defense argument that the plaintiff's losses were caused in part by the plaintiff's own careless behavior.

directors and officers insurance Insurance purchased by a corporation to indemnify its directors and officers from losses suffered as a result of good-faith performance of their official duties.

negligence rule A damages assignment rule that holds a professional responsible for damages from breach of contract by not performing as promised in the contract.

INDEX